MASONRY AND CONCRETE

Masonry and Concrete

FOR RESIDENTIAL CONSTRUCTION

Christine Beall

McGraw-Hill

New York   Chicago   San Francisco   Lisbon   London
Madrid   Mexico City   Milan   New Delhi   San Juan
Seoul   Singapore   Sydney   Toronto

Library of Congress Cataloging-in-Publication Data

Beall, Christine.
    Masonry and concrete / Christine Beall
        p.   cm.
    Includes bibliographical references.
    ISBN 0-07-006706-6
    1. Masonry.   2. Concrete construction.   3. Dwellings—Materials.   I. Title.

TH5311.B43   2000
693'.1—dc21   00-056104

McGraw-Hill

A Division of The McGraw·Hill Companies

4 5 6 7 8 9 0   DOC/DOC   9 0 9 8 7 6 5 4 3

ISBN 0-07-006706-6

The sponsoring editor for this book was Zoe G. Foundotos, the editing supervisor was Sally Glover, and the production supervisor was Pamela Pelton. It was set in Melior per the CMS design specs by Michele Pridmore of McGraw-Hill's Professional Book Group Hightstown composition unit.

Printed and bound by R. R. Donnelley & Sons Company.

 This book is printed on recycled, acid-free paper containing a minimum of 50% recycled de-inked fiber.

McGraw-Hill books are available at special quantity discounts to use as premiums and sales promotions, or for use in corporate training programs. For more information, please write to the Director of Special Sales, McGraw-Hill, Two Penn Plaza, New York, NY 10121-2298. Or contact your local bookstore.

TO PSYCHO, JESSIE, AND PUPPY

CONTENTS

MASONRY AND CONCRETE

Introduction to Concrete and Masonry

Concrete and masonry are two of the most widely used building materials in the world. Brick and stone structures date back to pre-historic times, and it is the durability of these materials which assured the survival of such architectural relics for thousands of years.

Concrete and masonry are almost always a part of contemporary residential construction. From simple, low-income housing with poured concrete slabs or foundations, to high-end custom residences with masonry veneers and elaborate carved or cast stone decorative elements, from sidewalks and driveways to retaining walls and patios, concrete and masonry are a prevalent part of the suburban landscape. Because of the variety of materials which masonry includes—brick, concrete block, adobe, glass block, natural and cast stone—residential masonry construction spans a range of economic markets, architectural styles, regional customs, and service applications.

In the chapters which follow, the most common residential applications of concrete and masonry are described in detail, including foundations, slabs, paving, veneers, retaining walls, and patios. The tools, techniques, and recommended practices for each material and system are discussed, as well as planning and estimating. This book is written as a reference for home builders and residential masonry contractors as well as a text for the apprentice wishing to learn more about concrete and masonry.

1.1   Characteristics and Performance

Concrete is a fluid mixture of cement, aggregates, and water which can be formed into different shapes and cures to a hard and durable construction material. Masonry is construction of natural building stone or manufactured units such as brick or concrete block.

All building materials expand and contract. Concrete and other cement-based products shrink permanently, and clay products expand permanently with changes in moisture content. Both materials (as well as wood, metal, glass, and plastics) expand and contract reversibly with changes in temperature. Since concrete and masonry are brittle, if construction does not accommodate this expansion and contraction, cracking and water penetration can result. Flexible anchorage and the installation of control joints in concrete and concrete masonry and expansion joints in clay masonry allow this natural expansion and contraction to occur without damage to the construction.

Concrete can be used as a structural and a finish material in slabs, walls, paving, and retaining walls. Masonry can be used as a structural system, as a veneer, or as a paving system and can be used to build fireplaces and retaining walls. Concrete and masonry are strong in compression but require the incorporation of reinforcing steel to resist tensile and bending stresses. Masonry veneers can be constructed over many types of structural frames and backing walls. Concrete and masonry also provide fire resistance, energy efficiency, and durability.

Fire Resistance: Concrete and masonry are *noncombustible*—they will not burn. This is a higher level of protection than mere *fire resistance*. Wood can be injected with chemicals to make it resistant to fire damage for a longer period of time than untreated wood, but ultimately wood becomes fuel for the fire. Steel is noncombustible, but it softens and bends when subjected to the high heat of a fire. In commercial construction, steel structural members must be protected from fire by sprayed-on mineral coatings, layers of gypsum board, plaster, or masonry. The highest level of protection and the highest fire protection ratings are associated with concrete and masonry.

Insurance companies recognize the value of noncombustible construction through reduced fire insurance premiums. *Newsweek* magazine published a photo after the wildfires in Oakland, California, several years ago destroyed hundreds of homes. It showed a neighborhood completely devastated by the fires—except for one house. An engineer who had spent his childhood in Vietnam during the war and learned firsthand the danger of spreading fire had designed his home of structural concrete and masonry. While nothing remained of his neighbors homes except the concrete slabs and masonry fireplaces, his home was intact and undamaged. Although most homes in the United States are built of wood frame rather than structural concrete, the use of noncombustible masonry veneers as a protective outer layer is recognized as an impediment to spreading fire and reduces the risk of property loss and the associated insurance premiums.

Durability: Concrete and masonry are durable against wear and abrasion and weather well for many years with little or no maintenance. Wood is highly susceptible to moisture damage and requires protective coatings to prolong service life. Properly designed and constructed concrete and masonry will provide many years of service to the homeowner without any additional investment of time or money.

Energy Efficiency: For centuries the thermal performance characteristics of masonry have been effectively used in buildings. Large masonry fireplaces used during the day for heating and cooking were centrally located within a structure. At night, the heat stored in the masonry radiated warmth until dawn. In the desert Southwest of the United States, thick adobe masonry walls provided thermal stability. Buildings remained cool during the hot summer days, and heat stored in the walls was later radiated outward to the cooler night air. Until recently, however, there was no simple way of calculating this behavior.

We now know that heat transfer through solid materials is not instantaneous. There is a time delay in which the material itself absorbs heat. Before heat transfer from one space to another can be achieved, the wall which separates the two spaces must absorb heat and undergo a temperature increase. As temperatures rise on one side of the wall, heat begins to migrate toward the cooler side. The speed with which the wall will heat up or cool down is dependent on its thickness, density, and conductivity, and the amount of thermal energy necessary to produce an increase in temperature is directly proportional to the weight of the wall. Although most building materials absorb at least some heat, higher density and greater mass cause slower absorption and longer retention. Metals heat up and cool down very quickly. Concrete and masonry are heavy, so they can absorb and store heat and substantially retard its migration through a wall. This characteristic is measured by the elapsed time required to achieve equilibrium between inside and outside wall surface temperatures. The midday sun load on the south face of a building will not completely penetrate a 12-in. solid masonry wall for approximately 8 hours. It is this thermal lag, in fact, which contributes to concrete and masonry fire safety by delaying heat transfer through the walls of burning buildings.

The effectiveness of wall mass on heat transfer is dependent on the magnitude of the daily temperature range. Warm climates with cool nights benefit most. Climates in which there is only a small daily temperature range benefit the least. In any climate where there are large fluctuations in the daily temperature cycle, the thermal inertia of masonry walls can contribute substantially to increased comfort and energy efficiency. The time lag created by delayed heat transfer through the walls reduces peak cooling demands to a great extent, and may reduce the size of air conditioning and heating equipment required.

1.2   Job Site Safety

Portland cement is alkaline in nature, so wet concrete and other cement-based mixes are caustic and will burn the skin after prolonged contact. Contact with wet concrete, masonry mortar, cement, and cement mixes can cause skin irritation, severe chemical burns, and serious eye damage. Wear sturdy work gloves, long sleeves, and full-length trousers to protect your hands, arms, and legs. Indirect contact through clothing can be as serious as direct contact, so promptly rinse out wet concrete or mortar from clothing. Wear rubber boots when placing and handling concrete for slabs and flatwork, because you may sometimes have to stand in the wet mix to spread and screed the concrete. Make sure the boots are high enough to prevent concrete from getting inside them. To protect your eyes from cement dust and from splattered mortar or concrete, wear safety glasses or goggles. Since masonry involves heavy lifting, be careful to avoid back strain and injury—always bend your knees, keep your back straight, and lift with your legs.

1.3 Building Codes

One of the most commonly used residential building codes in the United States is the CABO *One and Two-Family Dwelling Code* published by the Council of American Building Officials. The CABO code was developed cooperatively by the three major model building code authorities in the United States for use in conjunction with the BOCA *National Building Code,* the ICBO *Uniform Building Code,* and the SBCCI *Standard Building Code.* The CABO residential code will be used throughout this book as a reference document for minimum design and construction standards. Unless otherwise noted, any reference made to code requirements or to "the code" means the CABO *One and Two-Family Dwelling Code.*

1.4 How to Use This Book

This is not a step-by-step, do-it-yourself manual for weekend construction warriors. It is intended to be a useful tool for professional builders who want to expand their knowledge of different building systems. You will not only learn how to pour concrete and lay masonry, you will gain an understanding of critical issues, master the skills needed to produce high-quality workmanship, and learn what is necessary to achieve long-term performance. Whether you are doing the work with your own crew or directing the work of subcontractors, this book will help assure that the end results provide durable and lasting performance for your customers with a minimum number of callbacks.

Understanding Concrete

Residential construction today nearly always includes concrete in some form and to some extent. Concrete is used in footings, foundation walls, floor slabs, retaining walls, sidewalks, driveways, and patios. Concrete is a strong, durable, and economical material whose appearance can be altered in many ways to make it decorative as well as functional. Concrete is a controlled mixture of cement, aggregates, and water. Because it is a fluid mix, concrete can be formed into almost any shape and finished with a variety of textures.

Concrete strength and durability are easier to achieve with an understanding of how concrete is mixed and cured, how strength develops, and how variations in materials and mix design can accommodate different seasonal weather conditions and project requirements. An understanding of concrete properties and ingredients will produce better projects with greater efficiency and economy, higher profits, and fewer callbacks. This chapter discusses the essential properties of fresh and hardened concrete, the characteristics of different cements and aggregates, the role of admixtures, the processes of hydration and curing, basic concrete mix designs, and the critical importance of water-cement ratio. Some discussion is also given to the cause of common problems and how to avoid them.

2.1   Basic Properties of Concrete

The term *fresh* concrete refers to the wet mix of ingredients before they begin to cure. When the material begins to set but is not fully cured, it is called *green* concrete. After it has fully cured, it is called *hardened* concrete. Fresh concrete must be workable, and hardened concrete must be strong and durable. The quality of the ingredients, the proportions in which they are mixed, and the way the concrete is handled, placed, and cured affect these properties.

2.1.1   Properties of Fresh Concrete

Concrete *workability* is the relative ease with which a fresh mix can be handled, placed, compacted, and finished without segregation or separation of the individual ingredients. Good workability is required to produce concrete that is both economical and high in quality. Fresh concrete has good workability if it can be formed, compacted, and finished to its final shape and texture with minimal effort and without segregation of the ingredients. Concrete with poor workability does not flow smoothly into forms or properly envelop reinforcing steel and embedded items, and it is difficult to compact and finish. Depending on the application, though, a mix that has good workability for one type or size of element may be too stiff or harsh for another, so the term is relative. Each mix must be suitable for its intended use, achieving a balance among required fluidity, strength, and economy. Workability is related to the consistency and cohesiveness of the mix and is affected by cement content, aggregates, water content, and admixtures.

Concrete workability is increased by *air entrainment.* Entrained air is different from entrapped air. Entrapped air usually accounts for about 1 to 2% of the volume of fresh concrete and its inclusion is not intentional. Small amounts of air are inadvertently entrapped in the concrete mixing process. Air content can be *intentionally* increased by a controlled process called air entrainment, which uses either a special cement or a chemical admixture to introduce evenly distributed, microscopic air bubbles. In fresh concrete, the tiny air bubbles act almost like ball bearings or a lubricant in the mix, and in hardened concrete they increase winter durability. Too much air reduces the strength of concrete, though, so air content is generally recommended to be within the ranges shown in Figure 2-1.

Maximum Aggregate Size, in.	Air Content, % by Volume
$\frac{3}{8}$	6 to 10
$\frac{1}{2}$	5 to 9
$\frac{3}{4}$	4 to 8
1	$3\frac{1}{2}$ to $6\frac{1}{2}$
$1\frac{1}{2}$	3 to 6

FIGURE 2-1

Recommended air content for various maximum aggregate sizes. *(From Waddell,* Concrete Manual, **International Conference of Building Officials, 1989. Based on** *Uniform Building Code* **Table 26-B).**

Consistency is the aspect of workability related to the flow characteristics of fresh concrete. It is an indication of the fluidity or wetness of a mix and is measured by the slump test. Fresh concrete is placed in a metal cone. When the cone is removed, the concrete slumps a certain amount, depending on how fluid it is. A wet, soft mix slumps more than a drier, stiffer one. A *high-slump* concrete is one that is very fluid, and a *low-slump* concrete is drier and more stiff. A high-slump mix may cause excessive bleeding, shrinkage, cracking, and dusting of the hardened concrete. There is a certain range of consistency which is appropriate for each type of work. Workability is at a maximum in concrete of medium consistency with a slump between 3 and 6 in (Figure 2-2). Both very dry (low slump) and very wet (high slump) mixes are less workable.

Cohesiveness is the element of workability which indicates whether a mix is harsh, sticky, or plastic. Plasticity is a desirable property in concrete, indicating that a mix can be molded and hold a shape when formed. A *harsh* mix lacks plasticity and the ingredients may tend to separate. Harshness can be caused by either an excess or deficiency of mixing water (high- or low-slump mixes), a deficiency of cement (lean mixes), or a deficiency of fine aggregate particles. Harshness may also be caused by an excess of rough, angular, flat, or elongated aggregate particles. Harsh mixes can sometimes be improved by air entrainment or by increasing the fine aggregate or cement content,

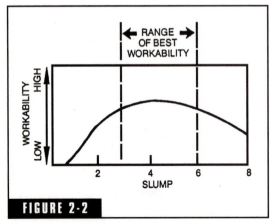

FIGURE 2-2

Concrete workability is best at a slump between 3–6 inches *(From Waddell, Concrete Manual, International Conference of Building Officials, Whittier, California)*.

but adjustments must be made to the overall mix to maintain the proper proportion of all ingredients. A *sticky* mix may have a high cement content (fat mixes) or large amounts of rock dust, fine sand, or similar fine materials (oversanded mixes). Sticky mixes do not segregate easily, but because they require a lot of water to achieve even minimal workability, sticky mixes often develop excessive shrinkage cracking. A *plastic* mix is cohesive without being either sticky or harsh, and the ingredients do not easily segregate unless the concrete is handled improperly.

2.1.2 Properties of Hardened Concrete

Fully cured, hardened concrete must be strong enough to withstand the structural and service loads which will be applied to it and must be durable enough to withstand the environmental exposure for which it is intended. When concrete is made with high-quality materials and is properly proportioned, mixed, handled, placed, and finished, it is one of the strongest and most durable of building materials.

When we refer to concrete *strength,* we are generally talking about compressive strength which is measured in pounds per square inch (*psi*). Concrete is strong in *compression* but relatively weak in *tension* and *bending.* It takes a great deal of force to crush concrete, but very little force to pull it apart or cause bending cracks (Figure 2-3). Compressive strength is determined primarily by the amount of cement used but is also affected by the ratio of water to cement, as well as proper mixing, placing, and curing. Tensile strength usually ranges from 7 or 8% of compressive strength in high-strength mixes to 11 or 12% in low-strength mixes. Both tensile strength and flexural bending strength can be increased by adding steel or fiber reinforcement.

Structural engineers establish required compressive strengths for various building elements based on an analysis of the loads which will be applied and the soil conditions at the project site. Actual compressive strength is verified by testing samples in a laboratory using standardized

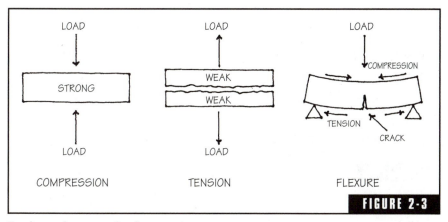

Tension and compression in concrete.

equipment and procedures. On commercial projects, numerous samples are tested throughout construction to verify that the concrete being put into place actually has the specified strength. Laboratory testing is not often required in residential work, except perhaps on large, high-end projects or on projects with difficult sites where special foundation designs make concrete strength critical. For most residential projects, required concrete strength will be in the range of 2,500 to 4,000 psi, depending on the intended use (Figure 2-4). A concrete that is stronger than necessary for its intended use is not economical, and one that is not strong enough can be dangerous. The primary factors affecting concrete compressive strength are the cement content, the ratio of water to cement, and the adequacy and extent of hydration and curing, all of which are discussed later in this chapter.

Durability might be defined as the ability to maintain satisfactory performance over an extended service life. Satisfactory performance is related to intended use. Concrete that will be walked or driven on must be abrasion resistant so that it doesn't wear away. Concrete that will be exposed on the outside of a building must be weather resistant so that it doesn't deteriorate from repeated freezing and thawing. Concrete in which steel reinforcement is embedded must resist excessive moisture absorption in order to protect the metal from corrosion. Natural wear and weathering will cause some change in the appearance of concrete over time, but in general, durability also includes the maintenance of aesthetic as well as functional characteristics. Just as concrete

Construction Element	Compressive Strength, psi
Basement and foundation walls and slabs	2,500–3,000
Driveways, garage slabs	2,500–3,500
Reinforced concrete beams, slabs, patios, sidewalks, and steps	2,500–3,500

FIGURE 2-4

Typical compressive strength requirements for residential concrete.

mix designs can be adjusted to produce a variety of strengths, appropriate concrete ingredients, mix proportions, and finishes can and should be adjusted on the basis of required durability.

In cold climates, exterior concrete is exposed to repeated freeze-thaw cycles which can potentially be very damaging. Freeze-thaw deterioration, in fact, is one of the most serious threats to concrete durability, but resistance to damage can be significantly increased by air entrainment. A network of fine voids formed by air entrained cement or an air-entraining admixture absorbs the expansive force of freezing water to prevent the hardened concrete from fracturing or scaling over repeated cycles of winter freezing and thawing. Air entrainment improves the durability of horizontal elements such as sidewalks, driveways, patios, and steps, which are most frequently exposed to rainwater, melting snow, and deicing salts. For vertical elements, which are less often saturated with rain, and in mild climates where freeze-thaw cycles are infrequent, air entrainment adds little value to hardened concrete but still may be used to increase the workability of fresh concrete. Air entrainment is sometimes credited with increasing the watertightness of concrete, but this is probably because the increased workability of the mix is conducive to better placement, consolidation, and finishing.

Another important aspect of concrete durability is volume stability. All materials expand and contract with changes in temperature, and porous materials like concrete also expand and contract with changes in moisture content. In addition to reversible thermal expansion and contraction, cement-based products such as concrete, concrete masonry, and stucco experience initial *shrinkage* as the cement hydrates and excess construction water evaporates. This initial shrinkage is permanent, and is in addition to reversible expansion and contraction caused by later temperature or moisture changes. Excessive shrinkage can cause concrete to crack. The cracks allow moisture to penetrate, and a vicious cycle of deterioration may begin. Shrinkage cracking can be restrained to some extent by steel or fiber reinforcement, and the location of shrinkage cracks can be controlled through the use of special joints that divide the concrete into smaller panels or sections. However, the mix design and ingredient proportions also have an effect on the potential for shrinkage cracking. The higher the cement content, the greater the tendency for shrinkage cracks to form while the concrete is curing and hardening.

2.2   Concrete Ingredients

The basic ingredients in concrete are cement, aggregates, and water. The type, quality, and proportioning of these ingredients affect the curing rate, compressive strength, and durability of the concrete. Chemical admixtures can be used to enhance one or more properties of the concrete or to improve its handling and placing characteristics.

2.2.1   Cement

Cement is not the same thing as concrete. Many people mistakenly refer to "cement" sidewalks or "cement" driveways and the like, but cement is only one of the ingredients in concrete. It is also an ingredient in masonry mortar, stucco, and other materials.

- Cement + water = cement paste
- Cement + water + sand = cement mortar
- Cement + water + sand + lime = masonry mortar
- Cement + water + sand + coarse aggregate = concrete

Cement is a powdery substance which reacts with water to form a *cement paste,* which is the actual cementing or binding medium in concrete. The cement paste must completely coat each aggregate particle, and as it cures in a process called *hydration,* the concrete hardens into a strong, stonelike mass.

There are many natural and manufactured cements, some of which date back to Roman builders of the first centuries A.D. Since its development in England in the early 1800s, though, *portland cement* has become the most widely used cement in the world. Portland cement got its name because the cured concrete it produced was the same color as a gray stone quarried in nearby Portland, England. There are five types of portland cement, each with different characteristics.

- Type I is a general-purpose cement and is by far the most commonly used, especially in residential work. Type I portland cement is suitable whenever the special characteristics of other types are not required.

- Type II cement has moderate resistance to sulfates, which are found in some soil and groundwater, and generates less heat during hydration than Type I. This reduced curing temperature can be particularly helpful in large structures such as piers and heavy retaining walls, especially when the concrete is placed in warm weather.

- Type III is a "high early strength" cement. High early strength does not mean higher strength—only that strength develops at a faster rate. This can be an advantage during winter construction because it reduces the time during which fresh concrete must be protected from the cold. Early strength gain can also permit removal of forms and shoring more quickly.

- Type IV cement produces less heat during hydration than Type I or Type II and is used only in massive civil engineering structures such as dams, large highway pilings, or heavy bridge abutments. Its strength development and curing rates, though, are much slower than Type I.

- Type V cement is used in concrete exposed to soil or groundwater that has high sulfate concentrations. This type of cement is usually available only in areas where it is likely to be needed. In the United States, Type V cement is common only in the southwestern states.

Types I, II, and III portland cement can also be made with a foaming agent that produces millions of evenly distributed microscopic air bubbles in the concrete mix. When manufactured in this way, the cements are said to be *air entrained,* and are designated as Types IA, IIA, and IIIA. Air-entrained cements require mechanical mixing.

Finely ground cement increases the workability of harsh mixes, making them more cohesive and reducing tendencies toward segregation. Coarsely ground cement reduces stickiness. Cement packages that are marked ASTM A150 meet industry standards for both physical and chemical requirements.

Portland cement comes in three colors—grey, white, and buff. The white and buff are more expensive and typically used in commercial rather than residential projects to achieve special color effects. Liquid or powder pigments can be added to a concrete mix, and liquid stains can be used to color the surface of cured concrete, but both will add to the cost. For most applications, ordinary gray concrete made with gray cement is suitable. Colored concrete should be reserved for special areas like a front entrance, a patio, or a pool deck.

In the United States, portland cement is packaged in bags containing exactly one cubic foot of material and weighing exactly 94 lbs. This standardized packaging, which all American manufacturers use, allows consistency in proportioning and mixing concrete by either weight or volume measurement. Bags should be stored on wooden pallets and covered to prevent wetting. Portland cement must remain dry and free-flowing until it is ready for use. If the bags get wet or absorb moisture from the soil or from a concrete slab, the cement will begin to harden prematurely and will produce weak, slow-curing concrete. Hard lumps which cannot be easily pulverized by hand indicate excessive wetting, and the cement should be discarded or used only for minor work such as setting fence posts.

Packaged concrete mixes contain cement, sand, and gravel in appropriate proportions and require only the addition of water to produce fresh concrete. These packaged mixes, marketed under a variety of trade names, are very convenient for small items like setting a single mailbox post or doing minor repairs. The most commonly available sizes are 40-, 60-, and 80-lb. bags. The 40-lb. bag makes about $1/3$ cu. ft. of concrete. A 60-lb. bag makes about $1/2$ cu. ft., and an 80-lb. bag about $2/3$ cu. ft. of concrete.

2.2.2 Aggregates

The *aggregates* most commonly used in concrete are sand, gravel, crushed stone, crushed slag, and pumice. Cement and water are mixed with aggregates to produce concrete. Concrete contains both fine and coarse aggregates. When cement is mixed only with fine aggregate, it is called *cement mortar,* which is used typically for patching and small repairs, or for coating a concrete surface to provide a smooth, even finish. Masonry mortar is different from a simple cement mortar because it contains other ingredients as well (see Chapter 3).

Cement paste coats the aggregates, binding them together and curing to form concrete. Aggregates add strength to concrete and reduce its potential for shrinkage. Aggregates actually make up 60 to 80% of the volume of hardened concrete, so their properties and characteristics are very important.

The *coarse aggregates* most commonly used in residential concrete are gravel and crushed stone. Aggregates must be sound, volume stable, nonreactive, abrasion resistant, suitably shaped, rough textured, well graded, and clean. Each characteristic of the aggregate has an effect on the resulting concrete (Figure 2-5). Unsound aggregates produce unsound concrete which is weak, has poor appearance, low durability, and may experience cracking, popouts, and spalling. Chemical reactivity, especially with the alkalis in cement, causes internal expansion, cracking, and disintegration of the concrete. Low abrasion resistance results in low strength and excessive wear in floors and pavements. Particle shape affects workability, and surface texture affects bond of the cement paste to the aggregate. Aggregate that is too absorptive produces concrete that has low durability and may suffer from scaling, popouts, and excessive shrinkage. Dirty or contaminated aggregate bonds poorly with the cement paste, can increase mixing water requirements, delay setting and hardening of the concrete, cause stains or popouts, lower strength and durability, and increase shrinkage.

Gravel generally has smoother, more rounded shapes than crushed stone and thus produces concrete with better workability. The workability of concrete made with crushed stone, however, can be improved by air entrainment. Regardless of the type of aggregate or its particle shape, coarse aggregate should include a well-graded range of sizes from small (1/4 in.) to large (3/4, 1, or 1-1/2 in.). Smaller particles fill in the spaces between the larger ones, making the mix both stronger

Characteristic	Significance in Concrete
Soundness, volume stability	Strength, durability, appearance
Chemical reactivity	Alkali-silica reaction, popouts, disintegration, appearance
Abrasion resistance	Wear resistance of floors, hardness
Particle shape	Workability, economy, shrinkage, strength
Surface texture	Bond, strength, durability
Grading	Workability, density, economy, shrinkage
Maximum size of aggregate	Economy, shrinkage, density, strength
Percentage of crushed particles	Workability, economy, strength
Specific gravity	Durability, density, needed for mix computations
Absorption	Durability, needed for mix computations and control
Moisture content	Needed for mix computations and control

FIGURE 2-5

Characteristics of concrete aggregate. *(Based on Waddell,* Concrete Manual, *International Conference of Building Officials)*.

and more economical (Figure 2-6). Maximum recommended aggregate size is based on the dimensions of the finished concrete and the spacing of reinforcing steel. Maximum aggregate size should not exceed any of the following (Figure 2-7):

- One-third the depth of a concrete slab
- Three-fourths the minimum clear distance between reinforcing bars or between reinforcing bars and forms
- One-fifth the narrowest dimension between sides of forms

For a 4-in.-thick concrete slab, maximum aggregate size should be about 1 in., and for a 6-in. slab, maximum aggregate size could be as

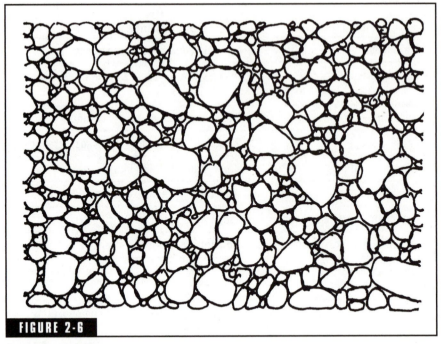

FIGURE 2-6

Aggregate gradation.

large as 1-½ in. Coarse aggregate with the largest allowable maximum size produces the most economical concrete mix. However, it is not necessary on any single project to use concrete with different maximum aggregate sizes for slabs, beams, piers, and so on. For convenience, the smallest recommended allowable aggregate size may be used throughout the project. In practice, aggregate of 3/4-in. or 1-in. maximum size is most commonly available and therefore most commonly used in all structural concrete. Figure 2-8 shows the American Concrete Institute (ACI) recommendations for maximum aggregate size for various types of construction.

The *fine aggregate* in concrete is sand. By definition, sand particles are 3/16-in. diameter and smaller. The sand fills in the voids between coarse aggregate particles. Like coarse aggregate, sand for use in concrete should include a well-graded mix of large and small sizes. Sharp, angular sand manufactured by crushing rock produces harsher concrete mixes with poor workability. Natural sand from river banks or pits has rounded particles, which increase workabil-

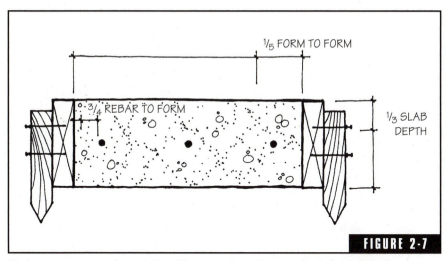

1/5 FORM TO FORM

3/4 REBAR TO FORM

1/3 SLAB DEPTH

FIGURE 2-7

Maximum aggregate size relationship to concrete forms and reinforcing steel.

ity and make slab surfaces easier to finish. Masonry sand is generally not appropriate for concrete because it contains only the smaller particle sizes and can cause the mix to be sticky rather than plastic.

Sand should be free of contaminants that can be harmful to concrete such as silt, clay, and organic materials such as leaves and roots. The cleanness of coarse aggregate can usually be judged by visual inspection, but sand contamination is a little more difficult to detect. There are sophisticated laboratory tests which can determine the exact type and amount of contaminants in concrete aggregates, but there is also a simple field test. Put 2 inches of sand in a quart jar, add water until the jar is about three-fourths full, shake it for one minute, then let it stand for an hour. If more than 1/8 in. of sediment settles on top of the sand, it should be washed by drenching with a garden hose the day before it will be used (Figure 2-9).

Gravel and crushed stone are sold by the ton or half ton, and can be purchased from an aggregate company or a ready-mix producer. Order a clean, graded mix ranging from 1/4 in. to either 3/4-, 1-, or 1-1/2-in. diameter as appropriate for the project. Small quantities of sand can usually be purchased at building supply yards. Larger quantities of sand are sold by the ton or half ton by aggregate suppliers and ready-mix producers. Order clean, natural, concrete sand.

Minimum dimension of section, in.	Max. Size of Aggregate, in.		
	Reinforced walls, beams, and columns	Heavily reinforced slabs	Lightly reinforced slabs
$2^1/2$–5	$^1/2$–$^3/4$	$^3/4$–1	$^3/4$–$1^1/2$
6–11	$^3/4$–$1^1/2$	1-$^1/2$	$1^1/2$–3
12–29	$1^1/2$–3	$1^1/2$–3	3
30 or more	$1^1/2$–3	$1^1/2$–3	3–6

FIGURE 2-8

Maximum sizes of aggregate recommended for various types of construction. *(from American Concrete Institute, Concrete Primer, Detroit).*

2.2.3 Water

As a rule of thumb, water used for mixing concrete should be drinkable. Any water that is drinkable is generally free of harmful impurities. In urban areas where municipal water supplies are available, contaminated water is usually not a problem. The same is true in most rural areas where well water is usually tested by local health officials to assure that it is fit for human consumption. In general, if water is reasonably clear and does not have a foul odor, or a brackish or salty taste, it is acceptable for mixing concrete.

2.2.4 Admixtures

Admixtures are substances other than cement, water, or aggregates which are added to concrete mixes for the purpose of altering properties of the fresh or hardened concrete. Admixtures are not generally required to produce high-quality, low-cost concrete, but they may sometimes be necessary or desirable to alter specific properties of the concrete for specific conditions or circumstances. They must be carefully controlled, however, to avoid adversely affecting the concrete, so it is best to use admixtures only in concrete supplied by an experienced and reputable ready-mix producer. Accurate job-site mixing can be difficult to achieve, and the ready-mix producer has the advantage of batching and mixing in a controlled environment with precisely calibrated equipment. The admixtures most commonly used in residential construction are chemical admixtures, air-entraining agents, and coloring pigments. The three most commonly used chemical admixtures are set accelerators, set retarders, and water reducers.

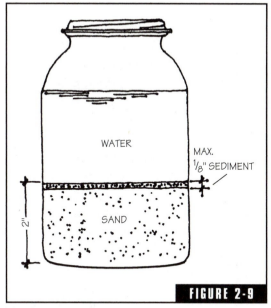

Field test for sand contamination.

Chemical Admixtures: Set *accelerators* speed up the setting time and early strength development of concrete. This can be helpful in winter weather to reduce the length of time required for curing and protection and to compensate for the effects of low temperatures on strength development. Setting time can be reduced by one-third to one-half. Calcium chloride is the most widely used chemical accelerator, but it has a corrosive effect on embedded steel reinforcement and should never be used in concentrations exceeding 2% of the weight of the cement. Other chemicals such as calcium nitrite and calcium formate have a less corrosive effect but are not as widely available. So-called "antifreeze compounds" for concrete are actually set accelerators. Antifreeze mixtures manufactured for the automotive industry will severely damage concrete and should never be used.

Set *retarders* slow down the hydration process so that the concrete stays plastic and workable for a longer time after mixing. This can be helpful in hot weather where high temperatures tend to speed up the normal setting time, and for complicated pours where placement takes a little longer than usual.

Water reducers lower the amount of mixing water required without decreasing workability. This can be helpful when the available materials simply will not produce concrete of adequate workability and consistency without exceeding recommended water-cement ratios. In practice, water-reducing admixtures are typically used only on commercial projects because they require the testing of trial batches of concrete to determine their effect on other properties.

Admixtures marketed as "dampproofing" or "waterproofing" compounds are of little practical use and may, in fact, be detrimental to the concrete. Most water leakage problems can be traced to poor construction practices, cracks, or lean, high-slump mixes. No admixture or surface-applied treatment is a substitute for high-quality ingredients and good workmanship.

Air-Entraining Agents: Both natural and chemical admixtures can be used to improve workability. Lean or harsh concrete mixes can be improved by the addition of finely ground material such as fly ash or natural or manufactured pozzolans. Some set-retarding or water-reducing admixtures also improve workability, but they are not used primarily for this purpose. *Air-entraining agents* improve workability and are particularly effective in lean mixes and in mixes containing poorly graded or sharp, angular aggregate. Air entrainment reduces segregation, slows the rate of bleeding, and shortens finishing time. Either a separate air-entraining agent or an air-entrained cement may be used, but total air content is generally recommended not to exceed 4 to 7% of the total concrete volume. Better control of air content is achieved using a separate air-entraining admixture batched at a ready-mix plant. For job-site mixing, air-entrained cements are easier to use but require mechanical rather than hand mixing.

Coloring Pigments: One of the ways to introduce color to concrete is the addition of natural or synthetic mineral *coloring pigments* to the mix. The pigments must be insoluble in water, free from soluble salts and acids, colorfast in sunlight, chemically stable in the alkaline cement paste, and have no adverse effect on the setting time, strength development, or durability of the concrete. Synthetic oxide pigments are stronger than natural oxide pigments so less is required, but the cost is higher. Many manufacturers package their pigments in amounts appropriate to color one cubic yard of concrete containing six bags of cement. Both liquid and powder pigments are available. Using white portland cement instead of grey produces cleaner, brighter, more vivid colors. Figure 2-10 lists various colors that can be achieved using different pigments.

Concrete Color	Pigment Used
Black, Gray	Black iron oxide, mineral black, carbon black
Brown, Red	Red iron oxide, brown iron oxide, raw umber, burnt umber
Rose and Pink	Red iron oxide (varying amounts)
Buff, Cream, Ivory	Yellow ocher, yellow iron oxide
White	White cement and white sand
Green	Chromium oxide, phthalocyanine green
Blue	Cobalt blue, ultramarine blue, phthalocyanine blue

FIGURE 2-10

Pigments for various concrete colors.

2.3 Concrete Mix Designs

For work requiring more than one cubic yard of material, concrete is usually ordered from a ready-mix supplier for delivery to the job site. The supplier will need to know the minimum compressive strength, the maximum aggregate size, and any special requirements such as air entrainment for added freeze-thaw durability. The supplier will then select a mix design that is appropriate for your needs. If you are mixing small batches of concrete on site, you will need to understand the basic principles of concrete mix design yourself. The proportion of dry ingredients and the ratio of water to cement are the two most important factors.

Cement and aggregates provide strength, durability, and volume stability in concrete, but too much or too little of one in relation to the other reduces quality.

- *Lean* or *oversanded* mixes with low cement content and high aggregate proportions are harsh and have poor workability.

- *Fat* or *undersanded* mixes with high cement content and low aggregate proportions are sticky and expensive.

Within the range of normal concrete strengths, compressive strength is inversely related to water content. That is, the more water you use, the lower the concrete strength. But increasing water content increases fluidity and workability. Since water is required for workability, and since workability is required for high-quality concrete, the low water requirements for strength and high water requirements for workability must be balanced. The ratio of water to cement is the weight of water divided by the weight of cement. Water-cement ratio affects the consistency of a concrete mix. The consistency, in turn, affects how easily the concrete can be poured, moved around in the forms, compacted, and finished. Up to a point, a mix with more water is easier to work with than one that has less water and is therefore stiffer. Too much water, though, will cause the ingredients to separate during the pouring, placing, and handling and will destroy the integrity of the concrete. Too much water also lowers strength, increases the porosity and water permeability of the cured concrete, and makes it more prone to shrinkage cracking. The trick is to use enough water to make the fresh concrete workable, but not so much that it creates weak or porous structures.

Air content for ready-mix concrete should generally be 3 to 6-$1/2$%, depending on the maximum aggregate size (Figure 2-1). Concrete that is batched on site can be made with either an air-entrained cement or an air-entraining admixture. Using an air-entrained cement will yield an air content within the proper range. When using a separate air-entraining agent, carefully follow the manufacturer's instructions to determine the correct amount to add to the mix. For job-site mixing, air-entrained cement is usually easier to work with.

It is easier to measure concrete consistency or *slump* than to calculate water-cement ratio. The concrete mix consistency produced by adding various amounts of water is measured by slump tests in which fresh concrete is poured into a special mold called a slump cone. You can buy one from a building supply yard. Place the concrete into the cone in three layers. Tamp each layer with a metal rod to assure that it is completely consolidated and does not contain air pockets. When the cone is full, scrape off any excess concrete, leaving a level top. Then remove the cone and measure the amount of slump or settlement with a rod and ruler (Figure 2-11). The wetter the mix, the higher the slump measurement, and the drier the mix, the lower the slump measurement. The slump recommended to assure proper water-cement ratio for residential concrete is 3 to 5 inches. Slump tests can also be used to ensure consistent mixes from batch to batch.

As a general guideline for ordering ready-mix concrete, Figure 2-12 shows recommended mix requirements for various exposure conditions. The weathering regions indicated on the map are intended only as a guide. Particularly in mountainous regions, local conditions can change within a very short distance and may be more or less severe than indicated by the region classification. Severe exposures are those in which deicing salts are used because of significant snowfall combined with extended periods in which natural thawing does not occur. If you are in doubt about which classification applies, always use the more severe exposure. Actual concrete ingredient proportions can be measured either by volume or by weight, as described in Chapter 3.

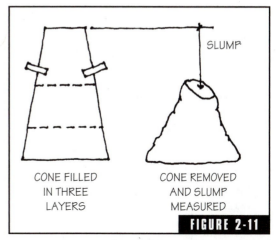

Concrete slump test *(from Concrete Construction Publications, Basics of Concrete,* **Concrete Construction Publications, Inc., Addison, Illinois).**

2.4   Formwork and Reinforcement

Formwork is used to shape the fluid concrete mixture and hold it in place while it cures. It must be strong enough to withstand the pressure of the wet mix, which can exert a considerable force until it begins to harden and hold its own shape. Reinforcement is used to add tensile strength to the concrete and to help resist shrinkage cracking.

2.4.1   Formwork Materials

Lumber and plywood are used to build forms or molds to contain the concrete mix and shape it. Usually, 2 × 4s, 2 × 6s or 2 × 8s are used for the actual form or mold, and 1 × 2s, 1 × 4s, or 2 × 4s for stakes and braces to hold it in place. Metal landscape edging or 1/4-in. plywood or hardboard can be used to form curved slab edges. Plywood used to form curves will bend more easily if it is cut in strips perpendicular to the face grain rather than along the grain. Form boards should be free of holes,

Element	Weathering Probability*	Minimum Compressive Strength, psi	Typical Maximum Coarse Aggregate Size, in.	Minimum Cement Content, sacks/ cu. yd	Air Content by Volume, %	Slump, in.
Foundations, basement walls, and slabs *not* exposed to weather (except garage slabs)	Severe	2,500		5½		
	Moderate	2,500	1	5½		3–5
	Mild	2,500		5½		
Foundations, basement walls, exterior walls and other vertical concrete work exposed to weather	Severe	3,000		6†	5–7	
	Moderate	3,000	1	5½†	5–7	3–5
	Mild	2,500		5½		
Driveways, garage slabs, walks, porches, patios, and stairs exposed to weather	Severe	3,500		6†	5–7	
	Moderate	3,000	1	5½†	5–7	3–5
	Mild	2,500		5½		

*See map for weathering probability (Alaska and Hawaii are classified as severe and negligible, respectively).

†Use air-entrained cement.

FIGURE 2-12

Recommended concrete mixes for various exposure conditions. *(Minimum required strength based on requirements of CABO One and Two Family Dwelling Code.)* Continued.

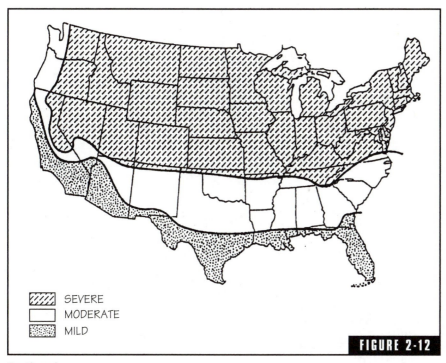

SEVERE
MODERATE
MILD

FIGURE 2-12

Continued

cracks, loose knots, and other defects that might reduce strength or mar the finished surface.

Any type of lumber that is straight and smooth can be used for temporary forms that will be removed when the concrete is cured. No. 2 or No. 3 grade yellow pine, spruce, or fir make good, sturdy form boards. Green lumber works better than kiln-dried lumber, which will swell when it absorbs water from the concrete mix. Forms that are too absorptive also reduce the quality of the concrete by removing too much water from the mix and leaving insufficient moisture for cement curing. Plywood for forms should be exterior type with grade B face veneers. For forms or divider strips that will stay in place, use redwood, cedar, cypress, or lumber that has been pressure-treated with a chemical preservative. Coat redwood, cypress, or cedar lumber with a clear sealer to protect it from the alkalis in the fresh concrete. Pressure-treated lumber does not require a sealer.

2.4.2   Concrete Reinforcement

Steel reinforcement helps control the natural shrinkage that occurs as concrete cures and dries, and it makes the concrete stronger and less likely to crack. There are two basic types of reinforcing steel—bars and mesh (Figure 2-13).

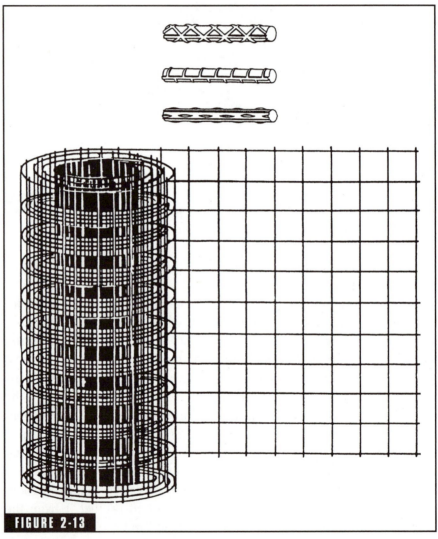

FIGURE 2-13

Steel reinforcing bars and reinforcing mesh.

Reinforcing Bars: Reinforcing bars range in size from ¼-in. to 1-in. in diameter and have surface ridges to provide better bond with the concrete paste. Reinforcing bars are numbered according to their diameter in eighths of an inch. A #3 bar, for example, is $3/8$ in. in diameter, a #4 bar is $4/8$ in. or $1/2$ in., a #5 is $5/8$ in., and so on. Reinforcing bars are used for concrete carrying heavy loads such as footings and foundation walls, slabs, and columns. There are several different types of steel used to make reinforcing bars, and there are two common grades, Grade 60 and Grade 40. Grade 60 has a higher yield strength and is required by building codes for some applications.

Reinforcing Mesh: Reinforcing mesh is made from steel wires woven or welded into a grid of squares or rectangles. The wires are usually 6, 8, or 10 gauge and may have smooth or deformed surfaces. Reinforcing mesh comes in rolls and mats and is used primarily in flatwork such as sidewalks, patios, and driveways. For most residential work, 6 in. × 6 in.–10 gauge mesh provides adequate strength and distributes shrinkage stresses to minimize cracking.

2.5   Control, Construction and Isolation Joints

Concrete shrinks irreversibly as it cures and dries out. After this initial shrinkage has occurred, concrete expands and contracts reversibly with changes in temperature and moisture content. This movement can cause concrete to crack uncontrollably unless it is reinforced with steel and built with special joints that are designed to control cracking locations.

The amount of expansion and contraction that concrete will experience is influenced by several things, including the water content of the mix, and the weather conditions during the curing period. Mixes made with a high water content are more prone to cracking from initial shrinkage than drier, stiffer mixes. Reinforcing steel increases the strength of concrete and absorbs the stress of expansion and contraction, but it cannot prevent cracking altogether—it can only distribute the stresses so that there will be many minute cracks instead of a few big ones. While reinforcement limits the amount of expansion and contraction to some extent, cracking and movement can also be regulated by subdividing the concrete into smaller sections with control joints and construction joints, and separating it from adjacent construction with isolation joints.

2.5.1 Control Joints

Control joints are used to prevent random shrinkage cracking and instead make the concrete crack in straight lines at predetermined locations. Control joints can be hand-tooled into fresh concrete with a special jointing tool, sawed into partially cured concrete with a circular saw, or formed with fixed divider strips of wood or of specially molded fiber, cork, or sponge rubber (Figure 2-14). The depths of tooled and saw-cut control joints are typically one-fourth the thickness of the concrete. This weakened section causes cracks to occur at the bottom of the joints where they will be inconspicuous. Divider strips that will remain in place should be the full thickness of a concrete slab so that they create separate panels that can expand and contract independently of one another.

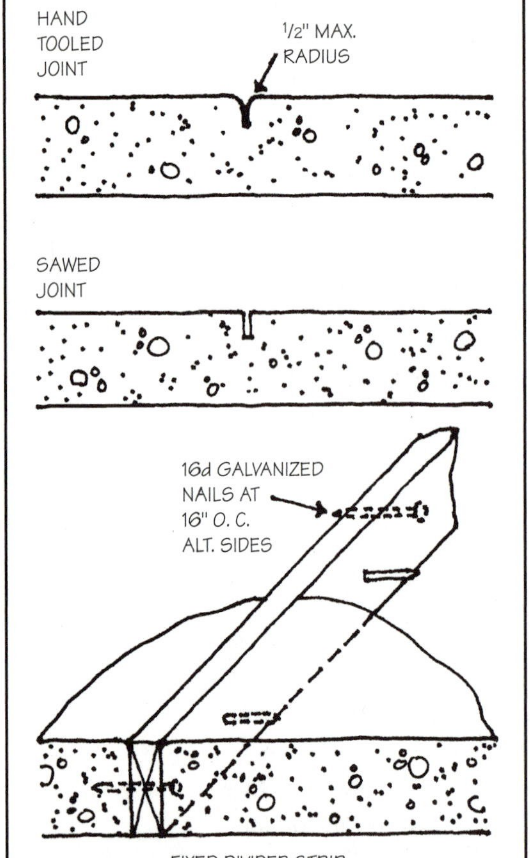

Figure 2-15 shows recommended maximum control joint spacing for concrete slabs based on concrete slump, maximum aggregate size, and slab thickness. Using the maximum spacing recommendations from the table as a guideline, it is best to subdivide concrete into panels that are square in shape rather than elongated. Rectangular areas that are more than one-and-a-half times as long as they are wide are prone to cracking. For a 10-ft.-wide driveway that is 4-in. thick, has a 5-in. slump and 1-in. maximum aggregate size, the table recommends control joints every 10 ft., which would result in square panels. For a 3-ft.-wide sidewalk with the same thickness, slump, and aggregate size, however, 10-ft. spacing would create elongated rectangular panels, so the spacing should be much closer than the maximum table recommendation. The sidewalk is less likely to crack if control joints are spaced 3 ft. apart to form square panels.

HAND TOOLED JOINT

1/2" MAX. RADIUS

SAWED JOINT

16d GALVANIZED NAILS AT 16" O. C. ALT. SIDES

FIXED DIVIDER STRIP

FIGURE 2-14

Concrete control joints.

Slab Thickness, in.	Slump 3–5 inches		Slump Less Than 4 in.
	Maximum size aggregate less than $3/4$ in.	Maximum size aggregate $3/4$ in. and larger	
4	8	10	12
5	10	13	15
6	12	15	18

FIGURE 2-15

Recommended concrete control joint spacing, ft.

2.5.2 Construction Joints

Construction joints are installed wherever a concrete pour is interrupted for more than half an hour or stopped at the end of the day. Construction joints are usually coated with oil to prevent bond with the next pour, and located so that they can also act as control joints. For slabs that are only 4-in. thick, a straight-edged butt joint is adequate, but for thicker slabs, a tongue-and-groove joint is required (Figure 2-16). The tongue-and-groove joint transfers loads in such a way that the adjoining panels remain level with one another but can still expand and contract independently. A tongue-and-groove joint is shaped by attaching a beveled wood, metal, or molded plastic form to a temporary wooden bulkhead. Construction joints should be square or rounded at the surface to match saw-cut or tooled control joints, respectively.

2.5.3 Isolation Joints

Isolation joints are used to separate new concrete from existing or adjacent construction, which might expand and contract differently or experience different soil settlement or other movement. If the fresh concrete were not separated from these elements by an isolation joint, a crack could form where the two meet. Isolation joints should be $1/4$ in. to $1/2$ in. wide, and filled with a molded fiber, cork, or rubber strip that is set $1/4$ in. below the surface (Figure 2-17). Do not use caulking or materials that might be squeezed out of the joint when it contracts, as this could cause someone to trip and fall. Figure 2-18 shows an example of control joint and isolation joint locations.

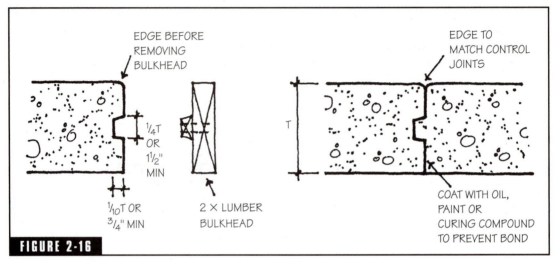

FIGURE 2-16

Construction joints.

2.6 Cement Hydration and Concrete Curing

Concrete curing is not simply a matter of the concrete hardening as it dries out. In fact, it is just the opposite. Portland cement is a *hydraulic* material. That is, it requires water for curing and can, in fact, fully cure to a hardened state even if it is completely submerged in water. Portland cement is *anhydrous*—it contains no water or moisture at all. The moment it comes in contact with water, a chemical reaction takes place in which new compounds are formed. This reaction is called

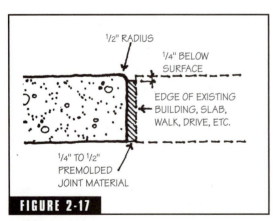

FIGURE 2-17

Isolation joints.

cement hydration. The rate of hydration varies with the composition of the cement, the fineness of the cement particles, the amount of water present, the air temperature, and the presence of admixtures. If the mixing water dries out too rapidly before the cement has fully hydrated, the curing process will stop and the concrete will not harden to its intended strength. Curing will resume if more water is introduced, but at a slower rate. Hydration occurs more rapidly at higher air temperatures.

Cement hydration itself generates heat, too. This heat of hydration can be helpful during cold-weather construction, and potentially harmful during hot-weather construction. The chemical reaction between water and cement first forms a paste which must completely coat each aggregate particle during mixing. After a time, the paste begins to stiffen or *set,* and after a few hours has lost is plasticity entirely. The rate of this *setting,* however, is not the same as the rate of *hardening.* A Type-III high-early-strength cement may set in about the same time as

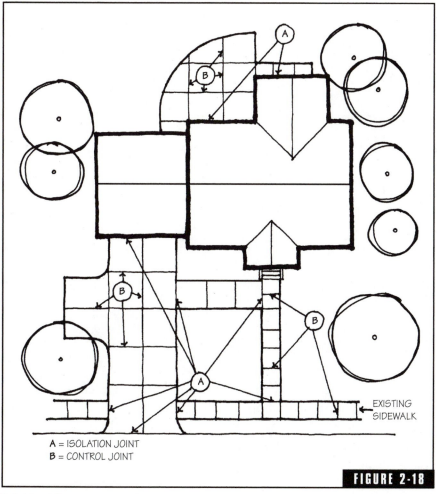

A = ISOLATION JOINT
B = CONTROL JOINT

FIGURE 2-18

Joint locations.

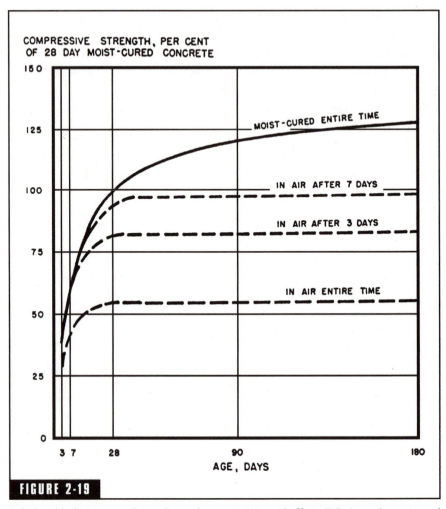

COMPRESSIVE STRENGTH, PER CENT
OF 28 DAY MOIST-CURED CONCRETE

FIGURE 2-19

Relationship between moist curing and concrete strength *(from U.S. Army,* Concrete and Masonry. *Technical Manual No. 5-742. U.S. Government Printing Office, Washington, D.C.).*

a Type-I general-purpose cement, but the Type III hardens and develops compressive strength more rapidly after it has set.

Concrete normally cures to its full design strength in 28 days. Curing is slower in cold weather, and at temperatures below 40°F, the concrete can be easily and permanently damaged if it is not properly protected. Concrete must be kept moist for several days after it is placed to allow the portland cement in the mix to cure and harden properly. Concrete that is not kept moist reaches only about 50% of its design strength. Figure 2-19 shows the differences in concrete strength for various periods of moist curing. If it is kept moist for at least three days, it will reach about 80% of its design strength, and for seven days, 100% of its design strength. If the concrete is kept moist for the full 28-day curing period, it will reach more than 125% of its design strength.

Concrete Construction Techniques

Concrete construction consists essentially of six stages—excavating, formwork, reinforcement, pouring, finishing, and curing. Work begins with material estimating, site preparation, and layout.

3.1 Estimating Materials

Small batches of concrete can be mixed at the job site, but for quantities of one cubic yard or more, it is usually more convenient to order ready-mix concrete delivered to the site. Ready-mix concrete is sold by the cubic yard, and most suppliers require a minimum order of one yard. The cost of ready-mix varies with the distance it must be hauled for delivery, the size of the order, unloading time, and type of mix. The construction drawings will give you the shape and dimensions needed for various concrete elements such as a slabs-on-grade, basement walls, footings, driveways, sidewalks, and so on. If small quantities of concrete are ordered from a ready-mix supplier, it will only be necessary to calculate the total quantity of concrete needed. If concrete is being mixed on site, it will also be necessary to calculate the quantity of each ingredient needed to produce the required volume of concrete.

3.1.1 Estimating Total Concrete Volume

To estimate the cubic yardage of concrete needed, first calculate the area in square feet, then use the graph in Figure 3-1 to find the volume of concrete needed. Locate the calculated square footage along the top of the graph. Then follow the vertical line down until it intersects the diagonal line for the required concrete thickness. Read horizontally to the right to find the volume in cubic yards and to the left to find the volume in cubic feet. If the area is larger than 300 sq. ft., first find the volume for 300 sq. ft., then find the volume for the remainder of the square footage, and add the two together. To allow for slight irregularities in concrete thickness and for some spillage and waste, round up at least to the next whole or half-cubic yard measure, allowing a minimum of 5–10% extra.

Ready-mix suppliers will need to know minimum compressive strength and maximum aggregate size for the concrete mix, and any special requirements such as air entrainment for added freeze-thaw durability. As a general guideline for ordering ready-mix concrete, Figure 3-2 shows recommended requirements. The weathering regions indicated on the map are intended as a general guideline. Local conditions can change within a very short distance, particularly in mountainous regions, and may be more or less severe than indicated by the regional classification. Severe exposures are those in which deicing salts are used because of significant snowfall combined with extended periods in which natural thawing does not occur. If you are in doubt about which classification applies, always use the more severe exposure.

3.1.2 Estimating Individual Ingredients

The actual ingredient proportions in concrete can be measured either by volume or by weight. To estimate the volume of concrete *and* the volume of the various ingredients needed for the mix, first calculate the total area in square feet as above, and use the graph in Figure 3-1 to find the volume of concrete needed. From the intersection of the vertical line for area and the diagonal line for thickness, read horizontally to the left to find the volume in cubic feet. Then use Figure 3-3 to determine the proportions of cement, sand, gravel, and water required. Table A in Figure 3-3 shows the required weight of each ingredient

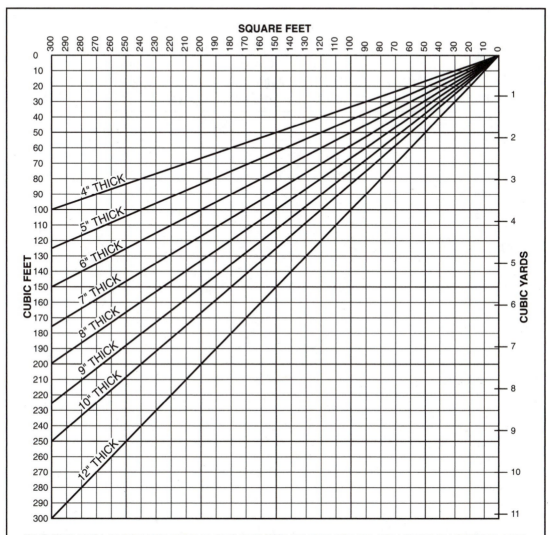

FIND THE AREA IN SQUARE FEET ALONG THE TOP OF THE GRAPH. FOLLOW THE VERTICAL LINE DOWN UNTIL IT INTERSECTS THE DIAGONAL LINE FOR THE APPROPRIATE THICKNESS. READ HORIZONTALLY TO THE LEFT TO FIND THE VOLUME IN CUBIC FEET. READ HORIZONTALLY TO THE RIGHT TO FIND THE VOLUME IN CUBIC YARDS (27 CU.FT. = 1 CU.YD.).

FIGURE 3-1

Calculating concrete quantity.

Element	Weathering Probability*	Minimum Compressive Strength, psi	Typical Maximum Coarse Aggregate Size, in.	Minimum Cement Content, sacks/ cu. yd	Air Content by Volume, %	Slump, in.
Foundations, basement walls and slabs not exposed to weather (except garage slabs)	Severe	2,500		5½		
	Moderate	2,500	1	5½		3–5
	Mild	2,500		5½		
Foundations, basement walls, exterior walls, and other vertical concrete work exposed to weather	Severe	3,000		6†	5–7	
	Moderate	3,000	1	5½†	5–7	3–5
	Mild	2,500		5½		
Driveways, garage slabs, walks, porches, patios, and stairs exposed to weather	Severe	3,500		6†	5–7	
	Moderate	3,000	1	5½†	5–7	3–5
	Mild	2,500		5½		

*See map for weathering probability (Alaska and Hawaii are classified as severe and negligible, respectively).

†Use air-entrained cement.

FIGURE 3-2

Recommended concrete mixes for various exposure conditions. *(Minimum required strength from CABO One and Two Family Dwelling Code.) Continued.*

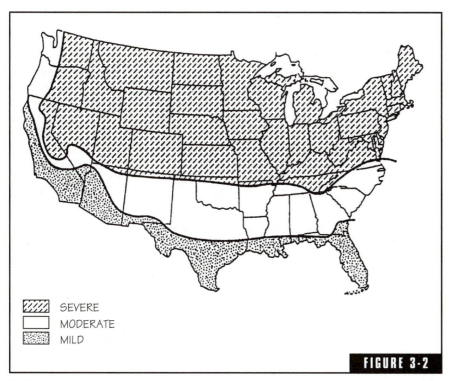

SEVERE
MODERATE
MILD

FIGURE 3-2

Continued

needed to produce one cubic foot of concrete. Multiply each ingredient weight times the total cubic footage of concrete required to figure out how much of each ingredient is needed. The standard weights of each ingredient are shown below the table. The calculated weights of each material will have to be converted to appropriate units such as gallons, cu. ft., bags of cement, and so on. If you are mixing by hand, 1-cubic-foot batches are a good size to work with. If you are using a mixing machine, multiply each ingredient by the capacity of the mixer to determine the amount of materials per batch. For example, multiply each ingredient by three for a 3-cu.-ft. mixer.

Table B in Figure 3-3 is based on a proportional volume mix. The volume of the concrete is equal to about $2/3$ the sum of the volumes of the individual ingredients because the sand particles and cement paste fill in the voids between the coarse aggregate. For job-site mixing, it is usually easier to proportion by volume rather than by weight

A. Proportions by Weight‡ to Make One Cubic Foot of Concrete

	Air-Entrained Cement				Non-Air-Entrained Cement			
Max. size coarse agg., in.	Cement, lb.	Sand,* lb.	Coarse Agg.†, lb.	Water, lb.	Cement, lb.	Sand*, lb.	Coarse Agg.†, lb.	Water, lb.
$\frac{3}{8}$	29	53	46	10	29	59	46	11
$\frac{1}{2}$	27	46	55	10	27	53	55	11
$\frac{3}{4}$	25	42	65	10	25	47	65	10
1	24	39	70	9	24	45	70	10
$1\frac{1}{2}$	23	38	75	9	23	43	75	9

‡Portland cement weighs 94 lbs./bag. Sand weighs 90 lbs./cu. ft. Coarse aggregate weighs 100 lbs./cu.ft. Water weighs 62.4 lbs./cu.ft. One gallon of water weighs 8.34 lbs.

*Proportions are based on wet sand. If you are using damp sand, decrease the quantity of sand by one pound and increase the water by one pound. If your sand is very wet, increase the quantity of sand by one pound and decrease the water by one pound.

†If crushed stone is used, decrease coarse aggregate by three pounds and increase sand by three pounds.

B. Proportions by Volume*

	Air-Entrained Cement				Non-Air-Entrained Cement			
Max. size coarse agg., in.	Cement	Sand	Coarse Agg.	Water†	Cement	Sand	Coarse Agg.	Water†
$\frac{3}{8}$	1	$2\frac{1}{4}$	$1\frac{1}{2}$	$\frac{1}{2}$	1	$2\frac{1}{2}$	$1\frac{1}{2}$	$\frac{1}{2}$
$\frac{1}{2}$	1	$2\frac{1}{4}$	2	$\frac{1}{2}$	1	$2\frac{1}{2}$	$2\frac{1}{2}$	$\frac{1}{2}$
$\frac{3}{4}$	1	$2\frac{1}{4}$	$2\frac{1}{2}$	$\frac{1}{2}$	1	$2\frac{1}{2}$	$2\frac{1}{2}$	$\frac{1}{2}$
1	1	$2\frac{1}{4}$	$2\frac{3}{4}$	$\frac{1}{2}$	1	$2\frac{1}{2}$	$2\frac{3}{4}$	$\frac{1}{2}$
$1\frac{1}{2}$	1	$2\frac{1}{4}$	3	$\frac{1}{2}$	1	$2\frac{1}{2}$	3	$\frac{1}{2}$

*Combined volume is approximately two-thirds of the sum of the original bulk volumes of the individual ingredients.

†One cubic foot of water is 7.48 gallons. One gallon of water is 0.134 cu. ft.

FIGURE 3-3

Estimating individual ingredients for concrete *(from Portland Cement Association,* The Homeowner's Guide to Building With Concrete, Brick and Stone, *PCA, Skokie, Illinois)*.

using a convenient unit of measure such as a plastic bucket. If the concrete will be made with maximum $3/8$-in. aggregate and air-entrained cement, the correct proportions would be one bucket of cement, 2-$1/4$ buckets of sand, $1/2$ bucket of coarse aggregate, and $1/2$ bucket of water. The proportions remain the same relative to one another, regardless of the size of the container used for batching. Depending on the amount of moisture in the aggregates, the water content may have to be adjusted slightly. Make a small trial batch to check the workability of the mix and add more or less water if necessary.

3.2   Site Preparation

Site preparation will include a carefully measured layout of the size and shape of the concrete, and excavating the existing soil or placing structural fill to the required elevation.

3.2.1   Size and Layout

The layout for a floor slab or perimeter footings should be very precise because it affects the layout of all the work which follows. Once you have determined how to position a house on the site, roughly locate each corner with wooden stakes, and then erect *batter boards* two to three feet beyond the corners on each side (Figure 3-4). Use 2 × 4s for the batter board stakes and 1 × 4s for the crosspieces. Drive the stakes well into the ground and use braces if needed to secure them against displacement from accidental bumps. If the site slopes, begin at the highest corner of the building area and set the top of the first crosspiece at 24 in. above the ground. Use a transit, a string-and-line level, or a water level to mark the elevation on the other batter board stakes and then set all of the crosspieces to the same reference elevation.

Place nails in the tops of the batter boards and run string lines to mark the exact size and shape of the concrete (Figure 3-5). Using a plumb bob, mark the intersection of the strings by driving a length of steel-reinforcing bar into the ground to temporarily mark the exact corner of the concrete (Figure 3-6). Repeat this process at every inside and outside corner, being sure to square each corner so that the dimensions required by the drawings are exactly the same as those marked on the ground. If the last dimension in the perimeter does not match the drawings, then one or more of the corners is not square.

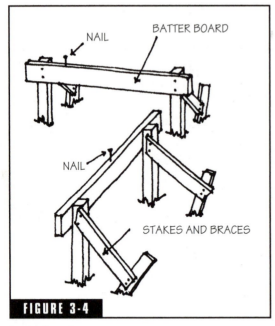

NAIL

BATTER BOARD

NAIL

STAKES AND BRACES

FIGURE 3-4

Batter boards.

The corner reinforcing bar stakes mark the outline of the slab or footing, and excavations should extend one or two feet beyond these limits to allow room for building the forms. Untie the string lines and pull them aside so that the excavation work can be done.

3.2.2 Excavating or Filling

Concrete footings, slabs, driveways, patios, and sidewalks will usually require some excavating or filling to establish the finished work at the proper elevation above or below the finish grade. Structural fill to support foundations or slabs-on-grade must be specified by the engineer as to the required type, compaction, and moisture content. This is work which should be performed by a qualified subcontractor with the proper equipment to achieve the strength and stability necessary for structural fill.

Excavation for a sidewalk or patio will usually consist of removing a few inches of topsoil. For grade beams or footings, excavation may be much deeper. The actual depth of foundations and footings will be indicated on the drawings by the project engineer or dictated by building code. In cold climates, footings must be placed below the winter frost line so that they are not destabilized by frost heave as the moisture in the soil freezes and expands. The map in Figure 3-8 gives winter frost depths in inches for the continental United States. This will give you a general idea how deep the bottoms of footings or grade beams must be set. The local building official can tell you exactly what the requirements are in a given area. In the northern tier of states and in the Rockies, foundations must be dug so deep that it is usually economical to excavate for a full or half basement.

QUICK»TIP To make sure that corners are square, use the 3-4-5 triangle method. From the outside corner point, measure 4 ft. along one string and 3 ft. along the other. The string lines are square when the diagonal between the two points measures exactly 5 ft. (Figure 3-7). To square a string line against an existing wall, use a steel carpenter's square.

Concrete slabs and footings must be supported on soil that is hard, uniformly graded, and well drained. A poorly or improperly prepared subgrade can cause uneven settlement and cracking. Remove all vegetation, roots, and large rocks from an area at least two to three feet wider than the slab or footing perimeter. Remove the soil to the necessary depth, allowing plenty of room around the outside to build the formwork. If you are digging very deep, leave a generous slope on the outer soil walls to prevent dangerous cave-ins. Dig out any soft or spongy areas in the subgrade and fill them with compacted

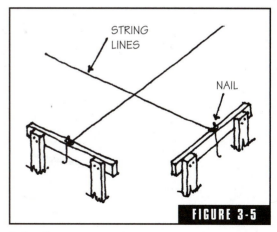

String lines.

soil, or with gravel, crushed stone, or sand. Loosen and tamp hard spots to provide uniform support for the concrete, but wherever possible, leave the subgrade undisturbed. Smooth loose surface soil and fill in holes left by stones or roots with sand or gravel. Level the subgrade surface and then compact it by hand, with mechanical rollers or vibratory compactors. In areas with poor drainage, excavate deeply enough to place a 4- to 6-inch layer of crushed rock or gravel under the concrete. Crushed rock is better than smooth gravel because it compacts firmly and provides more stable support for the concrete.

This aggregate drainage layer will stop the capillary rise of soil moisture into the bottom of the concrete.

Only small areas should be excavated by hand because the work is labor intensive and backbreaking. Larger areas are more economically excavated with heavy equipment or subcontracted to an excavation company.

3.3 Building Formwork

Small, shallow concrete footings can sometimes be formed by earth trenches if

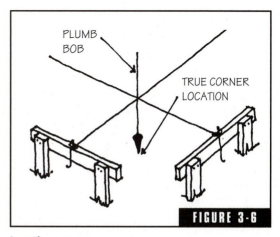

Locating corners.

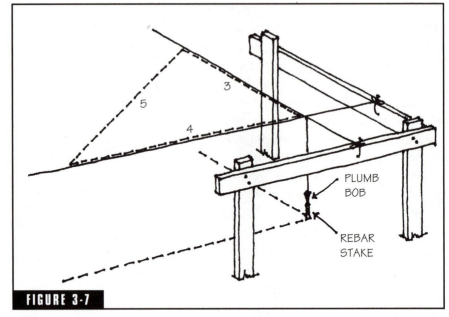

FIGURE 3-7

Squaring corners.

the soil is stable, but most concrete work requires building forms to shape and hold the mix until it hardens. Forms for concrete must be strong, tightly fitted, and rigidly constructed.

3.3.1 Temporary Formwork

Most formwork is removed after the concrete has hardened enough to support its own weight. The formwork materials can often be reused several times. The sides of residential concrete forms are usually constructed of 2× lumber or plywood held in place by wooden stakes or braces and stakes driven into the ground, depending on the height of the form (Figure 3-9). Removable forms must be built in such a way that the green concrete is not damaged by the form removal process.

Once the concrete size and shape have been laid out and the corners marked with the temporary reinforcing bars, the elevation of the top of the finished concrete must be established and a string line erected to set the form boards and supporting stakes correctly. The string lines should be attached to stakes set just beyond the corners. The strings themselves should be 1½ in. outside the corner markers to allow for the thickness of the 2× form boards (Figure 3-10). Stretch the string tightly from corner to corner using a line level to keep the elevation the same throughout its length. Braided nylon twine works best because it's strong enough to pull tightly without breaking. For forms that are only one or two boards high, supporting stakes should be spaced along the outside of the string beginning at the corners, at 3- to 4-foot intervals, depending on the height of the form, and at the intersection of abutting form boards. The deeper the concrete, the greater the pressure it will exert on the formwork, so don't be afraid to use an extra stake or two to help ensure that forms won't bulge or bow out of shape during the pour. Drive supporting stakes slightly below the height of the string so they won't interfere with leveling or finishing the concrete surface.

Set the forms so the tops of the boards are aligned on the inside of the string line and at the same height as the string (Figure 3-11). Butt

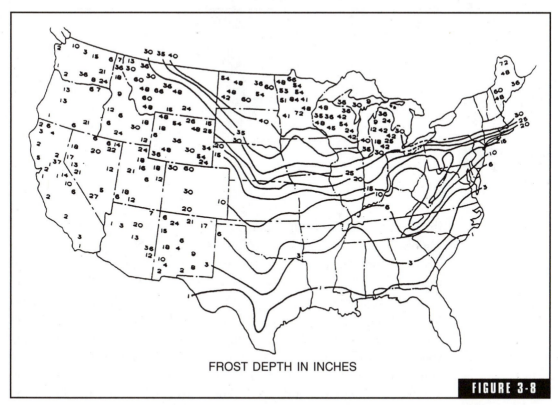

FROST DEPTH IN INCHES

FIGURE 3-8

Average annual frost depth for continental United States *(from* Architectural Graphic Standards, *9th ed.)*.

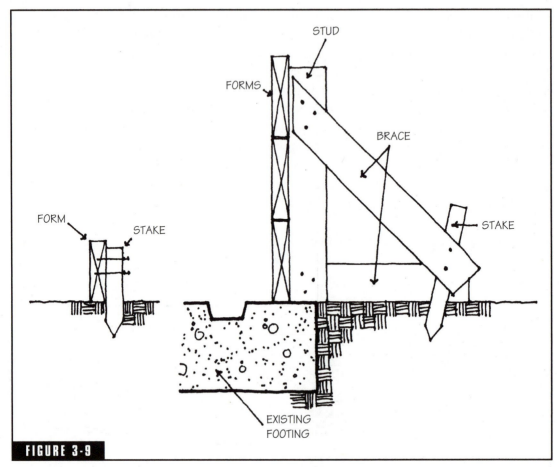

FORMS

STUD

BRACE

FORM

STAKE

STAKE

EXISTING
FOOTING

FIGURE 3-9

Bracing forms.

the form boards tightly together to prevent the wet concrete from leaking out. Where the ends of two boards adjoin, drive a stake so that it supports the ends of both boards. Hold the form boards firmly against the stakes and nail through the stakes into the form. Use double-headed nails or screws to make it easier to take the forms apart without hammering or prying against the finished concrete. The tops of narrow forms can be checked using an ordinary carpenter's level (Figure 3-12). For sidewalks, patios, or driveways, plan the locations of control joints and mark them on the tops of the form boards with a wax crayon or other marker that will show up easily when the forms are wet and splattered with concrete.

For taller forms, additional bracing to support the pressure of the concrete is needed. Vertical 2 × 4 studs and horizontal 2 × 4 wales are used for wall forms, and 2 × 4 yokes for column forms (Figure 3-13). In large forms, the lateral pressure of the concrete can be well over 1000 psf, so the spacing of supports must be close together to resist the tremendous weight without collapse. For wall forms, the studs should about 24 in. on center if you're using 2× form boards, or 12 in. to 16. in on center if you're using 3/4-in. plywood. Supporting wales should

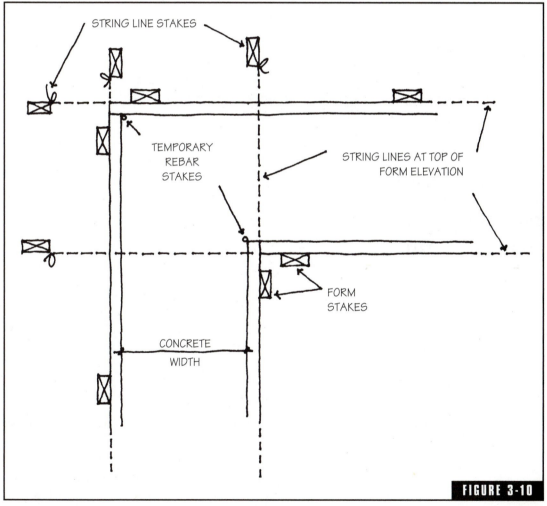

FIGURE 3-10

Corner forms and stakes.

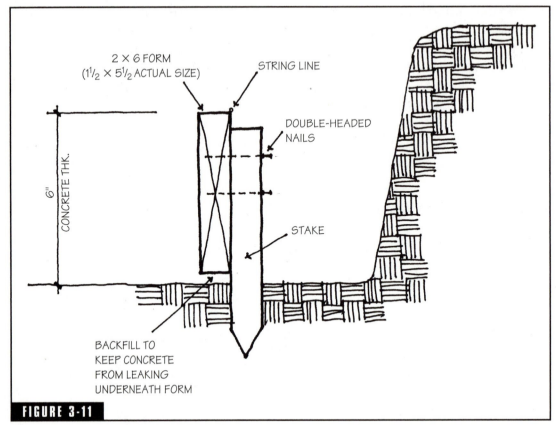

2 × 6 FORM
(1½ × 5½ ACTUAL SIZE)

STRING LINE

DOUBLE-HEADED NAILS

CONCRETE THK.

6"

STAKE

BACKFILL TO KEEP CONCRETE FROM LEAKING UNDERNEATH FORM

FIGURE 3-11

Form boards set to string line.

be 12 in. to 16 in on center. For columns up to 24 in. wide and 16 ft. tall, Figure 3-14 shows recommended yoke spacing. You can also buy round cardboard forms for columns, but you will have to build some supporting framework to hold them firmly in place during the concrete pour.

3.3.2 Permanent Formwork

In patios and sidewalks, form boards are sometimes left in place to serve as decorative dividers and edging. Corners and intersections should be formed as neat butt joints or miter joint. Stakes should be located inside rather than outside the form and driven well below the surface so they will be adequately covered by the concrete. Drive 16-d galvanized nails through the outside of the form boards at about 16 in.

on center to anchor the boards to the concrete and keep them in place. A finishing nail with a small head can be driven slightly below the surface of the wood so that it will not show in the finished construction. Redwood, cypress, and cedar are often used for permanent forms, but they must be coated with a clear sealer to protect them from the alkalis in fresh concrete. Pressure-treated lumber can also be used but does not have to be sealed because it is protected by chemical preservatives. Temporarily cover the tops of all permanent forms with masking tape to protect them from damage or staining during the concrete pour (Figure 3-15).

3.3.3 Curved Formwork

To form a radius corner on concrete, you'll have to build curved forms. For short-radius curves, it is easiest to use hardboard or plywood for the curved section. Cut strips of plywood to the same height as the 2× forms used for the straight sections, being sure to turn the grain of the plywood face veneer vertical so it will bend more easily (Figure 3-16). Space supports at 1-ft. or 2-ft. intervals. For long-radius curves, use 1× lumber. Wet the wood first to make bending easier, and space stakes at 2-ft. to 3-ft. intervals. It is more difficult to bend 2× lumber, but if you are building forms that will remain in place as decorative elements,

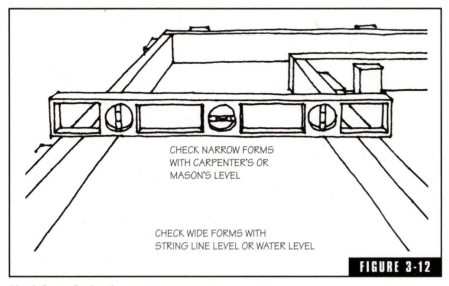

CHECK NARROW FORMS
WITH CARPENTER'S OR
MASON'S LEVEL

CHECK WIDE FORMS WITH
STRING LINE LEVEL OR WATER LEVEL

FIGURE 3-12

Check forms for level.

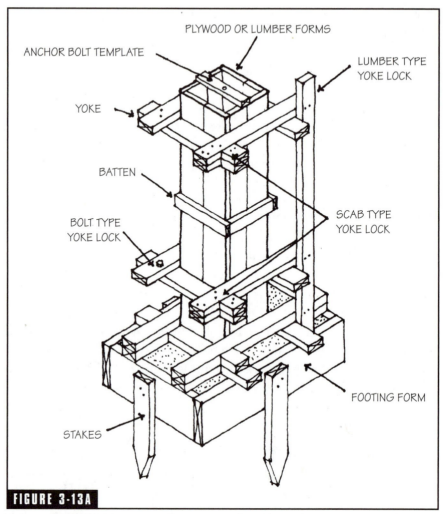

ANCHOR BOLT TEMPLATE

PLYWOOD OR LUMBER FORMS

LUMBER TYPE YOKE LOCK

YOKE

BATTEN

SCAB TYPE YOKE LOCK

BOLT TYPE YOKE LOCK

FOOTING FORM

STAKES

FIGURE 3-13A

Bracing tall concrete forms *(from U.S. Army,* **Concrete and Masonry.** *Technical Manual No. 5-742. U.S. Government Printing Office, Washington, D.C.).*

you may occasionally have to bend a 2 × 4 or 2 × 6 to form a long-radius curve. Saw the board one-half to two-thirds through, spacing the cuts two or three inches apart, then bend the board so that these "kerf" cuts are on the inside radius. As you bend the board, the kerfs will close up. At curves, nail the form from the inside to hold it securely, but use common nails here so the heads will not be embedded in the concrete (Figure 3-17).

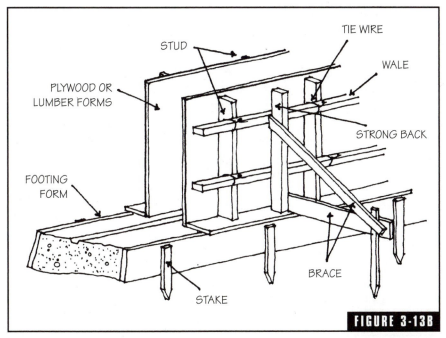

TIE WIRE

STUD

WALE

PLYWOOD OR
LUMBER FORMS

STRONG BACK

FOOTING
FORM

BRACE

STAKE

FIGURE 3-13B

Bracing tall concrete forms *(from U.S. Army,* **Concrete and Masonry.** *Technical Manual No. 5-742. U.S. Government Printing Office, Washington, D.C.).*

3.4 Placing Reinforcement

After the excavations are completed and the forms built, steel reinforcement is put in place to provide tensile strength for the cured concrete. Wire reinforcing mesh is used for shallow elements like sidewalks, patios, and driveways, and steel reinforcing bars are used for heavier elements like footings, slabs, walls, and columns.

3.4.1 Placing Steel Reinforcing Bars

Reinforcing steel must be completely embedded in concrete to develop full-strength and structural bond, and to provide adequate protection against corrosion. To keep steel reinforcing up off the ground or the bottom of the form so the concrete can surround it, use small stones or pieces of concrete block or special wire stilts to support the bars or mesh (Figure 3-18). The reinforcement should be located about one-third up from the bottom of the form. Where two pieces of reinforcing bar must be spliced together, lap them 30 times

Column Height, feet	Largest Dimension of Column, L, in inches			
	16	18	20	24
1	31	29	27	23
2	31	29	27	23
3	31	28	26	23
4	31	28	26	23
5	31	28	26	23
6	30	28	26	23
7	30	28	24	22
8	30	26	24	16
9	29	26	19	16
10	29	20	19	14
11	21	20	16	13
12	21	18	15	12
13	20	16	15	11
14	18	16	14	10
15	18	15	12	9
16	15	13	11	9

FIGURE 3-14

Column form yoke spacing, inches. *(Adapted from U.S. Army Corps of Engineers,* Concrete, Masonry and Brickwork.*)*

the diameter of the bar, or a minimum of 12 in. and tie them securely together with wire (Figure 3-19). For example, if the bar is $1/2$-in. diameter (No. 4 bar), 30 × $1/2$ in. = 15-in. lap. Intersecting steel reinforcing bars should also be tied to hold them together when the concrete is poured. The wire used to tie reinforcing should be a soft annealed wire, usually 16- or 14-gauge thickness.

For some applications, reinforcing bars will have to be bent to certain shapes. Figure 3-20 shows some typical bar shapes and end hooks, as well as minimum diameter of bend for various bar diameters. Reinforcing bars can be cut to size and bent on site or ordered from a steel fabricator in the sizes and shapes required by the drawings.

Provide a minimum distance of $1^{1}/2$ in. between reinforcing bars and the sides or bottoms of forms, and 3 in. between the rebar and the soil for slabs and footings. This will assure that the steel is fully embedded in the concrete and protected from the corrosive effects of moisture.

3.4.2 Placing Steel Reinforcing Mesh

Steel reinforcing mesh is a grid of steel wires welded together at the wire intersections and used to distribute shrinkage stresses in thin concrete sections like sidewalks and driveways. Light-gauge, welded wire mesh comes in rolls and heavier-gauge mesh in flat sheets. Like steel reinforcing bars, wire mesh reinforcing must be completely embedded in concrete to develop full strength and structural bond, and to provide adequate protection against corrosion of the metal. Since reinforcing mesh is often used in thin 4-in. slabs for sidewalks and patios, it is not always possible to place it as precisely as the reinforcing bars used in thicker slabs and footings. Reinforcing mesh is usually located in the center of the concrete thickness with a minimum of 1½ inches between the wire and the soil, and supported on small stones or pieces of concrete block. At splices, reinforcing mesh must be lapped one full row of squares and tied with soft steel tie wire (Figure 3-21).

3.5   Mixing Concrete on Site

If you're mixing concrete on site, the mixing area should be close to the pour area if possible, and your ingredients stockpiled nearby. Store bags of cement off the ground and cover them with plastic to keep them dry. Small quantities of sand can usually be purchased in bags at building supply yards. Larger quantities of both sand and gravel are sold by the ton or half-ton by aggregate suppliers and delivered to the site in dump trucks. Spread tarps on the ground before the sand is dumped so that the moisture content of the sand is not affected by the moisture content of the soil, and so that rocks or soil are not accidentally shoveled up with the sand.

One of the most important things in mixing concrete is consistency from batch to batch. The ingredient weights and proportions in the tables in Figure 3-3 are based on "wet" sand. Most sand that is sold for construction uses is "wet" sand, and the moisture that it contains has been accounted for in the recommended amounts of mixing water. If the sand you are using is "damp" rather than "wet," and you are mixing ingredients by weight, reduce the quantity of sand in Table A by one pound, and increase the quantity of

FIGURE 3-15

Permanent forms *(Photo courtesy PCA).*

QUICK»»TIP

- Damp sand falls apart when you try to squeeze it into a ball in your hand.

- Wet sand forms a ball when squeezed in your hand, but leaves no noticeable moisture on the palm.

- Very wet sand, such as sand exposed to a recent rain, forms a ball if squeezed in your hand, and leaves moisture on the palm.

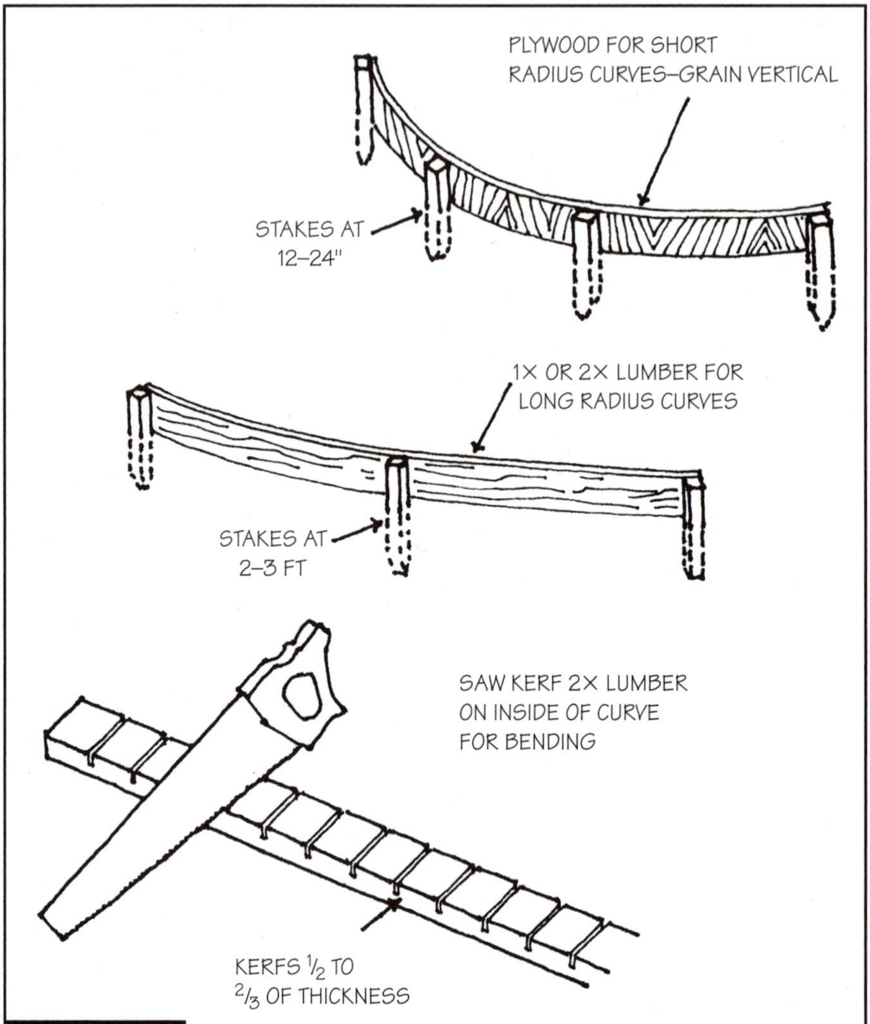

PLYWOOD FOR SHORT
RADIUS CURVES–GRAIN VERTICAL

STAKES AT
12–24"

1X OR 2X LUMBER FOR
LONG RADIUS CURVES

STAKES AT
2–3 FT

SAW KERF 2X LUMBER
ON INSIDE OF CURVE
FOR BENDING

KERFS $\frac{1}{2}$ TO
$\frac{2}{3}$ OF THICKNESS

FIGURE 3-16

Curved forms *(from Portland Cement Association,* **The Homeowner's Guide to Building With Concrete, Brick and Stone,** *PCA, Skokie, Illinois).*

water by one pound. If your sand is "very wet," increase the quantity of sand in Table A by one pound and decrease the water by one pound. The moisture content of sand is more difficult to adjust for when proportioning mixes by volume rather than weight. Up to a point, wet sand "bulks" to a greater volume than dry sand, and the amount of volume increase depends not only on the amount of moisture, but also on the fineness of the sand grains. If the volume of your sand is more or less than that assumed in Table B of Figure 3-3, your concrete may be over- or undersanded and therefore difficult to handle and finish. The volume of wet sand can be as much as $1\frac{1}{4}$ times the volume of the same sand if it were dry. All the variables involved in sand bulking make it difficult to adjust volume measurements, so if you are using the volume method of proportioning ingredients, always use wet sand. If your sand is too dry, wet it thoroughly with a garden hose the day before you

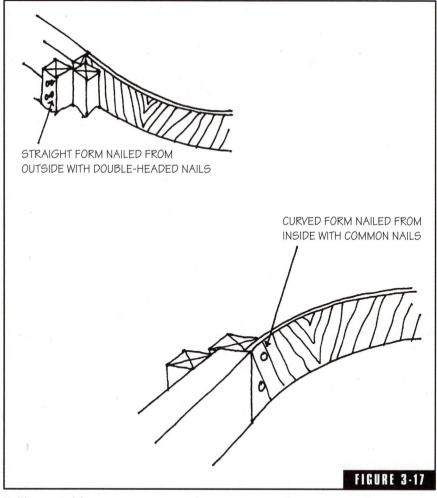

STRAIGHT FORM NAILED FROM
OUTSIDE WITH DOUBLE-HEADED NAILS

CURVED FORM NAILED FROM
INSIDE WITH COMMON NAILS

FIGURE 3-17

Nailing curved forms.

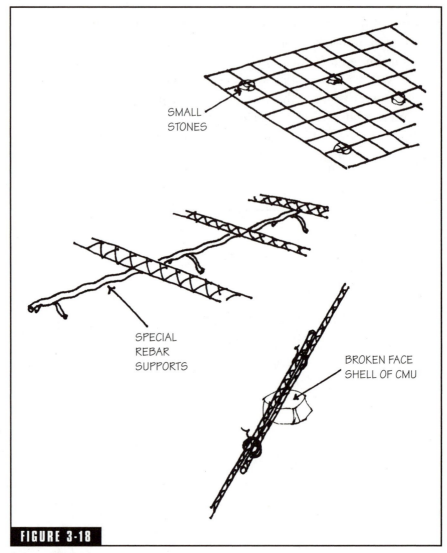

SMALL
STONES

SPECIAL
REBAR
SUPPORTS

BROKEN FACE
SHELL OF CMU

FIGURE 3-18

Reinforcing bar supports.

begin work. Keep the sand pile covered with a sheet of plastic when you're not working to minimize moisture evaporation.

3.5.1 Hand Mixing

If you need less than a cubic yard of concrete, or if ready-mix concrete is not available at the job site, you can mix your own concrete. For very small projects, like setting a post or doing minor repairs, it's easiest to buy a packaged concrete mix containing cement, sand, and gravel. The ingredients are already in the correct proportions, and all you have to do is add water to make fresh concrete. Packaged mixes are very convenient but are economical only for very small quantities of concrete. For batches requiring more than a few bags of packaged mix but less than the one cubic yard minimum which ready-mix suppliers usually require, it is more economical to mix concrete on site using portland cement and bulk aggregates.

Hand mixing concrete is very simple. Usually a large and sturdy wheelbarrow is the best container to use because you can mix in it, transport the concrete, and pour it into the forms. Clean and rinse the wheelbarrow before adding your materials. Place the correct proportion of each dry ingredient, and mix them together in the wheelbarrow with a mason's hoe. Make a depression in the middle, pour part of the water in, and mix it with the dry ingredients. Add the rest of the water, and mix all the ingredients thoroughly again. Hand mixing is not vigorous enough to produce proper air entrainment, so hand mixing should not be used for concrete which requires air-entrained cement or air-entraining admixtures.

3.5.2 Machine Mixing

Machine mixing is faster and a little less backbreaking than hand mixing. You can rent a small concrete mixer with a capacity ranging from $1/2$ to 6 cubic feet. The size of the concrete batch is usually only about 60% of the total volume of the mixer. This allows room for proper mixing and rotation without spilling. Never load a mixer beyond its maximum batch size. For volume proportions, use a bucket or shovel to measure

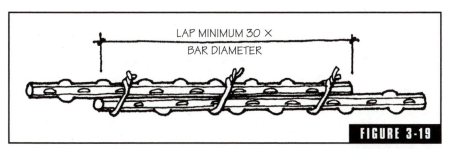

FIGURE 3-19

Reinforcing bar lap splices *(from Adams, J. T., The Complete Concrete, Masonry and Brick Handbook, Van Nostrand Reinhold, New York)*.

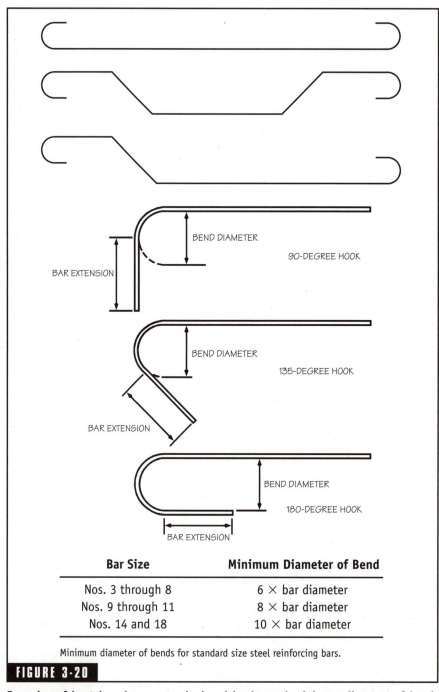

Bar Size	Minimum Diameter of Bend
Nos. 3 through 8	6 × bar diameter
Nos. 9 through 11	8 × bar diameter
Nos. 14 and 18	10 × bar diameter

Minimum diameter of bends for standard size steel reinforcing bars.

FIGURE 3-20

Examples of bent bar shapes, standard end hooks, and minimum diameter of bends *(from Waddell,* Concrete Manual, *International Conference of Building Officials, Whittier, California).*

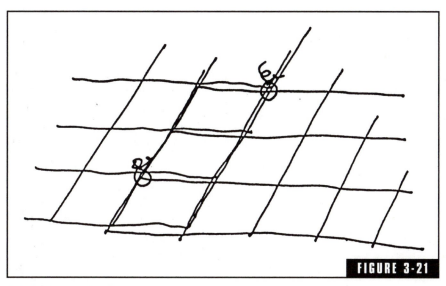

FIGURE 3-21

Reinforcing mesh splices.

ingredients accurately for each batch. For best results in mechanical mixing, load concrete ingredients into the mixer as follows:

1. With the mixer stopped, add all the coarse aggregate and half the mixing water.

2. Start the mixer, then add the sand, cement, and remaining water with the mixer running.

3. After all ingredients are in the mixer, continue mixing for at least three minutes, or until the ingredients are thoroughly mixed and the concrete has a uniform color. Do not overmix, or the ingredients will begin to separate.

Always clean the mixer thoroughly as soon as possible after you have finished using it. Add water and a few shovels of coarse aggregate to the drum while it is turning. This will scour the inside of the mixer. Dump the water and gravel, and hose out the drum.

3.6   Pouring Concrete

There are several rules to follow when pouring concrete. The first is that concrete should be placed in the forms as soon as possible after it is mixed. Delays result in evaporation of moisture from the mix and a loss of both workability and strength. If the concrete is not placed within $1\frac{1}{2}$ hours and shows signs of stiffening, it should be discarded. Do not add water to a mix that has begun to stiffen. Even if you succeed in restoring some workability, the concrete will be of poor quality. To avoid delays, it's important to make sure that all the necessary preparations have been made before the ready-mix truck arrives or before you begin mixing. Preparations should include wetting the inside surfaces of plywood and kiln-dried lumber forms and the soil subgrade to keep them from absorbing too much water from the concrete mix. Linseed oil or commercial form release oil can be used. Oiled forms will also make form removal easier without damage to the concrete surfaces. Oiling or wetting the forms and soil is especially important on a warm and windy day when moisture evaporation is at its highest.

The second rule in pouring concrete is to place the mix as near to its final location as possible. A ready-mix truck is equipped with metal chutes which can be extended a moderate distance to deliver concrete directly into the forms, and concrete pumps are often used on large commercial projects. On residential projects, it is more common to use wheelbarrows or buggies to move the concrete from the mixer to the forms. You can build ramps and runways over the forms to keep from bumping the boards or reinforcing out of place. Deep forms may require pouring in more than one *lift* or layer. Work in lifts of 6-in. to 24-in. thickness, consolidating the concrete as you go to eliminate voids and large air pockets. Continue with successive lifts until the pour is completed. In wall or column forms, concrete should not be dropped vertically more than three to five feet without appropriate chutes or baffles to keep the concrete from segregating. Start placing concrete at the ends or corners of the walls and work toward the middle. In slabs and footings, start placing the concrete in the farthest corner of the forms, depositing each load against the previously placed concrete. Do not make separate piles of concrete and attempt to move the mix horizontally because this will also cause segregation of ingredients. Make sure you get enough concrete to fill the forms completely. Fill low areas with a shovel if necessary, and tamp the concrete to fill in corners. Settle concrete against the perimeter forms by tapping the outside of the form boards with a hammer.

As the concrete is placed, use a hook or a claw hammer to lift wire reinforcing mesh and make sure that concrete flows underneath to completely embed it. Be careful not to displace reinforcing bars or knock them off their supports.

The third rule in pouring concrete is to effectively compact or *consolidate* the fresh mix immediately after it is placed and before it begins to stiffen. Concrete must be consolidated to eliminate air pockets and voids and to get the concrete to flow around reinforcement and anchorages. In very small applications, adequate consolidation can be achieved by rodding or puddling by hand with shovels, metal rods, or tampers, but mechanical vibration is preferred on most applications. High-speed mechanical vibrators cause the mix to settle evenly down into the forms and brings enough fine material and cement paste to the surface to permit finishing operations when appropriate. Internal or immersion type vibrators are most commonly used (Figure 3-22). They are immersed to the bottom of the concrete for a few seconds and withdrawn when it levels itself like a liquid and a thin layer of cement paste forms at the surface. Over-consolidation will cause the ingredients to segregate.

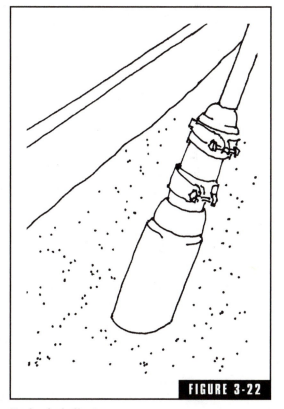

3.7 Concrete Finishing

The tops of concrete slabs, driveways, patios, and sidewalks must be leveled and finished to apply an appropriate surface texture. Surface finishes may be simple and utilitarian or more elaborate and decorative.

3.7.1 Floating, Troweling, and Brooming

The tops of footings and walls are left unfinished after the concrete has been vibrated, but flat concrete elements such as slabs, driveways, sidewalks, and patios must be leveled on top and an appropriate

FIGURE 3-22

Mechanical vibrator.

CONCRETE FINISHING TOOLS

A straight-edged board is used to strike off freshly poured concrete level with the tops of the forms (Figure 3-23). A tamper or "jitterbug" is used to consolidate stiff concrete mixes, settling the large aggregate and bringing fine material to the surface for easier finishing. A bull float is used to apply the first rough finish in large areas, or a darby in small areas. A wood float smooths and works the surface, a steel finishing trowel produces a final smooth finish, and an edging trowel gives a rounded edge that will not break off easily. A jointer or groover with a blade at least 1 in. deep or $1/4$ the thickness of the slab is used to form control joints. A stiff broom can be used to apply a nonslip finish, and other tools and techniques can be used to create decorative finishes.

---

finish applied. As soon as the first few feet or the first section of concrete is poured, you should begin striking off or *screeding* the excess concrete so that the surface is level with the top of the forms. Use a length of 2 × 4 that is slightly wider than the forms. Keep both ends of the strikeoff board pressed down on top of the forms and drag it along to roughly level the surface of the concrete (Figure 3-24). Fill any hollow areas that are left with shovels of concrete mix, and then strike them off. Wide elements like slabs and driveways next require a bull float with a long handle to begin smoothing the screeded concrete (Figure 3-25). You can make a bull float with a 4-ft. long 1 × 12 with a 12-ft. long 2 × 2 for a handle, or you can buy one. Place the float at the opposite edge of the slab from where you are standing, and draw it toward you. After you have finished a section, repeat the process from the opposite side. For smaller elements like sidewalks, a wooden darby can be used instead. *Do not do any more finishing until the water sheen is gone from the surface, and the concrete will hold your weight without your foot sinking more than $1/4$ in.* The time that this will take will vary depending on the temperature, wind and humidity, and the type of cement used.

For sidewalks, driveways, and patios, begin the concrete finishing operations by edging the slab. First, use the point of a small trowel to cut the top inch or so of concrete away from the face of the form (Figure 3-26), then edge the slab with an edging trowel to form an attractive, finished edge that will resist damage (Figure 3-27). Run the edger back and forth to smooth the surface, being careful not to gouge the concrete. Edging is not necessary on concrete slabs which will be covered by other construction. On sidewalks, driveways, and patios, use a jointing or grooving trowel to form control joints at the locations you

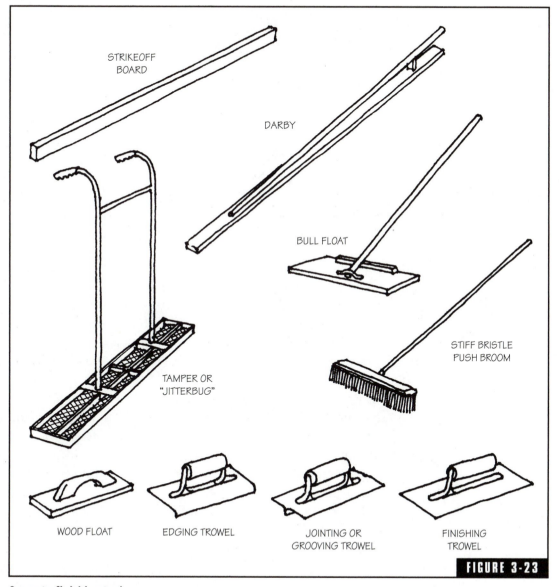

STRIKEOFF BOARD

DARBY

BULL FLOAT

STIFF BRISTLE PUSH BROOM

TAMPER OR "JITTERBUG"

WOOD FLOAT

EDGING TROWEL

JOINTING OR GROOVING TROWEL

FINISHING TROWEL

FIGURE 3-23

Concrete finishing tools.

FIGURE 3-24

Strike-off board.

previously marked on top of the form boards (Figure 3-28). Lay a 2 ×
12 across the tops of the forms to kneel on while you work, and use the
edge as a guide to assure that the joints are straight. If you want to saw
rather than tool your control joints, wait until the concrete has hardened for about three hours. Use a circular saw with a masonry cutting
blade, and saw grooves to a depth of about one-fourth the slab thickness (Figure 3-29). Use a straight piece of 2 × 4 as a guide.

After forming the control joints, use a float to smooth the concrete
surface and bring a sand and water mixture to the top of the slab. Hand
floats are made of wood, plastic, or composition materials. Magnesium
floats are light and strong and slide easily over the surface. Magnesium
floats are recommended for air-entrained concrete. Wood floats drag on
the surface and thus require greater effort, but they produce a surface
with relatively good skid resistance. Hold the float nearly flat and move
it in wide sweeping motions (Figure 3-30), smoothing over any marks or
gouges left from edging or jointing. If water comes to the surface when
you begin the floating, stop and wait awhile before trying again. After
floating the surface, go back over the edges and control joints with the

edger and jointing tool respectively to touch up. Wherever tile or pavers will be used as a flooring, leave the concrete with this float finish so that it will provide a good bond with the setting bed. Wherever carpet or hardwood floors will be laid, a float finish provides an adequate substrate without any further finishing work. A float finish also provides moderate slip-resistance for exterior surfaces such as driveways, patios, and sidewalks. For a nonslip finish on exterior sidewalks, patios, steps, or driveways, pull a damp broom across the floated concrete surface perpendicular to the direction of traffic (Figure 3-31). For a fine texture, use a soft bristled brush. For a coarser texture, use a broom with stiffer bristles. You will get best results if you buy a broom made especially for concrete finishing.

Bull float (*Photo Courtesy PCA*).

Where resilient tile or sheet flooring will be applied, the concrete surface must be very smooth so that imperfections will not "telegraph" through the flooring. Where the concrete will be left exposed in garages, utility rooms, and other areas, the surface must be smooth so that cleaning or waxing is easier. For a smooth, dense surface, a trowel finish is applied with a steel finishing trowel. Hold the blade nearly flat against the surface. Sweep it back and forth in wide arcs, overlapping each pass by one half the trowel blade length (Figure 3-32). This basically trowels the surface twice in one

Darby. (*Photo Courtesy PCA*).

operation. For an even smoother finish, go back over the surface again after you have finished the initial troweling. Go back over edges and control joints in outdoor work with the edger and jointing tool respectively to touch up after troweling.

FIGURE 3-26

Cutting edge of concrete from form. *(Photo courtesy PCA).*

On large slabs where it is not possible to reach the entire surface from the perimeter, floating and troweling requires the use of knee boards. Knee boards can be made from 24-in. long 1 × 10s with 1 × 4 handles on the ends (Figure 3-33), and are used to distribute the weight of the finisher without leaving deep depressions in the surface. Start in the least accessible areas and work your way backwards to the edge. When working on knee boards, troweling is typically done immediately after floating. This requires waiting until the concrete has hardened enough that water and fine material are not brought to the surface. Too long a delay will mean the surface is difficult to finish, but the tendency is to begin too early. Premature floating and troweling can cause scaling, crazing, or dusting of the concrete surface. For outdoor concrete subject to the extremes of weather, this is particularly harmful because the concrete is less durable and less wear resistant.

Power floats can be used to reduce finishing time on large slabs, and by changing blades, the same equipment can be used for troweling. Power floats can be rented at many tool rental stores.

3.7.2 Special Finishes

An *exposed aggregate finish* will add color and texture to a driveway, sidewalk or patio, as well as a nonslip finish. The concrete should be poured in small, manageable areas so that the aggregate can be seeded into the surface before the concrete becomes too hard. The seeding method of creating an exposed aggregate finish takes about three times longer than normal finishing so it is usually done in smaller sections.

FIGURE 3-27

Edging concrete. *(Photo Courtesy PCA).*

Formed control joints. (*Photo courtesy PCA*).

Sawed control joints. (*Photo courtesy PCA*).

Choose an aggregate that has a fairly narrow range of size variation such as $1/4$ in. to $1/2$ in., $3/8$ in. to $5/8$ in., or $1/2$ in. to $3/4$ in. You will get a more uniform texture if the stones are all similar in size. For best results, select rounded river gravel, and avoid crushed stone that is sharp or angular. After the concrete has been bull floated or darbied,

FIGURE 3-30

Wood float. *(Photo courtesy PCA).*

spread the gravel aggregate over the slab by hand or shovel so that the surface is completely and uniformly covered with a single layer of stones. Embed the seeded aggregate in the fresh concrete by tapping with a darby, a wood float, or a flat board until the aggregate is completely and uniformly covered by the concrete (Figure 3-34). Be careful not to embed the aggregate too deeply, and keep the finished surface flat. When the concrete has cured enough to bear the weight of a person kneeling on a flat board without leaving marks in the surface (anywhere from one to three hours, depending on conditions), begin brushing away the top surface of the concrete to expose the seeded aggregate. First, lightly brush the surface with a stiff-bristled nylon broom. Work carefully so that you do not dislodge the stones. If dislodg-

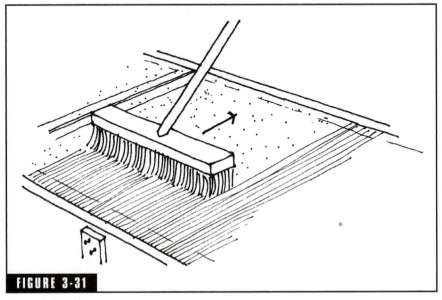

FIGURE 3-31

Broom finish.

ing occurs, wait until the concrete has cured a little longer. After the initial brushing, brush the surface again while simultaneously washing away the loosened concrete with a garden hose. The water spray should be strong enough to remove the loosened concrete, but not so strong as to blast the aggregate loose or gouge the surface. Continue washing and brushing the surface until the runoff water is clear and the top one-third to one-half of the aggregate is uniformly exposed.

To produce a *flagstone pattern,* bend a length of $1/2$-in. or $3/4$-in. diameter copper pipe into an "S" shape. After the concrete has been bull floated or darbied, use the pipe to cut a random flagstone pattern

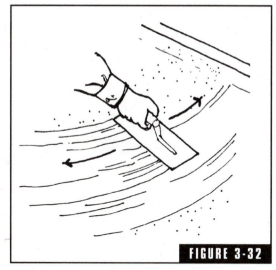

FIGURE 3-32

Steel finishing trowel.

into the concrete surface, forming grooves that are about $1/2$-in. deep (Figure 3-35). When the surface water has evaporated, float the surface and retool the grooves. When you are finished, brush out the

FIGURE 3-33

Knee boards. *(Photo courtesy PCA).*

Seeding aggregate for exposed aggregate finish. *(Photo courtesy PCA).*

Tamping aggregate for exposed aggregate finish. *(Photo courtesy PCA).*

FIGURE 3-34C

Embedding aggregate for exposed aggregate finish. *(Photo courtesy PCA).*

grooves carefully with a small, stiff-bristled brush to bristled remove any burrs or particles of concrete that remain.

In warm climates where winter freezing is not a problem, you can apply a *rock salt texture* to concrete. After troweling the surface smooth, scatter rock salt crystals evenly over the surface at a rate of 3 to 6 lbs. per 100 sq. ft. Roll a length of PVC pipe across the concrete, pressing the salt into the surface until only the tops of the crystals are exposed. After curing the concrete for seven days, wash and brush the surface to dissolve the salt, leaving a pattern of pits or holes that resembles travertine marble. In cold climates, water that freezes in these holes will expand and damage the surface, so rock salt finishes should be used only in areas that are not subject to winter freezing.

Pattern stamped finishes can create the look of masonry pavers in concrete. Special stamping tools can be rented or texture mats purchased in a variety of patterns from bricks to slate flagstones (Figure 3-36). For this type of work, the maximum aggregate size in the concrete should not be greater than $3/8$ in. After the surface has been troweled once, the stamping pads are pressed into the concrete surface, forming impressions that resemble paver joints. If the concrete is also colored

FIGURE 3-35

Flagstone pattern concrete. *(Photo courtesy PCA).*

and the joints filled with gray mortar, the effect is strikingly similar to masonry pavers but at a lower cost.

For *colored concrete,* a special powdered pigment is applied to the floated concrete surface after it has been edged and jointed. On the first application, dry-shake about two-thirds of the recommended amount of pigment uniformly onto the surface by hand. As the pigment absorbs moisture from the concrete, float it into the surface, apply the balance of the pigment, float the surface again, and then apply a smooth trowel finish. Tool control joints and edge the slab again after applying the color.

3.8 Curing Concrete

Concrete must be kept moist for several days after it is placed to allow the portland cement in the mix to cure and harden properly. The most common methods of curing concrete are as follows:

- Cover the surface completely with large sheets of plastic. Be sure to keep the plastic flat on the surface of the concrete, or it will cause uneven coloring. Weight down edges and joints with pieces of lumber.

- Cover the surface with roofing felt. Tape the joints and edges or weight them down with pieces of lumber to help seal moisture in and retard evaporation.

- Cover the surface with burlap bags, using a garden hose to keep the bags wet.

- Sprinkle or fog the concrete with a garden hose or sprinkler.

- Apply a chemical curing compound.

Plastic sheeting and roofing felt can cause uneven discoloration of the concrete surface if they are not kept flat. On large surfaces, it is difficult to smooth out all of the wrinkles in a covering, so if the concrete will be exposed to view and its appearance is important, use another method for curing. Wet burlap curing should not be used on colored

FIGURE 3-36

Pattern stamped concrete. *(Photo courtesy PCA)*.

concrete surfaces because it can cause the color to become splotchy. Keep the concrete moist for seven days.

After concrete slabs have cured for 24 hours, and concrete walls and footings for three days, remove the forms, but do not pry or hammer against the concrete itself. The concrete will continue to cure slowly for another month until it reaches full strength, but slabs are safe to use for foot traffic after the first day and for light rubber-tired vehicles after the first week. Heavy traffic areas should be protected with plywood. Foundation walls and footings should cure for at least two weeks before substantial framing loads are added.

3.8.1   Cold Weather Concreting

Cold weather can have damaging effects on freshly placed concrete. Both setting time and rate of strength gain are slower in cold weather, and if the concrete freezes during the first few days of curing, it will suffer reduced strength and weather resistance, and increased moisture permeability. When it is necessary to work in cold weather, certain precautions must be taken to assure the quality of the finished concrete.

Cold weather is defined as a period when the mean daily temperature drops below 40°F for more than three consecutive days. On commercial projects, heated enclosures are often provided to protect concrete and masonry work during cold weather. Although this is not usually done on residential work because of the expense, the following protective measures can and should be taken.

- For slabs and other flatwork such as driveways, sidewalks, and patios, reduce the amount of mixing water so that the concrete has a slump of 4 in. or less. This will minimize bleeding of mix water to the surface and decrease the time until initial set.

- Use air-entrained cement or an air-entraining admixture even if the concrete will not be exposed to freeze-thaw cycling in service.

- Use either an extra bag of cement per cubic yard of concrete, a high-early-strength cement (Type III), or a nonchloride set accelerator to develop strength faster.

- If you are ordering from a ready-mix supplier, specify heated concrete with a minimum temperature as recommended in Figure 3-37.

- Remove ice and snow from inside forms and thaw frozen subgrade before concrete placement.

- If you are mixing concrete on site, store ingredients in a heated area if possible, and use heated water for mixing.

- Reduce the time between mixing and placing as much as possible to reduce heat loss. Work with smaller batches if necessary.

- Keep concrete temperatures above the minimum recommended in Figure 3-37 for the number of days recommended in Figure 3-38. Place insulation blankets on slabs immediately after concrete has set sufficiently so that concrete surface is not marred. Provide double or triple thickness of insulation at corners and edges of slabs where concrete is most vulnerable to freezing. Use windscreens to protect slabs and other flatwork from rapid cooling.

- Delay form removal as long as possible to minimize evaporation and to reduce damage to formed surfaces caused by premature form stripping.

Condition	Sections Less Than 12 in. Thick	Sections 12 to 36 in. Thick
Minimum temperature } above 30°F	60	55
of concrete *as mixed* } 0°F to 30°F	65	60
in weather indicated } below 0°F	70	65
Minimum temperature of concrete *during placement and curing*	55	50
Maximum gradual temperature drop allowed in first 24 hours after protection is removed	50	40

FIGURE 3-37

Recommended temperatures for cold weather concrete, degrees F (*Adapted from American Concrete Institute Standard ACI 306R*).

Construction and Service Conditions	To Protect from Damage by Freezing		For Safe Form Removal	
	Type I or II Cement	Type III Cement	Type I or II Cement	Type III Cement
Not loaded during construction, not exposed to freezing in service	2	1	2	1
Not loaded during construction, exposed to freezing in service	3	2	3	2
Partially loaded during construction, exposed to freezing in service	3	2	6	4

FIGURE 3-38

Days of protection required for cold weather concrete. *(Adapted from American Concrete Institute Standard ACI 306R.)*

■ Wrap protruding reinforcing bars with insulation to prevent heat drain.

Whenever you can schedule concrete pours during milder weather, it is best to do so, but in some climates this is impractical. When cold weather concreting cannot be avoided, quality does not have to be sacrificed if proper precaution is exercised.

3.8.2 Hot Weather Concreting

Hot weather can also be damaging to concrete. The fresh mix will require more water than usual to achieve the required slump and workability, will set faster and have reduced working time, will more likely experience plastic shrinkage cracking on the surface, and will suffer variations in air content. The hardened concrete will have lower strength, more drying shrinkage and tendency to crack, less durability in freeze-thaw exposures, and less uniform surface appearance. The adverse effects of hot weather increase as temperatures rise, relative humidity falls, and wind increases, and the damage can never be completely undone. There are, however, a number of recommendations which can help avoid problems. The following protective measures should be taken when temperatures are 90°F or above, especially when accompanied by windy conditions or relative humidities below 25%.

- To decrease the possibility of plastic shrinkage cracking, use the largest size and amount of coarse aggregate compatible with the job requirements and, if ordering from a ready-mix supplier, specify a water-reducing admixture.

- Locate control joints at slightly closer intervals than when concreting in milder temperatures, and plan the locations of construction joints ahead of time with smaller working areas in mind.

- Use sunshades or windbreaks as appropriate, and avoid working during the hot afternoon.

- Have enough workers on hand to keep the job running smoothly and quickly.

- If you are mixing concrete on site, sprinkle aggregate stockpiles ahead of time for evaporative cooling and use ice as part of the mixing water.

- Reduce the time between mixing and placing as much as possible and avoid excessive mixing. Do not add water to ready-mixed concrete at the job site.

- Moisten the forms and reinforcement and moisten soil subgrades before placing the concrete.

- Cure the concrete for at least three days, but preferably for one week. When forms are removed, provide a wet cover for newly exposed surfaces.

The primary concern of hot-weather concreting is the rapid loss of mixing water to evaporation. All of the protective measures outlined are aimed at preserving the moisture needed for cement hydration and curing. If adequate moisture can be maintained in the concrete for at least three and preferably seven days, there will be no decrease in the quality of the concrete compared to that placed and cured in milder weather.

3.9 Avoiding Common Problems

There are a number of problems which can occur in concrete as a result of improper mixing, placing, or curing. The following are common problems that are easily avoided if proper procedures are followed.

Segregation is the tendency of the various constituents of a concrete mix to separate, especially the separation of the large aggregate particles from the cement mortar. Segregation can result in rock pockets or honeycombs in the hardened concrete, sand streaks, porous layers, scaling, laitance, and bond failure at construction joints. Harsh mixes have a tendency to segregate, usually those that are too wet but sometimes those that are too dry. A well-proportioned mix with a slump of 3 to 4 in. resists segregation, but any mix can segregate if it is not properly handled, transported, and placed. Once segregation has occurred, the aggregate cannot be reintegrated and the mix must be discarded. Segregation can be caused by overmixing or by improper handling during placement operations.

Bleeding occurs when the cement and aggregate in newly placed concrete begin to settle and surplus water rises to the top surface of the concrete. Bleeding continues until the cement starts to set, until bridging develops between aggregate particles, or until maximum settlement or consolidation occurs. Mix proportions, sand grading, sand particle shape, the amount of aggregate fines, the fineness of the cement, water content of the mix, admixtures, air content, temperature, and depth or thickness of the concrete all influence the rate and total amount of bleeding. A slab placed on a plastic vapor retarder will bleed more than one placed directly on soil because the soil absorbs some of the surplus water. Some bleeding is a normal part of concrete curing, but excessive bleeding can decrease the durability of the surface, interfere with the bond of cement paste to reinforcing bars, and increase porosity of the hardened concrete. Air entrainment reduces bleeding, as does a well-graded sand, an increase in cement content, or a reduction in water content. If changes are made to some ingredient quantities, the mix must be adjusted to maintain the proper proportions required for strength and durability. Bleed water must be allowed to dry naturally, as there is little way to remove it from the soft surface of the fresh concrete. Excessive bleeding will delay the start of finishing operations.

Plastic shrinkage cracking is usually associated with hot-weather concreting. It is caused by rapid evaporation of surface moisture from a slab or other flatwork. The procedures recommended for hot-weather concreting will alleviate the possibility of plastic shrinkage cracking.

Dusting is the wearing away of hardened concrete surfaces under traffic. Dusting is caused by mixes with too much water, segregation during the placement and consolidation of the concrete, dirty aggregate, applying water to the concrete surface during finishing operations, or premature or prolonged finishing operations which cause the formation of a weak surface layer called laitance. *Laitance* is a white or light gray substance which appears on the surface of concrete after it is consolidated and finished and which consists of water, cement, and fine sand or silt particles. Laitance prevents good bond of subsequent layers of concrete and adhesion of other materials to the concrete such as finish flooring. In an exposed slab, laitance will scale and dust off after the floor is in use, and it can contribute to hairline cracking and checking. Excessive amounts of rock dust, silt, clay and other similar materials can also contribute to laitance. The same measures that are used to reduce bleeding will also reduce the occurrence of laitance.

Scaling is the flaking or peeling away of a thin layer of cement mortar on the surface of concrete. The aggregate below is usually clearly exposed in patchy areas and often stands out from the remaining surface. Scaling can be paper thin or as deep as $1/4$ in. One type of scaling is caused by the same things that cause dusting and laitance: mixes with too much water, segregation during the placement and consolidation of the concrete, applying water to the concrete surface during finishing operations, or premature or prolonged finishing operations. Another type of scaling is caused by the use of deicing salts on non-air-entrained concrete, and can be prevented by the use of air-entrained cement or air-entraining admixtures.

In *false set,* concrete appears to set or harden after only a few minutes. This is a temporary condition caused by hydration of unstable gypsum (calcium sulfate) in the cement. It usually disappears with prolonged mixing or remixing and is generally not a problem with ready-mixed concrete. Do not add more water. After a few more minutes, with or without additional mixing, false set will usually disappear on its own.

Understanding Masonry

Masonry consistently ranks among consumers as the first choice in residential cladding materials. Studies conducted by the National Association of Home Builders have found that 60% of home buyers prefer masonry homes, that the homes command higher selling prices, and that masonry homes produce higher profit margins for the builder.

Brick and stone masonry have been favorites of builders and homeowners for hundreds of years, and concrete block is becoming popular for residential construction as well. Masonry symbolizes strength, durability, and prestige and at the same time adds warmth, color, and scale to a home. Masonry is most visible in building walls, but is also used in foundations, fireplaces, garden walls, retaining walls, floors, sidewalks, patios, and driveways. This chapter covers basic materials and properties of masonry.

4.1 Basic Properties of Masonry

The term *masonry* includes many different materials and types of construction. Natural stone as well as manufactured units of clay brick, concrete block, cast stone, structural clay tile, terra cotta, adobe, and glass block are all masonry materials. Brick, concrete block, and stone are the most popular and most widely used. Brick and concrete block are usually laid with mortar, but some block can be "dry-stacked" without mortar if the units have an interlocking shape or if a special surface-bonding mortar is applied to hold the units together. Natural stone is also usually set in mortar, but can be dry-stacked for walls of modest height used in landscaping applications. In addition to units and mortar, most masonry projects will include accessory items such as anchors, ties, flashing, or joint reinforcement. These accessories are as important to successful structural and functional performance as the units, mortar, and workmanship.

Masonry that is used as a facing material over a nonmasonry backing wall is called *veneer* (Figure 4-1). Veneers are typically only one unit in thickness. Freestanding masonry walls may be one unit or more in thickness depending on the type of masonry and the wall design. Walls that are only one unit in thickness and are not anchored to a backing wall are called *single-wythe walls. Double-wythe walls* are two units in thickness. If the space between the wythes is less than one inch, it is called a *collar joint* and is filled solidly with mortar or cement grout. A space wider than one inch between wythes is called a *cavity,* and may be either open or filled with grout or grout and steel reinforcing bars. Double-wythe walls with an ungrouted cavity are called *cavity walls.* Both cavity walls and veneer walls are designed to drain water through the open space between wythes or the space between the veneer and its backing wall. Insulation can also be installed in this space to increase the thermal resistance or R-value of the wall.

In most residential construction in the United States, masonry is used as a veneer over wood stud or metal stud framing. Veneers are nonstructural and support only their own weight while transferring wind loads to the backing wall. Masonry is strong enough to serve as a loadbearing structural wall which supports the floors and roof of a structure. Loadbearing masonry was once very common in both residential and commercial construction but was gradually surpassed in popularity by concrete, steel, and wood framing after the turn of the century. Contemporary loadbearing masonry is stronger and more economical than historic loadbearing masonry, and new structural masonry systems are gaining popularity again among home builders.

Like concrete, masonry is strong in compression but requires the incorporation of reinforcing steel to increase resistance to tension (pulling) and flexural (bending) stresses (Figure 4-2). Masonry will not burn, so it can be used to construct fire walls between units or areas of

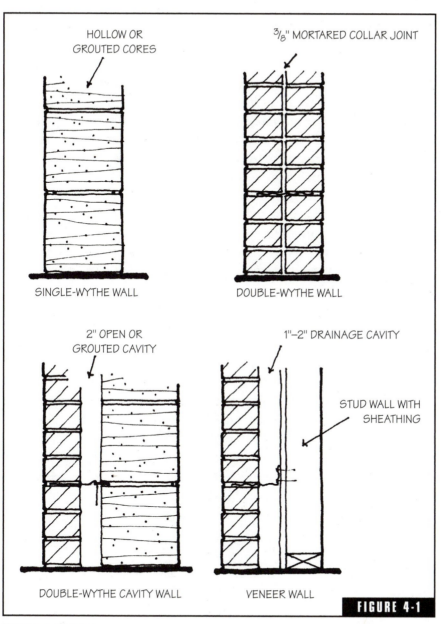

HOLLOW OR
GROUTED CORES

SINGLE-WYTHE WALL

$3/8$" MORTARED COLLAR JOINT

DOUBLE-WYTHE WALL

2" OPEN OR
GROUTED CAVITY

DOUBLE-WYTHE CAVITY WALL

1"–2" DRAINAGE CAVITY

STUD WALL WITH
SHEATHING

VENEER WALL

FIGURE 4-1

Masonry wall types.

multifamily housing or closely built single-family homes or town-houses. It is durable enough against wear and abrasion to serve as a paving material, and most types of masonry weather very well without any kind of protective coating. Masonry can provide efficient thermal and acoustical resistance, and when it is properly designed and constructed to meet current building codes, masonry is also resistant to earthquakes. In both the Loma Prieta and Northridge earthquakes in California, building officials documented the excellent performance of properly designed masonry in resisting significant seismic loads. The same is true for hurricane winds. When properly designed and constructed according to current building code requirements, even south Florida's Hurricane Andrew had little damaging effect on masonry structures. Almost any masonry material or combination of materials can be used to satisfy many different functional requirements, but specific masonry materials are usually selected on the basis of aesthetic criteria such as color, texture, and scale.

Like all building materials, masonry expands and contracts with changes in temperature, but masonry is relatively stable compared to metals and plastics. Concrete, masonry, and wood also expand and contract with changes in moisture content. Flexible anchorage, reinforcement, control joints, and expansion joints are used to accommodate the combined effects of thermal and moisture movements so that the masonry will not crack. Expansion, contraction, and weather resistance are discussed in more detail later in this chapter.

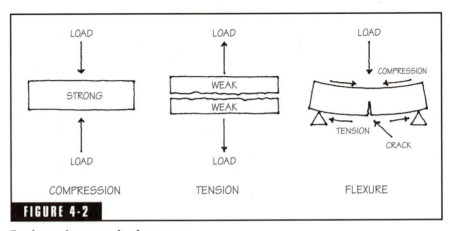

FIGURE 4-2

Tension and compression in masonry.

4.2 Brick

Brick can be made of several different materials, but the most common type of brick is made from ordinary clay soil. Clay brick is the oldest manufactured building material in the world, and it is still one of the most widely used. Sun-dried mud bricks are estimated to have been in use for about 10,000 years, and fired bricks since about 3,000 B.C. Sun-dried bricks are a traditional residential construction material in dry climates and are still used in many countries. The *adobe* construction of the Southwestern United States is made of sun-dried clay brick protected from the weather by a stucco coating. More typically, modern clay brick is fired at over 2,000°F in a large kiln to produce units that are very dense, hard, and durable. The color of the clay determines the color of the brick, and more than one clay can be combined to produce a variety of colors. Brick textures vary depending on the molding and forming process. Most brick are shaped by extruding wet clay through a die and slicing it to the appropriate size. Extruded brick may have holes cored through the middle which makes them lighter in weight and allows mortar to physically interlock with the brick. Even though they may contain core holes, if the cores account for 25% or less of the cross sectional area of the brick, the units are still considered to be solid. By this definition, most bricks are considered solid masonry units. Molded bricks are actually solid and do not have core holes, but they may have an indentation called a *frog* in one or both bed surfaces. When building codes make reference to solid masonry, they are referring to either masonry constructed of solid units (i.e., brick), or of solidly grouted hollow units such as concrete block.

4.2.1 Brick Sizes, Shapes, and Colors

Brick are rectangular in shape but come in many different sizes. The easiest size to work with is called *modular* brick because its height and length are based on a 4-in. *module.* The measured dimensions of a masonry unit are called the *actual dimensions,* and the dimensions of a masonry unit plus one mortar joint are called the *nominal dimensions.* The actual dimensions of a modular brick are 3-$\frac{5}{8}$ in. wide $\times$ 2-$\frac{1}{4}$ in. high $\times$ 7-$\frac{5}{8}$ in. long. The nominal length of one modular brick plus one $\frac{3}{8}$-in. mortar joint is 8 in. Three bricks laid one on top the other with three mortar joints is also equal to 8 in. If the height and length of masonry walls are multiples of 4 in. and doors and windows are located and sized on the 4-in. module, only whole and half-length modular brick will be needed and a minimum amount of cutting and fitting required. Modular bricks are easy to combine with other types of modular masonry units such as concrete block, which have nominal dimensions of 8 in. × 8 in. × 16 in. (Figure 4-3). Modular layout and planning are discussed in more detail in Chapter 5.

Some manufacturers make special brick shapes for both decorative and functional applications (Figure 4-4). Special shapes cost more but can add distinction to a home. The color of special-shape brick will not be an exact match to standard size brick of the same color because they are usually produced in a different run and there are always slight variations in clay color from one batch to another.

Colors and textures vary depending on the clay and the methods used to form the brick. Reds, browns, tans, pinks, and buff colors are common. Brick manufacturers also sell color blends which combine light and dark shades, and more than one color of brick to create different effects. It is very important with brick blends to distribute the different colors and shades evenly throughout the wall to avoid odd patterns or blotches of color. Brick from four different pallets should be used at the same time, and most manufacturers provide instructions for taking brick from the pallets in a way that will achieve the right color distribution. The wider the range of colors or shades, the more noticeable uneven visual effects can be (Figure 4-5).

Brick comes in three types. Architectural bricks (Type FBA) are the most popular for residential and some small commercial construction because they often resemble old brick. Type FBA includes hand-molded brick as well as extruded bricks that have been tumbled or rolled before firing to soften the edges or dent the surfaces (Figure 4-6b). FBA bricks have substantial size variations and may also be warped or have relatively large chips and cracks. Standard bricks (Type FBS) have a more uniform look (Figure 4-6a). The dimensions do not vary as much from one brick to the next, the edges are sharper, and there are fewer and smaller chips and cracks. Type FBX are more expensive precision brick with tight limits on size variation, chips, and cracks (Figure 4-6c). The edges are sharp and crisp, which gives them a very contemporary look. Type FBX is not very popular, even for commercial projects, and is not widely available. Type FBA, FBS, and

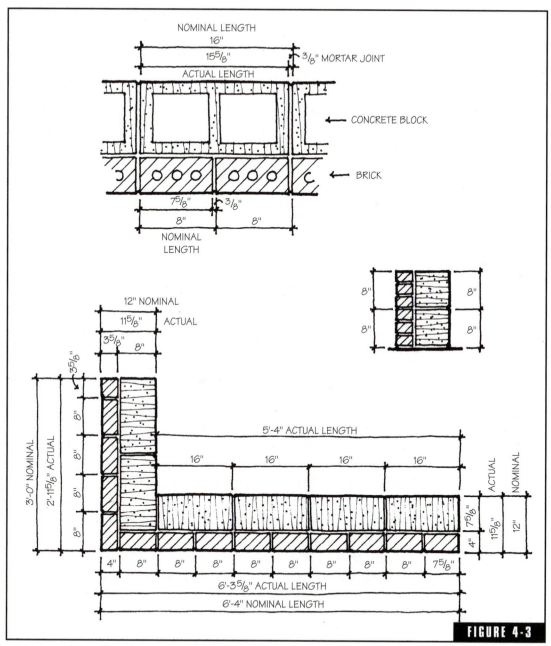

Modular masonry layout.

FIGURE 4-3

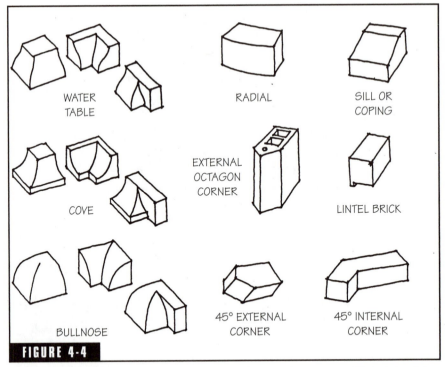

WATER TABLE

RADIAL

SILL OR COPING

COVE

EXTERNAL OCTAGON CORNER

LINTEL BRICK

BULLNOSE

45° EXTERNAL CORNER

45° INTERNAL CORNER

FIGURE 4-4

Special shape bricks. *(from Beall, Christine,* Masonry Design and Detailing, *4th edition, McGraw-Hill, New York).*

FBX brick are all required to meet the same strength and durability standards and differ only in appearance.

The best way to choose brick is to visit a brick plant or brick distributor to look at samples. If there are large sample panels or photographs of completed projects available, these will give the best idea of what the finished masonry will look like when combined with different mortar colors. Choose brick based on what goes with the style of the home, what seems most appropriate to the type of project, or simply what you like the best. There will always be some price variation, but even for a large home, the cost difference is very small compared to the overall construction budget. Always buy from a reputable manufacturer or distributor because cheap imported brick are often not very durable.

4.2.2 Brick Properties

Brick has many properties which make it a good building material. It is strong, hard, fireproof, abrasion resistant, and provides some degree

of thermal and acoustical resistance. Three
of the most important properties of brick
are strength, absorption, and freeze-thaw
resistance.

Strength: Brick are much stronger than
they need to be for simple one- and two-
story construction. Compressive strength
can range from 1,500 to 22,500 psi. The
majority of brick produced in the United
States and Canada exceeds 4,500 psi. Mortar is not as strong as brick, so when mortar
and brick are combined, the compressive
strength of the masonry drops to about
1,000-2,000 psi, depending on the mortar
mix and the exact brick strength. Even at a
very modest 1,000 psi, a brick wall could
theoretically support its own weight for a
height of more than 600 feet without crushing. To resist the bending stress of wind
loads, though, the wall also needs flexural
strength. Flexural strength requires good
bond between the mortar and the units,
and good bond is a function of brick tex-

FIGURE 4-5

Uneven color distribution. *(from Beall, Christine,* Masonry Design and Detailing, *4th edition, McGraw-Hill, New York).*

ture and absorption, mortar quality, and workmanship.

Absorption: When fresh mortar comes in contact with a brick, the
mortar paste is absorbed into the surface pores, contributing to the
strength of the bond between brick and mortar. Brick that is very
moist cannot properly absorb the mortar paste, and the lower bond
strength reduces resistance to wind loads and cracking. Brick that is
very dry absorbs too much water so that the mortar cannot cure properly and develop adequate bond strength. Moist brick should be
allowed to dry before use so that its absorption is increased, and dry
brick should be hosed down so its absorption is reduced. The mortar
could also be mixed with a little more or a little less water. Too much
or too little water in the mortar, however, decreases its workability so
it is better to adjust the moisture content of the brick instead of the

FIGURE 4-6A

Type FBS brick.

FIGURE 4-6B

Type FBA brick.

FIGURE 4-6C

Type FBX brick.

water content of the mortar. Ideally, the body of the brick should be moist and the outer surfaces dry to the touch (Figure 4-7). Sprinkle dry brick with a garden hose at least one day ahead of time so the surfaces will dry off before you use them, and allow wet brick to dry to the same condition.

Weathering Grade: There are two grades of brick, Grade MW (Moderate Weathering) and Grade SW (Severe Weathering), which are indicative of the brick's ability to withstand freezing and thawing over a long period without damage. In warm climates like south Florida, south Texas, southern Arizona and southern California, Grade SW will provide better performance for horizontal work where the brick is in contact with the soil. In all other areas of the United States, Grade SW is recommended for *all* outdoor uses because it has better resistance to damage from repeated freezing and thawing.

4.2.3 Brick Pavers

Brick for use in streets, walks, patios, and driveways must be strong, hard, and very dense. Used brick, although popular for residential

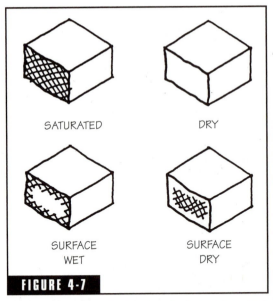

SATURATED   **DRY**

SURFACE WET   **SURFACE DRY**

FIGURE 4-7

Moisture content of brick. *(from* **Technical Note 17C,** *Brick Industry Association, Reston, VA).*

paving, may not always be durable enough for paving in cold climates. Paving bricks are manufactured to meet special needs with high compressive strength, resistance to abrasion, and low moisture absorption to increase durability against winter freezing and thawing cycles.

Paving brick that are designed to be laid *with* mortar have the same 3-5/8-in. width × 7-5/8-in. length as modular brick. Paving bricks that are designed to be laid *without* mortar are a full 4 in. × 8 in. so that patterns will still lay out to a 4-in. module. Paving brick come in several thicknesses, the most common of which are 1-5/8 in. for light traffic areas such as patios and sidewalks, and 2-1/4 in. for heavy traffic areas such as driveways and streets (Figure 4-8).

4.2.4 Fire Brick

Fireplaces and barbecue pits have special requirements because of the high temperatures to which the firebox brick are exposed. Special *fire brick* are made from fire clay which has a much higher melting point than ordinary clay or shale. Fire brick can tolerate long exposure to high temperatures without cracking, decomposition, or distortion. Fire brick are usually heavier, softer, and larger than ordinary brick. They are laid with very thin joints of mortar made from fire-clay instead of cement. Fire clay produces brick that are white or buff color. The units must be 100% solid, with no cores or frogs.

4.3 Concrete Masonry Units

Concrete masonry units (CMUs) include both large block and smaller brick size units. Concrete masonry units are made from cement, sand, and crushed stone or gravel aggregate that is molded and cured at a manufacturing plant. The basic ingredients are the same as those used for cast-in-place concrete, except that the aggregate is smaller. Concrete

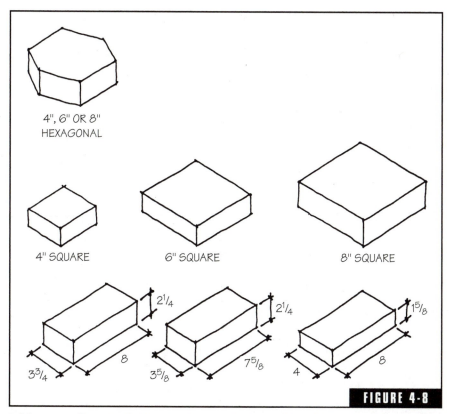

FIGURE 4-8

Brick pavers. *(from Beall, Christine,* Masonry Design and Detailing, *4th edition, McGraw-Hill, New York).*

block is quite common in commercial construction and has gained a larger share of the residential market as a wider variety of textures and colors have become available. Traditional gray concrete block are quite plain but can be painted or plastered to improve their appearance and to protect them from moisture absorption. Many manufacturers also produce colored and textured block which are usually treated with a clear water repellent so that they may be exposed to the weather without any additional protective coating. Concrete brick are made in sizes and shapes similar to clay brick, but they are not used as widely used.

4.3.1 Block Sizes and Shapes

Most concrete block are nominally 8 in. high $\times$ 8 in. thick $\times$ 16 in. long and are cored with two or three large holes per unit to reduce the weight as much as possible. The long exterior sides of the blocks are called face shells, and the short sections connecting the face shells are called webs. The core holes are tapered slightly to make it easier to remove the block from the manufacturing molds, and to provide a better grip for handling in the field. The wider surface should always be on top when the units are placed in a wall because it also gives a larger area for spreading mortar (Figure 4-9).

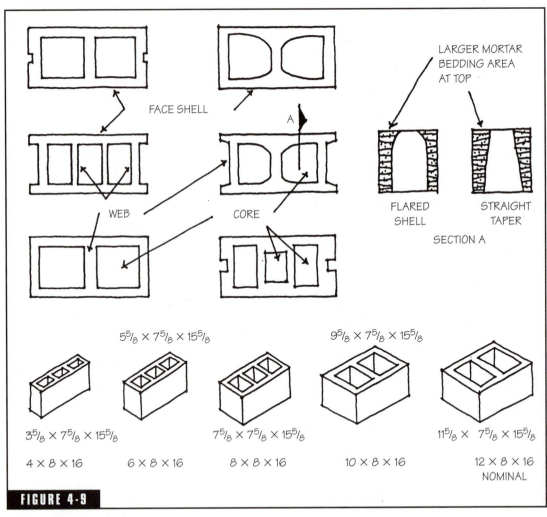

FACE SHELL

LARGER MORTAR BEDDING AREA AT TOP

WEB

CORE

FLARED SHELL

STRAIGHT TAPER

SECTION A

$5\frac{5}{8} \times 7\frac{5}{8} \times 15\frac{5}{8}$

$9\frac{5}{8} \times 7\frac{5}{8} \times 15\frac{5}{8}$

$3\frac{5}{8} \times 7\frac{5}{8} \times 15\frac{5}{8}$

$7\frac{5}{8} \times 7\frac{5}{8} \times 15\frac{5}{8}$

$11\frac{5}{8} \times 7\frac{5}{8} \times 15\frac{5}{8}$

4 × 8 × 16

6 × 8 × 16

8 × 8 × 16

10 × 8 × 16

12 × 8 × 16
NOMINAL

FIGURE 4-9

Concrete block terminology.

Standard concrete block measure 7-5/8 in. × 7-5/8 in. × 15-5/8 in. actual size. The actual dimensions, plus the thickness of a 3/8-in. mortar joint, equal 8 in. × 8 in. × 16 in. nominal dimensions. The most commonly used block thickness is also nominally 8 in., but nominal 4-, 6-, 10-, and 12-in. thicknesses are also available. Three modular bricks with mortar joints are the same height as one modular 8-in. block with one mortar joint, and two modular brick lengths with one joint equals one modular block length (see Figure 4-3). This makes it very easy to use brick and concrete masonry units together in the same project. It is quite common, particularly in commercial construction, for concrete masonry walls to serve as a structural backing for brick veneer walls or for brick and block to be used side by side in a veneer.

4.3.2 Special-Purpose Blocks

Plain rectangular block units are called stretchers, but there are also a number of special shapes used in CMU construction (Figure 4-10). A few of these shapes are fairly common, including the channel or lintel block and bond beam block, both of which can be used to build a steel-reinforced beam to span across window and door openings. Another special shape which can be very useful is called an open-end or "A" block because it is shaped like the letter "A." Masonry walls containing vertical reinforcing steel are easier to build by placing A-block around the reinforcing bar rather than lifting and threading standard stretcher units over the top of the bar or trying to drop the steel down into the block core after the units are in place. The end webs of stretcher units can also be cut away for the same ease of placement.

The newest type of concrete masonry units are interlocking retaining wall blocks, which are designed to be laid without mortar. There are several different types of systems marketed under a variety of trade names (Figure 4-11). These new systems greatly simplify the construction of small landscape retaining walls. The cost per unit is higher than for standard block but the savings in time and labor is substantial.

4.3.3 CMU Colors and Finishes

Ordinary concrete block are grey and have flat face shells with textures that may range from coarse to relatively fine, depending on the aggregate used and the density of the block. *Architectural block* come in a

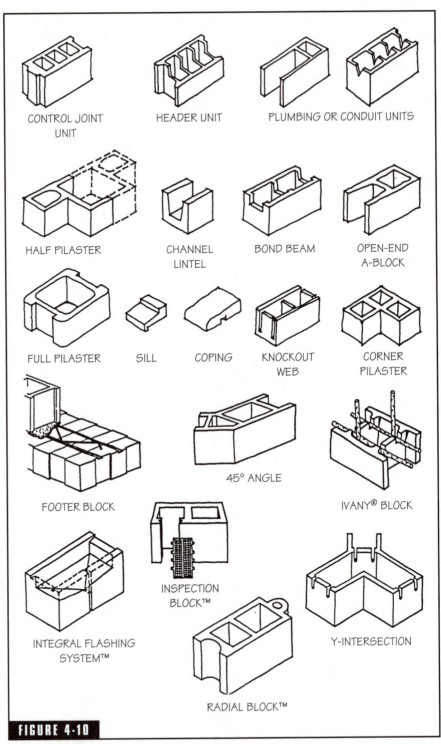

CONTROL JOINT UNIT

HEADER UNIT

PLUMBING OR CONDUIT UNITS

HALF PILASTER

CHANNEL LINTEL

BOND BEAM

OPEN-END A-BLOCK

FULL PILASTER

SILL

COPING

KNOCKOUT WEB

CORNER PILASTER

FOOTER BLOCK

45° ANGLE

IVANY® BLOCK

INTEGRAL FLASHING SYSTEM™

INSPECTION BLOCK™

Y-INTERSECTION

RADIAL BLOCK™

FIGURE 4-10

Special shape CMUs. *(from Beall, Christine, Masonry Design and Detailing, 4th edition, McGraw-Hill, New York).*

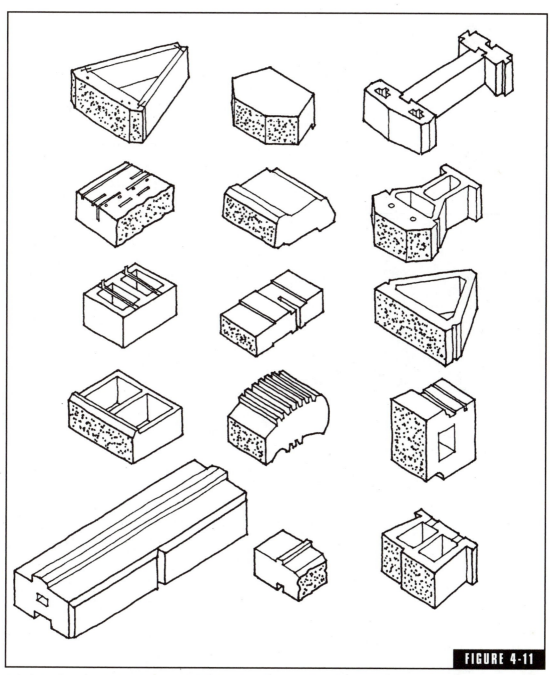

FIGURE 4-11

A variety of segmental retaining wall (SRW) units. *(from National Concrete Masonry Association,* Design Manual for Segmental Retaining Walls, *NCMA, Herndon, VA).*

FIGURE 4-12A

Split-face block.

variety of colors and textures. Most manufacturers now produce "split-face" or "rock-face" units which resemble a natural stone texture, as well as ribbed block, fluted block, scored block, and units with raised geometric patterns or smooth ground faces (Figure 4-12). Architectural block colors range from creams, buffs, and browns to reds, pinks, and even greens. Some colors are produced by using colored aggregates, while others are made by adding natural or synthetic pigments. Units made with colored aggregates are often brighter, and the color will not fade in the sun. Those made with pigments come in a greater variety of colors, but some may fade a little with time.

4.3.4 CMU Properties

Unit Strength: Aggregate type, size, and gradation as well as water-cement ratio are important in determining the compressive strength of concrete masonry units. Manufacturers determine optimum ingredient proportions to obtain a balance among moldability, handling, breakage, and strength. For non-loadbearing CMU, compressive strength may be as little as 500 psi and still adequately serve its purpose. For loadbearing applications, CMU should have a minimum average compressive strength of 1,900 psi. Typically, compressive strengths range from about 1,000 to 3,000 psi.

Unit Weight: Concrete block can be made with aggregates that are light, medium, or heavy in weight. The heavy block are made with sand and gravel or crushed stone and can weigh more than 40 lbs. each. Lightweight units made with coal cinders, slag, and other aggregates may weigh as little as 22 lbs. apiece. The lightweight block have higher thermal and fire resistance but also have higher moisture absorption.

4.3.5 Concrete Pavers

Concrete masonry pavers are popular for residential applications but are strong and durable enough to be used in commercial and even municipal paving. Concrete pavers come in a number of shapes (Figure 4-13) and are designed to be laid on a sand bed with no mortar between units. The small units interlock for stability under traffic loads. The openings in the grid pavers are filled with gravel, or with soil and grass, and allow rainwater to percolate into the ground with virtually no runoff. Concrete pavers are much stronger and more dense than ordinary concrete block, so they will absorb little moisture and not be damaged by repeated freezing and thawing. For residential driveways, a thickness of about 3-$\frac{1}{8}$ in. is usually used. For patios and sidewalks, a 2-$\frac{3}{8}$-in. thickness is adequate.

FIGURE 4-12B

Ribbed block.

4.3.6 Coatings for Concrete Masonry

All concrete and masonry surfaces absorb moisture, some to a greater or lesser degree than others. A troweled concrete slab or a fired clay brick, for instance, are more dense and therefore less absorbent than concrete block. Coatings can be applied to concrete and masonry to increase resistance to water absorption. Although new brick construction does not usually require such treatment because of the density of the brick, concrete block is often treated with paint, plaster, or clear water repellents, particularly in climates with large amounts of rainfall or cold weather. Light-colored stone is also sometimes treated with a clear water repellent to help keep dirt from discoloring the surface. Concrete slabs are often treated with clear water repellents to reduce staining and to reduce freeze-thaw damage from absorbed water. Clear coatings are thin and do not have any elasticity, so they

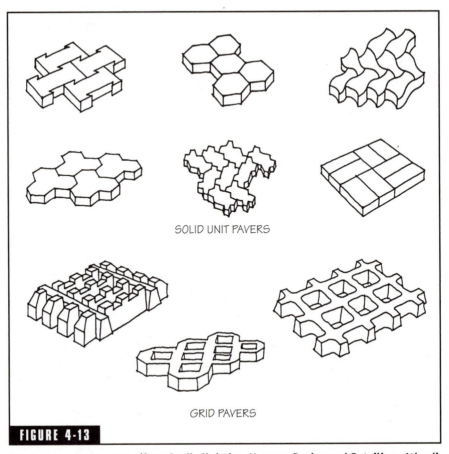

SOLID UNIT PAVERS

GRID PAVERS

FIGURE 4-13

Concrete masonry pavers. *(from Beall, Christine,* Masonry Design and Detailing, *4th edition, McGraw-Hill, New York).*

will not seal cracks in the surface. Water-repellent coatings come in a variety of proprietary formulations marketed under different trade names. The most common clear and opaque masonry coatings are available through masonry or building suppliers. Coatings usually require reapplication every few years. In order to maintain the weather resistance of the surface the homeowner must bear this expense periodically. To provide fundamental resistance to water penetration, however, requires more than just surface coatings. Other factors affecting the performance of masonry in resisting the harmful effects of water penetration are discussed in detail in the sections below on weather resistance.

4.4   Cast Stone and Cultured Stone

Cast stone is a fine-grained precast concrete product manufactured to resemble natural stone, with the same finish as stone which has been cut and dressed to precise shape and dimension. Despite its name, cast stone is more closely related to concrete and concrete masonry than to natural stone. Cast stone is used for decorative accessory elements in masonry construction. *Cultured stone* or "simulated" stone is another manufactured product which looks like rustic stone and is used as a veneer.

Cast stone is made of a carefully proportioned mix containing natural gravel, washed and graded sand, and crushed and graded stone such as granite, marble, quartz, or limestone. White portland cement usually is used to produce light colors and color consistency, although grey cement and color pigments are sometimes blended with the white cement. Because a rich cement-aggregate ratio of 1:3 is normally used, cast stone properly cured in a warm, moist environment is dense, relatively impermeable to moisture, and has a fine-grained, natural texture. Cast stone is relatively heavy, and its compressive strength is higher than ordinary cast-in-place concrete. Most cast stone manufacturers produce and stock standard items of architectural trim such as balusters, corner quoins, door pediments, and balcony rails (Figure 4-14). Any shape which can be carved in natural stone can generally be reproduced in cast stone at a lower cost. Cast stone may also simulate the appearance of small, roughly hewn quarried stone or weathered natural stone from fields or riverbeds. The color of the cement and the type of aggregate can be varied depending on the desired appearance. To produce a simulated white limestone, for instance, white portland cement and limestone dust are used (Figure 4-15). Cast rubble stone is generally less expensive than natural stone and easier to lay because it is more regular in size and shape and does not require field trimming.

4.5   Natural Stone

There are many different ways to describe stone. It can be identified by the form in which it is used—rubble, ashlar, or flagstone. It can be identified by its type or mineral composition—granite, limestone,

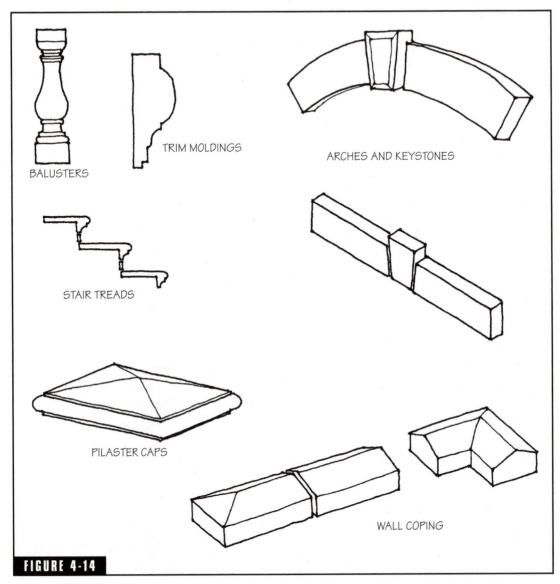

BALUSTERS

TRIM MOLDINGS

ARCHES AND KEYSTONES

STAIR TREADS

PILASTER CAPS

WALL COPING

FIGURE 4-14

Cast stone elements.

sandstone, slate, etc. It can be described by the way in which it is obtained—field stone gathered from the earth's surface in its natural state, or cut stone quarried and shaped with tools or mechanical equipment. It can also be described by method of geologic origin—igneous, sedimentary, or metamorphic. For building stone, the type of stone and the way in which it is used are the most important and most descriptive kinds of information.

4.5.1   Rubble, Ashlar, and Flagstone

Rubble stone is irregular in size and shape. *Fieldstone rubble* is harvested from fields in its natural form—smooth but irregular and uneven. *Quarried rubble* comes from the fragments of stone left over from the cutting and removal of large slabs from stone quarries. Fieldstone rubble is weathered on all its surfaces, while quarried rubble has freshly broken faces which may be sharp and angular (Figure 4-16). Rounded fieldstone and river-washed stone can be hard to work with because the smooth, curved surfaces make it difficult to stack with stability. Round or awkwardly shaped rubble can be roughly squared with a hammer to make it fit together more easily. Quarried rubble is more angular but may also require trimming with a mason's hammer for better fit. Rubble stone can be laid in a number of different patterns, depending on its size and shape and the desired appearance (Figure 4-17).

Ashlar is a type of cut stone processed at a quarry to produce relatively smooth, flat bedding surfaces that stack easily. Ashlar is generally

FIGURE 4-15A

Cast rubble stone.

FIGURE 4-15B

Cast rubble stone.

cut into small squares or rectangles and has sawn or dressed faces, but the face may also be left slightly rough. The free-form look of a rubble stone wall is quite different from the more formal pattern of an ashlar stone wall (Figure 4-18). Rubble and ashlar cut stone can be used together where their distinctly different appearance creates contrasting elements in a wall (Figure 4-19).

Flagstone may be a quarried material that has been cut into flat slabs for use as paving, a field stone that is naturally flat enough for paving, or a stone that naturally splits into thin layers. Flagstone ranges from $1/2$ in. to 2 in. thick and may be shaped in either rough mosaic form or geometric patterns (Figure 4-20).

4.5.2 Common Types of Natural Stone

Although there are many different types of natural stone, only a few are suitable for building. A good building stone must have strength, hardness, and durability, but also be workable. The degree of hardness of a stone dictates its relative workability as well as its ultimate form and cost, and determines its durability and weathering characteristics. A soft stone is easily workable with hand tools and therefore less expensive than a hard stone, which requires machine cutting. Soft stones are also more porous and have less resistance to damage from weathering. The most common stones that satisfy the requirements of building construction are granite, limestone, sandstone, and slate. While many others, such as quartzite, bluestone, brownstone, and serpentine, are available in some parts of the country, they are used less frequently.

Granite is an extremely hard, strong stone noted for its long term durability and resistance to weathering. Its color may be red, pink, brown, buff, green, gray, or black, depending on where it was quarried. Because it is so hard, granite must be cut and dressed at the quarry or

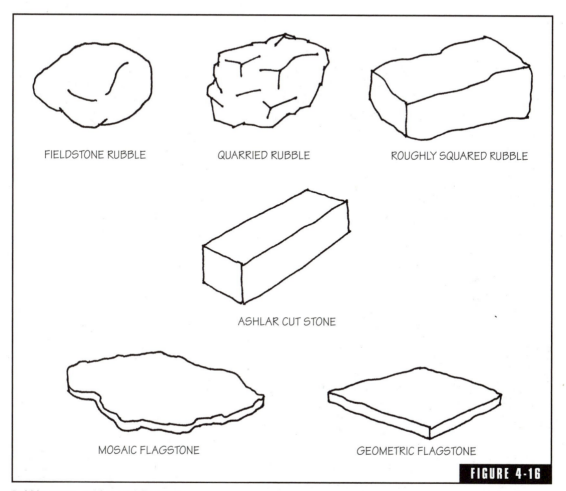

FIELDSTONE RUBBLE   QUARRIED RUBBLE   ROUGHLY SQUARED RUBBLE

ASHLAR CUT STONE

MOSAIC FLAGSTONE   GEOMETRIC FLAGSTONE

FIGURE 4-16

Rubble stone, ashlar, and flagstone.

at a fabricating plant, but the hardness also lends itself to producing highly polished surfaces. As an exterior facing material, granite is used primarily on high-end commercial projects. In custom homes, polished granite countertops provide an elegant but durable kitchen work surface. For outdoor garden and landscape applications, small chunks of quarried or fieldstone granite rubble are somewhat less expensive.

Limestone is relatively durable, easily worked, and widely available in many parts of the country. It's an attractive stone sometimes characterized by embedded shells and fossilized animals and

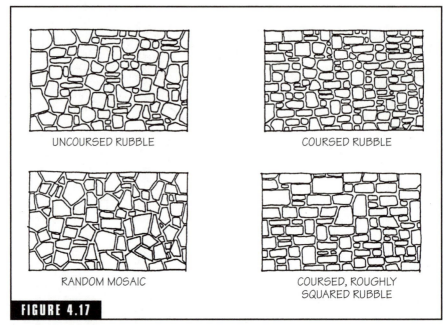

UNCOURSED RUBBLE

COURSED RUBBLE

RANDOM MOSAIC

COURSED, ROUGHLY
SQUARED RUBBLE

FIGURE 4.17

Rubble stone patterns. *(from Beall, Christine,* Masonry Design and Detailing, *4th edition, McGraw-Hill, New York).*

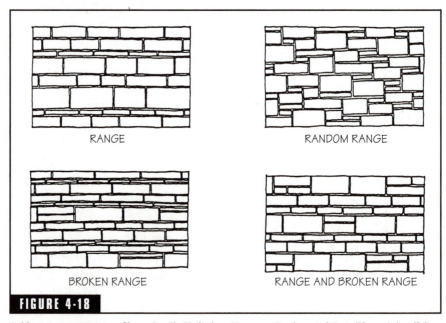

RANGE

RANDOM RANGE

BROKEN RANGE

RANGE AND BROKEN RANGE

FIGURE 4-18

Ashlar stone patterns. *(from Beall, Christine,* Masonry Design and Detailing, *4th edition, McGraw-Hill, New York).*

plants. Although soft when first quarried, limestone becomes harder with age and exposure to the weather. Because it's much more porous than granite, limestone is not as durable in cold and wet climates where it is exposed to repeated cycles of freezing and thawing. Limestone is generally cream or buff colored, but it may also be reddish or yellowish or have a grey tint.

Limestone is available as fieldstone and quarried rubble, as saw-cut ashlar, and sometimes as flagstone. Because it is softer and more porous than granite, limestone is also easier to work with and to shape with hand tools and small saws. Since its softness also makes it less expensive than granite, limestone is frequently used for both residential and commercial work.

Sandstone varies in color from buff, pink, and crimson to greenish brown, cream, and blue-gray. Light-colored sandstone is usually strong and durable. Reddish or brown sandstone is typically softer

FIGURE 4-19

Rubble stone and ashlar used together.

and more easily cut. Sandstone is available as fieldstone and quarried rubble, as ashlar, and as flagstone split into thin slabs for paving. Sandstone is easier to cut and work than granite, but more difficult than limestone.

Slate is usually split into slabs $1/4$ in. or more in thickness. It's used for flagstone, flooring tiles, and roofing. Small quantities of various mineral ingredients give color to different slates, ranging from black, blue, and gray, to red, purple, and green. "Select" slate is uniform in color and more costly than "ribbon" slate, which contains stripes of two or more colors. Slate is very durable as a paving material because it has low porosity and high resistance to the abrasion of repeated foot traffic. It is moderately easy to cut and shape, but is very brittle.

FIGURE 4-20

Flagstone walkway.

4.5.3 Selecting Stone

Stone for building construction is judged on the basis of appearance, durability, strength, economy, and ease of maintenance. In terms of practicality and long-term cost, durability is the most important consideration in selecting building stone. Suitability will depend not only on the characteristics of the stone, but also on climatic conditions. Repeated freezing and thawing is the most active agent in the natural destruction of stone. In warm, dry climates, almost any stone may be used to build with good results. Stones of the same general type may vary greatly in durability because of softness and porosity. Soft, porous stones, which are more liable to absorb water and then to flake or fracture when frozen, may not be suitable in cold, wet climates.

The costs of various stones will depend on the proximity of the quarry to the building site, the abundance of the material, and its workability. In general, stone from a local source is less expensive than imported stone; that produced on a large scale is less expensive than scarce varieties; and stone quarried and dressed easily is less expensive than those requiring more time and labor.

4.6 Masonry Mortar and Grout

Masonry mortar is similar in composition to concrete but different in properties and performance. Masonry mortar is a mix of cement, lime, sand, and water used to bond masonry units or individual stones in walls and other building elements. Masonry grout is a more fluid mixture of similar ingredients used to fill hollow cores and cavities and to embed reinforcing steel and accessories in masonry construction. The most important physical property of concrete is compressive strength, but compressive strength is usually less important in masonry mortar and grout than bond strength. Good bond between the mortar and units provides physical stability as well as resistance to wind loads and moisture penetration. A mortar or grout mix which produces good bond will have a lower compressive strength than concrete, but only moderate compressive strengths are required for most masonry construction.

Mortar makes up only a small part of masonry construction, but its influence on performance and appearance are much greater than the proportion implies. The ingredients used to make mortar and grout directly affect the performance of the finished masonry. Cement provides strength and durability. Lime adds workability, water retention, and elasticity. Sand serves as a strong and economical filler. High-quality mortar and grout require high-quality ingredients.

4.6.1   Mortar and Grout Properties

The term *fresh* mortar refers to the wet mix of ingredients before they begin to cure. When the material begins to set but is not fully cured, it is called *green* mortar and after it has fully cured, it is called *hardened* mortar. Fresh mortar and grout must be workable, and hardened mortar and grout must have good bond strength and durability. The quality of the ingredients, the proportions in which they are mixed, and the way the mix is handled, placed, and cured affect these properties.

Workability significantly influences most other mortar characteristics. Workability is not easy to define, but a workable mortar has a smooth consistency, is easily spread with a trowel, and readily adheres to vertical surfaces. Well-graded, smooth sand enhances mortar workability, as do lime, air entrainment, and proper amounts of mixing water. The lime gives plasticity and increases the capacity of the mix to retain water. Air entrainment introduces minute bubbles which act as lubricants in improving workability, but air entrainment must be limited in mortars because it reduces bond strength. Where concrete mixes perform best when mixed with the minimum amount of water necessary, masonry mortar is just the opposite. Mortar requires the *maximum amount of water* consistent with workability. Variations in units and in weather conditions affect optimum mortar consistency and workability. For example, mortar for heavier units must be more dense to prevent uneven settling and to keep excessive mortar from being squeezed out of the joints. Hot summer temperatures require a soft, wet mix to compensate for evaporation.

Mortar is subject to water loss by evaporation, particularly on hot, dry days. *Retempering* (the addition of mixing water to compensate for evaporation) is good practice in masonry construction. A partially dried and stiffened mortar will have lower bond strength if the evaporated water is not replaced. Mortar which has begun to harden as a result of cement hydration, however, should be discarded. Since it is difficult to tell whether mortar stiffening is due to evaporation or hydration, the suitability of mortar is judged on the time elapsed after initial mixing. When air temperatures are above 80°F, mortar may be safely retempered if needed during the first 1-1/2 to 2 hours after mixing. When temperatures are below 80°F, mortar may be retempered for 2-1/2 hours after mixing. Industry standards recommend that all mortar be used within 2-1/2 hours, and permits retempering as frequently as needed within this time period. Tests have shown that the decrease in compressive strength is minimal if retempering occurs within recommended limits, and that it is much more beneficial to the performance of the masonry to maximize workability and bond by replacing evaporated moisture.

For the majority of masonry construction, the single most important property of mortar is *bond strength* and integrity. For durability, weather resistance, and resistance to loads, it is critical that the bond between units and mortar be strong and complete. The term *mortar bond* refers to a property that includes

- Extent of bond or area of contact between unit and mortar

- Bond strength or adhesion of the mortar to the units

The mechanical bond between the mortar and the individual bricks, blocks, or stones holds the construction together, provides resistance to tensile and flexural stress, and resists the penetration of moisture. The strength and extent of the bond are affected by many variables of material and workmanship. The mortar must have good workability to spread easily and wet the unit surfaces. The unit surfaces must be rough enough to provide physical interlocking, and sufficient absorption to draw the wet mortar into these surface irregularities. The moisture content, absorption, pore structure, and surface characteristics of the units, the water retention of the mortar, and curing conditions such as temperature, relative humidity, and wind combine to influence the completeness and integrity of the mortar-to-unit bond. Voids at the mortar-to-unit interface offer little resistance to water infiltration and increase the chance of subsequent disintegration and failure if repeated freezing and thawing occurs.

Although a certain amount of surface absorption is desirable to increase the depth of penetration of the mortar paste, excessive suction reduces the amount of water available for cement hydration at the unit surface. *Moist curing* of masonry after construction assures complete hydration of the cement and improves the bond of mortar to high-suction brick and to dry, absorptive concrete masonry units. Clay brick with low absorption, dense stone, and nonabsorptive glass block provide little or no absorption of mortar paste into surface pores. These types of units require a relatively stiff, low-water-content mortar. Unit texture also affects bond. Coarse concrete masonry units and the wire cut surfaces of extruded clay brick produce a better mechanical bond than molded brick or the die-formed surfaces of extruded brick. Loose sand particles, dirt, coatings, and other contaminants also adversely affect mortar bond.

Workmanship is also critical in mortar bond. Full mortar joints must assure complete coverage of all contact surfaces, and maximum extent of bond is necessary to reduce water penetration. Once a unit has been placed and leveled, additional movement will break or seriously weaken the bond. Mortars with high water retention allow more time for placing units before evaporation or unit suction alters the moisture content of the mortar.

Masonry *compressive strength* depends on both the unit and the mortar. As with concrete, the strength of mortar is determined by the cement content and the water/cement ratio of the mix. Since water content is adjusted to achieve proper workability and flow, and since bond strength is ultimately of more importance in masonry construction, higher compressive strengths are sometimes sacrificed to increase or alter other characteristics. For loadbearing construction, building codes generally provide minimum allowable working stresses, and required compressive strengths may easily be calculated using accepted engineering methods. Strengths of standard mortar mixes may be as high as 5000 psi, but need not exceed either the requirements of the construction or the strength of the units themselves. Although compressive strength is less important than bond strength, simple and reliable testing procedures make it a widely accepted basis for comparing mortars. Basically, compressive strength increases with the proportion of cement in the mix and decreases as the lime content is increased. Air entrainment, sand, or mixing water beyond normal requirements also reduce compressive strength.

For residential construction, mortar compressive strength is not a critical design factor because both the mortar and the masonry are much stronger in compression than is typically needed. Compressive strength is important in loadbearing construction, but structural failure due to compressive loading is rare. More critical properties such as flexural bond strength are usually given higher priority. Masonry mortars generally should not have a higher compressive strength than is necessary to support the anticipated loads. An unnecessarily strong mortar with high cement content is brittle and may experience more cracking than a softer mortar with higher lime content, which is more flexible and permits greater movement with less cracking.

4.6.2 Cementitious Materials

The most common cementitious ingredients in masonry mortar and grout are portland cement and lime, but some proprietary masonry cement mixes contain other chemical or mineral additives in addition to or instead of some proportion of the basic portland cement and lime.

Portland Cement: There are five types of portland cement, each with different physical and chemical characteristics as described in Chapter 2. Not all of the five types are suitable for masonry construction. Type I is a general-purpose cement and is the most widely used in masonry construction. Type III is often used in cold weather because it gains strength rapidly and generates more heat during the hydration process. This can help keep fresh mortar or grout from freezing and shorten the time required for protection against low temperatures.

Air-entraining portland cements (designated as Types IA, IIIA, etc.) are made by adding a foaming agent to produce minute, well-distributed air bubbles in the hardened concrete or mortar. Increased air content improves workability and increases resistance to frost action and the scaling caused by chemical removal of snow and ice. Air-entrained mixes are not as strong as ordinary portland cement mixes, and excessive air is detrimental in mortar and grout because it reduces bond to masonry units and reinforcing steel.

Air-entrained cements are used primarily in horizontal applications where exposure to ponded water, ice, and snow is greatest. Entrained air produces tiny voids in concrete or mortar into which freezing water can expand without causing damage. Masonry paving with mortared joints may enjoy some of the benefits of air-entrainment in resisting the expansion of freezing water. Although masonry industry standards limit the air content of masonry mortar, the benefits of higher air contents in resisting freeze-thaw damage to paving may outweigh the decrease in bond strength. Since mortared masonry paving systems are generally supported on concrete slabs, the bond strength of the masonry is less important than its resistance to weathering. In paving applications, lower bond strength might be tolerated in return for increased durability.

In the United States, portland cement is packaged in bags containing exactly one cubic foot of material and weighing exactly 94 lbs. This standardized packaging allows consistency in proportioning and mixing mortar and grout by either weight or volume measurement.

Lime: The mortar used in most historic buildings was made only with lime and sand and did not contain any cement. Lime mortars were strong and durable but cured very slowly by a process called carbonation. Construction was also slow because the mortar had to gain strength before it could support very much weight. The invention of portland cement in the early 1800s changed the way mortar was made by substituting cement in the mix for a portion of the lime. Contemporary cement and lime mortars are now made with a higher proportion of cement than lime. Although this has reduced curing time and speeded up construction, the trade-off is that the higher portland cement content makes fresh mixes stiff and hardened mortar brittle. A cement mortar made without any lime is harsh and unworkable, high in compressive strength, but weak in bond and other required characteristics. The continued use of lime, although reduced in proportion, has many beneficial effects in masonry mortar and grout.

The type of lime used in building is a burned lime made from sedimentary limestone. Powdered hydrated lime is used today instead of lime putty. Only lime that is labeled "mason's lime" is suitable for masonry work. Lime adds plasticity to mortar, so it spreads easily into tiny surface indentations, pores, and irregularities in the units and develops a strong physical bond. Lime also improves water retention. Mortar with lime holds its moisture longer, resisting the suction of dry, porous units so that enough water is maintained for proper curing and cement hydration. Lime is packaged in bags containing exactly one cubic foot of material and weighing exactly 40 lbs. This packaging allows consistency in proportioning and mixing mortar and grout by either weight or volume measurement.

Masonry Cements and Mortar Cements: Masonry cements are proprietary mixes of cement with chemical or mineral additives. Masonry cements do not necessarily contain portland cement and hydrated lime, but may include combinations of portland cement, blended cements, plasticizers, and air-entraining additives. Finely ground limestone, clay, and lime hydrate are often used as plasticizers because of their ability to adsorb water and thus improve workability. Masonry cements are popular for residential construction because of their convenience and good workability. Since masonry cements have all the cementitious ingredients preblended and proportioned in a single bag, they are easier to mix on site. For small projects, masonry cements are more convenient because all that is required is the addition of sand and water. Masonry cements are manufactured as Type M, Type S, and Type N, to correspond with the mortar type in which they are intended to be used.

Like all proprietary products, different brands of masonry cements will be of different quality. Because of the latitude permitted for ingredients and proportioning, the properties of a particular masonry cement cannot be accurately predicted on the basis of compliance with industry standards. They must be established through performance records and laboratory tests. Some building codes do not permit the use of masonry cements in highly active seismic areas. In addition to mortars made from portland and lime or from masonry cement, some building codes include mortars made from *mortar cement.* Generally, proprietary masonry cements that can produce mortars which meet the performance requirements for labeling as "mortar cements" are considered to be the higher-quality masonry cements among those on the market. They combine the convenience of a one-bag mix with the higher quality typically associated with port-land cement and lime mixes.

For very small projects, you may find it most convenient to buy a *mortar mix* that includes both masonry cement and sand already prop-erly proportioned in a single bag. These mixes are more expensive, but they require only the addition of water at the project site (Figure 4-21).

4.6.3 Aggregates

Sand accounts for at least 75% of the volume of masonry mortar and grout. Manufactured sands have sharp, angular grains, while natural sands obtained from banks, pits, and riverbeds have particles that are smoother and more round. Natural sands generally produce mortars that are more workable than those made with manufactured sands. For

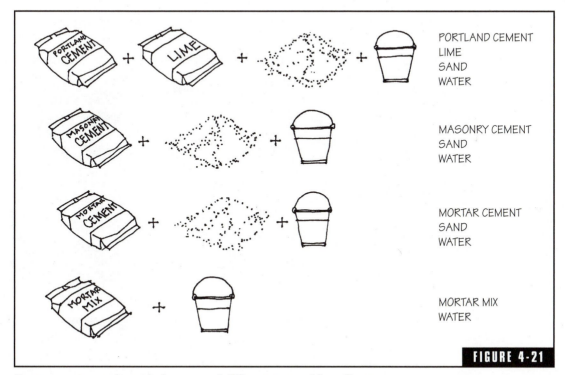

FIGURE 4-21

Masonry mortar can be made from several different types of ingredients.

use in masonry mortar and grout, sand must be clean, sound, and well graded with a variety of particle sizes.

The sand in masonry mortar and grout acts as a filler. The cementitious paste must completely coat each particle to lubricate the mix. Sands that have a high percentage of large grains produce voids between the particles and will make harsh mortars with poor workability and low resistance to moisture penetration. When the sand is well proportioned of both fine and coarse grains, the smaller grains fill these voids and produce mortars that are more workable and plastic. If the percentage of fine particles is too high, more cement is required to coat the particles thoroughly, more mixing water is required to produce good workability, and the mortar will be weaker, more porous, and subject to greater volume shrinkage. Figure 4-22 illustrates the range and distribution of particle gradation that is recommended, from the coarsest allowable gradation to the finest allowable gradation, with the ideal gradation shown in the middle. Both the coarse and fine gradations have a void content much higher than

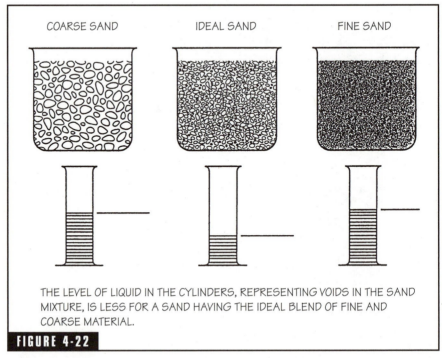

COARSE SAND   IDEAL SAND   FINE SAND

THE LEVEL OF LIQUID IN THE CYLINDERS, REPRESENTING VOIDS IN THE SAND MIXTURE, IS LESS FOR A SAND HAVING THE IDEAL BLEND OF FINE AND COARSE MATERIAL.

FIGURE 4-22

Sand particle gradation. *(from Portland Cement Association,* Trowel Tips—Mortar Sand*).*

that of the ideal gradation and will affect the amount of cement required to produce good mortar.

Sand particles should always be washed to remove foreign substances. Silt can cause mortar to stick to the trowel and can impair proper bond of the cementitious material to the sand particles. Clay and organic substances reduce mortar strength and can cause brownish stains varying in intensity from batch to batch. There is a simple field test which can determine the amount of contaminants in masonry sand. Put 2 inches of sand in a quart jar, add water until the jar is about 3/4 full, shake it for 1 minute, then let it stand for an hour. If more than 1/8 in. of sediment settles on top of the sand, it should be washed by drenching with a garden hose the day before it will be used (see Figure 2-9 in Chapter 2).

Masonry mortar is used to fill relatively small joints between units, so sand is the largest practical aggregate that can be used. But masonry grout is used to fill larger cores and cavities in masonry construction, so it is both practical and economical to include larger aggregate in addition to sand. Maximum aggregate size for masonry grout is usually limited to 3/8 inch so that the grout can still flow easily into unit cores and wall cavities even when they are crowded with reinforcing bars.

4.6.4 Mixing Water

Water for masonry mortar must be clean and free of harmful amounts of acids, alkalis, and organic materials. Whether the water is drinkable is not in itself a consideration, as some drinking water contains appreciable amounts of soluble salts, such as sodium and potassium sulfate, which can contribute to efflorescence. In general, though, water that is drinkable, is reasonably clear, and does not have a foul odor or a brackish or salty taste is acceptable for mixing masonry mortar and grout.

4.6.5 Mortar and Grout Admixtures

Although admixtures are often used with some success in concrete construction, they can have adverse effects on the properties and performance of masonry mortar and grout. Masonry industry standards do not incorporate, nor in fact even recognize, admixtures of any kind. A variety of proprietary materials are available which are reported by their manufacturers to increase workability or water retentivity, lower the freezing point, and accelerate or retard the set. Although they may produce some effects, they can also reduce compressive strength, impair bond, contribute to efflorescence, increase shrinkage, or corrode metal accessories and reinforcing steel.

Set accelerators, often mistakenly referred to as "antifreeze" compounds, are sometimes used in winter construction to speed cement hydration, shorten setting time, increase early strength development, and reduce the time required for cold-weather protection. Calcium chloride accelerators cause corrosion of embedded steel anchors and reinforcement. Nonchloride accelerators are a little more expensive but less damaging to the masonry. Chlorides should not be used in mortar or grout which contains embedded metals such as anchors, ties, or joint reinforcement. Automotive antifreeze should never be used in masonry mortar or grout.

Set retarders extend the board life of fresh mortar and grout for as long as four to five hours by helping to retain water for longer periods of time. Set retarders are sometimes used during hot weather to counteract the effects of rapid set and high evaporation rates. With soft, dry brick or block, set retarders are also sometimes used to counteract rapid suction and help achieve better bond. Mortar with set retarders *cannot* be retempered.

Integral water repellents reduce the water absorption of hardened mortar by as much as 60%. They must be used in mortar for concrete masonry units that have also been treated with an integral water repellent. Using water-repellent-treated masonry units with untreated mortar, or vice versa, can reduce mortar-to-unit bond and the flexural strength of the wall. Reduced bond also allows moisture to penetrate the wall freely at the joint interfaces, so the intended moisture resistance of the water repellent treatment is negated. To achieve good bond when using treated concrete block, the block manufacturer should supply a chemically compatible admixture for use in the mortar.

The most commonly used admixtures are natural and synthetic iron oxide *pigments* used to produce colored mortar. Iron oxides are nontoxic, colorfast, chemically stable, and resistant to ultraviolet radiation. Iron oxides come in yellows, reds, browns, and blacks. Carbon black and lampblack (used to make blacks and browns) are less weather resistant than the iron oxides used to make the same colors. Synthetic iron oxides have more tinting power than natural oxides, so less pigment is required to produce a given color. Synthetic oxides also produce brighter, cleaner colors than natural iron oxides. Beyond a certain point, called the saturation point, the color intensity of the mortar does not increase in proportion to the amount of pigment added. Synthetic iron oxides generally are saturated at about 5% of the weight of the cement, and natural oxides at about 10%. Adding pigment beyond the saturation point produces little additional color.

Colored mortar can be made at the job site from powdered or liquid pigments. Powdered pigments are used most frequently, and the majority are packaged so that one bag contains enough pigment to color one cubic foot of cementitious material (i.e., for each one-cubic-foot bag of masonry cement, portland cement, or lime, one bag of color is added). Pigment manufacturers supply charts which identify the exact number of bags of pigment required for various mortar proportions. Similarly, liquid colorants are generally packaged so that one quart of pigment is needed for each bag of cementitious material. Liquid pigments create less mess and blowing dust than dry powders, but they also cost more. The same pigments used to color mortars are used to produce colored concrete masonry units. Some manufacturers market colored masonry cements, mortar cements, and prebagged portland lime mortar mixes in which pigments are preblended in the bag with the other ingredients. These will generally produce mortar colors that range from white, cream, buff, tan, and pink to chocolate brown. This is the easiest way to get colored mortar.

Shrinkage-compensating admixtures (commonly called *grouting aids*) are often used in grout which typically shrinks 5–10% after placement as the surrounding masonry units absorb water. To minimize volume loss, maintain good bond, and give workers more time to vibrate the grout before it stiffens, these specially blended admixtures expand the grout, retard its set, and lower the water requirements. Admixtures can also be used to accelerate grout set in cold weather or retard set in hot weather. Superplasticizers may be used in hot weather to increase grout slump without adding water or reducing strength.

4.6.6 Mortar and Grout Mixes

For years there has been controversy over the relative merits of mortars made with portland cement and lime versus mortars made with masonry cement. Historically, portland cement and lime mortars have higher flexural bond strengths than masonry cement mortars. Higher flexural bond strengths not only increase resistance to wind loads, but to moisture penetration as well. Masonry cements are more widely used than portland cement and lime for masonry mortars, and the vast majority of projects which incorporate them perform very well. On projects which have flexural bond failures or excessive moisture penetration, the fault can seldom be attributed solely to the use of masonry cement instead of portland cement and lime in the mortar. Usually, there are other defects which contribute to the problems. Both masonry cement mortars and portland cement and lime mortars are capable of providing what the industry considers adequate flexural bond strength when they are properly designed, mixed, and installed.

There are five common mortar types, designated as M, S, N, O, and K. Each of the five types is based on standardized proportions of the various ingredients and has certain applications to which it is particularly suited. *Type M,* for instance, is a high-compressive-strength mix recommended for masonry which may be subject to high-compressive loads. *Type S* is a high-bond-strength mortar recommended for structures which require resistance to significant lateral loads from soil pressures, winds, or earthquakes. Because of its excellent durability, Type S mortar is also recommended for structures at or below grade and in contact with the soil, such as foundations, retaining walls, pavements, sewers, and manholes. *Type N* is a good general-purpose mortar for use in above-grade masonry. It is recommended for exterior masonry veneers and for interior and exterior loadbearing walls. This medium-strength mortar represents the best compromise among compressive and flexural strength, workability, and economy and is, in fact, recommended for most masonry applications. *Type O* is a high-lime, low-compressive-strength mortar. It is recommended for interior and exterior non-loadbearing walls and veneers which will not be subject to freezing in the presence of moisture. Type O mortar is often used in one- and two-story residential work and is a favorite of masons because of its excellent workability and economical cost. *Type K* mortar has a very low compressive strength and a correspondingly low flexural bond strength. It is seldom used in new construction and is recommended only for tuckpointing historic buildings constructed originally with lime and sand mortar.

For outdoor work that is above grade, use a Type N or Type O mix. For below-grade construction and for paving projects, use a Type S or Type M mix. The proportions used to produce the various mortar types are shown in Figures 4-23 and 4-24. Bags of masonry cement and mortar cement are marked as Type M, Type S, or Type N and should be mixed with sand in a 1:3 proportion, 1 part cement mix to 3 parts sand. For most residential masonry veneers, a Type N mortar is the best choice for overall structural and functional performance. The unnecessary use of a Type M or Type S mortar when the higher compressive strength is not needed will not only cost more because of the higher cement content, but it will reduce workability in the fresh mortar and elasticity in the hardened mortar and ultimately be detrimental rather than beneficial. For foundation and basement wall construction, a Type M or Type S mortar may be required by some building codes.

Grout mixes should be made from portland cement and lime because most building codes do not permit the use of masonry cement for grout. Masonry grouts are classified as fine or coarse according to the size of aggregate used. If the maximum aggregate size is less than $3/8$ inches, the grout is classified as *fine*. If the aggregate contains particles $3/8$ inches or larger, the grout is classified as *coarse*. Standard mix proportions are shown in Figure 4-25. Use of a fine grout or coarse grout is determined by the size of the grout spaces and the pour height as shown in Figure 4-26.

	Proportions by Volume		
Mortar Type	Portland Cement	Lime	Sand
M	1	$1/4$	$3\frac{1}{2}$
S	1	$1/2$	$4\frac{1}{2}$
N	1	1	6
O	1	2	9
K	1	3	12

FIGURE 4-23

Portland cement and lime mortar mixes. *(from ASTM C270 Standard Specification for Mortars for Unit Masonry, American Society for Testing and Materials, West Conshohocken, PA).*

	Proportions by Volume			
	Masonry Cement or Mortar Cement			
Mortar Type	M	S	N	Sand
M	1			3
S		1		3
N			1	3

FIGURE 4-24

Masonry cement and mortar cement mixes. *(from ASTM C270 Standard Specification for Mortar for Unit masonry, American Society for Testing and materials, West Conshohocken, PA).*

	Grout Proportions by Volume			
			Aggregate measured in damp, loose a condition	
Type	Parts by volume of portland cement	Parts by volume of hydrated lime	Fine	Coarse
Fine	1	0 to $\frac{1}{10}$	$2\frac{1}{4}$ to 3 times the sum of the volumes of the cement and lime	—
Coarse	1	0 to $\frac{1}{10}$	$2\frac{1}{4}$ to 3 times the sum of the volumes of the cement and lime	1 to 2 times the sum of the volumes of the cement and lime

FIGURE 4-25

Fine and coarse masonry grout mixes. *(from ASTM C476, Grout for Reinforced and Non-reinforced Masonry, American Society for Testing and Materials, West Conshohocken, PA).*

Grout Type	Grout Pour Height, Ft.	Minimum Width of Grout Space Between Wythes, Inches	Minimum Dimensions for Grouting Cores of Hollow Units, Inches × Inches
Fine	1	$\frac{3}{4}$	$1\frac{1}{2} \times 2$
	5	2	2×3
	12	$2\frac{1}{2}$	$2\frac{1}{2} \times 3$
	24	3	3×3
Coarse	1	$1\frac{1}{2}$	$1\frac{1}{2} \times 3$
	5	2	$2\frac{1}{2} \times 3$
	12	$2\frac{1}{2}$	3×3
	24	3	3×4

FIGURE 4-26

Grout space requirements for fine and coarse grout. *(from ACI 530/ASCE 5/TMS 402 Building Code Requirements for Masonry Structures, American Concrete Institute, American Society of Civil Engineers, The Masonry Society).*

4.7 Masonry Accessories

Some types of masonry construction require accessory items such as anchors, ties, flashing, and reinforcement which are as important to the successful performance of the masonry as the units and mortar themselves.

4.7.1 Anchors, Ties, and Fasteners

Anchors are used to connect a masonry veneer to a backing wall of some other type of construction such as wood framing, metal studs, or concrete. The most common masonry anchor used in residential work is the corrugated veneer anchor which can be nailed into wood studs or screwed into metal studs (Figure 4-27). Wire anchors for attachment to metal stud framing must be a minimum of 9 gauge. In areas with high earthquake risk, building codes usually require special seismic veneer anchors.

Ties are used to connect different wythes of masonry in a multi-wythe wall. A corrugated veneer anchor can be used as a multiwythe wall tie if it is laid flat in the bed joints, or stronger wire ties can be used. A Z-shaped wire tie is used for solid masonry units such as brick, and a rectangular wire tie is used for hollow masonry units such as concrete block. Corrugated metal ties are less expensive than wire ties, but they have to be spaced closer together, so more are needed.

Fasteners are used to connect other materials or objects to masonry walls and may be designed to insert into a mortar joint or penetrate through to a hollow core or cavity (Figure 4-28).

Wire ties for multiwythe walls must be 3/16-in. diameter. Corrugated anchors for residential work should be 7/8 in. wide and 22-gauge thickness. Wire anchors should be a minimum of 9 gauge. For extra protection against corrosion, use anchors and ties that are hot-dip galvanized.

4.7.2 Reinforcement

Like concrete, masonry requires the incorporation of steel reinforcement to increase flexural and tensile strength, and concrete masonry uses steel reinforcement to resist moisture shrinkage. There are two types of masonry reinforcement, prefabricated wire joint reinforcement and structural reinforcing bars. Prefabricated wire *joint rein-*

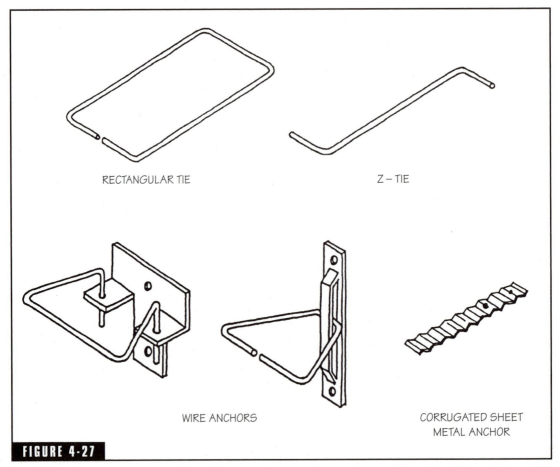

RECTANGULAR TIE

Z – TIE

WIRE ANCHORS

CORRUGATED SHEET
METAL ANCHOR

FIGURE 4-27

Masonry anchors and ties. *(from Beall, Christine,* Masonry Design and Detailing, *4th edition, McGraw-Hill, New York).*

forcement is used in the mortar beds of concrete masonry walls to help control shrinkage cracking (Figure 4-29). For residential projects, the long wires should be 9-gauge thickness. The width of joint reinforcement should always be about 1 in. less than that of the units so that it has $1/2$-in. to $5/8$-in. cover of mortar on each side of the wall. Joint reinforcement may also include flexible veneer anchors for the attachment of brick, CMU, or stone veneers over concrete block backing walls.

The second type of masonry reinforcement is heavy steel *reinforcing bars* like those used in concrete construction. Reinforcing bars are used in masonry to strengthen supporting members like pilasters, lintels, and bond beams. Steel reinforcement of either type must be embedded in and surrounded by mortar or grout so that it develops its full strength. Joint reinforcement is usually hot-dip galvanized to protect the thin wires against corrosion, and reinforcing bars generally should be Grade 60 steel.

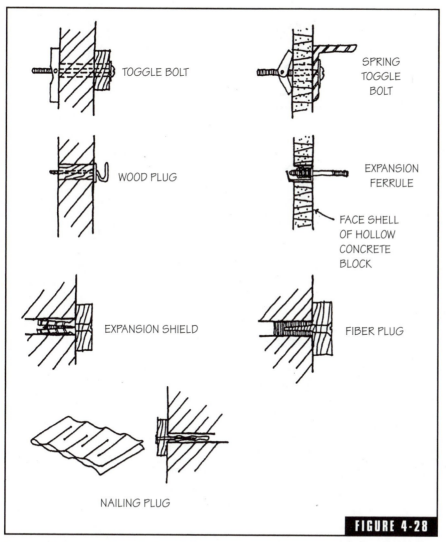

FIGURE 4-28

Masonry fasteners. *(from Technical Note Vol. 2, No. 10, Brick Industry Association, Reston, VA).*

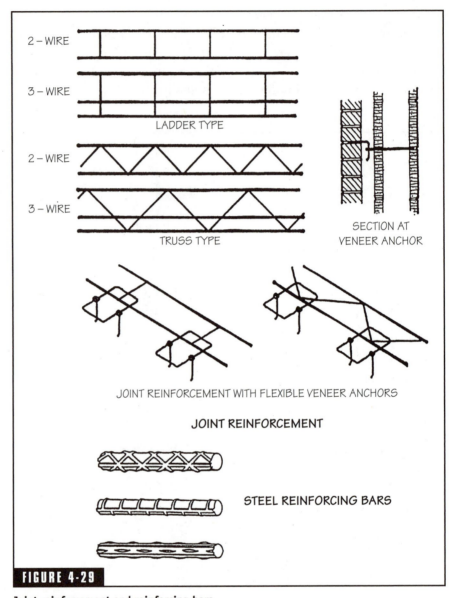

2 – WIRE

3 – WIRE

LADDER TYPE

2 – WIRE

3 – WIRE

TRUSS TYPE

SECTION AT
VENEER ANCHOR

JOINT REINFORCEMENT WITH FLEXIBLE VENEER ANCHORS

JOINT REINFORCEMENT

STEEL REINFORCING BARS

FIGURE 4-29

Joint reinforcement and reinforcing bars.

4.7.3 Flashing and Weep Holes

Masonry flashing can be made of metal, rubberized asphalt, sheet membranes, and other materials. It is used to control moisture in masonry walls either by keeping the top of a wall dry, or by collecting water inside a wall so that it can be drained out through weep holes (Figure 4-30). Rubber and plastic flashings are most often used in residential work because they are inexpensive and easy to work with. The thickness of these membrane flashings should be sufficient to prevent puncturing or tearing too easily with the point of a trowel. PVC flashings may become brittle over time and not serve the life of the building.

Weep holes are usually formed by leaving the mortar out of some of the mortar joints between units, but cotton wicks may also be used. Cotton wicks provide slower moisture drainage, but they are the least

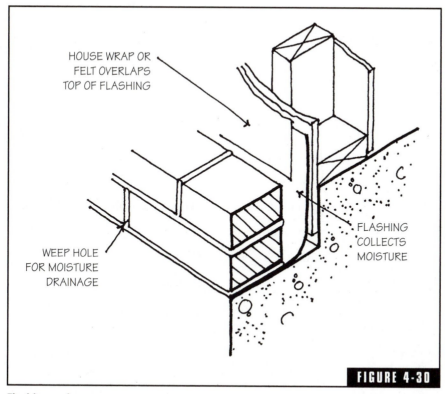

FIGURE 4-30

Flashing and weeps.

conspicuous visually. If the appearance of an open joint weep is objectionable, the openings can be fitted with a variety of ventilating screens or covers.

4.8 Weather-Resistant Masonry

One of the most important functions of any exterior building wall is resistance to weather and moisture. Moisture can penetrate masonry walls no matter who builds them or what materials they consist of. Brick, concrete block, stone, and mortar are porous and they absorb moisture easily, but they also dry out easily. Some masonry walls allow more water penetration than others, depending on the design, the detailing, materials, and workmanship. Most masonry walls are built with a drainage space between the facing and backing which is fitted with flashing and weep holes to facilitate rapid drying and to prevent the migration of moisture into the interior of the building.

To prevent excessive moisture penetration or prolonged saturation, it is important to limit the amount of water that can enter a wall and to prevent the accumulation of water within the wall. There are several specific steps which should be taken to assure good weather resistance of masonry walls.

- Limit moisture penetration
    - provide full mortar joints
    - control cracking
    - apply protective coating on porous materials
- Prevent moisture accumulation
    - install flashing to collect moisture
    - install weep holes to drain moisture

4.8.1 Limit Moisture Penetration

In certain climates high winds and frequent rains combine to create high-risk exposures where water can often penetrate buildings even though the materials and workmanship are good. In masonry construction, penetration of this wind-driven rain can be minimized by providing full mortar joints with good bond, by controlling cracking, and by the judicious application of protective coatings to very absorptive units.

Provide Full Mortar Joints: Full mortar joints and good bond between units and mortar are extremely important, not only to the strength and stability of masonry walls, but also to their weather resistance. Wind-driven rain of sufficient strength and duration can penetrate even well-built masonry walls, but if the joints are only partially filled, moisture penetration is substantially increased along with the likelihood of leakage to the interior of the building. Full mortar joints can easily be achieved with proper technique, but mortar bond is affected by the mortar materials, the mortar mixture, and the texture and absorption of the unit surface.

Both portland cement and lime mortars and masonry cement mortars allow water to penetrate through masonry walls. The amount of water entering the wall is generally higher with masonry cement mortars, but when workmanship is poor, joints are only partially filled, and flashing and weeps are not functional, either type of mortar can produce a leaky wall. There are no industry standards or guidelines identifying varying amounts of water penetration that are either acceptable or unacceptable. A wall system with well-designed and properly installed flashing and weeps will tolerate a much greater volume of water penetration without damage to the wall, the building, or its contents than one without such safeguards. Ultimately, the workmanship and the flashing and weep hole drainage system will determine the success or failure of most masonry installations.

Control Cracking: Masonry walls are very strong in compression and can support their own weight for a height of several hundred feet or support the weight of a building for 15 to 20 stories. Masonry walls are also relatively brittle and can bend very little without cracking. In unreinforced masonry, the bond between mortar and units is what holds the walls together and gives them a modest amount of resistance to pulling (tension) and bending (flexure). The bond between mortar and units is also the weakest link in masonry, and cracks usually occur along the lines of the mortar joints. A building may contain thousands of linear feet of mortar joints along which cracks can open if the masonry is not properly designed to accommodate compressive loads, wind loads, expansion and contraction, or dissimilar movement between the masonry and adjacent materials. Cracks can also occur as a result of foundation or soil movements, impact, and other catastrophic events. Large cracks may indicate serious structural problems, but even small cracks are unsightly and provide the potential for excessive moisture penetration, so understanding the cause and prevention of cracking is an important element in overall performance.

Cracking in masonry is most often related to the expansion and contraction caused by changes in moisture content. Some shrinking and swelling occurs alternately through normal wetting and drying cycles, but more important are the *permanent moisture expansion* of clay masonry and the *permanent moisture shrinkage* of concrete masonry. Clay masonry begins to reabsorb moisture from the atmosphere as soon as it leaves the firing kiln, and as the moisture content increases, the units expand permanently. Concrete masonry products are moist-cured to hydrate the portland cement in the mix. Once the curing is complete, residual moisture evaporates, causing the units to shrink permanently. Both clay and concrete masonry also expand and contract very slightly with changes in temperature, but these movements are always less than the initial moisture shrinkage or expansion. Much of the initial moisture shrinkage or expansion will take place before the masonry is used, but some almost inevitably occurs after the units are laid and can cause masonry walls to crack or bow out of place if the movement is not properly accommodated by flexible anchorage or fully restrained by reinforcing steel.

Normal shrinkage cracking in concrete masonry can be minimized by incorporating wire joint reinforcement in the mortar beds of single-wythe walls or steel bar reinforcement in the grouted cavity of double-wythe walls. This helps restrain the shrinkage and evenly distributes the stresses. Special joints can also be installed to force the cracking to occur at predetermined locations. *Concrete masonry control joints* are continuous, weakened joints designed to accommodate the shrinkage in such a way that cracking will occur in straight lines at predetermined locations rather than zig-zagging across the wall at random locations. The more joint reinforcement there is in the wall, the farther apart the control joints can be. The less joint reinforcement, the closer together the control joints must be.

A *brick masonry expansion joint* is a continuous, open joint without mortar that is designed to accommodate the natural expansion of brick. Unlike control joints in concrete masonry, expansion joints in clay masonry are intended to allow the adjacent units or wall sections to expand without pushing against each other. Because brick masonry always expands more than it contracts, expansion joints must be free of mortar or other hard materials. The walls of residences are relatively short in length compared to most commercial construction, so there is less accumulated expansion to accommodate. However, stress buildup can occur even in small structures if the expansion is not properly accommodated. One of the most obvious results of brick expansion occurs at the slab corners. The slab is made of concrete, which shrinks just like concrete masonry. At the same time, the brick is expanding so the two elements are trying to move in opposite directions. If the brick is not separated from the concrete by a flashing membrane or other sheet material, the expansive movement exceeds the tensile strength of the concrete, and the corner of the slab breaks off.

Despite common misusage, the terms *control joint* and *expansion joint* are not interchangeable. The two types of joints are very different both in the way they are constructed and in the function they serve. Several different forms of control joints and expansion joints will be discussed in Chapter 5, along with tables and rules of thumb on where to locate the joints in relation to windows, doors, and other building elements.

Apply Coatings: Most masonry materials do not need any sort of protective surface coating, and therefore require little or no maintenance for the first 20 to 30 years after construction. Concrete masonry units, however, can be very absorptive and in most climates will provide better moisture penetration resistance if they receive a protective coating. The most commonly used coatings are clear water repellents which must generally be reapplied every three to five years, depending on the coating manufacturer's recommendations, and paints which usually require recoating at about the same intervals. Decorative concrete block or "architectural" block are available from many manufacturers with an integral water repellent treatment which is claimed to last the life of the units. This eliminates the problem of coating maintenance but complicates the attainment of good bond between units and mortar. Any time that units with integral water repellent treatments are used, a similar and chemically compatible admixture from the same manufacturer must be used in the mortar to assure that good bond is achieved.

4.8.2 Prevent Moisture Accumulation

Water does not hurt masonry, and a wall that gets wet suffers no harm as long as it can dry out easily. Saturated masonry, however, is vulnerable to freeze-thaw damage and other problems, so draining penetrated moisture to prevent its accumulation is important. Cavity walls were initially conceived to provide drainage through a system of flashing and weep holes. Cavity walls and anchored veneer walls should have an open separation of at least two inches between the exterior masonry wythe and the backing. The open cavity, when it is properly fitted with flashing and weep holes, functions as a drainage system for moisture which penetrates from the exterior or is condensed from water vapor within the wall section. Single-wythe walls and multi-wythe solid walls must also be designed with a system of flashing and weep holes to divert moisture to the outside. Moisture protection is maximized when the flashing membrane is of sturdy material that is installed without gaps or voids and is turned up to form pans at horizontal terminations.

One of the most critical elements in the proper drainage of masonry walls is keeping the drainage cavity open and the weeps unobstructed. If the cavity is clogged with mortar droppings or other debris, drainage is ineffective and moisture will accumulate above the flashing. In cold climates, this saturation can lead to freeze-thaw damage, and in warm climates to the growth of mold and mildew as well as other vegetation. In any climate, prolonged saturation of masonry can cause *efflorescence,* which is a white, powdery stain, or *"lime run,"* which is a hard, crusty white streak. Recommendations on the placement of flashing and weeps are covered in the various chapters which follow, as appropriate to the type of construction involved. The removal of efflorescence and lime run are discussed in Chapter 7.

Masonry Construction Techniques

Residential masonry construction involves the laying of brick, concrete block, or stone in beds of mortar, the installation of accessory items, and sometimes reinforcement. One of the most important operations is mixing mortar batches that are correctly and consistently proportioned to produce mortar with adequate strength and durability. The functional and financial success of a project, however, are often determined before construction begins—based on proper planning and estimating.

5.1   Planning and Estimating

The design of buildings with masonry foundations, basements, and veneers must take into consideration the size of the units involved. The length and height of walls as well as the location of openings and intersections will greatly affect both the speed and cost of construction as well as the appearance of the finished masonry. The use of a common module in determining dimensions can reduce the amount of field cutting required to fit the masonry units together and to coordinate the integration of masonry elements with the size and dimensions of other systems such as concrete slabs or foundations and wood framing.

5.1.1 Modular Planning

Brick and concrete block walls are typically laid out based on a 4-in. or 8-in. module, respectively. The nominal length of one modular brick plus one mortar joint is 8 in. Three bricks laid one on top of the other with three mortar joints is also equal to 8 in. If the height and length of brick veneer walls are multiples of 4 in. and doors and windows are located and sized on a 4-in. module, only whole and half-length modular brick will be needed and a minimum amount of cutting and fitting will be required. For example, a brick wall should be 6 ft.-8 in. long rather than 6 ft.-6 in. because 6 ft.-8 in. (80 inches) is a multiple of 4 in. A brick sidewalk should be 3 ft.-0 in. wide rather than 2 ft.-6 in. because 36 in. is a multiple of 4 in. Concrete blocks have nominal face dimensions of 8 in. × 16 in., including one head and one bed joint. If the height and length of concrete block walls are multiples of 8 in. and doors and windows are located and sized on an 8-in. module, only whole and half-length blocks will be needed (Figure 5-1). In construction of brick veneer over concrete-block backing walls, modular sizes facilitate the coursing and anchorage as well as the joining and intersecting of the two types of units (Figure 5-2). When the brick and block units work together in both plan and section, it increases the speed with which you can lay up a wall and improves the general quality, workmanship, and appearance of the job. Figure 5-3 lists the heights and lengths for various brick and block courses. Corners and intersections in masonry walls can be critical both structurally and aesthetically, and proper planning can facilitate construction of these elements while maintaining proper coursing (Figure 5-4).

A brick that is laid lengthwise in the wall is called a stretcher (Figure 5-5). Standing upright with the narrow side facing out, it is called a soldier—with the wide side facing out, a sailor. A stretcher unit that is rotated 90° in a wall so that the end is facing out is called a header. If the unit is then stood on its edge, it's called a rowlock. With modular brick, no matter which way you turn the units, they will work to a 4-in. module. Turning a brick stretcher crosswise in a two-wythe wall to make a header is also easy if the units are modular. The header unit is exactly the same width as a wall built of two rows of brick with a 3/8-in collar joint in between. Two header units

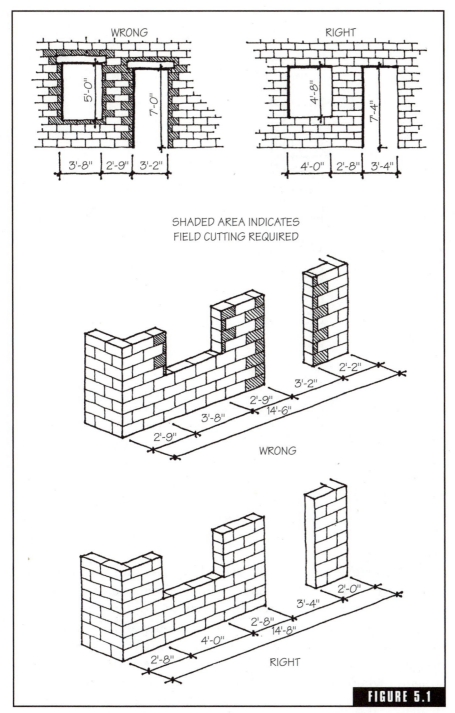

Modular layout of openings in masonry walls. *(adapted from NCMA, TEK 14, National Concrete Masonry Association, Herndon, VA).*

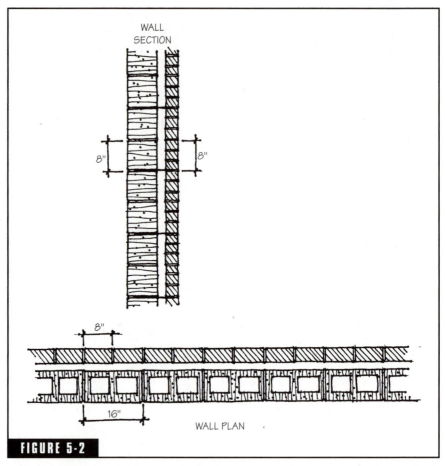

FIGURE 5-2

Brick and CMU coursing. *(from Beall, Christine,* Masonry Design and Detailing, *4th edition, McGraw-Hill, New York).*

or three rowlock units are the same length as one stretcher brick. One soldier course is the same height as three stretcher or header courses. Two rowlock courses are the same height as three stretcher courses or one soldier course, and so on (Figure 5-6). Using alternating stretcher and header units, you can easily create patterns and designs in a wall (Figure 5-7). In contemporary veneer wall construction where the masonry is only 4 in. thick, half-rowlocks and half-headers may be used to create the aesthetic effects of different pattern bonds on the exterior without the unit actually penetrating the full thickness of the wall (Figure 5-8).

Number of brick and mortar bed joint courses	Number of concrete block and bed joint courses	Wall height
1		2-$\frac{11}{16}$"
2		5-$\frac{5}{16}$"
3	1	8"
6	2	1'-4"
9	3	2'-0"
12	4	2'-8"
15	5	3'-4"
18	6	4'-0"
21	7	4'-8"
24	8	5'-4"
27	9	6'-0"
30	10	6'-8"
33	11	7'-4"
36	12	8'-0"
39	13	8'-8"
42	14	9'-4"
45	15	10'-0"
48	16	10'-8"
51	17	11'-4"
54	18	12'-0"
57	19	12'-8"
60	20	13'-4"
63	21	14'-0"
66	22	14'-8"
69	23	15'-4"
72	24	16'-0"

Number of brick and head joint courses	Number of concrete block and head joint courses	Wall length
1		0'-8"
2	1	1'-4"
3		2'-0"
4	2	2'-8"
5		3'-4"
6	3	4'-0"
7		4'-8"
8	4	5'-4"
9		6'-0"
10	5	6'-8"
11		7'-4"
12	6	8'-0"
13		8'-8"
14	7	9'-4"
15		10'-0"
16	8	10'-8"
17		11'-4"
18	9	12'-0"
19		12'-8"
20	10	13'-4"
21		14'-0"
22	11	14'-8"
23		15'-4"
24	12	16'-0"
25		16'-8"
26	13	17'-4"
27		18'-0"
28	14	18'-8"
29		19'-4"
30	15	20'-0"
36	18	24'-0"
42	21	28'-0"
48	24	32'-0"

FIGURE-5.3

Modular brick and block coursing.

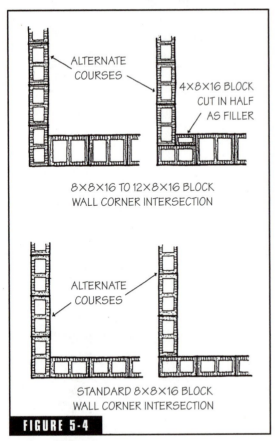

ALTERNATE COURSES

4×8×16 BLOCK CUT IN HALF AS FILLER

8×8×16 TO 12×8×16 BLOCK WALL CORNER INTERSECTION

ALTERNATE COURSES

STANDARD 8×8×16 BLOCK WALL CORNER INTERSECTION

FIGURE 5-4

Corner coursing. *(from Beall, Christine,* **Masonry Design and Detailing,** *4th edition, McGraw-Hill, New York).*

5.1.2 Estimating Materials

Estimate the number of bricks needed by multiplying the number of units in the wall length times the number of courses in the wall height, or figure 7 modular bricks for every square foot of wall area. For brick paving, estimate 4-1/2 modular bricks for every square foot when the units are laid flat on their broadest face and will be set with mortar joints, 5-1/2 units per square foot if laid tightly abutted without mortar joints. Estimate the number of concrete blocks needed by multiplying the number of units in the wall length times the number of courses in the wall height, or figure 1-1/4 units per square foot of wall area.

Stone is sold by the ton or by the cubic yard at quarries and stone suppliers. Cut stone will naturally be more expensive than rubble stone. To estimate how much stone will be needed, multiply the length × the height × the width of the wall in feet to get cubic feet, then divide by 27 to get cubic yards. To translate from cubic feet to tons, figure limestone and sandstone at about 140 lbs./cu. ft. and granite at 160 lbs./cu. ft. A stone supplier should be able to provide accurate conversions for each type of stone they sell. If the stone is sold by the ton, estimate 45–50 square feet of wall area from each ton for most types of stone. For cut ashlar stone, add about 10% extra for breakage and waste, and for rubble stone, add at least 25% extra. For flagstone to build a patio or walk, figure the square footage by multiplying length × width. The stone supplier will be able to estimate the amount of stone based on this figure and the type of stone selected.

Mortar should be estimated by the cubic yard for large projects. The amount of mortar required will depend on the type of masonry unit or stone. Figure 5-9 shows the approximate cubic yardage of mortar required for different types of masonry. Various mix proportions for both portland cement and lime mortars and for masonry cement mortars are included in Chapter 4, but for residential work, a Type N mortar is the most appropriate. The typical mix proportions for a portland cement and lime mortar are 1:1:6 (1 part portland cement : 1 part hydrated mason's lime : 6 parts masonry sand). To make one cubic yard of a Type N portland cement and lime mortar will require 4-$1/2$ sacks of cement, 4-$1/2$ sacks of lime, and 1-$1/2$ tons of sand. The typical mix proportions for a masonry cement mortar are 1:3 (1 part masonry cement : 3 parts sand). To make one cubic yard of Type N masonry cement mortar will require 9 sacks of Type N masonry cement and 1-$1/2$ tons of sand.

5.2   Construction Preparation

Before beginning construction, materials must be properly stored and protected from the weather and supporting elements inspected for completion and accuracy.

5.2.1   Material Delivery, Storage, and Handling

The methods used to store and handle materials affect both the performance and appearance of the finished masonry. Weather should not

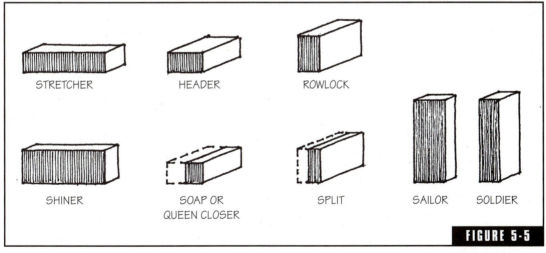

Terminology for various orientations of bricks. *(from Beall, Christine,* Masonry Design and Detailing, *4th edition, McGraw-Hill, New York).*

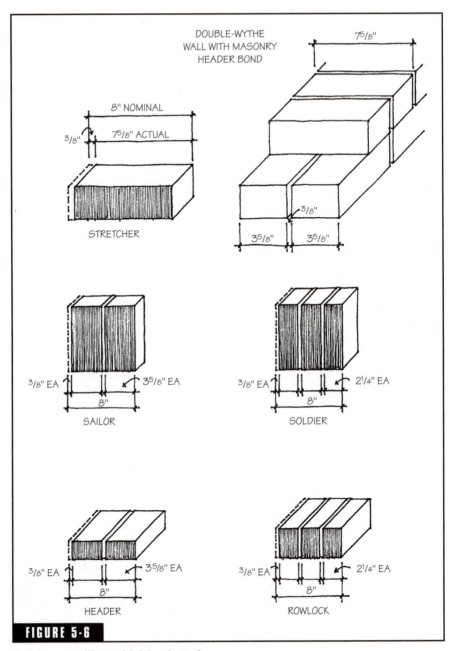

DOUBLE-WYTHE
WALL WITH MASONRY
HEADER BOND

7⁵/₈"

8" NOMINAL

3/8" 7⁵/₈" ACTUAL

STRETCHER

3/8"

3⁵/₈" 3⁵/₈"

3/8" EA 3⁵/₈" EA
8"
SAILOR

3/8" EA 2¹/₄" EA
8"
SOLDIER

3/8" EA 3⁵/₈" EA
8"
HEADER

3/8" EA 2¹/₄" EA
8"
ROWLOCK

FIGURE 5-6

Modular versatility and brick orientation.

affect properly stored and protected materials, but improper procedures can result in physical damage to units and accessories, or contamination of mortar ingredients. As a general rule, materials should
always be stored high and dry and protected from weather.

The color, texture, and size of units delivered to the job site should
be verified before the shipment is accepted. Masonry units should be
delivered and stored on wooden pallets to prevent moisture absorption from the soil, and covered with water-repellent tarps or plastic

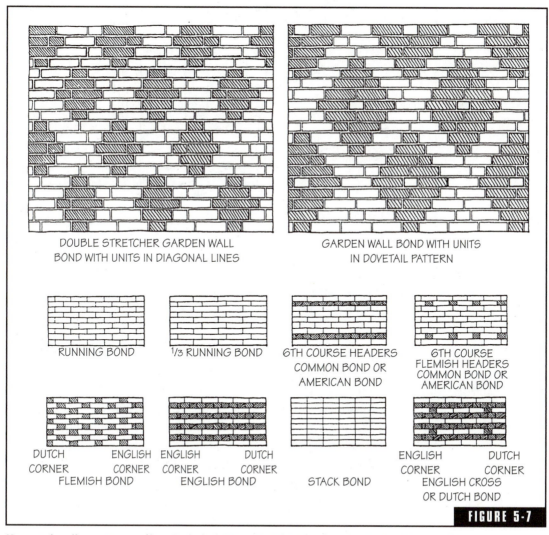

DOUBLE STRETCHER GARDEN WALL
BOND WITH UNITS IN DIAGONAL LINES

GARDEN WALL BOND WITH UNITS
IN DOVETAIL PATTERN

RUNNING BOND

1/3 RUNNING BOND

6TH COURSE HEADERS
COMMON BOND OR
AMERICAN BOND

6TH COURSE
FLEMISH HEADERS
COMMON BOND OR
AMERICAN BOND

DUTCH CORNER   ENGLISH CORNER
FLEMISH BOND

ENGLISH CORNER   DUTCH CORNER
ENGLISH BOND

STACK BOND

ENGLISH CORNER   DUTCH CORNER
ENGLISH CROSS
OR DUTCH BOND

FIGURE 5-7

Masonry bonding patterns. *(from Technical Note 30, Brick Industry Association, Reston, VA)*.

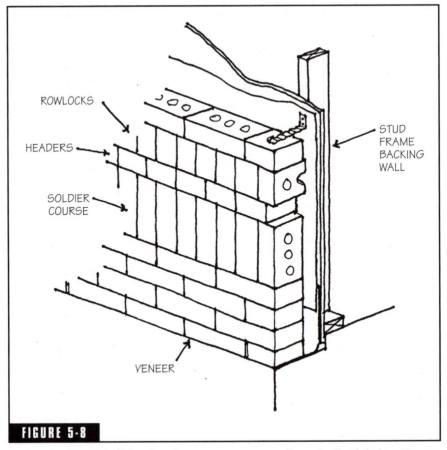

FIGURE 5·8

Half rowlocks and half headers in masonry veneers. *(from Beall, Christine,* **Masonry Design and Detailing,** *4th edition, McGraw-Hill, New York).*

covers to prevent wetting, staining, or discoloration. Masonry units that are kept dry but subjected to freezing temperatures while stored may be used in construction without damage to the units or to the masonry. Masonry units that have absorbed moisture from rain or snow and are then frozen, however, must be thawed before they can be used, so it is always easiest to keep the units covered and dry. Aggregates should be protected against contamination from rain, ice, and snow and from blowing dust and soil during construction so that they do not contribute to staining or reduced mortar bond strength. Different aggregates should be stored in separate stockpiles and all aggregate stockpiles covered with a waterproof tarp or plastic covering when not in use. This will prevent evaporation of moisture from sand aggregates as well as excessive wetting, both of which affect how much mixing water will be needed in the mortar. Packaged mortar ingredients such as cement, lime, admixtures, and pigments should be stored on pallets and covered with waterproof tarps or plastic covers to prevent moisture intrusion and damage.

5.2.2 Inspecting Surfaces to Receive Masonry

Concrete supporting elements should be inspected before starting the masonry work to assure correct layout and dimensions. Footings should be cleaned to remove laitance, loose aggregate, dirt, and other substances which would prevent mortar from bonding to the concrete. In veneer walls, the masonry is laid on flashing rather than directly on the concrete, but the concrete surface should be relatively smooth and clean to avoid puncturing the flashing.

5.2.3 Layout and Coursing

The laying up of unit masonry walls is a very ordered and controlled process. Units must remain in both vertical and horizontal alignment throughout the height and length of a wall in order to maintain structural stability and for the coursing to work out with opening locations, slab connections, anchorage to other structural elements, and so on.

Type of masonry	Mortar quantity, cu. yds.
3-$\frac{5}{8}$" $\times$ 2-$\frac{1}{4}$" $\times$ 7-$\frac{5}{8}$" modular brick with $\frac{3}{8}$" mortar joints	0.515 per 1000 brick
Nominal 8" $\times$ 8" $\times$ 16" concrete block with $\frac{3}{8}$" mortar joints	1.146 per 1000 block
4" $\times$ 1-$\frac{1}{2}$" $\times$ 8" paving brick	
$\frac{3}{8}$" mortar joints	0.268 per 1000 pavers
1" thick mortar setting bed	0.820 per 1000 pavers
Cut stone	0.04 to 0.10 per cu.yds. of stone
Fieldstone	0.15 to 0.40 per cu.yds. of stone

FIGURE 5-9

Estimating required mortar quantities. (*Adapted from Kolkoski*, Masonry Estimating.*)

TERMINOLOGY

A single horizontal row of units is called a course; a vertical section one unit wide is called a wythe. Horizontal joints are called bed joints, vertical joints between individual units are called head joints, and the longitudinal joint between wythes is called a collar joint if it is narrow and filled with mortar or grout, and called a cavity if it is an open air space for drainage (Figure 5-10). A unit whose length is cut in half is called a *bat*. One that is halved in width is called a "soap," and one that is cut to half-height is called a *split*.

Laying out of the first course is critical, since mistakes at this point would be difficult, if not impossible, to correct later. The first course must also provide a level and stable base on which the remainder of the walls can rest. It is important to coordinate the dimensions of concrete slabs and footings so that the masonry lays out properly with full and half-size units.

Before beginning work, the horizontal coursing can be checked by laying out a dry course of masonry units without mortar. Chalk lines are used to establish location and alignment of masonry on a concrete footing. A concrete slab will typically have a dropped brick ledge along its outer perimeter so that the bottom of the brick veneer is slightly lower than the finished floor height. A dry course layout should start from the wall ends or corners and work from both ends toward the middle. A piece of $^3/_8$-

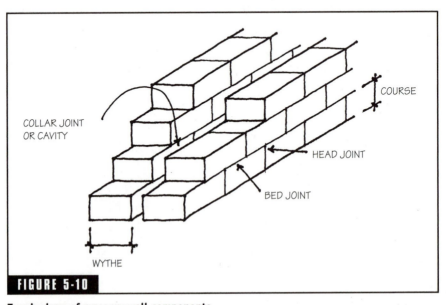

FIGURE 5-10

Terminology of masonry wall components.

> **QUICK»TIP** Bricks are cut with a wide mason's chisel called a *brickset*. Soft brick can usually be cut with one sharp blow. Harder brick must be scored on all sides, then severed with a final sharp blow. Concrete block and stone are cut with a power saw equipped with a masonry blade. For making only a few cuts, a circular saw may be adequate, but for larger projects, a table-mounted masonry saw can be rented or purchased. Stone is often wetted while sawing to cool the blade and control dust, but concrete masonry units should never be wetted because this will increase the moisture content and the possibility of shrinkage cracking in the wall.

in. plywood or the tip of a finger can be used to evenly space between units. If necessary, the size of the head joints between units can be adjusted to take up slight variations in brick size, footing length, or brick ledge dimensions. Each concrete block and head joint should measure 16 in., each modular brick and head joint should measure 8 in., and every three bricks with head joints should be 24 in. The size of "antiqued" Type FBA brick will vary more than those of smoother FBS brick, so the head joint width will also have to vary more to maintain the modular dimensions of a wall. The wall length should lay out using only whole and half-length units. Half-size brick units should be cut where needed for openings, wall ends, and corners. After the head joints are adjusted for even coursing, a few joint locations or opening locations or other critical dimensions can be marked along the chalk line on a footing or on the face of a brick ledge so that they can be used to check the spacing of the first course when the units are later laid in mortar.

5.2.4 Masonry Units

When brick is manufactured, it is fired in a high-temperature kiln which drives virtually all of the moisture out of the wet clay. Fired bricks are extremely dry until they absorb enough moisture from the air to achieve a state of moisture equilibrium with their surroundings. Brick that is very dry when it is laid causes rapid and excessive loss of mixing water from the mortar, which results in poor adhesion, incomplete bond, and water-permeable joints of low strength. Brick that is very dry and absorptive is said to have a high initial rate of absorption

To test a brick for excessive absorption, draw a circle the size of a quarter on the bed surface using a crayon or wax pencil. With a medicine dropper, place twelve drops of water inside the circle and time how long it takes to be absorbed (Figure 5-11). If the water is completely absorbed in less than one minute, the brick is too dry.

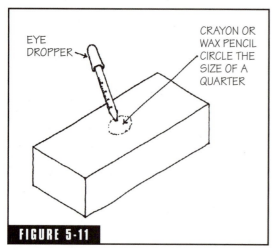

EYE DROPPER

CRAYON OR WAX PENCIL CIRCLE THE SIZE OF A QUARTER

FIGURE 5-11

Field test of brick absorption.

(IRA) or high suction. High-suction bricks should be wetted with a garden hose a day or so before they will be used so that moisture is fully absorbed into the units but the surfaces are dry to the touch before being laid. Some experts recommend that brick not be wetted in winter because some high-suction units produce better bond strength in cold weather than low-suction units. Even though it is very absorptive, *concrete block should never be wetted before placement* because this will increase unit shrinkage and the possibility of cracking in the finished wall. For this reason, it is particularly important to keep concrete block covered and protected at the job site. All masonry units should be clean and free of contaminants such as dirt, oil, or sand that might interfere with mortar bond.

5.2.5   Reinforcement, Connectors, and Accessories

Reinforcement and accessories should be checked for correct size and configuration and for adequate quantities to complete the work. Before placing reinforcing steel or metal accessories in the wall, oil, dirt, ice, and other contaminants should be removed so that a good bond can be achieved with the mortar or grout.

5.3   Mixing Mortar

Mortar is the cementitious material that bonds units, connectors, and reinforcement together for strength and weather resistance. Although it contributes to the compressive strength of the masonry, mortar's primary functions are in providing bond strength and in sealing the joints between units against the passage of air and water. To perform these functions, it must be properly mixed and placed to achieve intimate contact with the unit surface and form both a mechanical and chemical interlock.

Mortar mixes must be carefully controlled at the job site to maintain consistency in performance and appearance. Consistent measurement of mortar ingredients should ensure uniformity of proportions, yields, strengths, workability, and mortar color from batch to batch.

Volume rather than weight proportioning is most often used because it is simpler. Ingredient proportions for the various types of conventional mixes are shown in Figures 5-12 and 5-13. Portland cement, mason's lime, and masonry cement are packaged and labeled only by weight. Each bag of portland cement or masonry cement equals one cu. ft. regardless of its labeled weight, and each bag of hydrated mason's lime equals 1-1/4 cu. ft. regardless of its weight. Cement and lime are generally charged into the mixer in whole or half bags, depending on the mixer size and the batch size needed.

Volume measurements of sand are often miscalculated because of variations in the moisture content of the sand. Common practice is to use a shovel as the standard measuring tool for sand, but moisture in the sand causes a *bulking* effect. Wet sand occupies more volume than the same weight of dry sand. This often causes over- or undersanding of the mix, which affects both the strength and bonding characteristics of the mortar. Oversanded mortar is harsh and unworkable, provides a weak bond with the masonry units, and performs poorly in freeze-thaw conditions. The simplest method of consistently measuring and batching sand by volume is by

	Proportions by Volume		
Mortar Type	Portland Cement	Lime	Sand
M	1	$\frac{1}{4}$	3-$\frac{1}{2}$
S	1	$\frac{1}{2}$	4-$\frac{1}{2}$
N	1	1	6
O	1	2	9
K	1	3	12

FIGURE 5-12

Proportions for portland cement and lime mortars. *(from ASTM C270 Standard Specification for Mortar for Unit Masonry, American Society for Testing and Materials, West Conshohocken, PA).*

	Proportions by Volume			
	Masonry Cement or Mortar Cement			
Mortar Type	M	S	N	Sand
M	1			3
S		1		3
N			1	3

FIGURE 5-13

Proportions for masonry cement and mortar cement mortars. *(from ASTM C270 Standard Specification for Mortar for Unit Masonry, American Society for Testing and Materials, West Conshohocken, PA).*

using a one-cubic-foot measuring box made of plywood or lumber. The person at the mixer can then determine the exact number of shovels of sand which equal one cubic foot. Since the moisture content of the sand will vary constantly because of temperature, humidity, and evaporation, it is good practice to check the volume measurement at least twice a day and make adjustments as necessary to the number of shovels of sand being used. Some mechanical mortar mixers are equipped with a measuring box which is convenient to use because it is hinged to dump directly into the mixer.

Bond strength is an important physical property of masonry mortar, which depends on many things, including workability and water content. Unlike concrete, which is mixed with as little water as possible to produce acceptable workability, masonry mortar requires the *maximum* amount of water consistent with good workability. Mortar requires more mixing water than concrete because excess water is rapidly absorbed by the masonry units, immediately reducing the water-cement ratio to normal levels and providing a moist environment for curing. Unlike concrete, masonry mortar is never specified by water-cement ratio or slump limits. Optimum water content is best determined by the mason's feel of the mortar on the trowel. Dry mixes do not spread easily, produce poor bond, and may suffer incomplete cement hydration. Mixes that are too wet are also difficult to trowel and allow units to settle after placement. A mortar with good workability is mixed with the proper amount of water. Mortar with good workability should spread easily, cling to vertical unit surfaces, extrude easily from joints without dropping or smearing, and permit easy positioning of the unit to line, level and plumb. Thus, water content is essentially self-regulating—what is good for the mason on the scaffold is also good for the mortar itself. Quality control, therefore, should concentrate not on water content, but on assuring batch-to-batch consistency in the proportioning of cementitious ingredients and aggregate. Water should be added to the mortar mix by a consistent measure of known volume such as a plastic bucket. With a water hose, it is easy to get too much water. The water proportion will vary for different conditions of temperature, humidity, unit moisture content, unit weight, and so on. The necessary water content for grout is significantly higher than that for mortar because grout must flow readily into unit cores and cavities and around reinforcement and accessories. Grout consistency at the time of placement should produce a slump of 8 to 11 in. (Figure 5-14).

The amount of moisture in the sand will influence how much water is needed in a mortar mix to get the right consistency. Sand bought in bags for small projects will usually be very dry. Sand bought in bulk by the ton for larger projects will probably be damp or wet. Keeping sand piles covered with water-repellent tarps or plastic covers assures that the moisture content will not change drastically because of rain or evaporation.

QUICK»TIP **Masonry mortar should be the consistency of soft mud. To check for proper consistency, make a series of sharp ridges in the mortar with a hoe or trowel. If the ridges appear dry and crumbly, more water is needed. If the ridges stay sharp without slumping, the mortar is the right consistency. If you get too much water, add proportional amounts of each dry ingredient to bring it back to the proper consistency.**

To avoid excessive drying and stiffening, mortar batches should be sized according to the rate of use. With a big crew, large mortar batches will be used quickly, but with a small crew, large batches may dry out too much before they can be used. Loss of water by absorption and evaporation can be minimized on hot days by wetting the mortar boards and covering the mix in the mortar box. Within the first 1-1/2 to 2-1/2 hours of initial mixing, the mason may add water to replace evaporated moisture. This is called *retempering* and is accomplished by adding a little water to the mortar and thoroughly remixing. Mortars containing added color pigment should not be retempered because the increased water will lighten the color and cause variation from batch to batch.

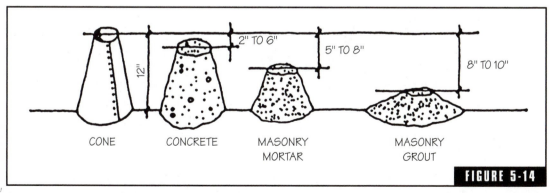

CONE   CONCRETE   MASONRY MORTAR   MASONRY GROUT

FIGURE 5-14

Masonry grout slump compared to typical concrete slump. *(from Beall, Christine, Masonry Design and Detailing, 4th edition, McGraw-Hill, New York).*

There are two traditional methods of mixing mortar on the job site. For small projects, *hand mixing* is most economical, using a mason's hoe and a mortar box or wheelbarrow. First, all of the dry ingredients are measured and mixed thoroughly with the hoe. Putting in half the sand first, then the cement and lime, and then the rest of the sand, makes blending a little quicker and easier. The materials are alternately pulled and pushed back and forth until the color is even. The mix is next pushed to one end of the mortar box or wheelbarrow, or a hole is made in the middle, and one or two gallons of water added to start. With a chopping motion of the hoe, the dry ingredients are mixed into the water, and the mix alternately pushed and pulled back and forth and more water added if necessary until the consistency and workability are judged to be satisfactory.

For larger projects, *machine mixing* is used to combine mortar ingredients. The mechanical drum or paddle-blade mixers used are similar to but of lighter duty than concrete mixers because they are not required to handle large-size aggregate. Capacities range from 4 to 7 cu. ft. About three-fourths of the mixing water, half the sand, and all of the cementitious ingredients are added first and briefly mixed together. The balance of the sand is then added, together with the remaining water. After all the materials and water have been combined, grout should be mixed a minimum of five minutes, and mortar a minimum of three and a maximum of five minutes. Less mixing time may cause nonuniformity, poor workability, low water retention, and lower-than-optimum air content. Overmixing causes segregation of materials and entrapment of excessive air, which may reduce bond strength. Pigments and admixtures are charged into the mixer last.

5.4   Unit Masonry Construction

Unit masonry construction consists of the placement of brick or block and mortar and the installation of accessory items such as anchors, ties, reinforcement, flashing, and weeps. The mechanics of brick and block laying are not difficult to learn, but skill and speed will improve only with time and practice. Increasing skill with trowel and mortar makes the work go faster and more efficiently and increases daily production rates. A skilled mason can lay an average of 530 modular brick or 125 heavyweight concrete block or 160 lightweight block in a day.

5.4.1 Unit and Mortar Placement

One of the most important elements of masonry construction is keeping the wall straight, level, and plumb and accurately maintaining the horizontal and vertical coursing. The initial layout of a wall discussed above included a dry run of units to establish horizontal coursing and adjust head joint spacing as necessary. Vertical coursing can be established by building leading sections or *leads* at the ends or corners of walls (Figure 5-16). Vertical coursing must be carefully measured for the leads to establish the correct bed joint thickness and height of each course for the whole wall. A *story pole* measured and marked ahead of time with the height of each course and the thickness of each mortar bed joint can be used to accurately and consistently maintain vertical coursing in the leads. A simple story pole can be made by marking the coursing heights on a straight piece of lumber that is long enough to mark the coursing for the full height of the wall.

The first course of a lead should be at least four or five units long and carefully aligned so the wall will be straight and not bowed or curved. Corners must be laid at true right angles of exactly 90 degrees. The second and successive courses of the lead are *racked back* one-half unit length in each course to establish a typical running bond pattern in which one unit overlaps the unit in the course below by half its length. A four-foot-long mason's level or straight 2×4 laid carefully along the "rack" of the lead should touch the corner of each brick or block (Figure 5-18). Leads are usually built four or five courses higher than the center of the wall, and as each course of the lead is laid, it should be carefully

> **TOOLS**
>
> A mason's tools include a steel framing square, 48-in. mason's level, folding rule, chalk line, line blocks or line pins, story pole, and string for layout; a bricklayer's hammer and brickset for breaking brick; a saw with a masonry blade for cutting block; a hawk or mortar board for holding small quantities of mortar; a trowel and jointing tools for placing mortar and finishing joints; and brushes to clean the surface of a wall (Figure 5-15). Jointing tools include rounded or convex jointers to produce concave joints, V-jointers, raking tools, and others.

> **QUICK TIP**
>
> A story pole for modular brick can be made by first marking a long 2 × 4 in 8-in. increments, then laying three bricks on edge, spacing 3/8 in. between them to allow for the mortar joints. Three modular brick and three mortar joints equals 8 in., so these three units can be used to mark the individual courses between each of the 8-in. increments (Figure 5-17). For concrete block, each 8-in. increment represents the height of one course of 7-5/8-in. modular units with one 3/8-in. bed joint.

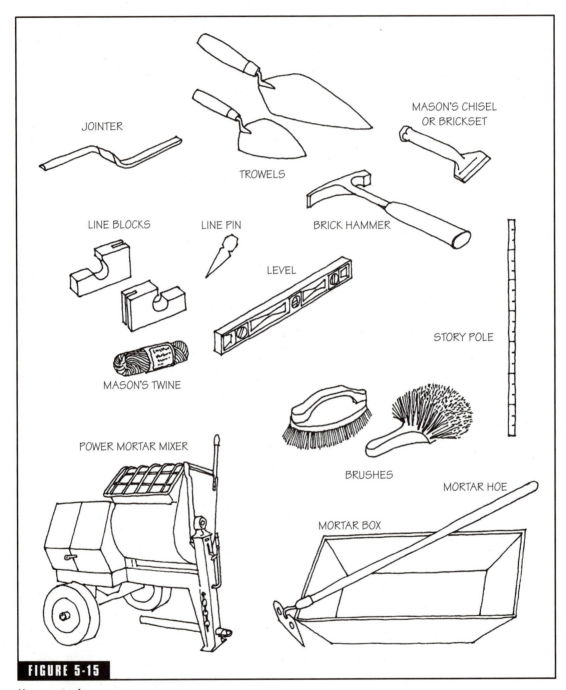

JOINTER

TROWELS

MASON'S CHISEL OR BRICKSET

LINE BLOCKS

LINE PIN

BRICK HAMMER

LEVEL

STORY POLE

MASON'S TWINE

POWER MORTAR MIXER

BRUSHES

MORTAR HOE

MORTAR BOX

FIGURE 5-15

Masonry tools.

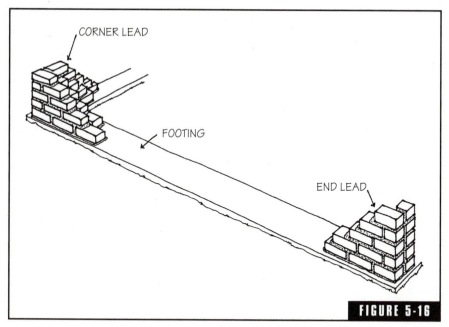

CORNER LEAD

FOOTING

END LEAD

FIGURE 5-16

Corner and end leads on a masonry wall.

checked to assure that it is level in both directions and plumb. A mason's level is used as a straightedge to check horizontal alignment. Units are brought to level and made plumb by light tapping with the trowel handle. This tapping, plus the weight of the unit and those above, helps form a good bond at the bed joint. Once the units have been laid, however, they cannot be adjusted or realigned by tapping without breaking the mortar bond. If it is necessary to reposition a unit, all the mortar must be removed and replaced with fresh.

For filling in the wall between leads, a string line is stretched from end to end and the top outside edge of each unit can then simply be aligned with the string. Nylon string is wrapped securely around two wooden line blocks. One line block is hooked on the corner of one lead so that the string is level with the top of the unit in the course being laid (Figure 5-19). The string is then stretched to the opposite corner lead and the other line block is hooked at the same height. The line blocks are held in place by the tension of the string. Steel line pins can also be used to run the string line. They are driven into the head joints of the leads and the string is wrapped around and pulled tightly. The

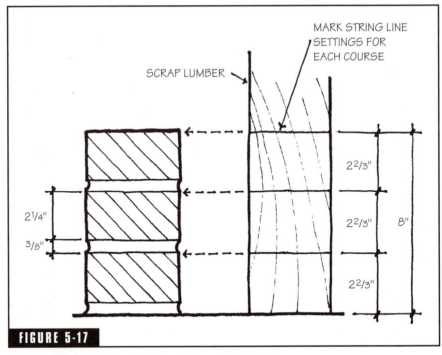

FIGURE 5-17

A story pole simplifies vertical coursing measurements.

line blocks should hold the string slightly away from the face of the wall so that the following units will not touch it or push it out of alignment. The masonry in between the leads can now be *laid to the line* to

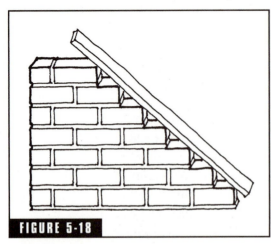

FIGURE 5-18

Racking back a partially completed masonry wall.

keep the wall straight and the brick course level. The string line should always be pulled tight enough to prevent sagging and should occasionally be checked with a line level. A mason's level is used to make sure the face of the wall is plumb. The line blocks and string are moved up the corners of the leads as each course of the wall is filled in, and the leads are continually built up several courses above the middle of the wall.

Commercial story poles are made of steel with adjustable coursing scales attached and are designed to eliminate the need for building leads. The poles attach to the structure at the corners or ends of the wall, and the string line is pulled from pole to pole. The poles must be rigid enough not to bend when the string is pulled taut from one side, and they must be easily plumbed and maintained for the height of the wall.

Brick masonry must be laid with full head and bed joints to assure adequate strength and resistance to moisture penetration. Bed joints should not be furrowed, but slightly beveled away from the cavity to minimize mortar droppings in the cavity (Figure 5-20). Bed joint mortar should be spread only a few feet at a time so that the mortar will not dry out too much before the next course of units is placed. The ends of the bricks should be fully buttered with mortar so that when they are shoved into place, mortar is squeezed from the joint (Figure 5-21). So-called *clip joints* in which only a thin section of mortar is placed at the face of the joint will allow excessive moisture to penetrate the masonry. Even though the joints look full and solid after the wall is completed and much less mortar is required to complete the work, callbacks from unhappy homeowners and the liability for water damage and cracking make this a risky practice.

FIGURE 5-19

A masonry line block holds the string in place so units can be laid to the line.

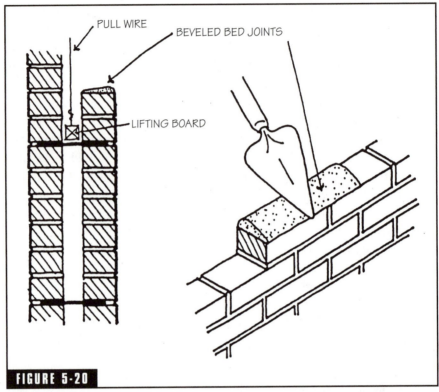

FIGURE 5-20

Beveled bed joint. *(from* Technical Note 21C, *Brick Industry Association, Reston, VA).*

Since concrete blocks are hollow, they are mortared differently than bricks. Concrete block walls are typically laid with what is called *face shell bedding,* in which the mortar head and bed joints are the same depth as the face shells and flanges (Figure 5-22). Because of their weight and difficulty in handling, masons often stand several blocks on end and apply mortar to the head flanges of three or four units at one time. Each block is then individually placed in its final position, tapped down into the mortar bed, and shoved against the previously laid block, thus producing well-filled vertical head joints at both faces of the masonry. When installing the

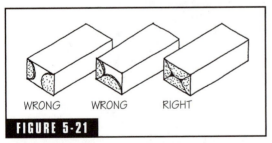

FIGURE 5-21

Full head joints improve mortar bond and limit moisture penetration. *(from* Technical Note 17C, *Brick Industry Association, Reston, VA).*

last brick or block in the middle of a course, all edges of the opening and all vertical edges of the unit should be buttered with mortar and the unit carefully lowered into place. If any of the mortar falls out, leaving a void in the joint, the closure unit should be removed and the operation repeated.

In cavity wall and veneer wall construction, it is extremely important that the cavity between the outer wythe and the backing wall be kept clean to assure proper moisture drainage. If mortar clogs the cavity, it can form bridges for moisture passage to the backing wall, or it may block weep holes. Some masons use a removable wooden strip to temporarily block the cavity as the wall is laid up and prevent mortar droppings. However, beveling the mortar bed as shown in Figure 5-20 allows little mortar to extrude toward the cavity.

To add visual interest to masonry walls, units may be laid in different positions as shown in Figure 5-5, and arranged in a variety of patterns as shown in Figure 5-7. The patterns were originally conceived in connection with masonry wall bonding techniques that are not widely used today. In older historic masonry, rowlock and header courses were used to structurally connect multiple wythes of a thick masonry wall together. Most contemporary buildings use the $1/3$ or $1/2$

FIGURE 5-22

Hollow masonry units are typically laid with face shell bedding. (Photo courtesy PCA).

running bond, or stack bond with very little decorative pattern work. Brick soldier and sailor courses create 8-in.-tall head joints. Because the bed surface of some brick can be relatively smooth, mortar will sometimes slump in a head joint of this height. Concrete block head joints do not have the same problem because the block surface is usually rougher and holds the mortar in place better. Brick soldier and sailor courses should be installed carefully to prevent voids in the head joints, which might be easily penetrated by moisture. Units used for sailor or shiner courses must be solid and uncored.

To achieve a consistent pattern on the wall, units with a pronounced color range from light to dark, or blends which contain more than one color of brick must be uniformly distributed. Brick manufacturers routinely attach instructions for unstacking and using each pallet of brick to assure that the colors are distributed uniformly in the wall. Working from more than one pallet at a time will also help assure good blending of slight inadvertent color differences. Narrow color ranges, however, present fewer potential problems than wider ranges or blends of more than one color (Figure 4-5).

Mortar color and joint type can be just as important in determining the appearance of a wall as the selection of a unit type or color, and variations in aesthetic effect can be achieved by using different types of mortar joints. There are several types of joints common today (Figure 5-23). *Rough-cut* or *flush* joints are used when other finish materials, such as stucco, gypsum board, or textured coatings, are to be applied over the masonry. These joints are formed by simply slicing off excess mortar with the edge of the trowel immediately after the units are laid. *Weathered* joints are more difficult to form since they must be struck off with the trowel point from below, but the mortar is somewhat compacted by the action, and the joint sheds water naturally. *Struck* joints are easily cut with a trowel point, but the small ledge created collects water, snow, and ice, which may then penetrate the wall. *Raked* joints are made by scraping out a portion of the mortar while it is still soft, using a square-edged tool. Even though the mortar is slightly compacted by this action, it is difficult to make the joint weather resistant, and it is not recommended where driving rain, high winds, or freezing are likely to occur. The cut of the joint does form a shadow and tends to give the wall a darker appearance. *Weeping* joints leave excess mortar protruding from the joint to give a rustic appearance, but again are not weather resistant. Other, more specialized effects can be achieved with tools to bead or groove a mortar joint. The most moisture-resistant joints are tooled *concave* and *V-shaped* joints. Mortar squeezes out of the joints as the masonry units are set in place, and the excess is struck off with a trowel. After the mortar has become "thumbprint" hard (i.e., when a clear thumbprint can be impressed and the cement paste does not stick to the thumb), joints are finished with a jointing tool slightly wider than the joint itself. As the mortar hardens, it has a tendency to shrink slightly and separate from the edge of the masonry unit. Proper tooling compresses the mortar against the unit and compacts the surface, making it more dense and more resistant to moisture penetration. Concave or V-tooled joints are recommended for use in areas subject to heavy rains and high winds. However, full head and bed joints and good mortar bond are more critical to moisture resistance than tooling. Less moisture-resistant joint treatments may be used in mild to moderate exposures *if* the workmanship is good, the bond between units and mortar is complete and intimate, and the flashing and weeps are properly designed and installed.

Horizontal joints should be tooled before vertical joints, using a long jointer sometimes called a *slicker* that is upturned on one end to

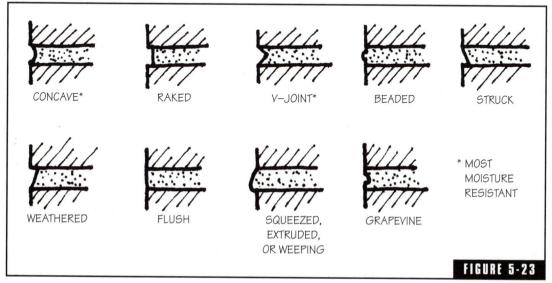

CONCAVE*   RAKED   V–JOINT*   BEADED   STRUCK

WEATHERED   FLUSH   SQUEEZED,   GRAPEVINE   * MOST
                         EXTRUDED,   MOISTURE
                         OR WEEPING   RESISTANT

FIGURE 5-23

Masonry joint profiles.

prevent gouging. Jointers for vertical tooling are small and S-shaped. Although the material most commonly used for these tools is steel, plastic jointers are used to avoid darkening or staining white or light-colored mortars. After the joints have been tooled, mortar burrs or ridges should be trimmed off flush with the face of the unit with a trowel edge, or by rubbing with a burlap bag, a brush, or a piece of carpet.

It is important that the moisture content of the mortar be consistent at the time of tooling, or color variations may create a blotchy appearance in the wall. Drier mortar tools darker than mortar that is wetter when tooled. Along with time and weather conditions, brick moisture content at the time of laying affects mortar curing time. An *inconsistent* unit moisture content therefore affects the color of the finished joint. If an unprotected pallet of brick, for instance, becomes partially wet during an overnight rain, the wet units will cause patches of lighter-colored joints because their higher moisture content keeps the mortar moist for a longer period of time than adjacent areas.

Even with high-quality workmanship, some routine patching or repair of damaged or defective mortar joints is to be expected. In addition, any holes left by line pins should be filled with fresh mortar before the joints are tooled. The troweling of mortar into joints after the units are laid is known as *pointing.* It is preferable that pointing and patching be done while the mortar is still fresh and plastic, and before final tooling of the joints is performed. If however, the repairs must be made after the mortar has hardened, the joint should be raked or chiseled out to a depth of about $1/2$ in. thoroughly wetted, and pointed with fresh mortar.

5.4.2   Flashing and Weep Holes

Flashing must be installed in continuous runs with all seams and joints lapped 4 to 6 in. and sealed with a nonhardening mastic or caulking material. Unsealed lap joints will allow water to flow around the end of the flashing and penetrate the wall. At lateral terminations where the flashing abuts other construction elements, and at terminations on each side of door jambs, flashing must be turned up to form an end dam. Flexible flashing can be simply folded into place (Figure 5-24).

Flashing should never be stopped short of the face of the wall, or water can flow around the front edge and back into the wall. Flexible flashing should be extended beyond the face of the wall and later trimmed flush with the face of the joint using a utility knife. The vertical leg of the flashing should be turned up several inches to form a back dam and be placed in a mortar joint in a concrete block backing wythe or behind the sheathing in a frame wall (Figure 5-25).

Weep holes are required in masonry construction at the base course and at all other flashing levels (such as window sills and lintels) so that water which is collected on the flashing can be drained from the wall as quickly and effectively as possible. Weep holes are formed by leaving the mortar out of the head joint between bricks at a spacing of 24 in. on center, or leaving the bottom portion of a concrete block head joint empty at a spacing of 32 in. on center. To function properly, weep holes must be unobstructed by mortar droppings or other debris. Blocked or missing weep holes can cause saturation of the masonry just above the flashing as moisture is dammed in the wall for longer periods of slow evaporation. Efflorescence, staining, corrosion of steel lintels, and freeze-thaw damage can result. To disguise the appearance of the open joints, they can be fitted with louvered metal or plastic grid weep vents (Figure 5-26).

5.4.3 Installing Accessories and Reinforcement

Metal ties, anchors, horizontal joint reinforcement, and steel reinforcing bars are all placed by the mason as the work progresses. Anchors, ties, and joint reinforcement must be properly spaced and placed in the mortar to assure complete encapsulation and good mortar bond. Since mortar is spread only a limited distance along bed joints to avoid excessive evaporation, long sections of joint reinforcement are usually

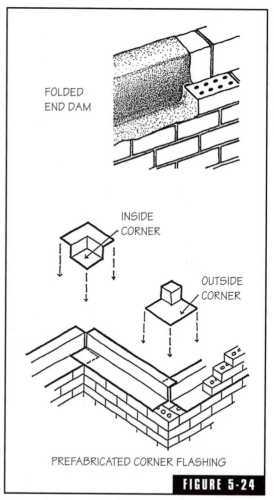

FOLDED END DAM

INSIDE CORNER

OUTSIDE CORNER

PREFABRICATED CORNER FLASHING

FIGURE 5-24

Flashing corners and end dams.

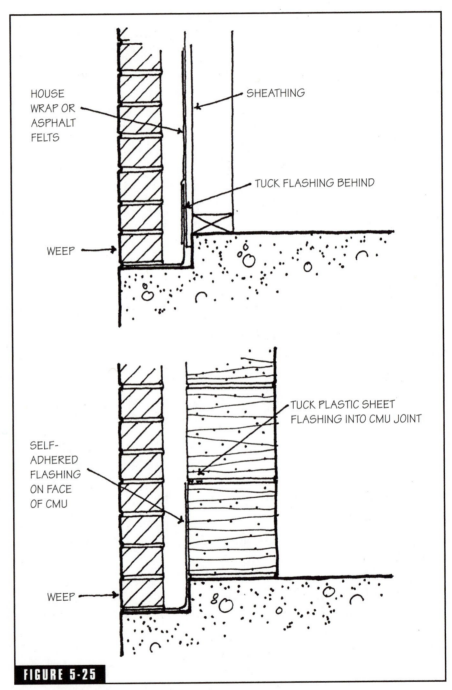

HOUSE WRAP OR ASPHALT FELTS

SHEATHING

TUCK FLASHING BEHIND

WEEP

SELF-ADHERED FLASHING ON FACE OF CMU

TUCK PLASTIC SHEET FLASHING INTO CMU JOINT

WEEP

FIGURE 5-25

Terminating back leg of masonry flashing.

laid directly on the units and lifted slightly with the fingers after the mortar is placed so that mortar can get underneath the wires. All metal accessories which are embedded in mortar joints should be kept a minimum of $5/8$-in. from the exterior face of the joint so they are well protected from wetting and corrosion.

Vertical steel reinforcement in a double-wythe wall is placed in the cavity and the masonry is built up around it. Spacers are used at periodic intervals to hold the reinforcing bars up straight and keep them in the correct location. Spacers can also be used to support horizontal bars (Figure 5-27). For single-wythe CMU walls with

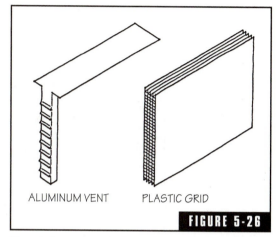

ALUMINUM VENT   PLASTIC GRID

FIGURE 5-26

Weep hole accessories. (from Beall, Christine, *Masonry Design and Detailing*, 4th edition, McGraw-Hill, New York).

steel reinforcement, special open-end units are made so that the block can be placed around the vertical bars rather than threaded over the top (Figure 5-28). Horizontal steel is placed in courses of special lintel or bond beam blocks.

5.4.4 Control and Expansion Joints

Allowances must be made in brick and concrete masonry construction for expansion and contraction of the units. All construction materials expand and contract with temperature changes, some to a greater or lesser degree than others. Clay brick also expands with the absorption of moisture, and concrete masonry shrinks with loss of residual moisture from the manufacturing and construction process. The exact locations of control and expansion joints will be affected by design features such as openings, offsets, and intersections. In brick walls, expansion joints should be located near corners because the opposing push of intersecting walls can cause cracking. For both brick and concrete masonry walls, joints should be located at points of weakness or high stress concentration such as abrupt changes in wall height; changes in wall thickness; columns and pilasters; and at one or both sides of windows and doors. Freestanding walls of relatively short length that are not connected to other structures may not require control or expansion joints if they are free to expand and contract without restraint.

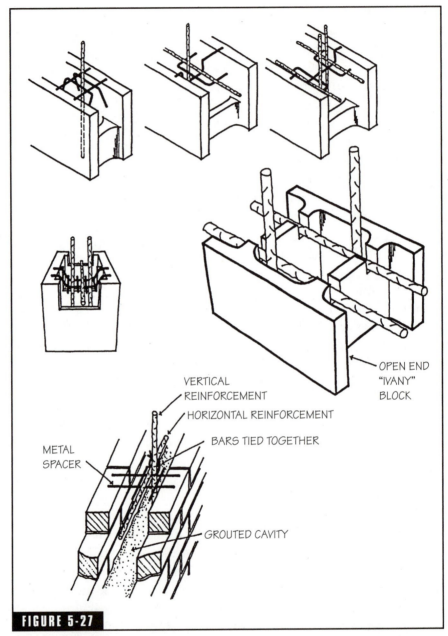

VERTICAL
REINFORCEMENT

HORIZONTAL REINFORCEMENT

BARS TIED TOGETHER

METAL
SPACER

OPEN END
"IVANY"
BLOCK

GROUTED CAVITY

FIGURE 5-27

Reinforcing bar spacers for hollow unit masonry. *(from Beall, Christine,* Masonry Design and Detailing, *4th edition, McGraw-Hill, New York).*

Steel reinforcement can also be used to restrain movement and reduce the need for control and expansion joints. Steel joint reinforcement is routinely used in concrete masonry walls to reduce shrinkage and is usually placed in every second or third bed joint.

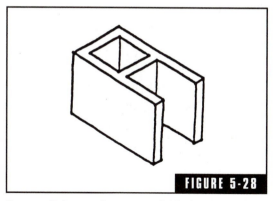

FIGURE 5-28

Open-ended concrete masonry A-block.

Expansion Joints: A masonry expansion joint is a soft joint without mortar that is designed to accommodate the natural expansion of brick. Any brick wall that is 20 ft. or more in length should have at least one expansion joint. Deciding where to put expansion joints will depend on the design. If either end of the wall is built against existing construction such as a house, garage, or another wall, an expansion joint can be placed between the two elements. If the wall is a long, straight section, an expansion joint should be located so that it divides the wall into sections that are no more than 20 ft. long. If the wall is an L or U shape, an expansion joint should be located near the corners (Figure 5-29).

Expansion joints should be $3/8$ in. to $1/2$ in. wide. To keep mortar from accidentally blocking the joint during construction, a soft foam pad can be placed in it, or a piece of temporary plywood that can be removed later. If a foam pad that will stay in place is used, its edge

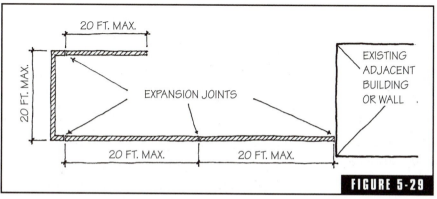

FIGURE 5-29

Brick masonry expansion joint locations.

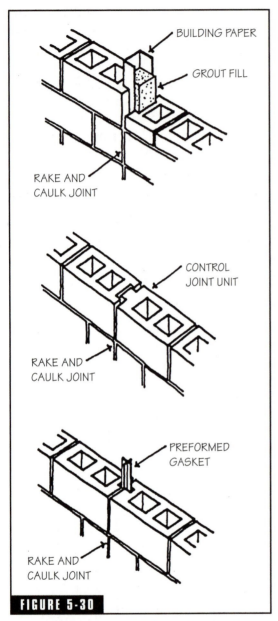

BUILDING PAPER

GROUT FILL

RAKE AND
CAULK JOINT

CONTROL
JOINT UNIT

RAKE AND
CAULK JOINT

PREFORMED
GASKET

RAKE AND
CAULK JOINT

FIGURE 5-30

Concrete masonry control joints. *(from Beall, Christine,* Masonry Design and Detailing, *4th edition, McGraw-Hill, New York).*

should be recessed from the face of the wall about $3/4$ in. so the joint can be caulked after the wall is finished.

Control Joints: Control joints are continuous, weakened joints designed to accommodate the natural shrinkage of concrete masonry in such a way that cracking will occur in straight lines at these joints rather than at random locations (Figure 5-30). Control joints also must incorporate a tongue-and-groove type key so that adjoining wall sections resist wind loads together, but still expand and contract independently. Control joints in concrete masonry walls that are required to keep out moisture must be sealed against leakage. To do this, the mortar is raked out before it hardens to a depth of 1/2 in. to 3/4 in., which will allow caulking for weather resistance. Concrete masonry always shrinks more than it expands, so even though control joints contain mortar, they can accommodate thermal expansion and contraction which occurs after the initial curing shrinkage.

If joint reinforcement is located in every other bed joint, space control joints at three times the wall height (e.g., for a 6-ft.-high wall, space control joints at 18 ft. on center). If joint reinforcement is located in every third bed joint, space control joints at 2-1/2 times the wall height (e.g., for a 6-ft.-high wall, space control joints at 15 ft. on center). *Joint reinforcement should stop on either side of a control joint. It should not continue through it.*

5.5 Stone Masonry Construction

Stone masonry is similar in many ways to unit masonry, but there are also some differences. Stone is a natural material, so its size and shape are not uniform, and it's also a very heavy material. Stone is dimensionally stable and does not expand and contract with changes in temperature or moisture content, so stone masonry construction does not require expansion or control joints.

5.5.1 Cutting and Shaping Stone

When rubble stone is laid in mortar, irregular shapes are taken up to some degree in the mortar joints themselves. When stone is dry-stacked without mortar, the fit of the stones must be more precise. For

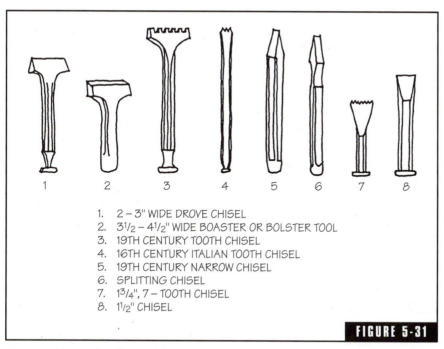

1. 2 – 3" WIDE DROVE CHISEL
2. $3^{1}/_{2}$ – $4^{1}/_{2}$" WIDE BOASTER OR BOLSTER TOOL
3. 19TH CENTURY TOOTH CHISEL
4. 16TH CENTURY ITALIAN TOOTH CHISEL
5. 19TH CENTURY NARROW CHISEL
6. SPLITTING CHISEL
7. $1^{3}/_{4}$", 7 – TOOTH CHISEL
8. $1^{1}/_{2}$" CHISEL

FIGURE 5-31

Stone working tools. *(from Harley J. Mckee,* Introduction to Early American Masonry— Stone, Brick, Mortar and Plaster. *The Preservation Press).*

both types of stonework, though, it will often be necessary to cut and shape individual stones to make them fit better.

Granite is the most difficult stone to cut, but limestone, sandstone, and slate are relatively easy to work with. To cut rubble, it is first laid on solid ground for firm, even support. Cutting should not be done on concrete surfaces because the hard concrete and uneven support may cause the stone to break in the wrong place. The cut is marked with chalk, crayon, or pencil, and scored with a chisel. Often, the stone will break along the line before it is scored all the way around. Small lumps or protrusions are removed with the pointing chisel. Flagstones can be cut by laying them over a small pipe and striking with the chisel. Small pieces can also be trimmed off of flagstone with a mason's hammer.

5.5.2 Mortar for Stone Masonry

The same types of mortar used for brick and block construction are suitable for stone masonry work as well. Sometimes the proportion of lime is reduced, and one popular mix uses 1 part lime, 2 parts portland cement, and 9 parts sand or 1 part masonry cement to 3 parts sand. Because stone is so heavy, the mortar should be mixed to a slightly stiffer consistency than that used with unit masonry, even though a stiffer mix is a little more difficult to work with. For light-colored stone, a light-colored mortar can be made using white portland cement instead of ordinary gray cement, or pigments can be added to create other colors.

5.5.3 Setting Stone

Ashlar stone that is laid in straight horizontal courses can be installed using string lines and line blocks just like unit masonry. For rubble stone that is less precise, pattern bonds are more like putting together a puzzle in which no two pieces are the same size or shape. There is an art to creating uniformity in pattern so that the front of the house looks the same as the sides and back. Colors must be blended and some regularity of coursing and placement is required. The necessary skills can be acquired only with hands-on experience and a good eye for the esthetics.

5.5.4 Flashing and Weep Holes

Even though stone is not as absorptive as brick or block, stone masonry walls still require flashing and weeps to drain moisture from the wall. Water entry in stone walls, like in brick and block walls, is most often through the mortar joints, and when the joints are irregular and difficult to tool, water penetration can be significant.

5.5.5 Accessories

Residential stone masonry usually is limited to veneer applications, garden walls, and retaining walls. Steel reinforcement is seldom necessary for these applications, so the accessories necessary for stone masonry construction are usually limited to wall ties and anchors. These need flexibility to accommodate the irregularities of the stone, and either wire or corrugated metal are most frequently used.

5.6 Grouting Masonry

Concrete block basement walls often require steel reinforcing for added strength. In reinforced concrete block construction, the cores of the hollow units are pumped with grout to secure the reinforcing steel and bond it to the masonry. All of the cores of a concrete block wall may be grouted with reinforcement spaced every few cores, or the grout may be limited only to the cores which contain reinforcement.

If only isolated cores of a concrete block wall will be grouted, the cores that will be grouted must be fully bedded in mortar, including the webs and face shell flanges. This will prevent the grout from flowing beyond its intended location. If the whole wall is to be grouted, the face shells are mortared as usual, but the webs are not. This allows the grout to flow laterally inside the wall for better bond. Spacers are used to maintain alignment of the vertical reinforcement to assure that grout completely surrounds the steel for full embedment and proper structural performance. Protrusions or fins of mortar which project into the cores will interfere with proper flow and distribution of the grout and could prevent complete bonding.

The *low-lift method* of grouting a wall is done in 8-in. lifts as the wall is laid up. Grout should be well mixed to avoid segregation of materials, and carefully poured to avoid splashing on the top of the units, since dried grout will prevent proper mortar bond at the succeeding bed joint. At least 15 minutes should elapse between pours to allow the grout to achieve some degree of stiffness before the next layer is added. If grout is poured too quickly, and the mortar joints are fresh, hydrostatic pressure can cause the wall to bulge out of plumb. A displacement of as little as $^1/_8$ in. will destroy the bed joint bond, and the work must be torn down and rebuilt. The joint rupture will cause a permanent plane of weakness and cannot be repaired by simply realigning the wall. Grout that is in contact with the masonry hardens more rapidly than that in the center of the grout space so it is important that consolidation or puddling of the grout take place immediately after the pour and before this hardening begins. Vibrators used in masonry grouting are usually smaller than those used in concrete work because the space they must fit into is smaller. In single-wythe, hollow-unit construction, walls may be built to a maximum 4-ft. height before grout is pumped or poured into the cores. Grout is placed in the cores and then consolidated by vibration to ensure complete filling and solid embedment of steel.

High-lift grouting operations are not performed until the wall is laid up to full story height. The cross webs of hollow units are fully embedded in mortar about every 25 ft. to form grout barriers. This limits the size of the pour to a manageable area and contains the grout within the designated area. Cleanouts must be provided at the base of the wall by leaving out every other unit in the bottom course of the section being poured. In single-wythe, hollow-unit walls, cleanout openings at least 3×4 in. are located at the bottom of every core containing dowels or vertical reinforcement, and in at least every second core that will be grouted, but has no steel. In solidly grouted, unreinforced single-wythe walls, every other unit in the bottom course should be left out. A high-pressure air blower is used to remove any debris which may have fallen into the cores. Cleanout plugs are filled in after cleaning the cavity, but before the grouting begins. The mortar joints in a wall should be allowed to cure for at least three days to gain strength before grouting by the high-lift method. In cold, damp weather, or during periods of heavy rain, curing should be extended to five days. Grout should be placed in a continuous operation with no intermediate horizontal construction joints within a story height. Four-foot maximum lifts are recommended, with 30 to 60 minutes between pours to allow for settlement, shrinkage, and absorption of excess water by the units. In each lift, the top 12 to 18 in. should be reconsolidated before or during placement of the next lift.

It is critical that the grout consistency be fluid, and that it be mechanically vibrated into place. When the grout is stiff, it hangs up on the side walls of the cores and the reinforcing bars, leaving voids in which the steel is not properly bonded or embedded and is much more susceptible to corrosion from moisture within the wall.

5.7 Protections

During construction, partially completed masonry work requires some protection from damage caused by weather or by other construction operations.

5.7.1 Bracing

High-lift grouting requires that walls be temporarily braced until the mortar and grout has fully set. Partially completed walls should also be braced during construction against lateral loads from wind or other forces applied before full design strength is attained or before permanent supporting construction is completed (Figure 5-32). Partially completed structures may be subject to loads which exceed their structural capabilities.

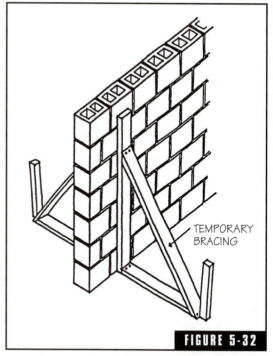

TEMPORARY BRACING

FIGURE 5-32

Bracing provides wind load resistance during construction. *(from NCMA, TEK 72, National Concrete Masonry Association, Herndon, VA).*

Wind pressure, for instance, can create four times as much bending stress in a new, freestanding wall as in the wall of a completed building. Fresh masonry with uncured mortar has no tensile strength to resist such lateral forces. Most codes require that new, uncured, unanchored walls be braced against wind pressure. Bracing should be provided until the mortar has cured and the wall has been integrally tied to the structural frame of the building. Bracing should be designed on the basis of wall height and expected wind pressures.

5.7.2 Coverings

Masonry walls should be covered at the end of each day and when work is not in progress. Excess moisture entering the wall during construction can cause saturation of units, which may take weeks or months to dry out. Such prolonged wetting may result in efflorescence, particularly if the cooler winter months lengthen the drying process. Extended wetting will also prolong cement hydration, producing large amounts of calcium hydroxide, which may also be taken into solution and leached to the surface to cause calcium carbonate stains.

Covers such as water-repellent tarps or heavy plastic sheets should extend a minimum of two feet down each side of uncompleted walls and be held securely in place. During construction, scaffold planks should also be turned on edge at the end of each day so that rain will not splash mortar droppings or dirt onto the face of the masonry.

5.7.3 Cold Weather

Cold weather causes special problems in masonry construction. Even with sufficient mixing water, cement hydration and strength development in mortar and grout will stop at temperatures below 40°F. Construction may continue during cold weather if the masonry mortar and materials are kept warm during placement, preventing the masonry from freezing during the initial hours after placement before cement hydration and mortar cure are complete. Frozen mortar looks like it is hardened, but it is not actually cured and will not develop full design strength or complete bond until it is thawed and liquid water is again available for hydration. Frozen mortar is easily scratched from joints, has a "crows feet" pattern on the surface of tooled joints, and may flake at the surface. Cement hydration will resume if the temperature of the masonry is raised above 40°F and its liquid moisture content exceeds 75%. When these conditions are maintained throughout the curing period, ultimate strength development and bond will be the same as those attained under moderate conditions.

The rate at which masonry freezes is influenced by the severity of temperature and wind conditions, the temperature and absorption characteristics of the units, the temperature of reinforcing steel and metal accessories, and the temperature of the mortar at the time of placement. Wet mortar mixes expand more when frozen than drier ones, and expansion increases as the water content increases. During freezing weather, low-moisture-content mixes and high-suction units are desirable, but regardless of the conditions, mortar and grout consistency must provide good workability and flow so that bond is maximized. During cold-weather construction, it may be desirable to use a

Type III, high-early-strength portland cement because of the greater protection it will provide the mortar.

In addition to normal storage and protection, consideration should be given to the method of stockpiling sand to permit heating the materials if required. As the temperature falls, the number of different materials requiring heat will increase. Mixing water is easily heated. If none of the other materials are frozen, mixing water may be the only ingredient requiring artificial heat. It should be warmed enough to produce mortar and grout temperatures between 40 and 70°F at the time of placement. Water temperatures above 180°F can cause cement to flash set, so sand and water should be mixed first to moderate high temperatures before the cement is added. Masonry sand, which contains a certain amount of moisture, should be thawed if frozen to remove ice. Sand should be warmed slowly to avoid scorching, and care should be taken to avoid contamination of the material from the fuel source. Dry masonry units should be heated if necessary to a temperature above 20°F at the time of use. Wet, frozen masonry units must be thawed without overheating.

The degree of protection against cold weather which is provided for the work area is an economic balance between the cost of the protection and the cost of not being able to work. Protective apparatus may range from a simple windbreak to a heated enclosure. Each job must be evaluated individually to determine needs and cost benefits, but some general rules do apply. Characteristics such as strength, durability, flexibility, transparency, fire resistance, and ease of installation should be considered when selecting protective materials. Canvas, vinyl, and polyethylene coverings are often used. In most instances, a windbreak or unheated enclosure will reduce the chill factor sufficiently to provide the degree of protection required. Precautions must also be taken to safeguard workers against injury, and enclosures must be adequate to resist wind, snow, and uplift loads. Cold-weather protection measures may be necessary when the ambient temperature or the temperature of the units is below 40°F. Figure 5-33 summarizes heating and protection requirements for various work temperatures.

5.7.4 Hot Weather

Although not as widely discussed as cold-weather problems, hot-weather conditions also pose special concerns for masonry construction.

Workday Temperature	Construction Requirement	Protection Requirement
Above 40°F	Normal masonry procedures	Cover walls with plastic or canvas at end of workday to prevent water entering masonry
40–32°F	Heat mixing water to produce mortar temperatures between 40–100°F	Cover walls and materials with plastic or canvas to prevent wetting and freezing
32–25°F	Heat mixing water and sand to produce mortar temperatures between 40–100°F	With wind velocities over 15 mph provide windbreaks during workday and cover walls and materials at end of workday to prevent wetting and freezing; maintain masonry above 32°F for 16 hours using auxiliary heat or insulated blankets
25–20°F	Mortar on boards should be maintained above 40°F	Provide enclosures and supply sufficient heat to maintain masonry enclosure above 32°F for 24 hours
20–0°F and below	Heat mixing water and sand to produce mortar temperatures between 40–120°F	

FIGURE 5-33

Cold weather construction requirements.

High temperatures, low humidity, and wind can adversely affect performance of the masonry.

Rapid evaporation and the high suction of hot, dry units can quickly reduce the water content of mortar and grout mixes so that cement hydration actually stops. Mortar workability and grout flow are inhibited and set occurs faster. High-temperature mortars have lower air contents, and air-entraining agents are less effective. Board life of mortars is shorter, and joints must be tooled sooner than normal. Evaporation at the exterior face of joints decreases durability and strength at the surface. When ambient temperatures are above 100°F, or above 90°F with wind velocities greater than 8 mph, protective measures should be taken to assure continued hydration, strength development, and maximum bond. Whenever possible, materials should be stored in a shaded location, and aggregate stockpiles covered with plastic sheets to retard moisture evaporation. High-suction brick can be wetted to reduce initial absorption, and metal accessories such as reinforcing steel, anchors and ties, mixers, mortar boards, and wheelbarrows can be kept cool by spraying with water.

Additional mixing water may be needed in mortar and grout, and additional lime will increase the ability of the mortar to retain water longer. Increasing the cement content in the mix accelerates early strength gain and maximizes hydration before evaporative water loss. Adding ice to the mixing water can also lower the temperature of the mortar and grout and slow evaporation. Water that is too hot can cause the cement to flash set. Set-retarding or water-reducing admixtures may also be used. Retempering should be limited to the first 1-1/2 hours after mixing. Mortar beds should not be spread more than 4 ft. ahead of the masonry, and units should be set within one minute of spreading the mortar. Sun shades and windscreens can modify the effects of hot, dry weather, but consideration should also be given to scheduling work during the cooler parts of the day.

5.7.5 Moist Curing

Cement hydration cannot occur if the temperature of the mortar or grout is below 40°F or if the moisture content of the mix is less than 75%. Both hot and cold weather can produce conditions which cause hydration to stop before curing is complete. These *dry outs* occur most frequently in concrete masonry construction and under winter conditions, but may also occur in brick construction and in hot, dry weather. Dry outs are naturally reactivated when temperatures rise above freezing and rainwater restores moisture to the wall, but until this occurs, the masonry is temporarily limited in compressive strength, bond, and weather resistance.

Moist curing methods similar to those used in concrete construction can help prevent masonry dry outs. Periodically wetting the finished masonry for several days with a fine water spray will usually assure that adequate moisture is available for curing, strength development, and good bond. Covering the walls with polyethylene sheets will also retard evaporation and create a greenhouse effect that aids in moist curing. Extreme winter conditions may also require the application of heat inside these enclosures to maintain temperatures above 40°F. Even though concrete masonry units cannot be wetted on site before they are installed, completed concrete masonry walls can be moist-cured because the restraining conditions of the joint reinforcement and surrounding construction minimize the effects of moisture shrinkage in the units.

5.8 Cleaning Masonry

Cleaning new brick and concrete masonry is easiest if some simple protective measures are taken during construction. The finished appearance of masonry walls depends to a great extent on the attention given to the surfaces during construction and during the cleaning process. Care should always be taken to prevent mortar smears or splatters on the face of the wall, but if such stains do occur, proper cleaning can help prevent permanent discoloration.

5.8.1 Construction Precautions

Precautions which should be taken during construction include the following:

■ protecting the base of the wall from rain-splashed mud or mortar droppings by using straw, sand, sawdust, or plastic sheeting spread out on the ground and up the wall surface;

■ turning scaffold boards on edge at the end of the day to prevent rain from splashing mortar or dirt directly onto the wall;

■ covering the tops of unfinished walls at the end of the day to prevent saturation or contamination from rain; and

■ protecting masonry units and packaged mortar ingredients from groundwater or rainwater contamination by storing off the ground, protected with waterproof coverings.

5.8.2 Methods of Cleaning

The cleaning process itself can be a source of staining if chemical or detergent cleansing solutions are improperly used, or if windows, doors, and trim are not properly protected from possible corrosive effects. New masonry may be cleaned by scrubbing with water, detergent, a muriatic acid solution, or proprietary cleaning compounds.

Detergent solutions will remove mud, dirt, and soil accumulations. One-half cup dry measure of trisodium phosphate and $1/2$ cup dry measure of laundry detergent dissolved in 1 gal. of water is recommended. *Acid cleaners* must be carefully selected and controlled to avoid both injury and damage. Hydrochloric acid (commonly called muriatic acid) dissolves mortar particles and should be used carefully in a diluted state. Muriatic acid should be mixed with at least nine parts clean water in a nonmetallic container, and metal tools or brushes should not be used. Acid solutions can cause green vanadium or brown manganese stains on some clay masonry and should not be used on light colored tan, buff, brown, black, pink, or gray brick which contains manganese coloring agents. *Proprietary cleaning compounds* should be carefully selected for compatibility with the masonry material, and the manufacturer's recommended procedures and dilution instructions should be followed.

Some contractors use *pressurized water or steam* cleaning combined with detergents or cleaning compounds. If the wall is not thoroughly saturated before beginning, high-pressure application can drive the cleaning solutions into the masonry, where they may become the source of future staining problems. High-pressure washing can also damage soft brick and mortar and accelerate deterioration. *Abrasive sandblasting* should not be used to clean masonry.

All cleaning solutions, even detergent, should be tested for adverse effects on a small, inconspicuous area of the wall. Some detergents contain soluble salts that can contribute to efflorescence. Muriatic acid can leave a white scum on the wall if the residue of dissolved cement is not thoroughly rinsed after a brief dwell time and light scrubbing. This white scum can only be removed with special proprietary compounds, or it may have to simply wear off. Detergent and acid solutions usually are applied by bucket and brush, but large jobs may require low-pressure spray application. The masonry should be thoroughly saturated from the top down before cleaning to prevent absorption of the acid or the dissolved mortar particles. Failure to adequately prewet a wall, or using an acid solution that is too strong will cause acid burn—a chemical reaction that changes the color of the masonry. Nonmetallic buckets, brushes, and tools must always be used with acid cleaners because metals react with acid, leaving marks on the wall that can oxidize and leave stains. Muriatic acid can also discolor pigmented mortars, so it should be pretested and used with caution on this type of work. Cleaning should be scheduled as late as possible in the construction.

Walls should be cleaned when they are in the shade rather than in the sun so that the cleaning solutions do not dry out too quickly. Confine cleaning to small areas that can be rinsed before they dry. For cleaning new masonry, the Brick Industry Association (BIA) has established guidelines for the selection of methods depending on the type of brick used (Figure 5-34).

5.8.3   Cleaning Fresh Mortar Smears

On brick and other clay masonry units, the mortar must be thoroughly set and cured before it can be properly removed. Trying to clean wet mortar from the surface presses the cement paste into the unit pores, making it harder to clean. Wooden paddles or nonmetallic scrapers should be used to remove large mortar droppings. For small splatters, stains, or the residue from larger pieces, a medium-soft fiber-bristle brush is usually adequate. Any motions that rub or press mortar particles into the unit face should be avoided. Mortar that cures too long is harder and more difficult to remove than fresh splatters, and may require acid cleaning. Mild acid solutions easily dissolve thin layers of mortar. Large splatters should be scraped off first and, if necessary, the residue removed with acid. Muriatic acid is suitable for cleaning clay masonry if it is diluted in a ratio of one part acid to nine parts water. Muriatic acid should never be used on light-colored tan, buff, gray, or pink brick because it can react with minerals in the clay and cause green vanadium or brown manganese stains.

Mud, dirt, and soil can usually be washed away with a mild detergent solution consisting of $1/2$ cup dry measure of trisodium phosphate (TSP) and $1/2$ cup dry measure of laundry detergent to one gallon of clean water. Dried mud may require the use of pressurized water or a proprietary "restoration" type cleaner containing hydrofluoric acid and phosphoric acid. Hydrofluoric acid, however, etches polished surfaces such as glass, so adjacent windows must be protected from accidental contact. Hydrofluoric acid is not suitable for cleaning mortar stains and splatters because it cannot dissolve portland cement products.

Brick Category	Cleaning Method	Remarks
Red and red flashed	■ Bucket and brush hand cleaning ■ High pressure water ■ Sandblasting	■ Hydrochloric acid solutions, proprietary compounds, and emulsifying agents may be used. ■ Smooth texture: Mortar stains and smears are generally easier to remove; less surface area exposed; easier to presoak and rinse; unbroken surface, thus more likely to display poor rinsing, acid staining, poor removal of mortar smears ■ Rough texture: Mortar and dirt tend to penetrate deep into textures; additional area for water and acid absorption; essential to use pressurized water during rinsing
Red, heavy sanded finish	■ Bucket and brush hand cleaning ■ High-pressure water	Clean with plain water and scrub brush or lightly applied high pressure and plain water. Excessive mortar stains may require use of cleaning solutions. Sandblasting is not recommended.
White, tan, buff, gray, specks, pink, brown and black	■ Bucket and brush hand cleaning ■ High-pressure water ■ Sandblasting	Do not use hydrochloric (muriatic) acid. Clean with plain water, detergents, emulsifying agents or suitable proprietary compounds. Manganese-colored brick units tend to react with muriatic acid solutions and stain. Light colored brick are more susceptible than darker unit to acid burn and stains.
White, tan, buff, gray, specks, pink, brown and black with sand finish	■ Bucket and brush hand cleaning ■ High pressure water	Do not use hydrochloric (muriatic) acid. Clean with plain water, or lightly applied detergents, emulsifying agents, or suitable proprietary compounds. Manganese-colored brick units tend to react with muriatic acid solutions and stain. Light colored brick are more susceptible than darker unit to acid burn and stains. Sandblasting is not recommended.
Glazed brick	■ Bucket and brush hand cleaning	Wipe glazed surface with soft cloth within a few minutes of laying units. Use soft sponge or brush plus ample water supply for final washing. Use detergents where necessary and acid solutions only for very difficult mortar stains. Do not use acid on salt glazed or metallic glazed brick. Do not use abrasive powders.
Colored mortars	■ Method is generally controlled by the brick unit	Many manufacturers of colored mortars do not recommend chemical cleaning solutions. Most acids tend to bleach colored mortars. Mild detergent solutions are generally recommended.

FIGURE 5-34

Brick masonry cleaning methods. *(from Technical Note 20 Rev, Brick Industry Association, Reston, VA).*

Although hydrochloric acid solutions are highly effective in removing mortar stains, they are not recommended for concrete masonry. Acid solutions remove the stain by dissolving the cement, but they also dissolve the cement matrix in the unit and etch the surface, leaving it porous and highly absorptive. As the cement is dissolved, more aggregate is exposed, changing both the color and the texture of the block.

Dry rubbing is usually sufficient for removing mortar stains from concrete masonry. To prevent smearing, mortar droppings and splatters should be almost dry before being removed. Large droppings can be pried off with a trowel point, putty knife, or chisel. The block surface can then be rubbed with another small piece of block, and finally with a stiff fiber-bristle or stainless steel brush.

Remove dried mortar splatters from stone with a trowel or by scrubbing with stone dust and fiber brushes wetted with white vinegar. Acids or chemical cleaners are not usually required to clean new stone. If stubborn dirt or other foreign substances are embedded in the stone surface, mild abrasive cleaners will usually remove them. If more aggressive methods are required, consult the stone supplier about the most appropriate cleaning chemicals and procedures.

5.8.4 Efflorescence and Calcium Carbonate Stains

Efflorescence and calcium carbonate stains are the two most common forms of surface stains on masonry. Both are white and both are activated by excessive moisture in the wall, but beyond that, there are no similarities. Efflorescence is a powdery salt residue, while calcium carbonate stains are hard, crusty, and much more difficult to remove.

Efflorescence is the white powdery deposit on exposed masonry surfaces caused by the leaching of soluble salts. Efflorescence occurs when soluble salts in the units or mortar are taken into solution by prolonged wetting. As the wall begins to dry, the salt solution migrates toward the surface through capillary pores. When the water evaporates, the salts are deposited on the face of the wall (Figure 5-35). If the units and the mortar ingredients contain no soluble salts such as sodium or potassium sulfate, and if insufficient moisture is present to effect leaching, efflorescence cannot occur. The source of moisture necessary to produce efflorescence may be either rainwater or the condensation of water vapor within the assembly. Water may also be present because unfinished walls were not properly protected from rain and snow during construction. "New building bloom" (efflorescence which occurs within the first year of the building's completion) is often traced to slow evaporation of such moisture. Hot summer months are not as conducive to efflorescence because the wetting and drying of the wall is generally quite rapid. In late fall, winter, and early spring, particularly after rainy periods, when evaporation is slower and temperatures cooler, efflorescence is more likely to appear. To minimize the possible contribution of mortar ingredients to efflorescence, use portland cements with low alkali content, clean washed sand, and clean mixing water.

Efflorescence will often disappear with normal weathering if the source of moisture is located and stopped. Efflorescence can also be dry brushed, washed away by a thorough flushing with clean water, or scrubbed away with a brush.

Calcium carbonate stains are hard encrustations which can be removed only with acid cleaners. Calcium hydroxide is present in masonry mortar as part of the hydrated lime in cement-lime mortars, and as a by-product of the portland cement hydration process itself. Portland cement will produce about 12—20% of its weight in calcium hydroxide at complete hydration. Calcium hydroxide is only slightly soluble in water, but extended saturation of the mortar prolongs the hydration process producing a maximum amount of calcium hydroxide and provides enough moisture to leach the calcium hydroxide to the surface. When it reacts with carbon dioxide in the air, the calcium hydroxide forms a concentrated calcium carbonate buildup, usually appearing as white streaks from the mortar joints and sometimes referred to as "lime deposits" or "lime run" (Figure 5-36). The existence of calcium hydroxide in cement-based mortar systems cannot be avoided. Preventing saturation of the wall both during and after construction, how-

FIGURE 5-35

Masonry efflorescence. *(from Beall, Christine, Masonry Design and Detailing, 4th edition, McGraw-Hill, New York).*

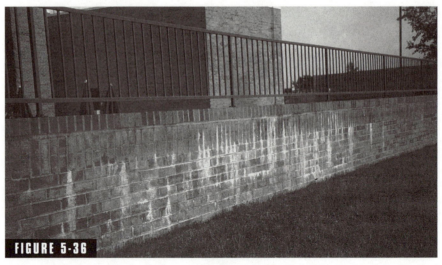

FIGURE 5-36

Calcium carbonate stains or "lime run." *(from Beall, Christine,* Masonry Design and Detailing, *4th edition, McGraw-Hill, New York).*

ever, will eliminate the mechanism needed to form the liquid solution and carry it to the masonry surface.

Before calcium carbonate stains can be removed, the source of moisture must be located and stopped. Once that is done, the stain and surrounding area should be saturated with water, and a dilute solution of one part muriatic acid to nine parts water applied. Using a stiff fiber-bristle brush, the stain can be scrubbed away and the wall thoroughly rinsed with water to remove the acid and residue.

5.9   Clear Water Repellents

Water-repellent coatings are often applied on architectural concrete block and on some light-colored stone, but their effectiveness is usually limited to a period of three to seven years, depending on the product selected. Water-repellent coatings can be applied in one of three ways, depending on the size of the surface being treated:

- With a synthetic bristle paint brush
- With a synthetic roller and plastic paint roller pan
- With low-pressure (20-psi) spray equipment with a stainless steel fan tip nozzle.

When water repellents are applied by sprayer, sheets of plastic should be used to protect adjacent surfaces and landscaping. The application of water-repellent coatings does not require any special skills or equipment, but manufacturer's label instructions should be followed for handling, application rates, cleanup, and disposal. Some products contain VOCs (volatile organic compounds), the use of which may be restricted in some areas, and the disposal of which is regulated in almost all areas.

The surface to which the coating will be applied must be clean and free of dirt or oils that would prohibit absorption of the coating into the surface. If general or spot cleaning is necessary, the surface should be allowed to dry thoroughly before proceeding. The mortar in new masonry walls (or freshly placed concrete) should fully cure for at least 28 days before applying a water repellent. Water-based coatings will have less odor than solvent-based products.

Spray applications should be made only when there is little or no wind to avoid damage from the spray drifting onto other surfaces. Regardless of whether the application is by brush, roller, or spray, the water repellent should be put on the wall from the bottom up with enough material applied to create a 6-in. to 8-in. rundown below the contact point. The coating should be allowed to penetrate the surface for two or three minutes and then reapplied in the same saturating manner. When the first coat is dry to the touch, or within two hours of the first application, a second saturating coat can be applied in the same way as described above.

Footings, Foundation Walls, Basements, and Slabs

Most residential construction today is supported on either concrete slabs-on-grade or on concrete or masonry foundations. There are a number of different foundation types, each of which must provide both the strength and stability to support the weight of the structure, its contents and occupants, as well as wind and snow loads that are transferred to the foundation by the structure.

6.1 Building Code Requirements

Most jurisdictions prescribe minimum building code requirements for the construction of residential foundations. The following basic requirements from the CABO *One and Two Family Dwelling Code* are fairly representative of those found in many municipalities.

- Fill material which supports footings and foundations must be designed, installed, and tested in accordance with accepted engineering practice.

- The grade away from foundation walls must fall a minimum of 6 in. within the first 10 ft. Where lot lines, walls, slopes, or other physical barriers prohibit the minimum slope, drains or swales must be provided to ensure drainage away from the structure.

- In areas likely to have expansive, compressible, or shifting soils or other unknown soil characteristics, the building official may require a soil test by an approved agency to determine soil characteristics at a particular location.

- When topsoils or subsoils are expansive, compressible, or shifting, they must be removed to a depth and width sufficient to assure stable moisture content in each bearing area or stabilized within each bearing area by chemical treatment, dewatering, or presaturation. Unstable soils that are removed may not be used as fill in other areas.

- Concrete must have a minimum compressive strength as shown in Figure 6-1.

6.1.1 Soil-Bearing Pressures

The soil which supports building foundations must be strong enough to withstand the loads that are applied to it. The Code provides that in lieu of a complete soils evaluation to determine bearing characteristics, the values in Figure 6-2 may be assumed. If you do not know what type of soil exists on a given site, the building official should be able to tell you what the code requirements are. You'll need to know what the soil bearing capacity is to determine minimum footing dimensions.

6.1.2 Frost Depth

The water in soil freezes and expands, then contracts again when it thaws. This phenomenon is called *frost heave.* Footings and foundations must be set below the winter frost line to avoid damage from frost heave. The depth to which the soil freezes depends not only on climate and geographic location, but also on soil composition, altitude, and weather patterns. The map in Figure 6-3 shows long lines of equal frost depth in the central and southern states, but in the west and north shows local frost depths that can vary widely within a small area. Along the Gulf coast, the frost depth is only 1 in., but in northern Maine a footing must be set 6 ft. deep to reach below the frost line.

6.2 Footings

Foundation walls can bear directly on the subsoil when the soil has a high bearing capacity. If the soil bearing capacity is lower, the wall

Type or location of concrete	Minimum Specified Compressive Strength Weathering Potential*		
	Negligible	Moderate	Severe
Basement walls and foundations not exposed to weather	2,500	2,500	2,500‡
Basement slabs and interior slabs on grade, except garage floor slabs	2,500	2,500	2,500‡
Basement walls, foundation walls, exterior walls and other vertical concrete work exposed to weather	2,500	3,000†	3,000†
Porches, carport slabs and steps exposed to weather, and garage slabs	2,500	3,000†§	3,500†§

*See map for weathering potential (Alaska and Hawaii are classified as severe and negligible, respectively).

†Use air-entrained cement.

‡Use air-entrained cement if concrete will be subject to freezing and thawing during construction.

§Minimum cement content 5-$\frac{1}{2}$ bags per cubic yard.

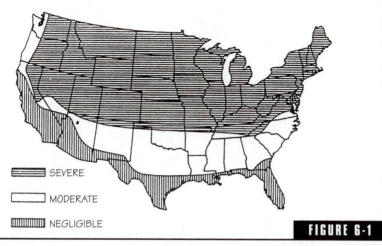

SEVERE

MODERATE

NEGLIGIBLE

FIGURE 6-1

Minimum required strength of concrete for footings, slabs, and foundations. *(from Council of American Building Officials* One and Two-Family Dwelling Code, *Falls Church, VA).*

Class of Material	Soil-Bearing Pressure, psf
Crystalline bedrock	12,000
Sedimentary rock	6,000
Sandy gravel or gravel	5,000
Sand, silty sand, clayey sand, silty gravel, and clayey gravel	3,000
Clay, sandy clay, silty clay, and clayey silt	2,000

FIGURE 6-2

Allowable bearing pressures for various types of soil. *(from Council of American Building Officials,* One and Two-Family Dwelling Code, *Falls Church, VA).*

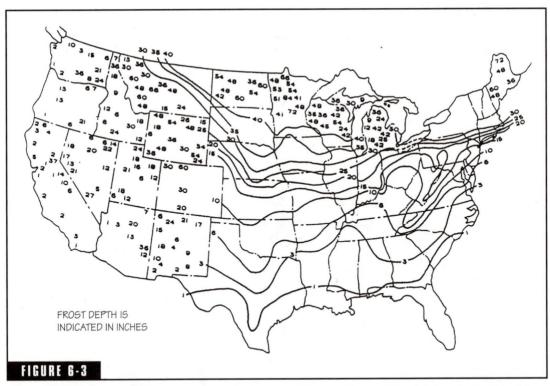

FROST DEPTH IS
INDICATED IN INCHES

FIGURE 6-3

Average annual frost depth for continental United States. *(from Architectural Graphic Standards, 9th ed.).*

may require a concrete footing that is wider than the wall itself and capable of distributing the weight of the structure over a larger area.

6.2.1 Concrete Footings

Concrete footings are used to support building walls, freestanding garden walls, and retaining walls for many types of construction. Footings that are wider than the walls they support are typically called *spread footings.* The Code requires that footings be:

- A minimum of 6 in. thick
- Supported on undisturbed natural soil or on engineered fill
- Set below the frost line unless otherwise protected against frost heave
- A minimum of 12 in. below grade regardless of frost depth

The required footing width (W) is based on the bearing capacity of the soil as indicated in Figure 6-4. Footing projections (P) on either side of the foundation wall must be a minimum of 2 in., but not more than the footing thickness. For a soil with moderate bearing capacity of 3,000 psf, in a conventionally framed 2-story house, the minimum required footing width is only 10 in. Soil with a relatively low bearing capacity of 2,000 psf, supporting a 2-story home of brick veneer over wood frame construction would require a footing 19 in. wide. The lower the soil-bearing capacity, the wider the footing required to spread the building's weight over a larger soil area. The footing widths shown in the tables are *minimum* dimensions. The wider the footing, the more stable it will be against overturning, rocking, or uneven settlement in any soil. Many industry professionals recommend using a rule of thumb which says that the footing thickness should be the same as the width of the foundation wall it supports, and the footing width should be a minimum of two times the thickness of the foundation wall it supports. For an 8-in. concrete block wall, this would mean a 16-in.-wide footing, 8 in. thick. The soil-bearing capacity may require a minimum footing width greater than or less than the rule of thumb, so the actual width should always be the larger of the two (Figure 6-5). In soils with high bearing capacity where the minimum required footing width is 8 in. or less, the foundation wall can be safely and economically constructed to bear directly on the subsoil without a spread footing. Once the width exceeds 8 in., it is usually more economical to build a spread footing than to unnecessarily increase the thickness of

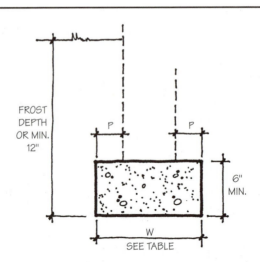

MINIMUM WIDTH (W) OF CONCRETE FOOTINGS, IN.

	Loadbearing Value of Soil, psf					
	1,500	2,000	2,500	3,000	3,500	4,000
Conventional Wood Frame Construction						
1 story	16	12	10	8	7	6
2 story	19	15	12	10	8	7
3 story	22	17	14	11	10	9
4-Inch brick veneer over wood frame or 8-inch hollow concrete masonry						
1 story	19	15	12	10	8	7
2 story	25	19	15	13	11	10
3 story	31	23	19	16	13	12
8-inch solid or fully grouted masonry						
1 story	22	17	13	11	10	9
2 story	31	23	19	16	13	12
3 story	40	30	24	20	17	15

FIGURE 6-4

Minimum requirements for concrete footings. *(from Council of American Building Officials One and Two-Family Dwelling Code, Falls Church, VA).*

the entire foundation wall, especially if its height is more than a foot or two.

For footings 12 in. or less in thickness, formwork is easiest to build of 2 × lumber because there is less cutting required than for making short plywood forms. Remember that the actual size of the lumber is $1/2$ in. less than its nominal dimension. Using 2 × 6s for a 6-in.-thick footing, for example, requires that the boards be set slightly off the ground to achieve the required dimension. To keep the concrete from running out the bottom of the forms, backfill with a little soil after the forms and braces are in place (Figure 6-6). If a footing is 8 in. or more in thickness, use 1 × 4 *spreaders* spaced about 4 ft. apart along the top of the forms to keep the concrete from bowing them out of shape (Figure 6-7). A beveled 2 × 4

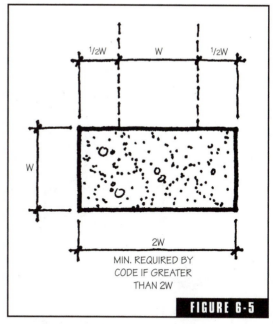

MIN. REQUIRED BY
CODE IF GREATER
THAN 2W

FIGURE 6-5

Rule-of-thumb footing size requirements.

should be inserted lengthwise along the top of the footing to form a *keyway* which will keep the wall from sliding. The keyway form should be well oiled so that it will be easy to remove after the concrete has hardened. Concrete walls set on top the footing will interlock physically along the indentation. The bottom course of a masonry wall should be set in a full bed of mortar which will also interlock slightly to prevent sliding.

6.2.2 Stepped Footings

Where the ground under a wall slopes slightly, you can build a footing that is level but is deeper in the ground at one end than the other. Where the ground slopes more steeply, though, it is best to step the form down the slope so that the footing is in a series of level sections (Figure 6-8). For footings with lumber forms, build two overlapping forms to create the change in height (Figure 6-9), making sure that the overlapping portion is at least as long as the footing is thick. That is, for an 8-in.-thick footing, overlap the two adjoining levels at least 8 in.

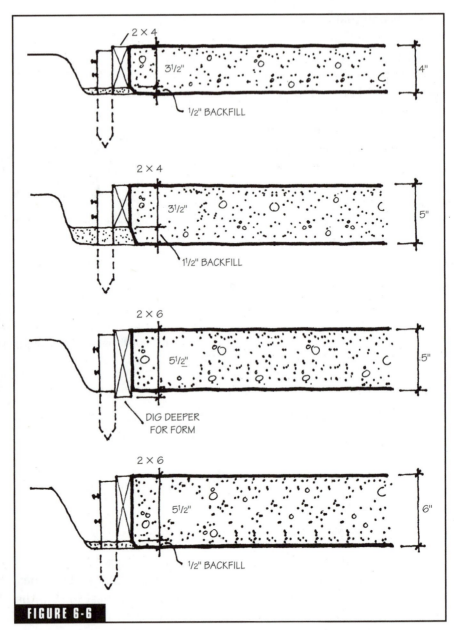

FIGURE 6-6

Backfill at bottom of concrete forms.

6.2.3   Footings Without Forms

For shallow footings in firm soil, wood forms can be eliminated and the concrete formed by the earth trench itself. The trench should be the exact width of the footing, excavated using a square-nosed shovel to keep the edges straight. The trench should be deep enough that the bottom of the footing will be at least 12 in. below grade as required by Code (Figure 6-10). A row of wooden stakes or short reinforcing bar lengths driven into the ground down the middle is used to indicate the required thickness of the concrete. A straight 2 × 4 and a level can be used to make sure the tops of the guide stakes are level. When the concrete is poured, simply strike and float the surface even with the tops of the stakes and then remove them. A

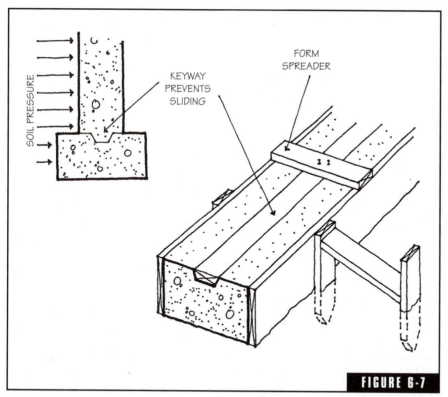

Footing spreaders and keyways. *(from Portland Cement Association,* **The Homeowner's Guide to Building with Concrete, Brick and Stone,** *PCA, Skokie, Illinois).*

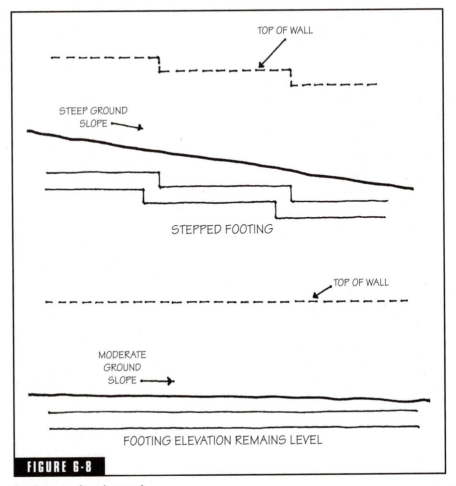

TOP OF WALL

STEEP GROUND
SLOPE

STEPPED FOOTING

TOP OF WALL

MODERATE
GROUND
SLOPE

FOOTING ELEVATION REMAINS LEVEL

FIGURE 6-8

Footings on sloped ground.

concrete with a 6-in. slump will flow easily and seek its own level
in the footing, but the high water-cement ratio reduces it compressive strength. Using a 6-sack mix (6 sacks of cement per cubic yard
of concrete) instead of a 5 or 5 1/2-sack mix will compensate for the
extra water and higher slump and still provide the 2,500 psi compressive strength required by Code. For stepped footings, step the
excavation down and form a dam with a board or piece of plywood
and wooden stakes driven firmly into the sides of the excavation
(Figure 6-11).

FIGURE 6-9

Stepped footing.

6.2.4 Steel Reinforcement

Footings for light loads are often built without steel reinforcing, but many footing designs require steel reinforcing bars to increase strength and help distribute heavier loads. The bars should be placed horizontally in the forms and supported off the ground in the position indicated by the drawings (bars are usually located one-third up from the bottom of the form, and at least 3 in. off the ground). If the footing is to support a reinforced concrete or masonry wall, it will also require short sections of reinforcing bar *dowels* that turn up and can be tied to the vertical reinforcement in the wall. The horizontal leg of the dowel should be at least 12 in. long, and the vertical leg at least 18 in. tall so that it will overlap horizontal reinforcing bars in the footing and vertical reinforcing bars in the wall a

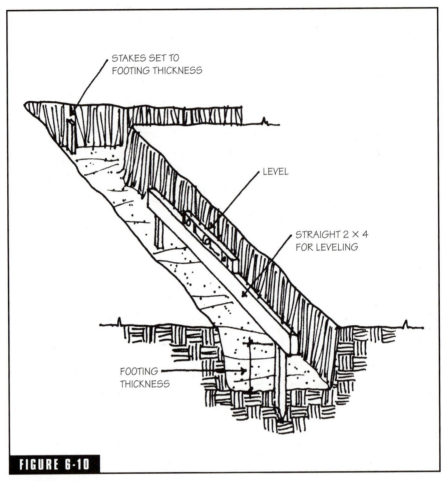

STAKES SET TO
FOOTING THICKNESS

LEVEL

STRAIGHT 2 × 4
FOR LEVELING

FOOTING
THICKNESS

FIGURE 6-10

Trenched footing without forms.

minimum of 12 in. or 30 times the diameter of the bars (Figure 6-12).
For foundation walls that are unreinforced, dowels can be used to
tie the footing and wall together instead of forming a keyway. If the
footing does not contain horizontal reinforcing bars, the dowels can
be tied to the spreaders on top of the footing forms to hold them in
place until the concrete hardens. Make sure the dowel spacing is
accurate, especially if the bars will have to align with the hollow
cores of a masonry unit wall. Provide a minimum distance of 1-1/2
in. between the footing reinforcement and the sides of the form, and
keep the bars at least 3 in. off the ground to assure that they are fully

embedded in concrete and protected from the corrosive effects of moisture in the soil. Bars can be supported on small stones or pieces of concrete block or tied to the 1 × 4 spreaders on top of the forms with a loop of twisted wire.

6.3 Foundation Walls and Basements

Basements are quite common in many parts of the country and almost unheard of in others. Where the frost line is relatively shallow and the footings are therefore close to the finish grade, only a short foundation wall (or stem wall as they are sometimes called) is needed to bring the construction above ground to provide support for the building frame. In cold climates where footings are required to be set deep in the ground to avoid frost heave, foundation walls may have to be several feet tall to reach above grade. With a little additional excavation, the footings can be set deeper and the foundation wall height extended sufficiently to accommodate construction of a habitable basement that is fully or partially below grade. The taller the foundation wall required by footing depth, the less additional work required to enclose a basement space.

FIGURE 6-11

Stepped footing without forms.

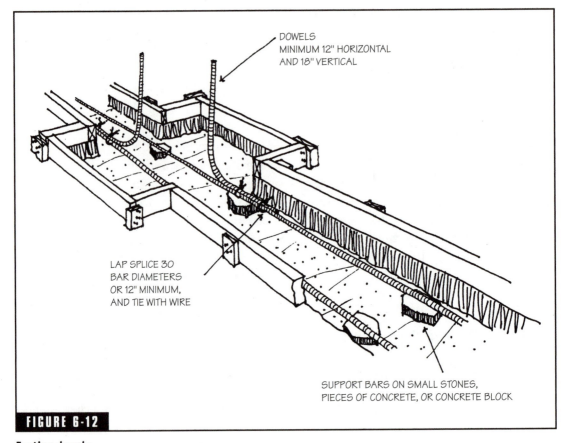

DOWELS
MINIMUM 12" HORIZONTAL
AND 18" VERTICAL

LAP SPLICE 30
BAR DIAMETERS
OR 12" MINIMUM,
AND TIE WITH WIRE

SUPPORT BARS ON SMALL STONES,
PIECES OF CONCRETE, OR CONCRETE BLOCK

FIGURE 6-12

Footing dowels.

6.3.1 Foundation Walls

Excavations for foundation walls may be done in one of two ways. If the foundation wall will be only a foot or two in height, the footing and the wall may be built in a trench that outlines the perimeter of the building and then backfilled from both sides. If the footing must be deeper because of the frost depth, it is often expedient to excavate the entire "footprint" of the building using heavy equipment. The wall is then backfilled from the outside only, leaving a crawl space on the inside of the wall. Walls that are backfilled on both sides are very stable because the soil pressures are balanced and help the wall to resist buckling from vertical loads. Tall walls that are backfilled on only one side must resist significant lateral loads from the unbalanced backfill. Trench excavations for short walls and crawl space excavations for taller walls can be roughly marked on the ground with a sack of mason's lime so the backhoe operator can see where to dig. The excavations should be wide enough to allow plenty of room for erecting the forms, with the sides sloped generously to prevent cave-ins.

Foundation walls are typically built of concrete or masonry. Masonry foundation walls can be constructed of brick or concrete block, but are usually built of block for its economy and because its utilitarian appearance is not typically exposed to view. Foundation walls must be strong enough to support the weight of the building superstructure and resist the lateral loads of the adjacent soil. They must also be durable enough to withstand years of exposure to moisture in the soil. Foundation walls may be unreinforced or *plain* as they are referred to in some codes, or they may be reinforced with steel bars for greater strength and load resistance. Building codes typically specify maximum height and backfill limits for unreinforced foundation walls and minimum reinforcing requirements for walls which exceed the limits for unreinforced walls.

The Code provides minimum design requirements based on the type of soil in which the foundation is built. Figure 6-13 lists soil properties according to the United States Soil Classification System, which is referenced in the Code. The minimum requirements of the CABO *One and Two Family Dwelling Code* for foundation walls include the following.

- Walls must extend a minimum of 4 in. above the adjacent finished grade where masonry veneer is used and a minimum of 6 in. elsewhere.

- The thickness of foundation walls may not be less than the thickness of the walls they support except that foundation walls of at least 8-in. nominal thickness are permitted under brick veneered frame walls and under 10-in. double-wythe masonry cavity walls as long as the total height of the wall being supported (including gables) is not more than 20 ft.

- Except for walls with less than 4 ft. of unbalanced backfill, backfilling may not begin until the foundation wall has cured to gain sufficient strength and has been anchored to the floor or sufficiently braced to prevent overturning or other damage by the backfill.

Soil Group	Unified Soil Classification System Symbol	Soil Description	Drainage[1]	Frost Heave Potential	Volume Change Potential Expansion[2]
Group I	GW	Well-graded gravels, gravel sand mixtures, little or no fines	Good	Low	Low
	GP	Poorly graded gravels or gravel sand mixtures, little or no fines	Good	Low	Low
	SW	Well-graded sands, gravelly sands, little or no fines	Good	Low	Low
	SP	Poorly graded sands or gravelly sands, little or no fines	Good	Low	Low
	GM	Silty gravels, gravel-sand-silt mixtures	Good	Medium	Low
	SM	Silty sand, sand-silt mixtures	Good	Medium	Low
Group II	GC	Clayey gravels, gravel-sand-clay mixtures	Medium	Medium	Low
	SC	Clayey sands, sand-clay mixture	Medium	Medium	Low
	ML	Inorganic silts and very fine sands, rock flour, silty or clayey fine sands, or clayey silts with slight plasticity	Medium	High	Low
	CL	Inorganic clays of low to medium plasticity, gravelly clays, sandy clays, silty clays, lean clays	Medium	Medium	Medium to Low
Group III	CH	Inorganic clays of high plasticity	Poor	Medium	High
	MH	Inorganic silts, microcaceous or diatomaceous fine sandy or silty soils, elastic silts	Poor	High	High
Group IV	OL	Organic silts and organic silty clays of low plasticity	Poor	Medium	Medium
	OH	Organic clays of medium to high plasticity, organic silts	Unsatisfactory	Medium	High
	Pt	Peat and other highly organic soils	Unsatisfactory	Medium	High

Notes:
1. The percolation rate for good drainage is over 4 in. per hour, medium drainage is 2–4 in. per hour, and poor is less than 2 in. per hour.
2. Soils with a low potential expansion have a plasticity index (PI) of zero to 15, soils with a medium potential expansion have a PI of 10 to 35, and soils with a high potential expansion have a PI greater than 20.

FIGURE 6-13

Properties of soils classified according to the Unified Soil Classification System *(from Council of American Building Officials One and Two-Family Dwelling Code,, Falls Church, VA).*

■ Concrete and masonry foundation walls must be constructed as set forth in Figure 6-14 or Figure 6-15 for unreinforced and reinforced walls, respectively.

Figure 6-16 shows four basic types of concrete and concrete masonry foundation walls. In areas with significant risk of earthquake, building codes typically require more stringent design standards for all types of construction, including foundations. The map in Figure 6-17 shows the seismic risk areas for the United States, with zero being the lowest risk and 4 being the highest risk. Foundation walls in Seismic Zones 3 and 4 which support more than 4 ft. of unbalanced backfill are required by Code to have a minimum nominal thickness of 8 in. and minimum reinforcement consisting of #4 vertical bars spaced a maximum of 48 in. on center, and two #4 horizontal bars located in the upper 12 in. of the wall (Figure 6-18). In concrete walls, horizontal reinforcing bars are simply tied to the vertical bars to hold them at the correct height. In masonry walls, horizontal reinforcing bars are placed in a course of bond beam units which form a continuous channel and are then grouted to bond the steel and masonry together (Figure 6-19).

The sill plate to which the floor framing will be attached must be anchored to the foundation with $1/2$-in.-diameter bolts spaced 6 ft. on center and not more than 12 in. from corners. The bolts must extend at least 7 in. into the concrete or masonry and have a 90° bend at the bottom. For concrete walls, the bolts can be placed into the concrete as it begins to set and develop enough stiffness to hold them in place. For concrete block walls, the cores in which anchor bolts will be located must be grouted to hold the bolts in place. To isolate the grout so that it will not flow beyond the core in which the anchor will be placed, the webs of that core should be mortared in addition to the face shells, and a piece of screen wire placed in the bed joint just below the top course (Figure 6-20). As the grout begins to stiffen, the bolt is inserted in the same way as for concrete. Make sure the bolt spacing is accurate so that it does not interfere with stud spacing, and leave the threaded end exposed sufficiently to penetrate the full thickness of the plate with allowance for a nut and washer. If the wall will have stucco or siding applied, the bolt should be located so that the plate is toward the outside of the foundation wall. If the wall will have a brick or stone veneer, the bolt should be located so that the plate is toward the inside

UNREINFORCED CONCRETE AND UNREINFORCED MASONRY FOUNDATION WALLS[1]

Max. Wall Height, ft	Maximum Unbalanced Backfill Height[4], ft	Plain Concrete Minimum Nominal Wall Thk, Inches			Plain Masonry[2] Minimum Nominal Wall Thk, Inches		
		Soil Classes[3]					
		GW, GP, SW and SP	GM, GC, SM, SM-SC and ML	SC, MH, ML-CL and Inorganic CL	GW, GP, SW and SP	GM, GC, SM, SM-SC and ML	SC, MH, ML-CL and Inorganic CL
5	4	6	6	6	6 solid[5] or 8	6 solid[5] or 8	6 solid[5] or 8
	5	6	6	6	6 solid[5] or 8	6 solid[5] or 8	6 solid[5] or 8
6	4	6	6	6	6 solid[5] or 8	6 solid[5] or 8	6 solid[5] or 8
	5	6	6	6	6 solid[5] or 8	8	10
	6	8	8	8	8	10	12
7	4	6	6	6	6 solid[5] or 8	8	8
	5	6	6	8	6 solid[5] or 8	10	10
	6	8	8	8	10	12	10 solid[5]
	7	8	8	10	12	10 solid[5]	12 solid[5]
8	4	6	6	6	6 solid[5] or 8	6 solid[5] or 8	8
	5	6	6	8	6 solid[5] or 8	10	12
	6	8	8	10	10	12	12 solid[5]
	7	8	10	10	12	12 solid[5]	Note 6
	8	10	10	12	10 solid[5]	12 solid[5]	Note 6
9	4	6	6	6	6 solid[5] or 8	6 solid[5] or 8	8
	5	6	8	8	8	10	12
	6	8	8	10	10	12	12 solid[5]
	7	8	10	10	12	12 solid[5]	Note 6
	8	10	10	12	12 solid[5]	Note 6	Note 6
	9	10	12	Note 7	Note 6	Note 6	Note 6

NOTES:

1. Use of this table for sizing concrete and masonry foundation walls in Seismic Zones 3 and 4 shall be limited to the following conditions:

   a. Walls shall not support more than 4 feet of unbalanced backfill.

   b. Walls shall not exceed 8 feet in height.

2. Mortar shall be Type M or S and masonry shall be laid in running bond. Ungrouted hollow masonry units are permitted except where otherwise indicated.

3. Soil classes are in accordance with Unified Soil Classification System (Figure 6-13).

4. Unbalanced backfill height is the difference in height of the exterior and interior finish ground levels. Where an interior concrete slab is provided, the unbalanced backfill height shall be measured from the exterior finish ground level to the top of the interior concrete slab.

5. Solid grouted hollow units or solid masonry units.

6. Wall construction shall be in accordance with Figure 6-15 or an engineered design shall be provided.

7. Engineered design is required.

8. Thickness may be 6 in., provided minimum specified compressive strength of concrete is 4,000 psi.

FIGURE 6-14

Minimum code requirements for unreinforced concrete and masonry foundation walls. *(from Council of American Building Officials One and Two-Family Dwelling Code,, Falls Church, VA).*

REINFORCED CONCRETE AND MASONRY FOUNDATION WALLS[1]

Max. Wall Height, ft	Maximum Unbalanced Backfill Height[5], ft	Maximum Vertical Reinforcement Size and Spacing[2,3] for 8-inch Nominal Wall Thickness — Soil Classes[4]		
		GW, GP, SW and SP	GM, GC, SM, SM-SC and ML	SC, MH, ML-CL and Inorganic CL
6	5	#4 @ 48″ o.c.	#4 @ 48″ o.c.	#4 @ 48″ o.c.
	6	#4 @ 48″ o.c.	#4 @ 40″ o.c.	#5 @ 48″ o.c.
7	4	#4 @ 48″ o.c.	#4 @ 48″ o.c.	#4 @ 48″ o.c.
	5	#4 @ 48″ o.c.	#4 @ 48″ o.c.	#4 @ 40″ o.c.
	6	#4 @ 48″ o.c.	#5 @ 48″ o.c.	#5 @ 40″ o.c.
	7	#4 @ 40″ o.c.	#5 @ 40″ o.c.	#6 @ 48″ o.c.
8	5	#4 @ 48″ o.c.	#4 @ 48″ o.c.	#4 @ 48″ o.c.
	6	#4 @ 48″ o.c.	#5 @ 48″ o.c.	#5 @ 40″ o.c.
	7	#5 @ 48″ o.c.	#6 @ 48″ o.c.	#6 @ 40″ o.c.
	8	#4 @ 40″ o.c.	#6 @ 40″ o.c.	#6 @ 24″ o.c.
9	5	#4 @ 48″ o.c.	#4 @ 48″ o.c.	#5 @ 48″ o.c.
	6	#4 @ 48″ o.c.	#5 @ 48″ o.c.	#6 @ 48″ o.c.
	7	#5 @ 48″ o.c.	#6 @ 48″ o.c.	#6 @ 32″ o.c.
	8	#5 @ 40″ o.c.	#6 @ 32″ o.c.	#6 @ 24″ o.c.
	9	#6 @ 40″ o.c.	#6 @ 24″ o.c.	#6 @ 16″ o.c.

NOTES:
1. Mortar shall be Type M or S and masonry shall be laid in running bond.
2. Alternative reinforcing bar sizes and spacings having an equivalent cross-sectional area of reinforcement per lineal foot of wall shall be permitted provided the spacing of the reinforcement does not exceed 72 in.
3. Vertical reinforcement shall be Grade 60 minimum. The distance from the face of the soil side of the wall to the center of the vertical reinforcement shall be at least 5 in.
4. Soil classes are in accordance with Unified Soil Classification System (Figure 6-13).
5. Unbalanced backfill height is the difference in height of the exterior and interior finish ground levels. Where an interior concrete slab is provided, the unbalanced backfill height shall be measured from the exterior finish ground level to the top of the interior concrete slab.

FIGURE 6-15

Minimum code requirements for reinforced concrete and masonry foundation walls. *(from Council of American Building Officials,* One and Two-Family Dwelling Code, *Falls Church, VA).*

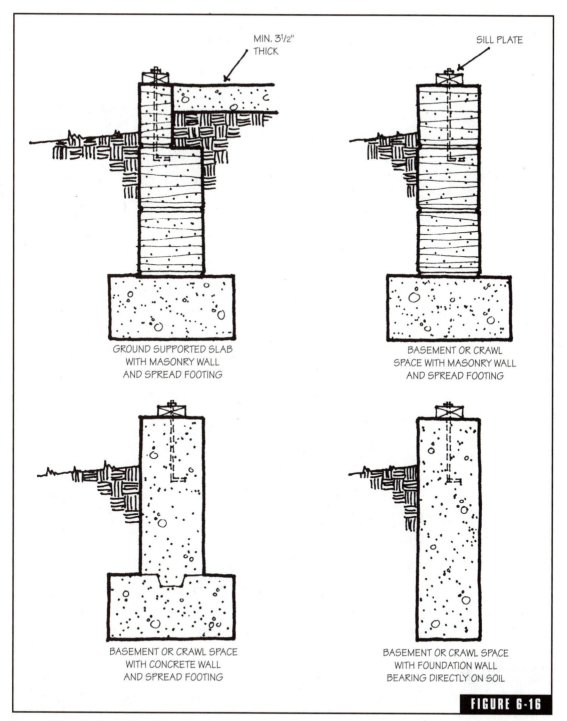

MIN. 3¹/₂"
THICK

SILL PLATE

GROUND SUPPORTED SLAB
WITH MASONRY WALL
AND SPREAD FOOTING

BASEMENT OR CRAWL
SPACE WITH MASONRY WALL
AND SPREAD FOOTING

BASEMENT OR CRAWL SPACE
WITH CONCRETE WALL
AND SPREAD FOOTING

BASEMENT OR CRAWL SPACE
WITH FOUNDATION WALL
BEARING DIRECTLY ON SOIL

FIGURE 6-16

Types of foundation walls. *(from Council of American Building Officials* One and Two-Family Dwelling Code, *Falls Church, VA).*

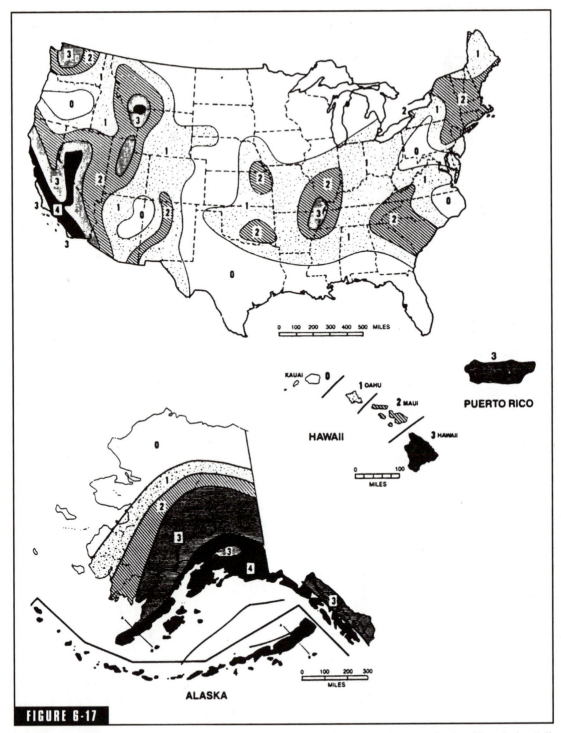

Seismic risk map. *(from Council of American Building Officials* One and Two-Family Dwelling Code, *Falls Church, VA).*

of the foundation wall (Figure 6-21). This will allow room for support of the veneer on the top of the foundation wall.

Figure 6-14 or 6-15 may be used to design concrete and masonry foundation walls except when any of the following conditions exist:

- The building official has determined that suitable backfill material is not available.

- Walls are subject to hydrostatic pressure from groundwater.

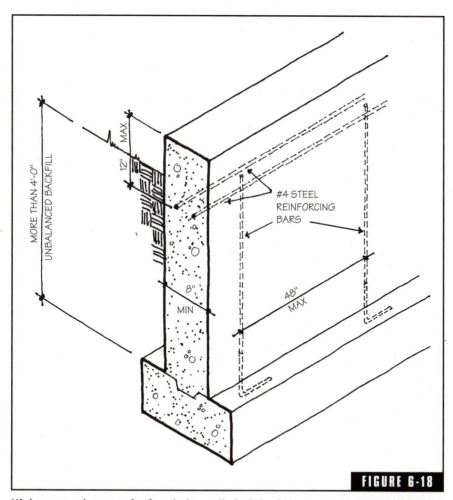

FIGURE 6-18

Minimum requirements for foundation walls in Seismic Zones 3 and 4 supporting more than 4 ft. of unbalanced backfill. *(from Council of American Building Officials* One and Two-Family Dwelling Code, *Falls Church, VA).*

FIGURE 6-19

Grouted and reinforced bond beam.

■ Walls support more than 48 in. of unbalanced backfill and do not have permanent lateral support at the top and bottom.

When any of these conditions exist, walls must be designed in accordance with accepted engineering practice and in accordance with the requirements of an approved standard such as ACI 530/ASCE 5/TMS 402 *Building Code Requirements for Masonry Structures,* or ACI 318 *Building Code Requirements for Reinforced Concrete.*

6.3.2   Basement Walls

Basement walls are essentially just tall foundation walls which will enclose habitable space instead of a crawl space. Their construction is essentially the same, and the minimum requirements discussed above for foundation walls apply equally to basement walls. The taller the wall, though, the greater the lateral load it must resist as the backfill soil pushes against it. Lateral support at the top of the wall is provided by the first-floor framing, and at the bottom by the footing and basement floor slab. Since the first floor helps resist soil pressures, backfilling should be delayed until the floor construction is in place. If earlier backfill is unavoidable, temporary bracing must be provided to prevent possible collapse of the wall. Walls should be allowed to cure for at least three weeks so that sufficient strength is gained before any backfilling may begin. The gravel and soil backfill should be placed in depths of 12 to 24 in. at a time to avoid large impact loads against the wall.

6.3.3 Formwork

Forms for concrete walls may be built of lumber or of plywood, so long as they have sufficient strength to resist the pressure of the wet concrete. The taller the wall, the greater the force exerted by the wet concrete and the stronger the forms must be. For short walls, lumber forms are easy to assemble and are economical, especially if the form boards can be reused in framing the structure or for future formwork. For taller walls, 3/4-in. or 1-in. plywood braced with 2 × 4 frames are more economical. Lumber forms should be fitted tightly together so the concrete can't leak out, and braced with vertical 2 × 4 studs at 24 in. on center. Plywood forms should be braced with vertical 2 × 4 studs at 16 in. on center. For plywood forms, double 2 × 4 wales should be placed horizontally at 18 in. on center, beginning 12 in. from the bottom of the form (Figure 6-22 right). For lumber forms, double 2 × 4 wales should be spaced 24 in. on center, also beginning 12 in. from the bottom of the form (Figure 6-22 left). At the corners, alternating wales should run long so they can be nailed or srewed together for added strength (Figure 6-23).

Wall forms must incorporate ties or spreaders to keep the sides from bowing. One of the simplest methods uses wire snap ties which simultaneously hold the side walls of the forms together to prevent bulging and keep them spread apart at the right dimension. Snap ties should be located on 16-in. or 24-in. centers midway between each vertical stud and arranged in horizontal rows at the same height as the wales. The forms are drilled with 5/8-in. diameter holes at the proper

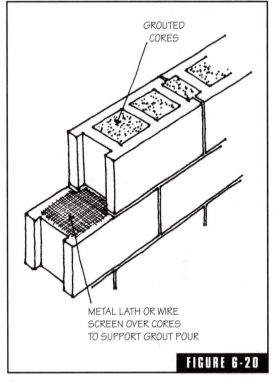

GROUTED CORES

METAL LATH OR WIRE SCREEN OVER CORES TO SUPPORT GROUT POUR

FIGURE 6-20

Grout screen.

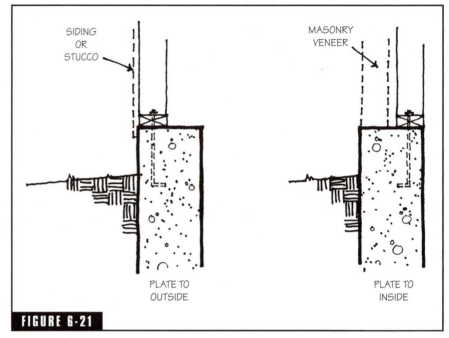

SIDING OR STUCCO

MASONRY VENEER

PLATE TO OUTSIDE

PLATE TO INSIDE

FIGURE 6-21

Attaching plates to foundation wall.

locations and the ties installed after one side of the form is in place. The second side of the form is then erected, fitting the form boards or plywood over the ties. Once the second set of wales is in place, metal wedges are used to secure the ties snugly (Figure 6-24). Snap ties can also support horizontal reinforcing bars in concrete walls, using wire to tie the bars in place. Forms can be stripped after two or three days the protruding wire of the snap ties broken off and the plastic cones pried out. If the wall will be exposed to view, the holes left by the cones can be patched with cement paste.

6.3.4 Reinforcement

Reinforcing steel is used in concrete and masonry walls to increase stiffness and resistance to lateral loads. The Code permits unreinforced walls where lateral loads are moderate, increasing the wall thickness requirements as the height of the wall and the lateral loads increase. The Code also prescribes minimum vertical reinforcement size and spacing for walls with greater height or unbalanced backfill than is permitted for unreinforced walls. Vertical steel reinforcing bars

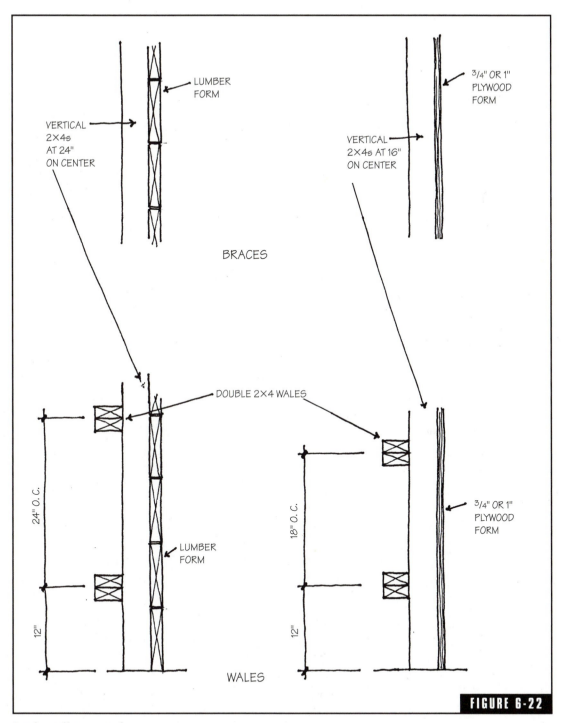

Bracing tall concrete forms.

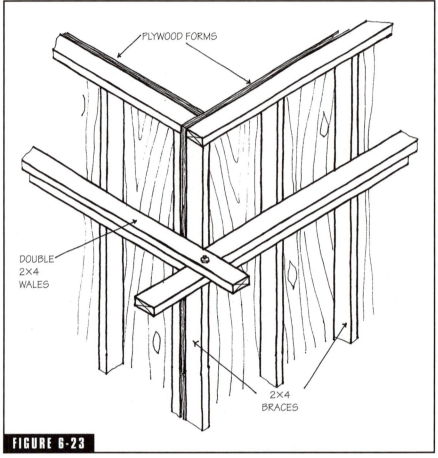

PLYWOOD FORMS

DOUBLE
2×4
WALES

2×4
BRACES

FIGURE 6-23

Corner wales for tall concrete forms.

in the wall must always be tied to the footing (Figure 6-25). Vertical stiffness in unreinforced masonry walls can also be increased by adding thickened sections called *pilasters* (see Figure 6-26). Pilasters are formed by turning concrete blocks perpendicular to the wall and bonding the projecting units into the wall, overlapping them with the adjacent blocks in alternating courses. Where pilasters project from one or both faces of a wall, the footing should be wider as well to accommodate the extra wall thickness.

Reinforcing steel in concrete and masonry walls not only increases strength, but it also helps control shrinkage cracking by distributing shrinkage stresses more evenly throughout the wall. Prefabricated joint reinforcement also controls shrinkage cracking in concrete masonry walls and can be used when codes do not require the wall to be structurally reinforced. Controlling shrinkage cracking in basement walls is important in maintaining the integrity of waterproofing materials applied to the wall and preventing water penetration through the cracks.

6.3.5 Basement Slabs

Basement floor slabs are usually supported on a gravel drainage bed with the edges resting on the perimeter footing (Figure 6-27). The CABO *One and Two Family Dwelling Code* requires only that the minimum slab thickness be 3-$\frac{1}{2}$ in. and the concrete strength a minimum of 2,500 psi. The Code does not include any requirements for reinforc-

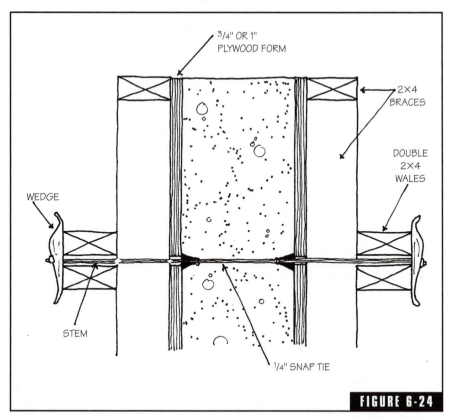

Snap ties for concrete forms. *(from Portland Cement Association,* The Homeowner's Guide to Building with Concrete, Brick and Stone, *PCA, Skokie, Illinois).*

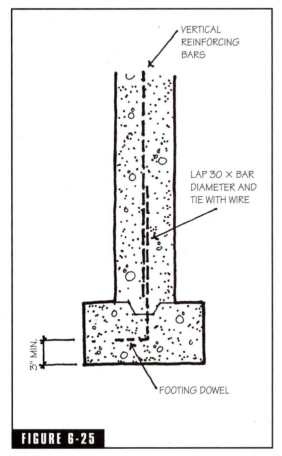

VERTICAL
REINFORCING
BARS

LAP 30 X BAR
DIAMETER AND
TIE WITH WIRE

3" MIN.

FOOTING DOWEL

FIGURE 6-25

Footing-to-foundation wall connections.

ing steel in slabs, but reinforcing may be required by some engineered designs. In thin slabs, steel cannot be set the recommended 3 in. above the subgrade, so it should be placed at the midpoint of the slab thickness. If the basement is properly designed for good drainage of soil moisture, the reinforcing should be protected well enough to prevent corrosion. Drainage and waterproofing, insulation, and vapor retarders are discussed later in this chapter.

6.4 Slabs-on-Grade

In warm climates where the frost depth is minimal, shallow concrete foundations are often designed and poured monolithically with the floor slab. These are referred to as *slabs-on-grade* or *slabs-on-ground.* The Code still requires that the bottom of the footing be set a minimum of 12 in. below the adjacent grade, that its minimum width is appropriate to the type of soil (refer to the table in Figure 6-4), that the slab be at least 3-1/2 in. thick, and the concrete at least 2,500 psi. Interior bearing walls require an integral footing with the same required width at the bottom as the perimeter footing, but usually with a reduced depth (Figure 6-28). For masonry veneers, a perimeter ledge allows the masonry to sit below the level of the finish floor (Figure 6-29). All top soil and vegetation must be removed from the area within the footings and replaced with a compacted fill material that is free of vegetation and foreign material.

There are no requirements for steel reinforcing, but sill plates must be anchored to the foundation with 1/2-in-diameter bolts spaced 6 ft. on center and not more than 12 in. from corners. The bolts must extend at least 7 in. into the concrete and have a 90° bend at the bottom. The top of the slab must be at least 4 in. above the adjacent finished grade where masonry veneer is used and at least 6 in. above grade elsewhere. The ground must slope away from the slab a minimum of 6 in. within the first 10 ft. If lot lines, adjacent walls, natural slopes, or other physical barriers prohibit the mini-

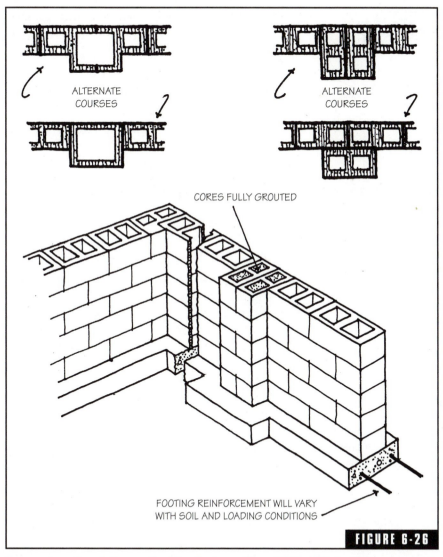

ALTERNATE COURSES

ALTERNATE COURSES

CORES FULLY GROUTED

FOOTING REINFORCEMENT WILL VARY WITH SOIL AND LOADING CONDITIONS

FIGURE 6-26

Basement or foundation wall with pilasters. *(from NCMA, TEK 1, National Concrete Masonry Association, Herndon, VA).*

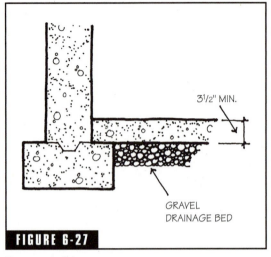

FIGURE 6-27

3¹/₂" MIN.

GRAVEL
DRAINAGE BED

Basement slabs.

mum slope, area drains or earth swales must be provided to ensure drainage away from the structure. Like basement floor slabs, slabs-on-grade are often supported on gravel drainage beds. Because the footings are shallow and the slabs set above grade, soil moisture is usually not a problem except on poorly drained sites or where the water table is very close to the ground surface, but water vapor diffusion from the soil must be considered, and perimeter insulation may be necessary in colder climates. Soil moisture, insulation, and vapor retarders are discussed below.

6.5   Drainage and Waterproofing

Water moves through the soil by gravity flow and capillary action and exerts hydrostatic pressure against basement walls and slabs which

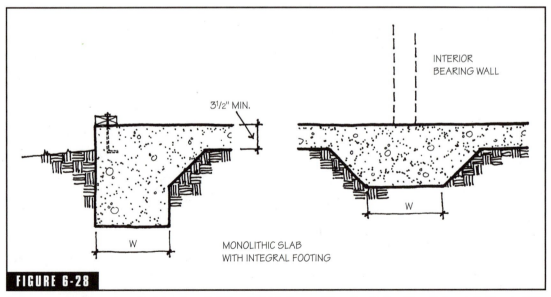

INTERIOR
BEARING WALL

3¹/₂" MIN.

W

W

MONOLITHIC SLAB
WITH INTEGRAL FOOTING

FIGURE 6-28

Slabs on grade. *(from Council of American Building Officials One and Two-Family Dwelling Code,, Falls Church, VA).*

are at or below the level of the groundwater. Water vapor diffuses through soil because of vapor pressure differentials between areas of higher and lower temperatures. To prevent moisture problems, both water and water vapor movement must be considered in the design of basements and slabs-on-grade.

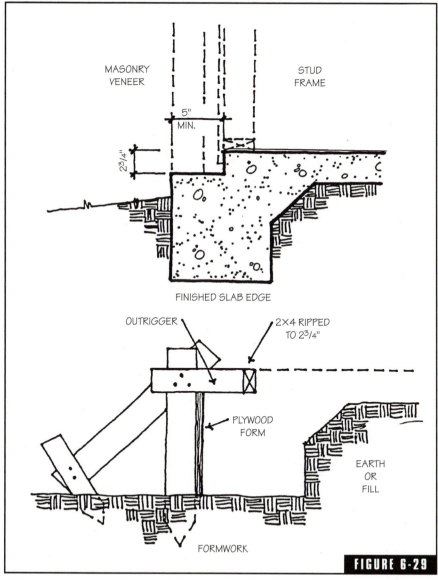

Recessed masonry ledge.

6.5.1 Water Movement in Soils

At some elevation below every building site, there is water in the ground because of rain seeping into the soil and because of the natural water content of the earth. This groundwater may be close to the surface or far below grade. The top elevation of groundwater is called the groundwater level or *water table.* Water table varies with climate, amount of rainfall, season, and, to some extent, with type of soil. The water table follows the general contours of the land but is closer to the surface in valleys and farther from the surface on hills and ridges. Water moves laterally through the soil by gravity flow to lower elevations. The direction of groundwater flow is always in the direction of lower elevations until the water emerges in a spring, stream, or other open body of water (Figure 6-30).

A soil boring test can identify the soil types which will be encountered below a building site, as well as the elevation of the water table. Since the water table can vary with climate and amount of rainfall, it is important to understand that the water table listed in a geotechnical report should not be taken as an absolute. If soil tests are performed during the rainy season, the elevation of the water table may be at its highest expected level, but if the tests are done during a period of drought, the water table may be unusually low and not representative of the normal conditions which would be encountered. If data from a

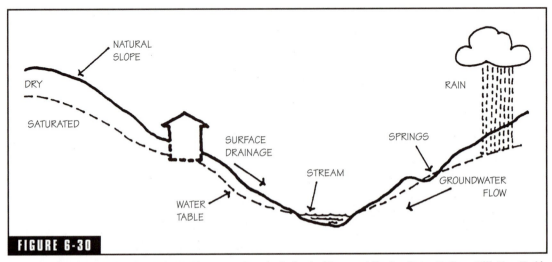

FIGURE 6-30

Groundwater. *(from Callendar, John H.,* **Timesaver Standards for Architectural Design Data,** *McGraw-Hill, New York).*

soil test is not available, excavations at the site can provide some contemporaneous information. Water which seeps into an excavation will rise to the level of the current water table. If the excavations are made during the dry season, the water table is probably lower than normal. If the excavations are made during the rainy season, the water table may be at its highest. Planning for drainage and waterproofing a basement space should be based on worst-case scenario because it is very difficult and very expensive to correct below-grade moisture problems after the backfill is in place. The cost of adding an extra measure of protection up front is minimal and can reduce or eliminate the callbacks required to deal with leaky or damp basements.

Hydrostatic pressure is the pressure exerted by the weight of a fluid such as water. The hydrostatic pressure exerted by groundwater at any point against a basement wall is equal to the depth of that point below the water table times the unit weight of water (which is 62.4 pcf). If the bottom of the wall is 8 ft. below the water table, the hydrostatic pressure at that point is $8 \times 62.4 = 499.2$ lbs. per square foot of wall area. The lateral pressure of the soil itself is slightly reduced because of the buoyancy of the water it contains, but the added hydrostatic pressure significantly increases the structural load on the wall. The hydrostatic uplift pressure on the bottom of a basement slab is calculated in the same way. Both structures and waterproofing membranes must be able to withstand the lateral and uplift loads created by hydrostatic pressure. As an alternative to resisting the full force of the hydrostatic load, groundwater can be diverted away from a basement by installing subsurface drains to lower the water table. Draining water away from a building reduces structural loads on walls, footings, and slabs as well as hydrostatic pressure on waterproofing membranes.

In addition to lateral gravity flow, water can move upward through soil from the water table by *capillary action*. The rate at which this capillary rise occurs depends on particle size and distribution and the resulting size of voids or pores between soil particles. Clay soils have the finest pore structure and can draw capillary moisture upward from a water table many feet below. Coarse, sandy soils generally have a pore structure so large that capillary rise is minimal. The capillary moisture content of soil varies in direct proportion to the fineness of the soil. Capillary moisture cannot be drained out of soil because the surface tension within the pore structure of the soil holds the water tightly. Soil particles less than ¹/₄₈₀ in. are called *fines.* Laboratory tests of soils containing 56% fines showed moisture constantly rising to the surface and evaporating at an average rate of about 12 gallons per 1000 sq. ft. per 24 hours with a water table as much as 30 in. below the surface. Field tests have also shown that substantial amounts of moisture migrate upward through fine soil even when the water table is as much as 20 ft. below the surface. Figure 6-31 indicates the height of capillary moisture rise which can be expected with various soil types. Any basement or slab-on-grade built without protection on moist soil would be exposed to a continuous capillary migration of moisture toward the structure. Since both concrete and

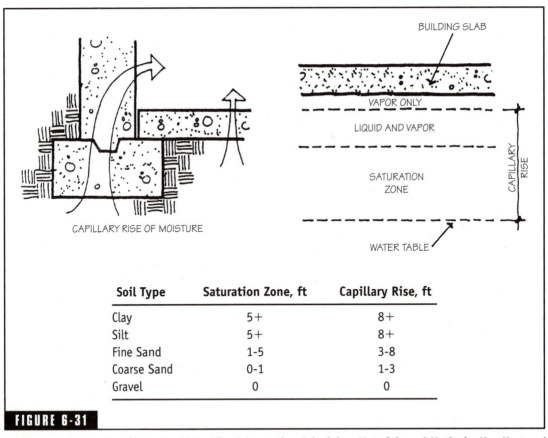

Soil Type	Saturation Zone, ft	Capillary Rise, ft
Clay	5+	8+
Silt	5+	8+
Fine Sand	1-5	3-8
Coarse Sand	0-1	1-3
Gravel	0	0

FIGURE 6-31

Capillary moisture rise. *(from Harold B. Olin,* Construction Principles, Materials and Methods, *Van Nostrand Reinhold).*

masonry are absorptive materials with a fine pore structure, the water rising through the soil by capillary action would be picked up by the concrete or masonry and continue its capillary migration.

To prevent the capillary rise of water into a slab-on-grade or below-grade slab, an intervening layer of material must be added which is either impervious to moisture penetration or has a pore structure large enough to prevent capillary suction. Gravel and crushed rock are the materials most commonly used to provide a capillary break under a slab-on-grade or below-grade slab. The aggregate should be mostly single graded and of $3/4$ in. maximum size. Capillary water penetration can also be prevented by installing dampproofing or membrane waterproofing as a barrier against capillary movement (Figure 6-32).

6.5.2 Water Vapor Movement in Soils

Below-grade vapor pressures within the soil, particularly if capillary moisture is present, are usually higher than vapor pressures within buildings. This pressure differential creates a flow of vapor from the soil toward the structure, regardless of season or interior heating or cooling cycles (Figure 6-33). Vapor can then migrate through a con-

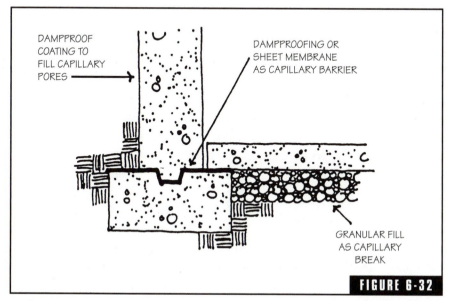

DAMPPROOF COATING TO FILL CAPILLARY PORES

DAMPPROOFING OR SHEET MEMBRANE AS CAPILLARY BARRIER

GRANULAR FILL AS CAPILLARY BREAK

FIGURE 6-32

Capillary barrier. *(from Beall, Christine,* Thermal and Moisture Protection Manual, *McGraw-Hill, New York).*

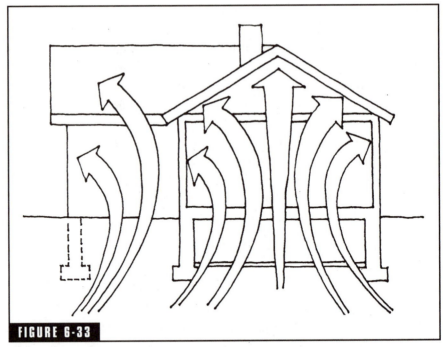

Vapor flow from soil. *(from W. R. Meadows, Inc. The Hydrologic Cycle and Moisture Migration)*.

crete slab or framed floor structure into the building. Vapor migration from the soil, if unimpeded, can provide a continuous supply of below-grade moisture flowing into the structure and then migrating outward through the walls and roof. If cooled below its dewpoint, this continuous supply of moist air will condense to liquid on interior surfaces, or condense as liquid or frost within the walls or roof of the building envelope. Vapor flow into buildings from the soil is a primary cause of the damp feeling often associated with basements.

6.5.3   Surface and Subsurface Drainage

Surface drainage should be the first line of defense in every residential moisture protection system. Groundwater can be controlled to a great extent by reducing the rate at which rainwater and surface runoff enter the soil adjacent to a building. Roofs typically concentrate collected rain water at a building's perimeter where it can cause serious groundwater problems (Figure 6-34 top). Water that is drained quickly away from a building at the ground surface cannot enter the soil and contribute to below-grade moisture problems. Roof overhangs, gutters, and downspouts provide effective control for sloped roofs by diverting the runoff away from the building (Figure 6-34 bottom). Site selection, building orientation, and grading should provide slopes away from the building, and ground swales and troughs can also be used to redirect surface runoff.

Backfill adjacent to a building should be compacted sufficiently to prevent settlement and the possibility of ponding water, which might drain toward the foundation wall. Backfill materials that contain a high percentage of fines may absorb and hold surface water and rain water, concentrating the moisture immediately adjacent to the building. A low-permeance cap of compacted clay soil can be installed under grassy areas. Planting beds located next to the building walls should always be well drained to avoid concentrating moisture along the foundation line. Sidewalks located adjacent to a building can prevent groundwater absorption but may cause backsplash and soiling on the walls. Sidewalks should always be sloped away from the building a minimum of $1/2$ in. per foot. The joint between the sidewalk and the building should be sealed with a traffic-grade silicone or urethane sealant if substantial rainfall, accumulated snow drifts, or exposure to roof or site runoff is expected.

Subsurface drainage systems can collect and divert groundwater away from the walls and floor of a basement and relieve hydrostatic pressure. The most common method of keeping groundwater away from basement structures is to provide a *perimeter drain* or *footing drain* in the form of perforated, porous, or open-jointed pipe at the level of the footings. Perforated drains are generally preferable to the porous pipe and open-jointed systems. When perforated drains are used, they should be installed with the perforations on the bottom so that water rises into the pipe. Perimeter drains artificially lower the water table below the elevation of the floor and eliminate hydrostatic pressure against the walls and the bottom of the slab (Figure 6-35).

Perimeter drains must be placed below the floor level but above the bottom of the footing. As a rule of thumb, the bottom of the footing should be at least 4 in. below the bottom of the drain to prevent undermining the footing stability. Crushed stone or gravel should always be placed above and below perimeter drains to facilitate water flow. The

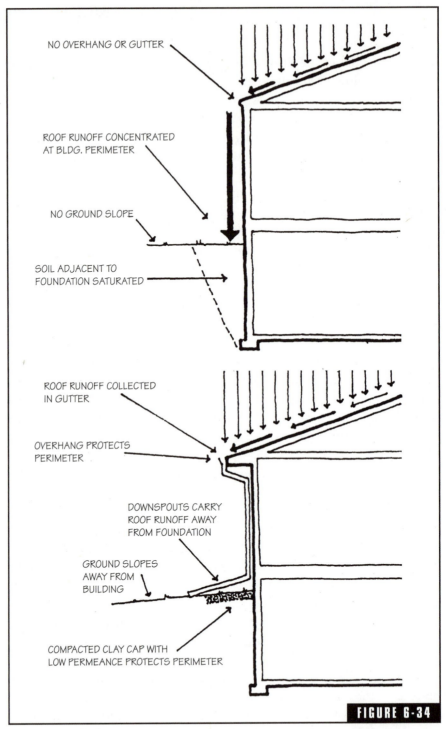

Roof runoff. *(from Joseph Lstiburek and John Carmody,* Moisture Control Handbook, Van Nostrand Reinhold*).*

gravel bed must be protected from soil clogging with a filtering cover made from landscape fabric. This will allow water to flow toward the drain but keep soil from clogging the voids between gravel particles. For clay soils, which have poor drainage and only limited amounts of groundwater flow, a 4-in. drain is usually adequate. For sandy soils with better drainage and more groundwater flow, a 6-in. drain is needed. For gravely soils with good drainage and large ground water flow, a drain as large as 8 in. may be necessary.

Subsurface drainage can also be used to relieve hydrostatic pressure against the full height of a basement wall. A free-draining gravel backfill that extends the height of the wall allows groundwater to flow by gravity down to the level of the drain (Figure 6-36 top). The gravel should be carried up the wall to within a few inches of the ground surface with only a covering of topsoil for landscaping purposes. Proprietary insulation board with vertical drainage channels can be used instead of the gravel backfill (Figure 6-36 bottom). These drainage mats are generally easy to install and help to insulate the basement as well. The insulation is a polystyrene board which is impervious to moisture damage.

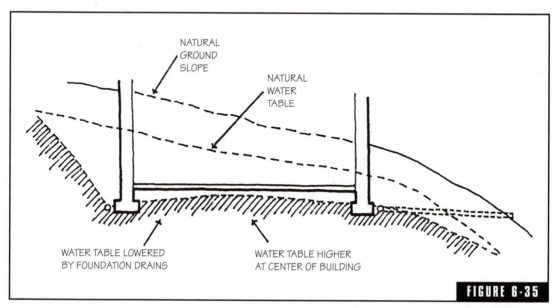

Drains lower water table. *(from Callendar, John H.,* Timesaver Standards for Architectural Design Data, *McGraw-Hill, New York)*.

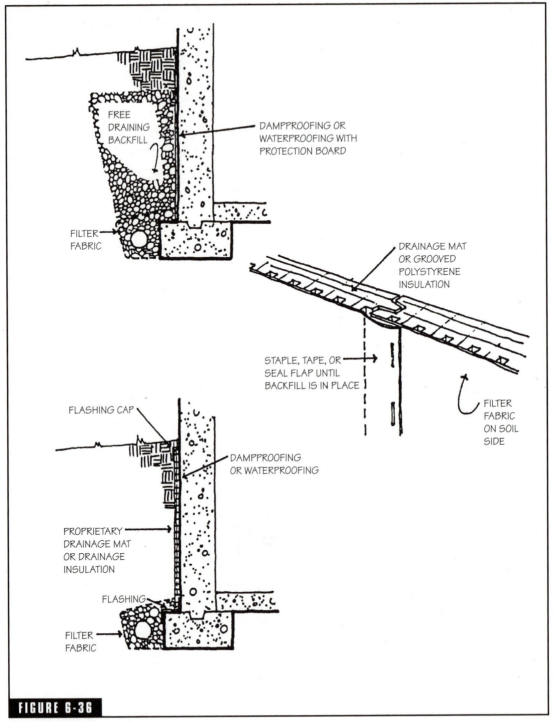

FREE DRAINING BACKFILL

DAMPPROOFING OR WATERPROOFING WITH PROTECTION BOARD

FILTER FABRIC

DRAINAGE MAT OR GROOVED POLYSTYRENE INSULATION

STAPLE, TAPE, OR SEAL FLAP UNTIL BACKFILL IS IN PLACE

FILTER FABRIC ON SOIL SIDE

FLASHING CAP

DAMPPROOFING OR WATERPROOFING

PROPRIETARY DRAINAGE MAT OR DRAINAGE INSULATION

FLASHING

FILTER FABRIC

FIGURE 6-36

Drainage backfill. *(from Beall, Christine,* **Thermal and Moisture Protection Manual, McGraw-Hill, New York).**

Water collected by perimeter drains should be drained by gravity outflow to an exposed lower elevation, to a dry well that is above the water table, or to an approved storm sewer system. When these disposal methods are not feasible or practical, it will be necessary to collect the water in a sump and pump it out mechanically. Perimeter drains are often located just inside rather than outside the footings, particularly when a sump is necessary. Weeps should be located every 32 in. along the base of the foundation wall or at the top of the footing to allow any water which builds up on the outside of the wall to flow into the gravel bed inside the footing and then into the drain (Figure 6-37). Floor slabs should be cast at a level above the weep holes.

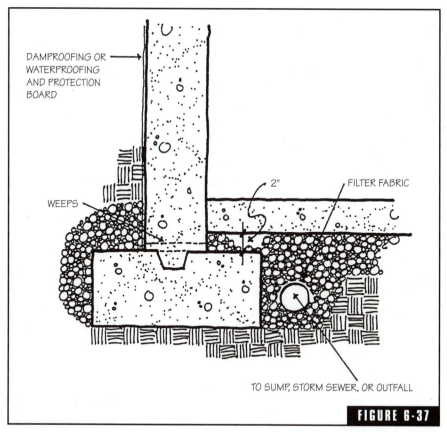

DAMPROOFING OR WATERPROOFING AND PROTECTION BOARD

WEEPS

2"

FILTER FABRIC

TO SUMP, STORM SEWER, OR OUTFALL

FIGURE 6-37

Interior drain for sump. *(from Beall, Christine,* Thermal and Moisture Protection Manual, McGraw-Hill, New York).

6.5.4   Waterproofing Membranes and Dampproof Coatings

The difference between waterproofing and dampproofing is one of degree. *Waterproofing* is the treatment of a surface or structure to prevent the passage of liquid water under hydrostatic pressure. *Dampproofing* is the treatment of a surface or structure to resist the passage of water in the absence of hydrostatic pressure. Where waterproofing is defined in absolute terms as *preventing* water infiltration even under extreme conditions, dampproofing is defined in relative terms as *resisting*—but not necessarily preventing—water infiltration under moderate conditions.

Some building codes dictate the use of either dampproofing or waterproofing on below-grade structures. Where no specific code mandates exist, the decision to provide footing drains, a drainage type backfill or drainage mat, dampproofing, or waterproofing should be based on the amount of moisture in the soil and the level of the water table. If the water table may fluctuate under different seasonal or weather conditions, protection should include a waterproof membrane in addition to subsurface drainage. If steel reinforcing is used in concrete or masonry basement walls (including joint reinforcement in concrete masonry), sufficient protection must be provided to prevent moisture absorption into the wall and corrosion of the metal.

In dry and moderate climates with deep water tables, or on well-drained sites with no history of groundwater problems and no possibility of a rising water table, a dampproof coating will inhibit the absorption of any groundwater which reaches the wall surface. Subsurface drainage can enhance the performance of the dampproofing by minimizing the amount of water which reaches the wall. Dampproof coatings provide resistance to moisture penetration by closing the capillary pores in concrete and masonry substrates. Dampproofing will not resist moisture penetration under hydrostatic pressure, and the cementitious and mastic materials typically used for these coatings do not have the ability to bridge across cracks. For dry or well-drained soils with low water tables, Figure 6-38 illustrates appropriate drainage and dampproofing measures.

Parging consists of a $3/8$-in. to $1/2$-in. thick coating of a portland cement and sand mortar mix applied in two layers of approximately equal thickness. The mix should be proportioned 1 part cement to 2-$1/2$ parts sand by volume. The wall surface should be dampened before

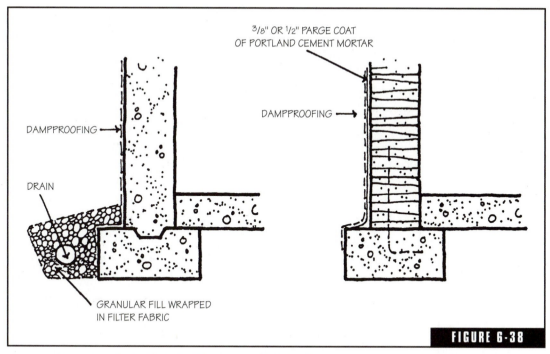

Dampproofing. *(from Beall, Christine,* Thermal and Moisture Protection Manual, McGraw-Hill, New York).

parging. The first coat, called a scratch coat, should be roughened or scratched to form a mechanical bond with the finish coat. The scratch coat should be allowed to cure for at least 24 hours, then dampened immediately before applying the second coat. This finish coat should be troweled to form a dense surface, and a cove should be formed at the base of the foundation wall to prevent water from accumulating at the wall/footing juncture. The finish coat should be moist cured for 48 hours to minimize shrinkage cracking and assure complete cement hydration.

Mastic or bituminous dampproofing can be applied directly to the surface of concrete or masonry walls, but CABO requires that dampproofing on masonry walls be applied over a parge coat. If a parge coat is to be applied, mortar joints in masonry walls should be struck flush. If a bituminous dampproofing is to be applied directly to the masonry, the joints should be tooled concave. Mastic dampproof coatings can be either sprayed, troweled, or rolled onto the surface. Some contractors apply them by hand, smearing the thick, gooey mastic onto the wall with a glove. Cracks and voids such as form tie holes should be patched or filled before applying the dampproofing. The vapor permeability of the interior coating of a dampproofed concrete or masonry wall should be higher than the vapor permeability of the exterior coating so that construction moisture and any soil moisture vapor which permeates the wall can evaporate to the inside (Figure 6-39). Gypsum board and latex paint finishes work well, but vinyl wallcoverings will trap moisture in the wall.

There are two general methods of waterproofing. In *positive side waterproofing,* the waterproofing is applied to the same side of the wall or floor on which the water source occurs (Figure 6-40a). In *negative side waterproofing,* the waterproofing is applied on the opposite side of the structure as the water source (Figure 6-40b). Positive side waterproofing is always preferable because the structure itself is protected from moisture penetration, as well as the interior spaces. This is

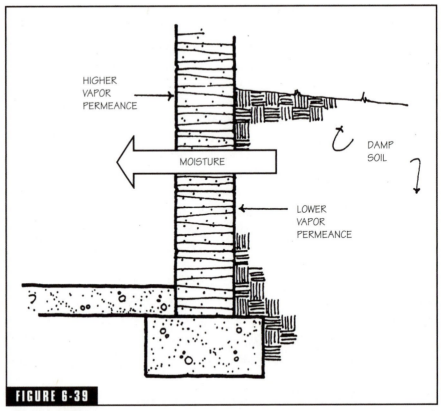

FIGURE 6-39

Vapor permeance. *(from Beall, Christine,* **Thermal and Moisture Protection Manual,** McGraw-Hill, New York).**

particularly important when reinforcing steel may be corroded by prolonged moisture exposure or chloride contamination from the soil. Negative side waterproofing is generally used only as a remedial measure in existing buildings where outside excavation and repair are impossible or prohibitively expensive.

Since a waterproofing membrane must withstand hydrostatic pressure, it is critical that all holes, cracks, and openings in the wall be eliminated. This is easier to do below grade than it is in above-grade walls because of the absence of doors and windows, because there are fewer joints, because thermal expansion and contraction is less with smaller temperature variations, and because there is no ultraviolet deterioration of materials. Perfect barriers, however, are still difficult to achieve, and the barrier concept is very unforgiving of application errors. When combined with effective subsurface drainage, however, a waterproofing membrane can provide good performance even though human error will inevitably introduce minor flaws into the system. In wet climates, or on sites with high water tables, fluctuating water tables, or poor drainage, a waterproofing membrane should be used in addition to subsurface drains, free-draining backfill, or drainage mats.

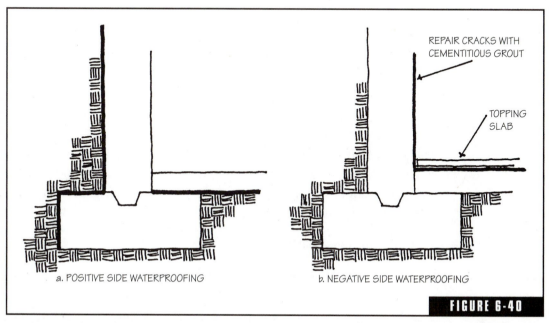

a. POSITIVE SIDE WATERPROOFING

b. NEGATIVE SIDE WATERPROOFING

REPAIR CRACKS WITH CEMENTITIOUS GROUT

TOPPING SLAB

FIGURE 6-40

Positive side and negative side waterproofing. *(from Beall, Christine,* Thermal and Moisture Protection Manual, McGraw-Hill, New York).

Waterproofing membranes must be fully adhered to the wall so that water cannot flow behind the membrane, and so that any leaks which occur will be easier to trace to the source. Membranes applied to concrete or concrete block must have sufficient flexibility to span cracks which will inevitably appear as a result of curing shrinkage, and enough elasticity to expand and contract with temperature changes. Steel reinforcement or control joints can be used to limit the amount of shrinkage cracking which will occur and to regulate the location of such cracks. If control joints are used, they must be sealed against water intrusion with an elastomeric sealant that will not deteriorate when submersed in water, that is chemically compatible with any membrane waterproofing or dampproofing which will be applied, and is resistant to any contaminants which may be present in the soil.

The CABO *One and Two Family Dwelling Code* requires waterproofing of foundation walls enclosing habitable space or storage from the top of the footing to the finish grade in areas where a high water table or other severe soil-water conditions are known to exist. Dampproof coatings are required in all other conditions. Waterproofing may consist of one of the following:

- 2-ply hot-mopped felts
- 55-pound roll roofing
- 6-mil polyvinyl chloride
- 6-mil polyethylene
- 40-mil polymer-modified asphalt

The joints in the membranes must be lapped and sealed with an adhesive compatible with the membrane itself. Dampproofing for masonry walls may consist of a $3/8$-in. portland cement parging covered with one of the following:

- bituminous coating
- 3 pounds per square yard of acrylic modified cement
- 1/8-in. coat of surface bonding mortar, or
- any material permitted for waterproofing.

Concrete walls may be dampproofed with any of the dampproofing or waterproofing materials listed above. Waterproofing membranes must be protected from punctures and tears during the backfilling process. Some materials such as polyethylene sheets are particularly vulnerable to damage. Special protection boards can be erected over the membrane, or insulating drainage mats can be used for this purpose.

For wet soils with a high water table or a water table which may fluctuate seasonally or under severe weather conditions, and for deep foundations in multistory below-grade structures, Figure 6-41 illustrates appropriate drainage and waterproofing techniques. Slabs can be waterproofed in different ways, depending on the type of membrane being used. Horizontal membranes for below-grade slabs are often cast on a thin "mud slab" and the structural slab is then cast on top, or the membrane is installed on the structural slab and a topping slab added as a wearing surface. This provides a stable subbase to support the

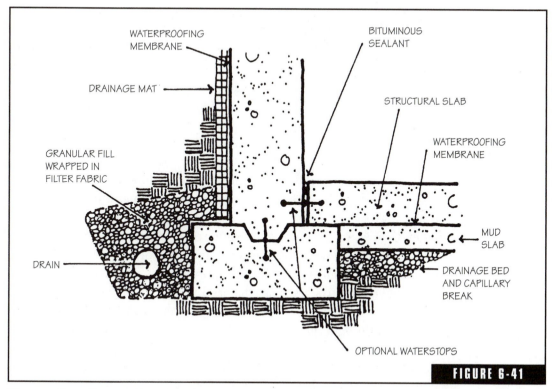

FIGURE 6-41

Waterproofing. *(from Beall, Christine,* **Thermal and Moisture Protection Manual, McGraw-Hill, New York).**

waterproofing and a protective wearing surface above it. Some types of waterproofing can be placed on compacted subgrade fill and a single structural slab cast on top of it.

6.6 Vapor Retarders

Where vapor migration from the soil is a potential problem, vapor retarders are necessary to protect the structure from a continuous flow of moisture. Where vapor-impermeable or moisture-sensitive floor-finishing materials are to be used, vapor retarders are particularly important in preventing loss of adhesion, peeling, warping, bubbling, or blistering of resilient flooring. Vapor retarders can also prevent buckling of carpet and wood flooring as well as fungal growth and the offensive odors and indoor air quality problems that accompany it.

In slabs-on-grade, polyethylene or reinforced polyethylene sheets of 6-, 8-, or 10-mil thickness are most commonly used in these applications. For maximum effectiveness, the vapor retarder must lap over and be sealed to the foundation; seams must be lapped 6 in. and sealed with pressure-sensitive tape; and penetrations for plumbing, electrical, or mechanical systems must be sealed. Vapor retarders under slabs-on-grade are usually installed over a base layer of free-draining gravel or crushed rock as a capillary break. Although vapor retarders themselves will prevent capillary moisture movement, they are usually used in conjunction with a drainage layer to provide a margin of safety in case of punctures or lap seam failures.

Figure 6-42 shows vapor retarder applications on basement slabs and slabs-on-grade. The granular base should be a minimum of 3 in. thick, and of compacted, mostly single-graded, coarse aggregate no larger than $3/4$ in. To protect the vapor retarder from puncture, a $1/2$-in. layer of fine, compactable sand fill may be rolled over the base. To keep the sand from settling into the gravel layer, a geotextile fabric can be placed over the coarse base material. Traditionally, a 2–4-in. layer of sand fill is added on top of the vapor retarder, but there are two schools of thought on whether this is necessary. In addition to providing a protection course on top of the vapor retarder, a layer of sand is thought by some to provide a cushion for the concrete and to act as a blotter to absorb excess moisture from the bottom of the slab. This supposedly promotes more even curing of the concrete, prevents exces-

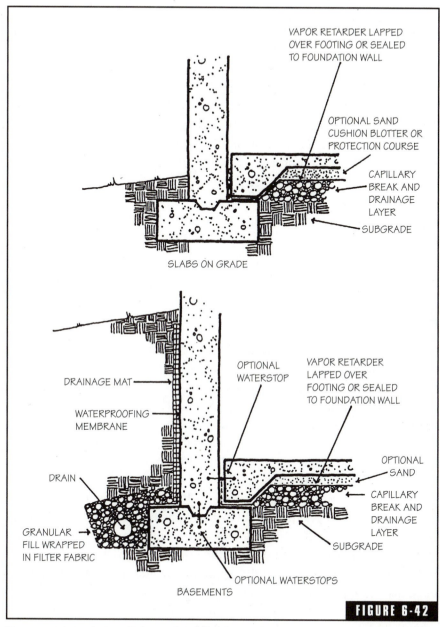

VAPOR RETARDER LAPPED OVER FOOTING OR SEALED TO FOUNDATION WALL

OPTIONAL SAND CUSHION BLOTTER OR PROTECTION COURSE

CAPILLARY BREAK AND DRAINAGE LAYER

SUBGRADE

SLABS ON GRADE

DRAINAGE MAT

WATERPROOFING MEMBRANE

DRAIN

GRANULAR FILL WRAPPED IN FILTER FABRIC

OPTIONAL WATERSTOP

VAPOR RETARDER LAPPED OVER FOOTING OR SEALED TO FOUNDATION WALL

OPTIONAL SAND

CAPILLARY BREAK AND DRAINAGE LAYER

SUBGRADE

OPTIONAL WATERSTOPS

BASEMENTS

FIGURE 6-42

Vapor retarders. *(adapted from ASTM E1643* **Standard Practice for Installation of Water Vapor Retarders Used in Contact with Earth or Granular Fill Under Concrete Slabs.** *Copyright ASTM).*

sive shrinkage cracking and slab curling, and permits earlier concrete finishing. Others feel that the vapor retarder can be better protected by a geotextile fabric rather than sand and that the blotter effect of the sand is not necessary to proper curing and finishing of the slab.

Reinforced polyethylene vapor retarders are more resistant to damage than unreinforced polyethylene and are manufactured in multiple plies for greater strength. If a sand cushion is not used, concrete mix designs should take into consideration the effect of a low-permeance vapor retarder on concrete curing, shrinkage, and drying time. Depending on the type of finish floor materials specified and the ambient conditions, concrete drying to acceptable moisture levels can take anywhere from 3 to 6 months. If scheduling is a potential problem, consider using a low-slump concrete so that there is a minimum amount of residual mixing water to evaporate after cement hydration has taken place.

6.7   Insulation

Soil is not a good insulating material, but it does have thermal mass which minimizes fluctuations in temperature. Daily temperature fluctuations affect only the top 1-$\frac{1}{2}$ to 2 ft. of soil. Annual temperature fluctuations affect the first 20–30 ft. of soil. Below this depth, the soil temperature is constant. Since average ground temperatures for most of the United States are below comfortable room temperatures, basements continuously lose some heat to the soil.

The thermal resistance of soil is generally estimated at R-1 to R-2 per foot of thickness. At an average of R-1.25, it takes 4 ft. of soil to equal the insulating value of 1 in. of extruded polystyrene insulation. Because heat flow from floor slabs and below-grade walls follows a radial path (Figure 6-43), however, the effective insulating value of soil is greater than would be initially apparent because the soil thickness is measured along the radial lines. This radial path of heat flow means that the perimeter of a slab-on-grade is subject to much greater heat loss than the interior floor. Figure 6-44 shows the heat flow from the perimeter of a floor slab to a cold exterior ground surface as a series of nearly concentric radial lines. As the length of the heat flow path increases, the effective insulating value of the soil increases, so thermal insulation is generally required only at the perimeter of the slab and not under the entire floor area. Placing this insulation vertically on the outside of the foundation provides the greatest protection from freeze-thaw stresses. Recommended R-values for perimeter insulation are shown in Figure 6-45.

Heat loss from a basement includes that which takes place through the wall above grade and that which takes place through the wall and floor below grade. In addition, there is heat loss in the movement of air. There is a potential path of significant air leakage through the joint between the top of the basement wall and the sill plate of the super-structure. With a hollow concrete block wall, part of which is exposed above grade, air in the block cores is cooled and sinks by convection, displacing warmer air in the lower parts of the wall. This causes additional heat loss from the basement as the lower portions of the wall are cooled. Insulating the outside of the wall will minimize this effect, and grouting the wall will eliminate the convective air spaces. Except in extreme northern climates where the ground temperature is colder, it is usually necessary to insulate only the first 3 to 6 ft. of below-grade

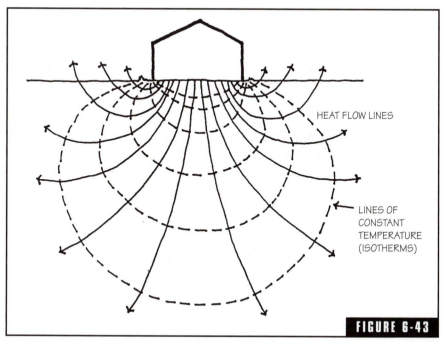

HEAT FLOW LINES

LINES OF CONSTANT TEMPERATURE (ISOTHERMS)

FIGURE 6-43

Radiant heat loss to soil. *(from Donald Watson and Kenneth Labs,* Climatic Building Design, *McGraw-Hill, 1983).*

walls. Below this level, the cumulative thermal resistance of the soil is sufficient to prevent serious heat loss.

6.8   Frost-Protected Shallow Foundations

Deep foundations required to reach below the frost line add cost to the construction of homes. Some codes, including the CABO *One and Two Family Dwelling Code* allow the construction of shallow slab-on-grade foundations for heated buildings in cold climates if certain precautions are taken to protect against frost heave. This type of foundation design is sometimes referred to as frost-protected shallow foundations, insulated footings, or frost-protected footings and was first developed in Scandinavia.

A layer of polystyrene insulation applied to the vertical stem of the foundation wall, and a horizontal "wing" of insulation placed outside

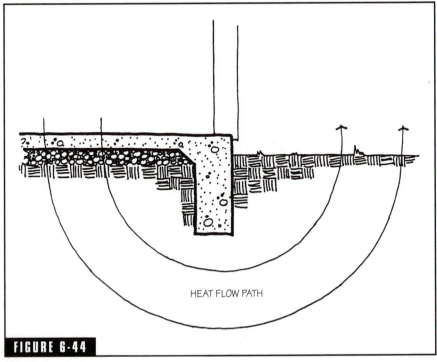

HEAT FLOW PATH

FIGURE 6-44

Heat loss at foundation perimeter. *(from Donald Watson and Kenneth Labs,* Climatic Building Design, *McGraw-Hill, 1983).*

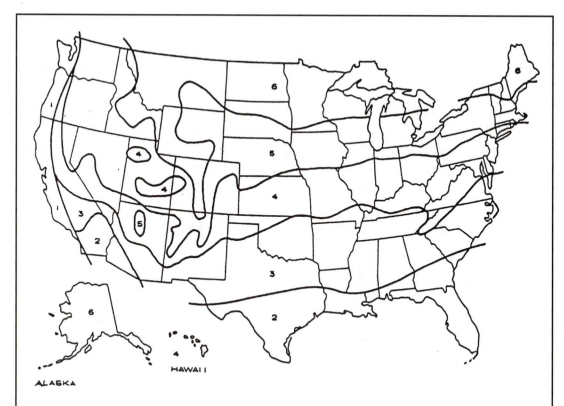

RECOMMENDED MINIMUM THERMAL RESISTANCE (R) OF INSULATION

ZONE	CEILING	WALL	FLOOR
1	19	11	11
2	26	13	11
3	26	19	13
4	30	19	19
5	33	19	22
6	38	19	22

NOTE: The minimum insulation R values recommended for various parts of the United States as delineated on the map of insulation zones.

FIGURE 6-45

Recommended R-values. *(from* Architectural Graphic Standards, *9th ed.)*

the perimeter of the building effectively blocks the natural radial heat flow paths (Figure 6-46). Heat migrating from the building interior elevates the soil temperature above its winter norm and artificially raises the frost depth. Seasonally fluctuating temperatures eventually stabilize since the heat cannot escape to the exterior ground surface. Code requirements for the use of frost-protected footings are based on climatic conditions. The air-freezing index in Figure 6-47 indicates the magnitude and duration of winter conditions in various parts of the country. The table and diagrams in Figure 6-48 list Code requirements for R-value and insulation dimensions based on air-freezing index ratings.

6.9   Ventilation and Radon Protection

Crawl spaces must be ventilated to dissipate soil moisture vapor and prevent its being drawn into the home. This means providing openings in the foundation walls of sufficient size and number to meet code

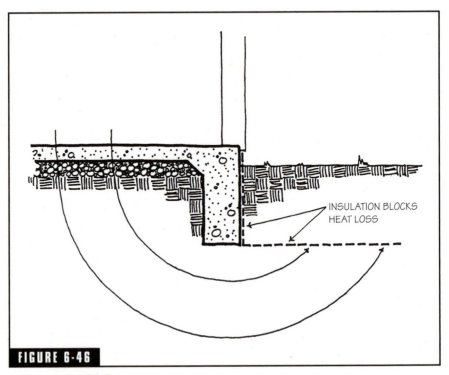

INSULATION BLOCKS HEAT LOSS

FIGURE 6-46

Frost protected footings.

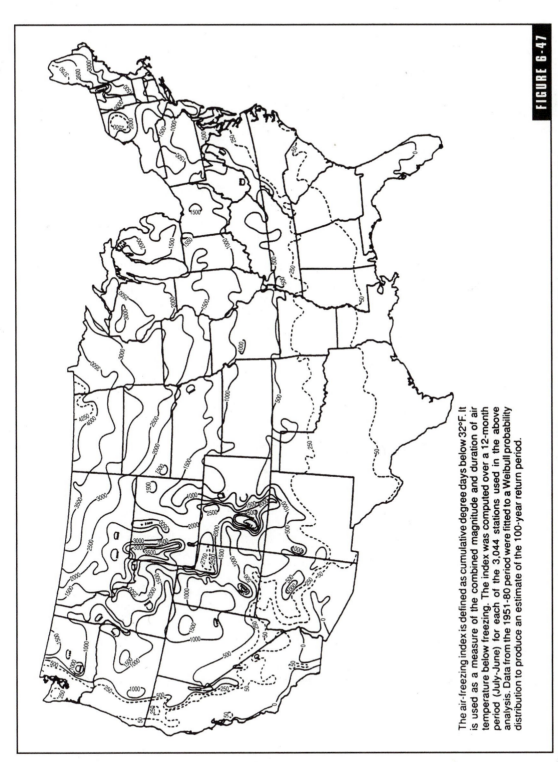

The air-freezing index is defined as cumulative degree days below 32°F. It is used as a measure of the combined magnitude and duration of air temperature below freezing. The index was computed over a 12-month period (July-June) for each of the 3,044 stations used in the above analysis. Data from the 1951-80 period were fitted to a Weibull probability distribution to produce an estimate of the 100-year return period.

FIGURE 6-47

Air freezing index. *(from Council of American Building Officials One and Two-Family Dwelling Code,, Falls Church, VA).*

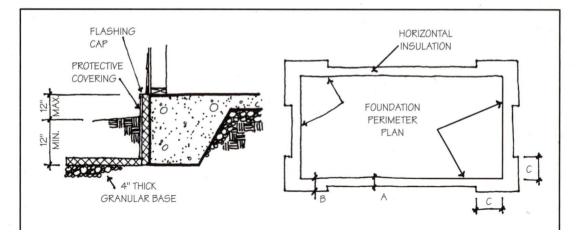

Minimum insulation requirements for frost-protected footings in heated buildings[1]

Air Freezing Index (°F Days)[2]	Vertical Insulation R-Value[3,4]	Horizontal Insulation R-Value[3,5]		Horizontal Insulation Dimensions Inches		
		along walls	at corners	A	B	C
1,500 or less	4.5	Not Required	Not Required	Not Required	Not Required	Not Required
2,000	5.6	Not Required	Not Required	Not Required	Not Required	Not Required
2,500	6.7	1.7	4.9	12	24	40
3,000	7.8	6.5	8.6	12	24	40
3,500	9.0	8.0	11.2	24	30	60
4,000	10.0	10.5	13.1	24	36	60

NOTES:
1. Insulation requirements are for protection against frost damage in heated buildings. Greater values may be required to meet energy conservation standards. Interpolation between values is permitted.
2. See Figure 6-47 for Air-Freezing Index values.
3. Insulation materials shall provide the stated minimum R-values under long-term exposure to moist, below-ground conditions in freezing climates. The following R-values shall be used to determine insulation thickness required for this application: Type II expanded polystyrene 2.4 R per inch; Type IV extruded polystyrene 4.5 R per inch; Type VI extruded polystyrene 4.5 R per inch; Type IX expanded polystyrene 3.2 R per inch; Type X extruded polystyrene 4.5 R per inch.
4. Vertical insulation shall be expanded polystyrene insulation or extruded polystyrene insulation, and the exposed portions shall have a rigid, opaque and weather-resistant protective covering to prevent the degradation of thermal performance. Protective covering shall cover the exposed portion of the insulation and extend to a minimum of 6 in. below grade.
5. Horizontal insulation shall be extruded polystyrene insulation.

FIGURE 6-48

Minimum insulation requirements for frost-protected footings in heated buildings[1] *(from Council of American Building Officials One and Two-Family Dwelling Code,, Falls Church, VA).*

requirements for crawl space ventilation. A minimum of four openings should be provided (one at each corner), placed as high in the foundation wall as possible. The CABO *One and Two Family Dwelling Code* requires a minimum net area of ventilation openings of 1 sq. ft. for each 150 sq. ft. of crawl space area, with one opening located within 3 ft. of each corner. Ventilation openings must be provided with corrosion-resistant wire mesh with the least dimension of the mesh being $1/8$ in. Net and gross ventilator areas for different types of screens and louvers are given in Figure 6-49. After calculating the required net area, multiply by the coefficient shown to determine the overall size or gross area of ventilators needed. Ventilation will dissipate soil moisture vapor, but it also will cool the underside of the floor sufficiently to require insulation to prevent winter heat loss. An alternative control measure is to cover the exposed soil. With a vapor retarder of polyethylene film, heavy roll roofing (55 lb.), or a proprietary membrane, the required net area of ventilation may be reduced to 1 sq. ft. for each 1,500 sq. ft. of crawl space area. Vents still should be placed within 3 ft. of each corner but may be omitted entirely from one side of the building.

In concrete foundation walls, blockouts can be provided for crawl space ventilation openings using either plywood or lumber to frame a penetration of the correct size through the formwork. Make sure the concrete flows around and fills in underneath the blockout by mechanical vibration or hammering against the forms. In concrete

Ventilator covering	Coefficient
$1/4$" mesh hardware cloth	1
Screening, 8 mesh.in.	1.25
Insect screen, 16 mesh/in.	2
Louvers plus $1/4$" mesh hardware cloth	2
Louvers plus screening, 8 mesh/in.	2.25
Louvers plus insect screening, 16 mesh/in.	3

*Gross ventilator area = required net area × coefficient

FIGURE 6-49

Net and gross ventilator area.

block foundation walls, screen block of the type described in Chapter 9 may be used if they are properly fitted with screen wire on the inside of the wall. An 18 in. × 24 in. minimum access opening must also be provided through the foundation wall to permit servicing and inspection of underfloor areas.

Where a crawl space is provided below wood-framed construction, the wood should be separated from the exposed soil by the minimum distances shown in Figure 6-50. In addition to separating the wood framing from the vapor source and allowing for ventilation, these clearances assure adequate access for periodic visual inspection. All formwork from footing and wall construction should be removed before proceeding with construction. The Code permits the finish grade in the crawl space to be at the bottom of the footings unless there is evidence of a rising water table or inadequate surface water drainage. In these cases, the finish grade in the crawl space must be the same as the outside finish grade unless an approved drainage system is provided.

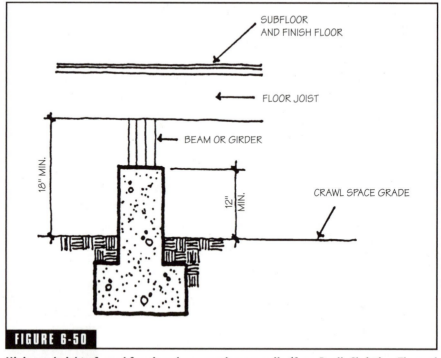

FIGURE 6-50

Minimum height of wood framing above crawl space soil. *(from Beall, Christine,* Thermal and Moisture Protection Manual, *McGraw-Hill, New York).*

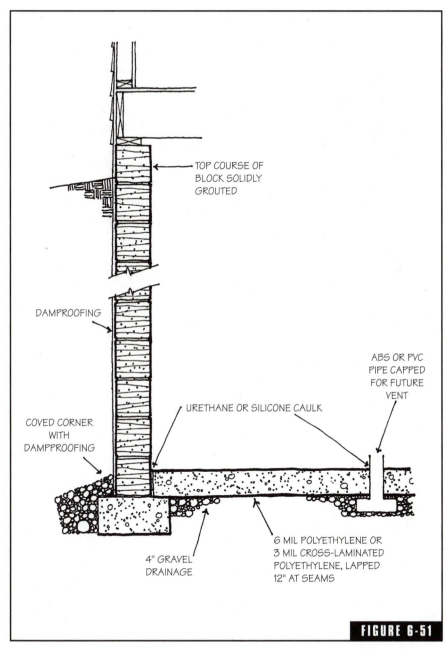

TOP COURSE OF
BLOCK SOLIDLY
GROUTED

DAMPROOFING

COVED CORNER
WITH
DAMPPROOFING

URETHANE OR SILICONE CAULK

ABS OR PVC
PIPE CAPPED
FOR FUTURE
VENT

4" GRAVEL
DRAINAGE

6 MIL POLYETHYLENE OR
3 MIL CROSS-LAMINATED
POLYETHYLENE, LAPPED
12" AT SEAMS

FIGURE 6-51

Radon protection. *(from NCMA TEK 6-15, National Concrete Masonry Association, Herndon, VA).*

In areas where radon gas from the soil is a potential problem, most building codes require that basements, crawl spaces, and slabs-on-grade be designed to resist radon entry and that the building be prepared for post-construction radon mitigation, if necessary. Figure 6-51 shows CABO requirements for basement construction. Similar details apply to crawl space and slab-on-grade foundations. One of the primary considerations is sealing the walls and slab to prevent gas entry. Dampproofing, perimeter caulk, and a below-grade air barrier are important elements. A 6-mil polyethylene sheet or a 3-mil cross-laminated reinforced polyethylene sheet is acceptable for this use. The top course of hollow concrete masonry foundation walls must be grouted solid to prevent air leakage to the interior space above, and a 4-in. layer of gravel below the slab acts as a gas-permeable layer which can be mechanically vented if needed. All control joints, construction joints, and isolation joints in concrete and masonry must be caulked.

Masonry Veneer

A veneer is a nonstructural facing used as a decorative or protective covering. Masonry veneers are among the most popular applications of masonry in the United States and Canada. Most of the masonry used in residential construction is used as a veneer attached to wood or sometimes to metal stud backing walls. Brick, concrete block, and stone are all used as masonry veneers, but brick veneer is by far the most common. Unlike masonry foundation and basement walls, masonry veneers are not designed to support the weight of the structure itself, but must resist lateral wind and earthquake loads and, in most cases, support their own weight. Masonry veneers must be carefully designed and constructed to accommodate moisture penetration through the facing without causing damage to the structure or leakage to the interior.

7.1 Veneer Anchorage

There are two basic methods of attaching masonry veneer. *Adhered veneer* is secured by adhering the veneer with mortar to a solid backing wall. This method of attachment is usually reserved for thin veneers that are not capable of supporting their own weight. In residential construction, adhered veneer is not common but might be used to attach thin stones to an exposed concrete or masonry foundation wall. *Anchored veneer* is secured by metal anchors attached to either a solid backing wall or a stud wall. An anchored masonry veneer supports its own weight, resting directly on the slab or foundation wall. Building codes regulate the design of masonry veneers by prescriptive requirements based on empirical data. The CABO *One and Two Family Dwelling Code* requires that masonry veneers be supported on non-combustible construction, and limits the height of masonry veneers over wood frame backing walls to 30 feet above the foundation with an additional 8 feet at gable ends.

Anchored masonry veneers transfer lateral loads to the backing wall through metal anchors and their fasteners. Flexible veneer anchors permit slight horizontal and vertical movement parallel to the plane of the wall but resist tension and compression forces perpendicular to it. Corrugated sheet metal anchors are typically used in residential construction. These should be 22-gauge galvanized steel, $7/8$ in. wide $\times$ 6 in. long. Corrosion-resistant nails should penetrate wood studs a minimum of $1\text{-}1/2$ in., exclusive of sheathing thickness. Galvanized or stainless steel screws should be used to attach corrugated anchors to metal studs. Corrugated anchors are relatively weak in compression compared to commercial veneer anchors, and they provide load transfer only if the horizontal leg is properly aligned in plane with the mortar bed joint and one of the two fasteners is positioned at the 90° bend (Figure 7-1). Anchors randomly attached to the backing wall and bent at odd angles to fit into the mortar joints are ineffective. Masonry veneer anchors must be embedded in the mortar joint a minimum of $1\text{-}1/2$ in. for lateral load transfer and have a minimum mortar cover of $5/8$ in. to the outside of the wall to prevent corrosion of the metal (Figure 7-2). Anchors should be placed within the mortar so that they are completely encapsulated for maximum pull-out strength. An anchor that is placed on the dry masonry and mortared only on top has only about half the strength of an anchor that is properly embedded.

Masonry veneer is typically connected to metal stud frames with 9-gauge corrosion-resistant wire anchors hooked through a slotted connector for flexibility (Figure 7-3). Anchors are attached to the studs with galvanized or stainless steel self-tapping screws. The use of brick veneer over metal stud backing is relatively recent in the long history of masonry construction. For one- and two-story buildings with lim-

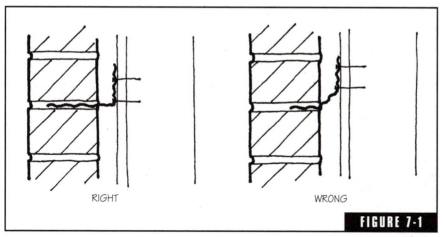

Corrugated anchor bending.

FIGURE 7-1

RIGHT   WRONG

ited floor-to-floor heights, the necessary stiffness might be achieved with 18-gauge studs, depending on wind load factors. Increased floor-to-floor heights, higher wind loads, and taller structures will generally require studs that are a minimum of 16 gauge. Stud spacing should not exceed 16 in. on center, and the studs should be hot-dip galvanized, especially in coastal climates and other corrosive environments.

Another method of masonry veneer attachment recognized by some building codes and by HUD "Minimum Property Standards" uses galvanized 16-gauge 2 ×2-in. paper-backed, welded wire mesh attached to metal studs with galvanized wire ties, or to wood studs with galvanized nails. Wire anchors are then hooked through the mesh, and the 1-in. space between veneer and backing is grouted solid (Figure 7-4). This is a much less common technique and offers no real advantage of performance or economy for unit masonry veneers. For construction of rubble stone veneer where coursing heights

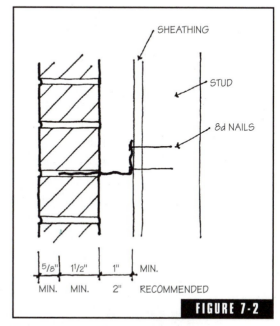

SHEATHING

STUD

8d NAILS

5/8" MIN.   1 1/2" MIN.   1" MIN.   2" RECOMMENDED

FIGURE 7-2

Veneer section with corrugated anchor.

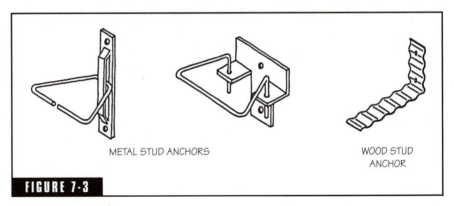

METAL STUD ANCHORS

WOOD STUD ANCHOR

FIGURE 7-3

Masonry veneer anchors.

are random, this method of attachment allows greater flexibility in the placement of anchors for proper alignment with mortar bed joints.

Where a masonry veneer is attached to concrete masonry backing, such as an above-grade foundation wall, the anchorage is usually in conjunction with the horizontal joint reinforcement used to control shrinkage cracking in the CMU. For walls in which the backing and facing wythes are both of concrete masonry, three-wire joint reinforcement can be used (Figure 7-5a). Two of the longitudinal wires are embedded in the face shell bed joints of the block and the third wire is embedded in the veneer bed joint. If the wythes are laid up at different times, however, the three-wire design makes installation awkward. Three-wire joint reinforcing should also not be used when insulation is installed in the cavity between wythes because the wires are too stiff to allow for differential thermal movement between the backing and facing wythes. For walls in which the backing and facing wythes are laid at different times, walls with clay brick facing and CMU backing, or walls which contain insulation in the cavity between wythes, joint reinforcement with adjustable ties allows differential movement between wythes and facilitates the installation of the outer wythe after the backing wythe is already in place (Figure 7-5b). The adjustable ties may be either a tab or hook and eye design.

In Seismic Zones 0, 1, and 2, masonry veneer anchors may be spaced not more than 32 in. on center horizontally and support not more than 2.67 square feet of wall area. Since the anchors are attached to the studs and must be embedded in the mortar joints, the stud spacing, unit size, and coursing heights affect the exact anchor placement. If the studs are spaced 24 in. on center, the maximum anchor spacing would be 24 in. on center horizontally × 16 in. on center vertically (every sixth course of brick or every second course of concrete block). If the stud spacing is 16 in. on center, the maximum anchor spacing would be 16 in. on center horizontally × 24 in. on center vertically (every ninth course of brick or every third course of concrete block).

Stone veneer is attached in the same way as brick veneer, but the anchor spacing must compensate for the irregularities of mortar bed height and still meet code requirements. An anchor spacing of 16 in. on center, for example, may not accommodate the coursing height of rough stone. If vertical spacing must be increased so that anchors align properly with the bed joints, horizontal spacing may have to be decreased to stay within the maximum allowable wall area supported by each anchor.

In Seismic Zones 3 and 4, and in areas subject to wind loads of 30 psf (108 mph) or more, each veneer anchor may support a maximum of 2 sq. ft. of wall area. This requires a stud spacing of 16 in. on center and an anchor spacing of 16 in. on center horizontally × 16 in. on cen-

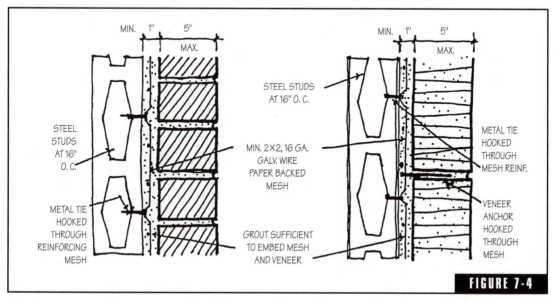

Alternate veneer attachment. *(from Beall, Christine,* Masonry Design and Detailing, *4th edition, McGraw-Hill, New York).*

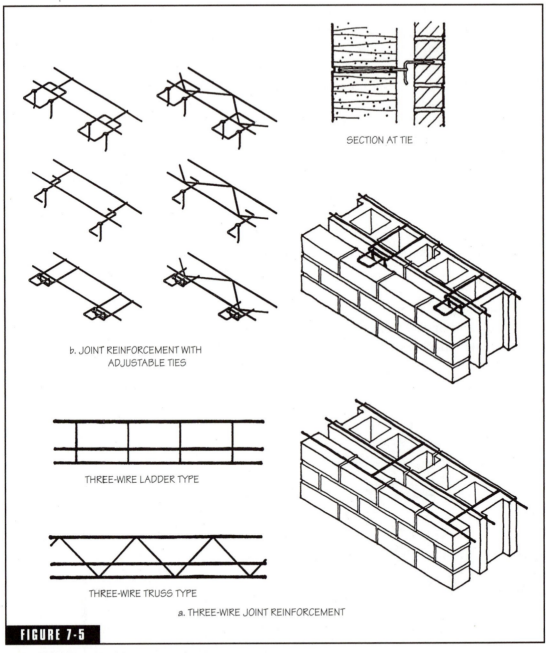

SECTION AT TIE

b. JOINT REINFORCEMENT WITH ADJUSTABLE TIES

THREE-WIRE LADDER TYPE

THREE-WIRE TRUSS TYPE

a. THREE-WIRE JOINT REINFORCEMENT

FIGURE 7-5

Joint reinforcement with veneer anchorage.

ter vertically. In Seismic Zones 3 and 4, veneer anchors must also be mechanically attached to continuous horizontal reinforcement of 9-gauge wire (W1.7). Special seismic anchors are made for such applications (Figure 7-6). Lap splices in the wire reinforcement should occur between veneer anchors. Some manufacturers also make prefabricated joint reinforcement with adjustable seismic veneer anchors for block walls with brick veneer.

7.2 Veneer Support Above Grade

Where a portion of a masonry veneer wall occurs over a lower roof area or balcony, support can be provided in one of two ways. The Code requires that a steel angle be installed to carry the masonry and that the angle either be attached to and supported by the stud frame, or resting on framing members sized to carry the additional load with a maximum deflection of $1/600$ of the span (Figure 7-7). The masonry should not rest directly on the wood framing or sheathing. Where veneer supported above grade adjoins masonry supported on the foundation, a control or expansion joint is required to prevent cracking caused by differential movement. If the masonry is above a sloping roof, the supporting angles may be attached to the studs as a series of short sections which step down the slope. Masonry installed on a sloping angle must be leveled with a mortar bed and will not be as stable.

7.3 Lintels and Arches

Noncombustible lintels of steel, reinforced masonry, stone, concrete, precast concrete, and cast stone are typically used to span openings in masonry veneer walls. Masonry arches perform the same function of supporting the masonry above the opening and transferring the weight to the wall sections on either side. Arches carry loads in compression, but lintels act as flexural members spanning horizontally from one support to the other (Figure 7-8). Lintels must resist compressive, bending, and shear stresses (Figure 7-9). Lintels and arches must be analyzed to determine the loads which must be carried and the resulting stresses which will be created in the member. Many of the cracks that appear over door and window openings result from excessive deflection of lintels which have been improperly or inadequately

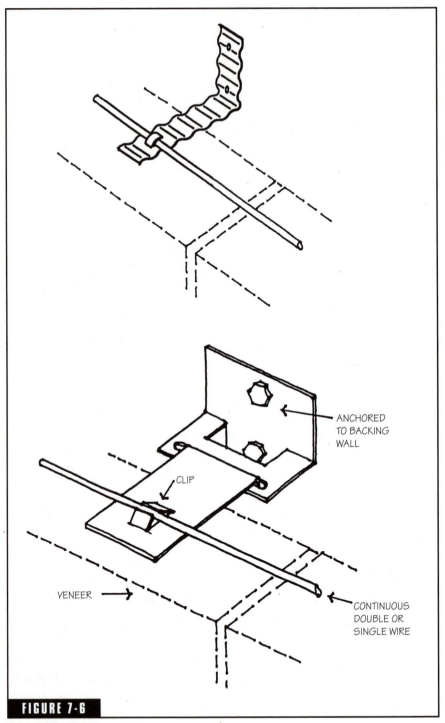

ANCHORED
TO BACKING
WALL

CLIP

VENEER

CONTINUOUS
DOUBLE OR
SINGLE WIRE

FIGURE 7-6

Seismic veneer anchors. *(from Beall, Christine,* Masonry Design and Detailing, *4th edition, McGraw-Hill, New York).*

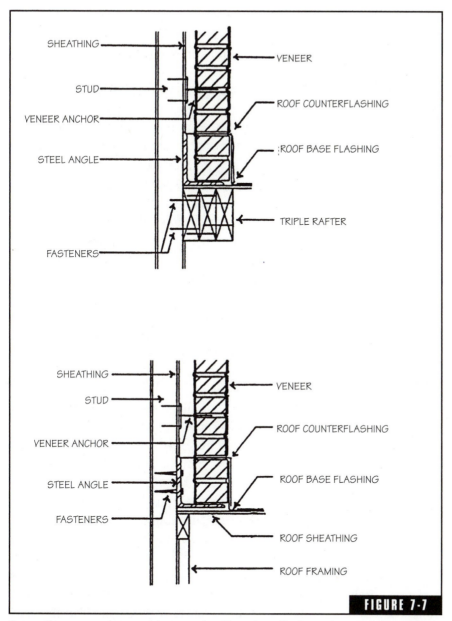

Supporting masonry veneer above grade. *(from Council of American Building Officials,* One and Two-Family Dwelling Code, *Falls Church, VA).*

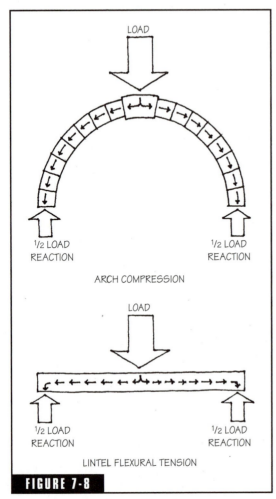

LOAD

½ LOAD
REACTION

½ LOAD
REACTION

ARCH COMPRESSION

LOAD

½ LOAD
REACTION

½ LOAD
REACTION

LINTEL FLEXURAL TENSION

FIGURE 7-8

Load transfer in arches and lintels.

designed, and arches may crack because of structural instability.

The most common method of supporting the masonry above openings is with loose steel angle lintels. A length of steel angle rests on the masonry on either side of the opening but is not attached to the backing wall. It should have a minimum bearing length of 4 in. on each side of the opening and be positioned so that it supports at least 2/3 of the masonry thickness. Loose steel lintels allow the work to proceed quickly without the need for temporary shoring or a curing period. Cast stone and precast concrete lintels also provide immediate support but require two workers or more for lifting the heavy sections in place. Cast stone lintels are popular because they add elegant detailing with greater strength and lower cost than natural stone. A minimum end bearing of 8 in. is recommended for cast stone, reinforced concrete, and CMU lintels.

When masonry is laid in running bond, it creates a natural, corbeled arch (Figure 7-10). In fact, before true masonry arches were invented, corbeled arches, vaults, and domes were used to span openings. Lintels must be designed to carry the weight of the masonry inside the triangle formed by the line of such arching action. This triangular area has sides at 45° angles to the lintel, and its height is therefore one-half the span length (Figure 7-11). Outside this area, the weight of the masonry is assumed to be carried to the supporting abutments by natural arching. For this assumption to be true, however, the arching action must be stabilized by 8–16 in. of masonry above the top of the triangle. If arching action cannot be assumed to occur because of inadequate height above the load triangle, or because the masonry is not laid in running bond, the lintel must be sized to carry the full weight of the wall above its entire length (Figure 7-12). When arching action is assumed, the lintel requires temporary support until the mortar has cured sufficiently to allow the masonry to assume its share of the load.

Arching action produces an outward horizontal thrust at each support or abutment. The abutments, therefore, must have sufficient mass to resist this force. If the opening is near a corner or close to another opening, or if an expansion or control joint occurs at the side of the opening, it may again be necessary to size the lintel large enough to carry all of the loads above its entire length, without assuming any arching action in the masonry. Once the total load on the lintel is known, it can be appropriately sized by an engineer to resist the calculated stresses. Lintel deflection should be limited to $1/600$ of the span to avoid cracking the masonry.

Steel angles are the simplest lintels to use for masonry veneers and are suitable for openings of moderate width such as windows and doors. For wider openings such as garage doors, double lintels or steel beams with suspended plates may be required (Figure 7-13). The horizontal leg of a steel angle should be at least 3 in. wide to adequately support a nominal 4-in. wythe of brick, block, or stone. Generally, angles should be a minimum of $1/4$ in. thick to satisfy code requirements for exterior steel members. Precast concrete, reinforced masonry,

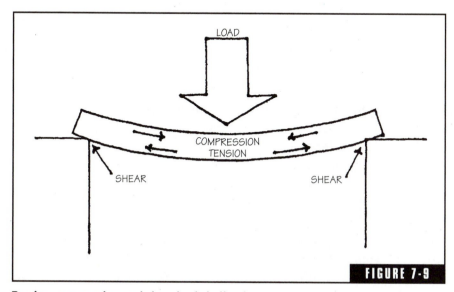

FIGURE 7-9

Tension, compression, and shear loads in lintels.

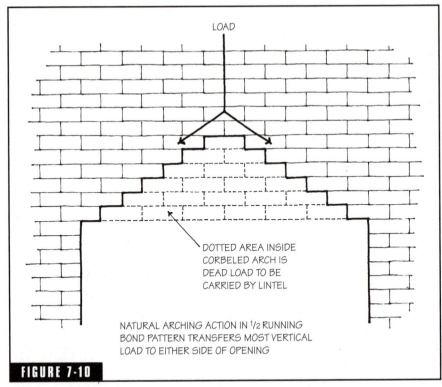

LOAD

DOTTED AREA INSIDE
CORBELED ARCH IS
DEAD LOAD TO BE
CARRIED BY LINTEL

NATURAL ARCHING ACTION IN ½ RUNNING
BOND PATTERN TRANSFERS MOST VERTICAL
LOAD TO EITHER SIDE OF OPENING

FIGURE 7-10

Corbeled arch created by arching action in running bond pattern. *(from Christine Beall,
"Lintel Design and Detailing,"* The Magazine of Masonry Construction, *March 1993).*

and cast stone lintels are also used to span openings in masonry veneer
walls. Span length for any type of lintel will depend on the strength of
the member. In steel lintels, increasing size and thickness provide
greater strength. In concrete and masonry lintels, reinforcing steel
increases strength and span capabilities. CABO requirements provide
that lintels in masonry veneer walls may have maximum spans as provided in Figure 7-14.

Arches may be constructed in various forms such as *segmental,
elliptical, Tudor, Gothic, semicircular, parabolic, flat* or *jack arches*
(Figure 7-15). The semicircular and segmental are perhaps the most
popular and widely used arch forms in contemporary design and construction. The primary structural advantage of an arch is that under
uniform loading conditions, the stress is principally compression
rather than tension. This is very efficient structurally since masonry's

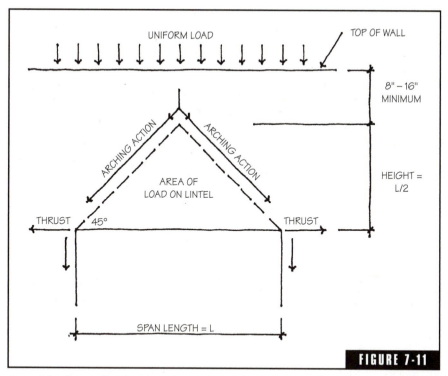

UNIFORM LOAD

TOP OF WALL

8" – 16" MINIMUM

HEIGHT = L/2

ARCHING ACTION

ARCHING ACTION

AREA OF LOAD ON LINTEL

THRUST

45°

THRUST

SPAN LENGTH = L

FIGURE 7-11

Area of load on a lintel with arching action. *(from Christine Beall, "Lintel Design and Detailing," The Magazine of Masonry Construction, March 1993).*

resistance to compression is greater than its resistance to tension. Arches generally are selected as an alternative to lintels not because of their efficiency, however, but because their style suits the architectural design of the home. Arches whose spans do not exceed 6 ft. are called minor arches, and they are most often used in building walls over door and window openings. Major arches whose spans are wider than 6 ft. require engineering design. The terminology used to describe the various parts of an arch are illustrated in Figure 7-16.

The steps in building a masonry arch are simple, but good workmanship is essential. Arches are constructed over temporary shoring or centering to carry the dead load of the material and other applied loads until the arch itself is completed and the mortar has cured to sufficient strength (Figure 7-17). Cut two $3/4$-in. plywood sections to the size and shape shown on the architectural drawings and nail them on either side of 2×4s (Figure 7-18). If the arch is a single brick wythe in

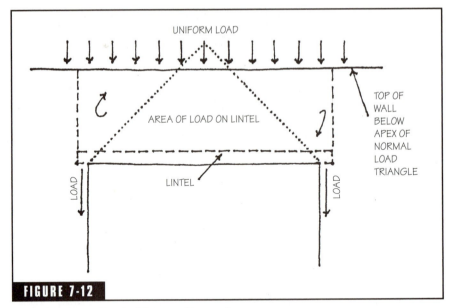

FIGURE 7-12

Area of load on a lintel without arching action.

thickness, lay the 2×4s flat. If the arch is more than one wythe thick with the soffit exposed such as at an entry porch, lay the 2×4s the other way. Place the centering flat on the ground and lay out the arch pattern by positioning the masonry units around it. There should always be an odd number of units or *voussoirs* so that the center unit or *key* falls exactly at the center of the arch. All units should be full size and the joints should be spaced evenly. Mark the position of the units on the plywood to serve as a guide during construction. Place a strip of roofing felt or polyethylene over the centering to keep mortar from sticking to it. Recess the centering from the face of the wall slightly so that the mortar joints can be tooled easily. Hold the centering in place with temporary wood posts and wedges until at least seven days after the arch is completed. Begin building the arch at the ends or abutments. Lay the brick or stone from each end toward the middle. In stone arches, take care to cut and lay the stone accurately with thin joints to prevent settling of heavy units.

Brick arches can be built of special wedge-shaped brick or stone so that the mortar joints are of uniform thickness, or they can be built of standard rectangular brick with joint thicknesses varied to obtain the

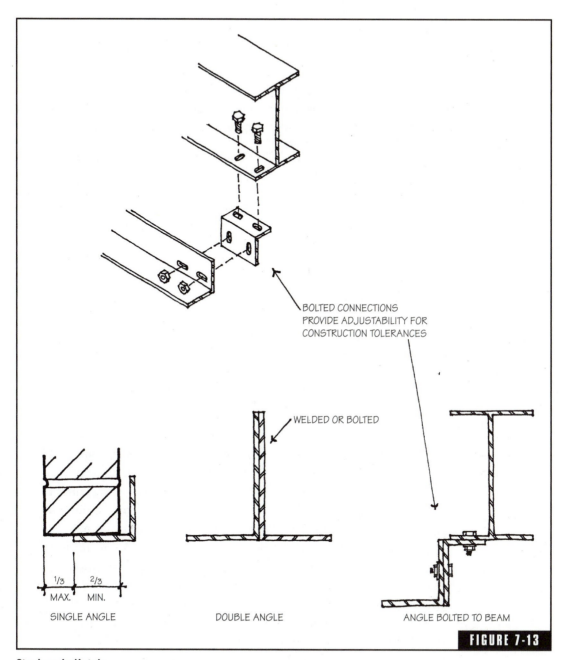

BOLTED CONNECTIONS
PROVIDE ADJUSTABILITY FOR
CONSTRUCTION TOLERANCES

WELDED OR BOLTED

1/3 | 2/3
MAX. | MIN.

SINGLE ANGLE   DOUBLE ANGLE   ANGLE BOLTED TO BEAM

FIGURE 7-13

Steel angle lintels.

Size of Angle*† For Steel Angle Lintels	Number of ½" or Equivalent Reinforcing Bars in Masonry or Concrete Lintels‡	Less Than One Story of Masonry Above Lintel	Lintel Supporting One Story of Masonry Above Opening	Lintel Supporting Two Stories of Masonry Above Opening
3 × 3 × ¼	1	6'-0"	3'-6"	3'-0"
4 × 3 × ¼	1	8'-0"	5'-0"	3'-0"
6 × 3½ × ¼	2	14'-0"	8'-0"	3'-6"
two 6 × 3½ × ¼	4	20'-0"	11'-0"	5'-0"

*Long leg of angle shall be in vertical position.

†Steel members indicated are adequate typical examples. Other steel members meeting structural design requirements may be used.

‡Depth of reinforced lintels shall not be less than 8 inches, and all cells of hollow masonry lintels shall be grouted solid. Reinforcing Bars shall extend not less than 8 inches into the support.

FIGURE 7-14

Allowable lintel spans. *(from Council of American Building Officials,* **One and Two-Family Dwelling Code,** *Falls Church, VA).*

required curvature. With standard brick the mortar joints are narrower at the bottom than at the top, but should be a minimum of ¼ inch. Units laid in a soldier course will have a more pronounced variance in the joint thicknesses. Two or more courses of rowlocks can be more attractive, particularly with arches of relatively short span (Figure 7-19).

Although the shape and placement of each unit are most important in the structural stability of an arch, mortar keeps the units from sliding, and it is especially important that the mortar joints be completely filled. It can be difficult to achieve full joints in soldier courses because the mortar tends to slump toward the bottom of the joint as the unit is placed. Full mortar joints are easier to achieve with rowlock courses. Mortar can be omitted from the bottom of the arch during construction and tuckpointed after the centering is removed. This will help avoid stains on the bottom brick surfaces and will also make it possible to tool the bottom joints properly. A wooden dowel of the

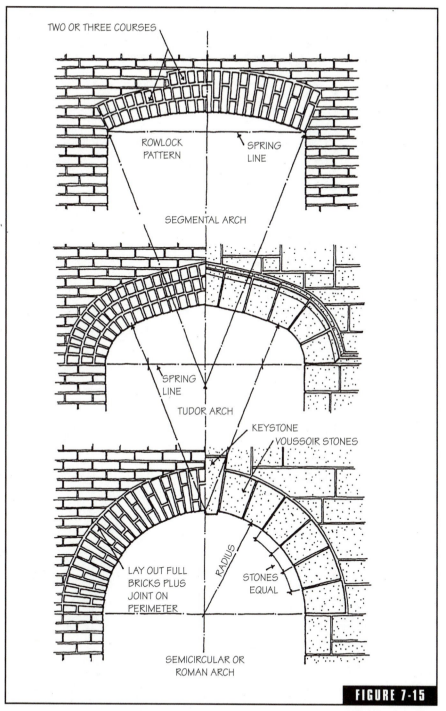

TWO OR THREE COURSES

ROWLOCK PATTERN

SPRING LINE

SEGMENTAL ARCH

SPRING LINE

TUDOR ARCH

KEYSTONE

VOUSSOIR STONES

LAY OUT FULL BRICKS PLUS JOINT ON PERIMETER

RADIUS

STONES EQUAL

SEMICIRCULAR OR ROMAN ARCH

FIGURE 7-15

Arch forms. *(from Beall, Christine,* **Masonry Design and Detailing,** *4th edition, McGraw-Hill, New York).*

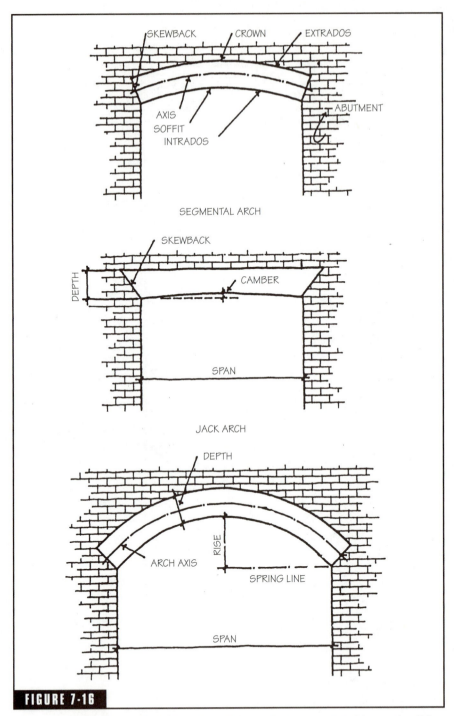

FIGURE 7-16

Arch terminology. *(from Beall, Christine, Masonry Design and Detailing, 4th edition, McGraw-Hill, New York).*

appropriate size placed at the bottom of the joint will maintain the correct joint width and unit spacing (Figure 7-20). Place a full 3/8-in. mortar joint along the top of the arch and cut adjacent units to fit against the curve.

7.4 Drainage Cavity

Most codes require a minimum 1-in. space between a masonry veneer and its backing and permit the space to be solidly grouted as the veneer is laid, or left open to form a drainage cavity. Anchored masonry veneers are usually designed with an open drainage cavity. Moisture will always penetrate a masonry veneer, even with good design, good detailing, and good workmanship. A certain amount of moisture penetration is expected in most climates. The greater the exposure to wind-driven rain, the more moisture will penetrate the wall. Drainage cavities increase the level of performance and the longevity of the wall system by removing moisture from the wall rapidly. This allows natural wetting and drying to occur without damage to the masonry or to the backing wall.

Wood stud walls behind a masonry veneer must be covered with either a water-repellent gypsum sheathing, a moisture-resistant insulating sheathing, or a plywood or OSB sheathing covered with moisture-resistant asphalt felt or polyolefin house wrap. Gypsum sheathing with a moisture-resistant facing is typically used over metal stud construction with additional protection against corrosion

FIGURE 7-17

Provide temporary support during arch construction. *(from Beall, Christine,* Masonry Design and Detailing, *4th edition, McGraw-Hill, New York).*

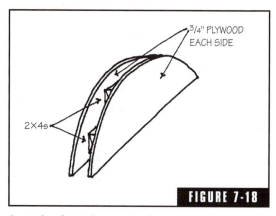

FIGURE 7-18

Centering for arch construction.

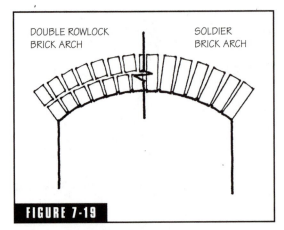

FIGURE 7-19

Soldier and rowlock arches.

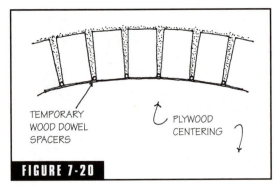

FIGURE 7-20

Blocking bottom joints for later tuck pointing.

provided by applying a layer of 15-lb. asphalt-saturated felt or polyolefin house wrap over the sheathing. The felt or house wrap should be lapped shingle style in horizontal layers to shed moisture (Figure 7-21). If the space between the masonry and the backing is grouted, paper-backed welded wire mesh may be attached directly to the studs in lieu of sheathing.

Where masonry veneers are installed over a concrete or concrete masonry backing wall, the cavity face of the backing wall should be coated with a mastic damp-proofing to provide increased moisture resistance. Mastics can be applied by brush, roller, or spray and should be carefully worked around anchors, plumbing, and electrical penetrations to provide an adequate seal (Figure 7-22).

The drainage cavity type of veneer construction provides the best long-term serviceability, but the cavity must be fitted with flashing and weep holes as described below, and kept clear of mortar droppings for drainage to be effective. The masonry industry recommends a minimum drainage cavity width of 2 in. because it is felt that a narrower cavity is difficult for a mason to keep clean during construction. A narrow cavity is also more easily bridged by mortar protrusions, which greatly increases the likelihood of moisture leakage through any defect which might exist in the backing wall. With a clean and unobstructed cavity, moisture which penetrates the face of the masonry runs down the back of the veneer and is collected on the flashing and drained through weeps.

7.5 Flashing and Weep Holes

Full head and bed joints and good bond of mortar to units will minimize moisture penetration directly through the face of a masonry veneer, but it is virtually impossible to entirely prevent moisture from entering a masonry wall. Masonry veneer walls require the installation of flashing and weep holes for the collection and discharge of moisture which penetrates the exterior wall face or condenses within the wall. This is true regardless of whether the space behind the veneer is intentionally left open for drainage or grouted solidly with mortar. The flashing is used to intercept and collect moisture at strategic locations within the wall, and weeps are used to direct the moisture to the outside of the wall.

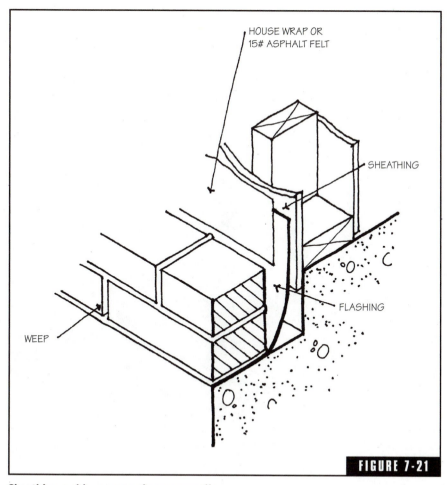

HOUSE WRAP OR
15# ASPHALT FELT

SHEATHING

FLASHING

WEEP

FIGURE 7-21

Sheathing and house wrap in veneer walls.

Masonry flashing can be made of metal, rubberized asphalt, plastic, or rubber sheet membranes and other composite materials. There are several criteria to consider in selecting flashing materials:

■ Imperviousness to moisture penetration

■ Resistance to corrosion from the caustic alkalies in mortar

■ Resistance to puncture, abrasion, and other damage during construction

■ Formability

■ Resistance to environmental deterioration

Cost should be considered only after other criteria are met. The quantity of flashing in a building is relatively small, and even a big savings in material cost is seldom significant in the overall project budget.

Plastic flashings are widely used in residential construction. They are inexpensive and easy to handle, and many are tough and resilient. Polyvinyl chloride (PVC) flashings are the most common among the plastic flashing materials. They are homogeneous and impermeable to

FIGURE 7-22

Mastic dampproofing.

moisture, and most retain good flexibility even in low temperatures. Thin plastic flashings are also easily torn or punctured during construction, so thickness should be a minimum of 20 mils, but preferably 30 mils or more. Puncture resistance can be added to plastic flashings with fiberglass scrim reinforcement when it is embedded between two sheets, and the overall required thickness is then greatly reduced. Metal foils can also be combined with fiberglass-reinforced plastics to form lightweight, durable flashings. Most recently, rubberized (or polymer modified) asphalt flashing materials have been introduced in the masonry industry and have enjoyed ready acceptance from design professionals and masons alike. The rubberized asphalt is self-adhering and self-healing of small punctures. Once the workers become accustomed to handling the material, it installs quickly and easily and is relatively forgiving of uneven substrates. Thorough cleaning of the substrate surface, however, is critical in obtaining good adhesion. Metal flashings such as copper and stainless steel are more commonly used in commercial construction, but on high-end homes, the extra durability provided may justify the additional cost.

FIGURE 7-23

Trim flexible flashing flush with face of wall after installation. *(photo courtesy Brick industry Association)*.

Lengths of flashing should be lapped 3–4 in. and sealed so that water cannot penetrate at the seams, and the flashing should be continuous around both internal and external corners. PVC and rubberized asphalt flashings cannot tolerate UV exposure, so they are typically brought beyond the face of the wall and then trimmed flush after the masonry is in place (Figure 7-23). It is important not to stop the flashing short of the exterior wall face, or water may not be properly drained from the cavity. Rubberized asphalt flashing, when properly adhered, prevents water from flowing back underneath the membrane and re-entering the wall. A formed drip edge on metal flashing also prevents water from flowing back into the wall. The inside leg of the flashing should turn up about 8 in. and be tucked underneath the felt paper or house wrap membrane, or underneath the sheathing itself (see Figure 5-25 in Chapter 5). If the backing wall is masonry, metal flashing should be tucked into a mortar joint and membrane flashings carefully adhered to the face of the block.

Flashing forms only half the moisture control system in a masonry wall. By itself, flashing collects water that enters the wall, but weep holes are necessary to provide the drainage mechanism that lets the water back out again. There are several types of weepholes commonly used. The most effective, but least attractive, are open head joints. Because mortar is left out of the head joint completely, the system has ample drainage and evaporative capacity for even the most severe coastal rain conditions, and so can be spaced at intervals of 24 in. Metal weephole ventilators and plastic grid type vents improve the aesthetics of the open joint without obstructing free drainage (Figure 7-24).

FIGURE 7-24

Weep hole vents.

Plastic tube weepholes are less conspicuous in the wall than open joints, but they are also much less effective. The smaller drainage capacity requires that spacing be reduced to 16 in. on center, and much greater care in construction is also required to avoid blocking the narrow tubes with mortar droppings (Figure 7-25). Cotton wick weeps avoid the problems associated with plastic tubes but still provide better aesthetics than open joints. A length of cotton rope 10–12 in. long is placed in head joints at 16 in. on center, extending through the veneer and up into the cavity well above the height of any possible mortar droppings (Figure 7-26). The rope can be tacked to the backing wall or adhered to it with a splash of mortar to keep it from falling over during construction. After installation, the exposed portion of the

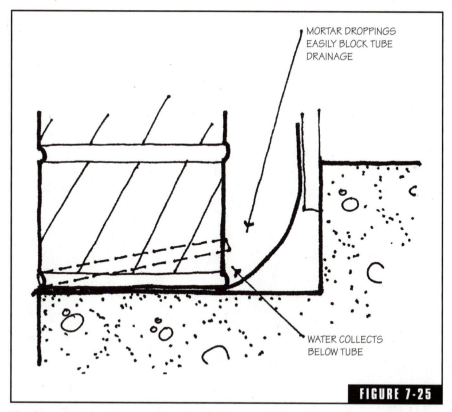

FIGURE 7-25

Plastic weep tubes are not recommended because they clog too easily. *(from Beall, Christine,* Masonry Design and Detailing, *4th edition, McGraw-Hill, New York).*

FIGURE 7-26A

Cotton wick weeps.

FIGURE 7-26B

Cotton wick weeps.

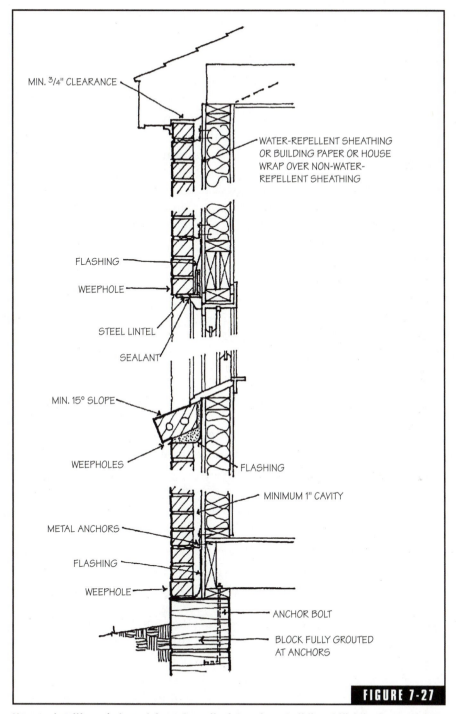

MIN. ³/₄" CLEARANCE

WATER-REPELLENT SHEATHING
OR BUILDING PAPER OR HOUSE
WRAP OVER NON-WATER-
REPELLENT SHEATHING

FLASHING

WEEPHOLE

STEEL LINTEL

SEALANT

MIN. 15° SLOPE

WEEPHOLES

FLASHING

MINIMUM 1" CAVITY

METAL ANCHORS

FLASHING

WEEPHOLE

ANCHOR BOLT

BLOCK FULLY GROUTED
AT ANCHORS

FIGURE 7-27

Veneer detailing. *(adapted from Council of American Building Officials,* **One and Two-Family Dwelling Code,** *Falls Church, VA).*

FIGURE 7-28

Expansion joint at change in wall height.

wick is clipped flush with the wall. Moisture in the cavity is absorbed by the cotton material and "wicked" to the outside face of the wall, where it evaporates. The rope will eventually rot, but it leaves an open hole for continued drainage. The rope must be cotton rather than nylon to be effective.

Through-wall masonry flashing must be installed at lintels above door and window openings, at window sills and ledges, and at the base of the wall. Weepholes must be installed in the first masonry course immediately above the flashing. The wall sections in Figure 7-27 illustrate basic requirements of the CABO *One and Two Family Dwelling Code.* Brick masonry sills should be sloped to drain water away from the window. The masonry industry recommends a minimum slope of 15 degrees. The flashing system must form a complete barrier to the passage of water. Masonry veneer should always rest on a ledge recessed below the finish floor line so that the flashing at the bottom of the drainage cavity collects and discharges moisture at this less-vulnerable location.

7.6   Expansion and Control Joints

As discussed in Chapters 4 and 5, cracking in masonry is most often related to the expansion and contraction caused by changes in moisture content. The walls of residences are relatively short in length compared to most commercial construction, so there is less accumulated movement stress to accommodate. However, stress buildup can occur even in small structures if not properly accommodated. Brick masonry expansion joints should be located near the external corners of long building walls because the opposing expansion of the intersecting walls can crack the brick. Brick masonry expansion joints and concrete masonry control joints should also be located at offsets and changes in wall height (Figure 7-28). If the brick is resting on a poured-concrete foundation, the bond break or slippage plane created by flashing at the base of a wall will prevent the opposing movement of brick expansion and concrete shrinkage from causing foundation cracking at outside building corners (Figure 7-29).

FIGURE 7-29

Cracking at building corner due to brick expansion restrained by concrete shrinkage.

Paving

Concrete and masonry provide durable and low-maintenance driveways, sidewalks, steps, and patios for homes of all sizes and styles. Although paving elements can be made of many different materials, concrete is still one of the most popular, with finishing options providing either a utilitarian or decorative appearance. Brick and concrete masonry pavers are more expensive than concrete but add an ornamental element that can enhance the value and appearance of high-end homes.

8.1 Design Guidelines

There are rule-of-thumb guidelines for the design of driveways, sidewalks, steps, and patios. Following are some basics for recommended width, thickness, drainage slope, turning radius, and so on.

Overall driveway size and shape will be dictated by the building site and its physical restrictions, but straight driveways for single-car garages and carports should be 10–14 ft. wide. Curved driveways should be a minimum of 14 ft. wide. A double-width driveway for two-car garages and carports should be 16–24 ft. wide. If the city or subdivision does not dictate requirements for aprons where the driveway meets the street, follow the basic guidelines given in Figure 8-1. If you want to provide room for turning a car around, follow the guidelines in Figure 8-2. If the house is on a hill, the driveway should not slope more than 14%—a rise or fall of 1-³/₄ in. per ft. of length—or a car's undercarriage and back bumper will scrape the ground at the top and bottom of the slope (Figure 8-3). If there is no slope to or from the street, flat driveways should be crowned or cross-sloped a minimum of ¹/₄ in. per foot to drain water off the surface (Figure 8-4). The top of a driveway slab should be 1–2 in. below the carport or garage slab and 1–2 in. above the street surface. Concrete driveways should be 4–6 in.

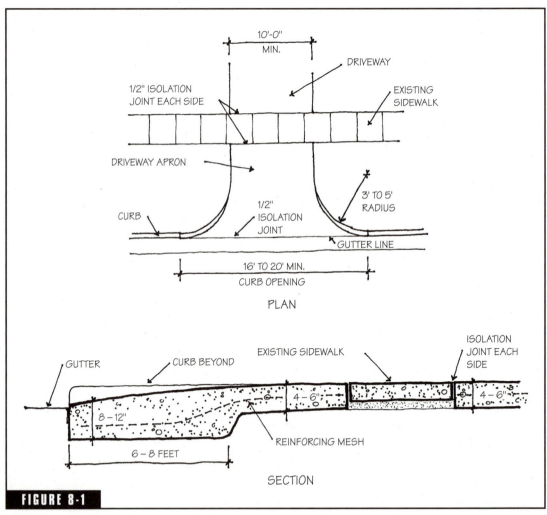

FIGURE 8-1

Driveway design guidelines. *(from Portland Cement Association,* **The Homeowner's Guide to Building With Concrete, Brick and Stone,** *PCA, Skokie, Illinois).*

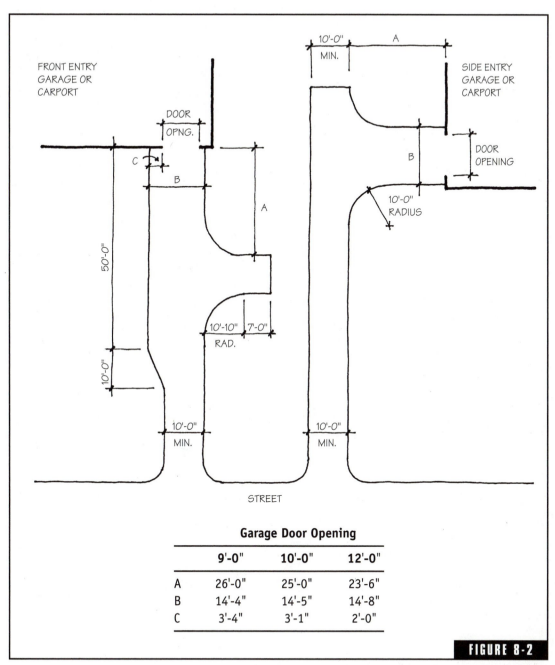

FRONT ENTRY
GARAGE OR
CARPORT

SIDE ENTRY
GARAGE OR
CARPORT

DOOR
OPNG.

10'-0"
MIN.

A

DOOR
OPENING

C

B

B

A

50'-0"

10'-0"
RADIUS

10'-0"

10'-10"   7'-0"

RAD.

10'-0"
MIN.

10'-0"
MIN.

STREET

Garage Door Opening

	9'-0"	10'-0"	12'-0"
A	26'-0"	25'-0"	23'-6"
B	14'-4"	14'-5"	14'-8"
C	3'-4"	3'-1"	2'-0"

FIGURE 8-2

Driveway turnaround. *(from* **Architectural Graphic Standards,** *9th ed).*

thick, with the apron thickness increased to 8–12 in. to support the impact loads of vehicles as they turn into the drive from the street.

If the driveway slopes downhill from the street toward the garage or carport, you will need to install a trench drain to intercept water and channel it away so that the garage doesn't flood when it rains.

The top of a sidewalk slab should be at least 1 in. below door sills leading to the house and about 2 in. above the adjacent ground. Sidewalks should generally be a minimum of 3 ft. wide. A narrower 2-ft. width could be used for a garden path or for service access, but primary entrance walks may look better at 4 ft. or even 6 ft., depending on

TOO STEEP

TOO STEEP

1³/4

12

MAXIMUM GRADE
14% OR 1³/4 FT. RISE
IN 12 FT. RUN

FIGURE 8-3

Driveway slope. *(from Portland Cement Association,* **The Homeowner's Guide to Building with Concrete, Brick and Stone,** *PCA, Skokie, Illinois).*

the size, style, and design of the house. Sidewalks should be 4 in. thick and sloped $1/4$ in. per foot to drain water off the surface. Sidewalks are typically supported on a 2-in.-thick sand bed over the subgrade.

The proportions of riser height and tread depth affect how easy or how difficult steps are to climb. There are some basic rules of thumb to follow. The height of two risers plus the depth of one tread should add up to 25 in. or less. The lower the riser, the deeper the tread should be, and vice versa. Many building codes prescribe a maximum riser height of 7-$1/2$ or 7-$3/4$ in. and a minimum tread depth of 10 in. Lower risers are easier to climb, particularly for the elderly or disabled, and steps with low risers and deep treads are also more gracious than those with steep risers and narrow treads. For flights of steps less than 30 in. high, a good riser height is 7 in. with an 11-in. tread. For flights of steps with a total rise of more than 30 in., individual risers should be about 6 in., with a 12-in. tread. A 5-in. riser and 14-in. tread combination is very comfortable to climb and can make steep grade changes easier to negotiate. A 1-in. nosing can be added to the tread depth as shown in Figure

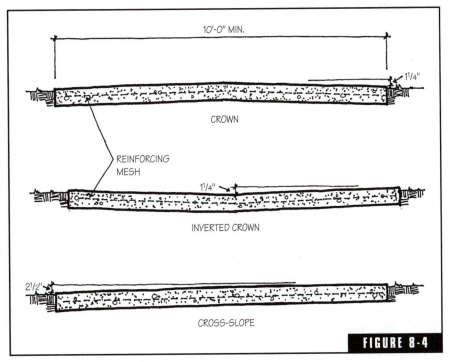

10'-0" MIN.

1$1/4$"

CROWN

REINFORCING MESH

1$1/4$"

INVERTED CROWN

2$1/2$"

CROSS-SLOPE

FIGURE 8-4

Slope to drain rain and melted snow.

8-5 to create a slanting riser face. If space is tight, this can help to accommodate a deeper tread than might otherwise fit.

To measure the total rise and run for steps, use wooden stakes and a string with a line level (Figure 8-6). Divide the total measured rise by the desired riser height to get the number of risers required. Adjust the length of the run as necessary to get the right tread depth for the riser height being used. If space is limited, adjust the riser height and tread depth proportionally until the steps fit within the available space. Flights of three or more steps need a footing, and in cold climates the footing should extend below the frost line for protection against frost heave (Figure 8-7). Steps with more than five or six risers can be broken into two runs separated by a landing that is at least 3 ft. in the direction of travel (Figure 8-8). For stepped ramps in sloping lawns, follow the guidelines in Figure 8-9 for either single or paired risers. Make each riser within a flight of steps the same height and each tread the same depth so that people don't trip.

Steps leading up to a door should have a landing at the top that is at least 3 ft. × 3 ft., but preferably larger for both safety and appearance. Whether the approach is from the front or from the side, the min-

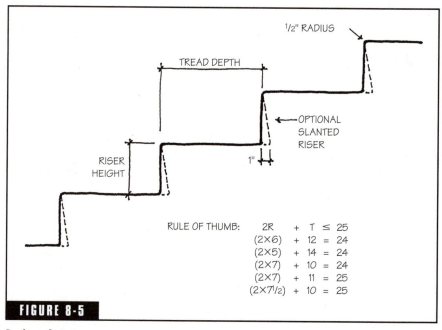

RULE OF THUMB:

$$2R + T \leq 25$$
$$(2 \times 6) + 12 = 24$$
$$(2 \times 5) + 14 = 24$$
$$(2 \times 7) + 10 = 24$$
$$(2 \times 7) + 11 = 25$$
$$(2 \times 7 1/2) + 10 = 25$$

FIGURE 8-5

Design of steps.

imum size must allow enough room for opening a typical screen or storm door safely (Figure 8-10).

The top of a patio slab should be at least 1 in. and preferably 2 in. below door sills leading to the house, and about 2 in. above the adjacent ground. Patio slabs should be 4 in. thick and should be sloped $\frac{1}{4}$ in. per foot to drain water away from the house. The slab should be supported on a 2-in.-thick sand bed as described above for sidewalks. To set the slope for proper drainage, calculate a $\frac{1}{4}$-in.-per-foot drop away from the house. If the patio is 12 ft. wide, for instance, the total slope would be 12 × $\frac{1}{4}$ in. = 3 in. The size and exact shape of the patio should be dictated by available space, existing landscape features, and physical relationship to the building. Square and rectangular shapes will be easiest and most economical to form, but curved shapes may create a more customized appearance.

8.2 Concrete Paving

The methods for installing concrete paving or *flatwork,* as it is sometimes called, is essentially the same for driveways, walks, and patios.

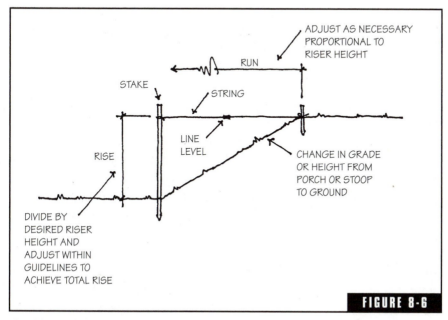

FIGURE 8-6

Figuring total rise and run for steps.

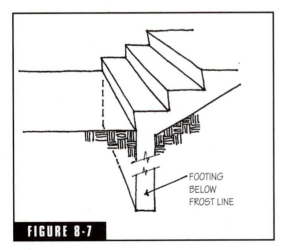

FIGURE 8-7

FOOTING
BELOW
FROST LINE

Footing for steps.

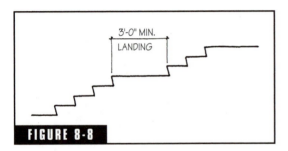

3'-0" MIN.
LANDING

FIGURE 8-8

Split steps.

Excavation, formwork, reinforcement, pouring, finishing, and curing vary only in size and shape. Broomed finishes provide an economical nonslip surface for concrete flatwork, but exposed aggregates, decorative patterns pressed or stamped into the surface, or coloring pigments can change the appearance of concrete paving from mundane to elegant. Minimum recommended concrete strength for exterior residential paving depends on weather exposure

- 2,500 psi in mild climates with no freeze-thaw exposure

- 3,000 psi in moderate climates with only a few freeze-thaw cycles per year and where deicer chemicals are not typically used

- 3,500 psi in severe climates with many freeze-thaw cycles per year and where deicer chemicals are used routinely.

In cold climates, air-entrained portland cement or air-entraining admixtures are required to provide extra freeze-thaw durability. Welded wire reinforcing mesh is typical in exterior concrete paving and should be located $1/3$ up from the bottom of the concrete for maximum strength. Control joints, construction joints, and isolation joints should be located as recommended in Chapter 3 to minimize shrinkage cracking. Exterior concrete paving should be slip-resistant when it's wet to avoid accidents. The most common surface treatments on exterior flatwork are the float finish and the broom finish. A float finish provides moderate slip resistance for flat and slightly sloped surfaces. A broom-finish is safer for surfaces with greater slope, and for maximum safety, the surface can be tooled with a series of parallel grooves running perpendicular to the direction of traffic. Decorative finishes can also be used if the additional cost is

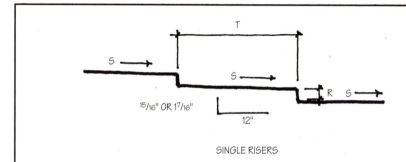

$^{15}/_{16}"$ OR $1^{7}/_{16}"$

12"

SINGLE RISERS

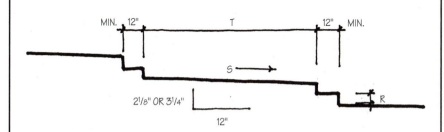

MIN. 12"   T   12" MIN.

$2^{1}/_{8}"$ OR $3^{1}/_{4}"$

12"

PAIRED RISERS

	Paired Risers		Single Risers	
	Minimum	Maximum	Minimum	Maximum
Riser height (R)	4 inches	6 inches	4 inches	6 inches
Tread length (T)	3'-0"	8'-0"	5'-6"	5'-6"
Tread slope (S)	$\frac{1}{8}"$ per ft.	$\frac{1}{4}"$ per ft.	$\frac{1}{8}"$ per ft.	$\frac{1}{4}"$ per ft.
Overall ramp slope	$2\frac{1}{8}"$ per ft.	$3\frac{1}{4}"$ per ft.	$^{15}/_{16}"$ per ft.	$1^{7}/_{16}"$ per ft.

Note: Recommended dimensions provide for one or three easy paces between paired risers and two easy paces between single risers.

FIGURE 8-9

Stepped ramps.

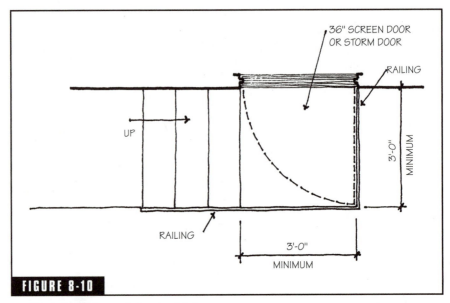

36" SCREEN DOOR OR STORM DOOR

RAILING

UP

3'-0" MINIMUM

RAILING

3'-0" MINIMUM

FIGURE 8-10

Landings should be a minimum of 3 ft.

warranted by a particularly competitive market, or if the home owner is willing to pay extra for this type of custom look.

8.2.1 Driveways

Lay out the rough size and shape of straight driveways using marker stakes at the corners and string lines along the length. Use garden hoses to outline the size and shape of curved driveways. Sprinkle sand or mason's lime, or use a can of spray paint to mark the concrete outline on the ground and excavate a foot or so wider to allow room to build the formwork. To mark the curve of the driveway apron at the street, set a pivot stake and use a string to mark a 3–5 ft. radius (Figure 8-11). In poorly drained areas that are frequently water soaked, excavate deep enough to place a 4–6-in. gravel drainage layer under the concrete, and plan to finish the driveway a little higher off the ground. If necessary, shape the surrounding grade so that runoff drains around rather than over the drive.

If the concrete will be poured directly on the subgrade without gravel, the subgrade should be leveled and the soil tamped with a hand tamper or a mechanical vibrating tamper. If a gravel bed will be

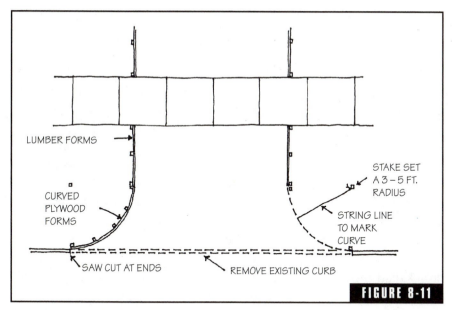

LUMBER FORMS

CURVED
PLYWOOD
FORMS

STAKE SET
A 3 – 5 FT.
RADIUS

STRING LINE
TO MARK
CURVE

SAW CUT AT ENDS

REMOVE EXISTING CURB

FIGURE 8-11

Laying out curve at driveway apron.

used, leave the subgrade undisturbed, smoothing loose surface soil
and filling holes left by stones or roots with sand or gravel. Once the
subgrade is prepared, set string lines to mark the finished concrete
height, drive stakes along the length of the string, and erect the formwork. If a gravel drainage layer is needed, form boards must be tall
enough to accommodate the depth of the gravel as well as the concrete.
Place about half the gravel inside the forms at one time and compact it
with a vibrating tamper, then place the other half and compact again.
If the driveway is large and will require more than one concrete pour,
erect temporary bulkheads where construction joints will separate
pours. Mark on the tops of the form boards the locations of control
joints that must be tooled or saw cut later.

If there is an existing concrete curb at the street, make a neat cut at
either side using a circular saw with a masonry blade, and remove the
curb manually or with a pneumatic hammer. Install an isolation joint
at the cut line on either side of the driveway to separate the existing
curb from the new concrete. If there is an existing sidewalk that will
cross the driveway, the top of the new concrete should be level with
the finish surface of the sidewalk. At the sides of a driveway with an
existing street curb, build curved plywood formwork tall enough to

allow for the thickness of the driveway slab and the drainage layer, plus the height of the curb. The concrete thickness tapers down from the edge of the curb to the flat surface of the driveway.

Start pouring concrete in the farthest corner of the forms. As soon as the first few feet of the driveway are poured, begin striking off or *screeding* the surface level with the top of the forms. Use a length of 2 × 4 that is slightly wider than the forms. For wide driveways, a 2 × 6 will be stronger, and a temporary screed may be needed down the middle for striking and leveling drives wider than 20 ft. Continue transporting and dumping and screeding the concrete until the forms are full. The easiest way to do the apron at a street with existing curbs is to set the formwork in two parts. Set temporary formwork at the sides of the flat center section of the apron to use as strike off boards (Figure 8-12). These will be removed as soon as the concrete in the center section is poured and struck, and the concrete in the side sections can be poured immediately afterwards. Shape the tapered concrete at the edges of the driveway apron by hand or with a wood float, tapering it from the top of the street curb and sloping it down into the flat surface of the driveway (Figure 8-13).

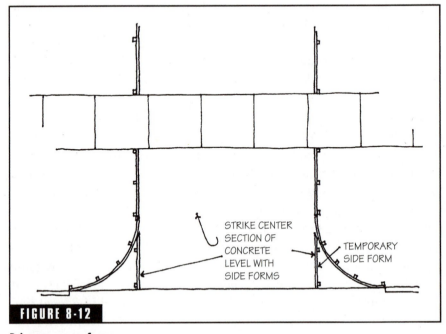

STRIKE CENTER SECTION OF CONCRETE LEVEL WITH SIDE FORMS

TEMPORARY SIDE FORM

FIGURE 8-12

Driveway apron forms.

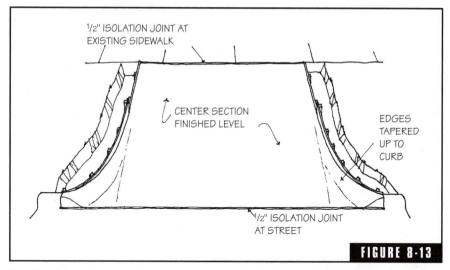

FIGURE 8-13

Forming driveway apron edges.

8.2.2 Sidewalks

The site preparation, formwork, pouring, and finishing operations for sidewalks are essentially the same as for driveways. Because they do not carry the weight of automobiles, gravel beds are not typically used under sidewalks unless drainage is very poor, but a layer of coarse sand is used as a cushion, leveling bed, and capillary break to keep soil moisture from continuously saturating the concrete and accelerating corro-

---

MAKING A SLOPED STRIKE OFF BOARD

If you want the driveway to be higher in the middle than the edges so that water will drain to both sides, or if you want it lower in the middle to channel water away, you will need to make a sloped strike off board. For a crowned driveway, lay a 2 × 4 and a 2 × 6 edge to edge and nail them together in the middle by overlaying a piece of scrap wood. Insert small wooden blocks or wedges at the ends to hold the boards apart the required distance (Figure 8-14). Nail a piece of scrap wood near each end to hold the shape. For a driveway that drains toward the middle, nail scraps of wood at the ends first, and then drive a wedge or block in the middle before nailing.

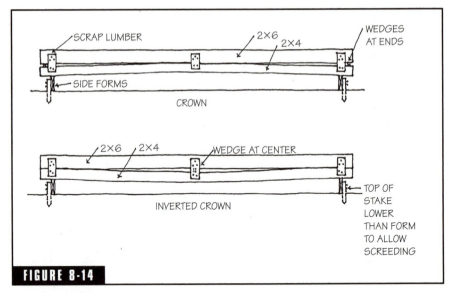

FIGURE 8-14

Sloped strikeoff board.

sion of the reinforcement. Some authorities also believe that a sand bed helps the concrete cure more evenly. The sand should be leveled to a 2-in. uniform thickness using two 2-×-4's nailed together so that one will slide along the top of the form boards and the other will drag the sand surface (Figure 8-15). Sidewalks on flat ground often slope $\frac{1}{8}$ to $\frac{1}{4}$ in. per foot from one side to the other to drain water. Calculate the amount of slope needed for the width, and set the string on one side lower by that amount. For example, a 3-ft. sidewalk sloped $\frac{1}{8}$ in. per foot should be $\frac{3}{8}$ in. lower on one side than the other, so the string should be set $\frac{3}{8}$ in. lower. Set the forms so that the tops of the boards align with the string (Figure 8-16). The depth of the sand bed should vary so that the concrete will be a uniform 4 in. thick. On the low side, the sand should be a minimum of 1-$\frac{1}{2}$ in. thick. Once the forms are set correctly for the slope, the sand can be struck to the same slope using the method described above with two 2-×-4s nailed together so that one will slide along the top of the form boards and the other will drag the sand surface.

8.2.3 Steps

Concrete steps provide a durable and low-maintenance approach to a porch or patio and can be used in conjunction with either concrete or

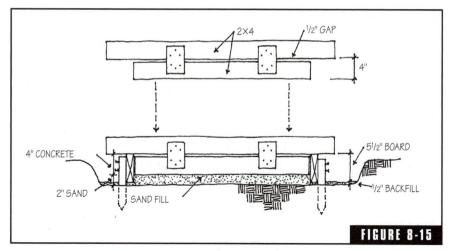

Leveling sand bed.

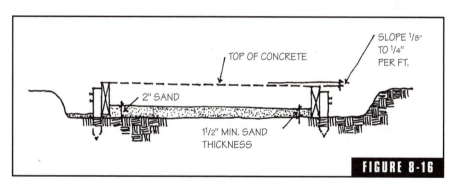

Sidewalk slope.

masonry sidewalks. First calculate the rise and run of the steps, add the landing depth, then excavate the necessary length and width, allowing extra room for building the forms. Dig out the excavation to a uniform 6-in. depth. If you need a footing at the bottom of the steps, form and pour it first as described in Chapter 6, and leave several steel reinforcing dowels sticking out of the top of the footing to tie the steps and footing together.

Forms for steps can be built of lumber or of plywood. The side forms for steps with sloped landings and treads are easiest to build out of 3/4-in. exterior-grade plywood. Measure from the bottom of the excavation up to about 1 in. below the door sill and mark this dimension on the short side of a full 4-ft. × 8-ft. sheet of plywood. Draw a straight line perpendicular to the long side of the plywood to equal the depth of the landing. Allow a slight slope away from the building of about 2% for drainage (approximately 1/4 in. per foot). If the landing is 3 ft. wide, this would be a total slope of 3/4 in. from back to front. For a 4-ft. landing, a total of 1 in. Measure down 1 in. and draw a line between this mark and the height of the landing at the edge of the plywood sheet (Figure 8-17). Next, use a carpenter's square to draw the outline of each riser and tread at the calculated height and depth. Remember that there will be an extra 6 in. of plywood at the bottom of the form that will be below grade. To create a slanted riser, angle the riser face backward 1 in. as shown. This will produce a "sawtooth"-shaped profile. To allow water to drain off the steps easily, each tread should also be sloped. Measure up 3/16 to 1/4 in. at the back corner of each tread to get a 2% slope and draw a line to the front edge (Figure 8-18). Cut the first plywood form, then use it to draw the profile for the form for the other side. With lumber side forms, slanted risers are created by using wood cleats at the sides to set the proper angle and hold the riser boards in place (Figure 8-19).

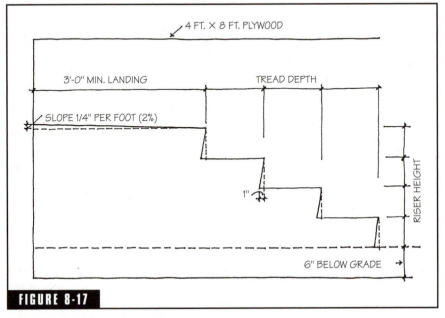

FIGURE 8-17

Making plywood forms for steps.

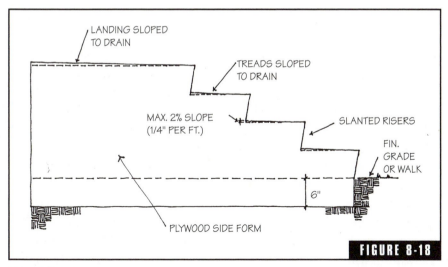

Sloped stair treads.

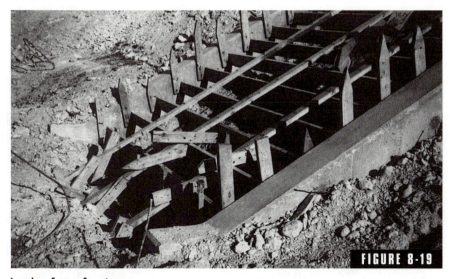

Lumber forms for steps.

Position the side forms for the steps using a carpenter's square to make sure they are at right angles to the walls of the house. Use a level to check for proper slope and plumb, then drive stakes into the ground 12–18 in. apart. Leave the stakes nearest the wall several inches taller than the tops of the forms because they will have to support a cross brace that will be added later.

The risers are formed by ripping 2 × 8 or 2 × 6 lumber to the exact riser height and cutting them to a length that will fit between the side forms. The bottom edge of the riser form must be beveled so that the entire surface of the tread is exposed for troweling and finishing. Starting with the top step, nail or screw the riser forms between the side forms using double-headed nails or screws to make form stripping easier. Step forms may often have to resist a considerable amount of weight from the concrete, so they should be braced and shored adequately. Shore the side forms with 1 × 4 or 2 × 4 braces, and for steps 3 ft. or more in width, reinforce the riser forms to prevent them from bulging. Drive a stake near the center of the bottom riser, nail a 2 × 6 to the stake, and use small cleats to hold the risers firmly in place (Figure 8-20). Finally, nail a cross tie between the two side form stakes nearest the wall.

To prevent the concrete from sticking to the wall of the house, paint or trowel a coat of mastic onto it. This will form an isolation joint and keep the concrete from cracking along this intersection when it shrinks as it cures. To reduce the volume of concrete that will be needed, you can fill the center portion of the step form with compacted soil, gravel,

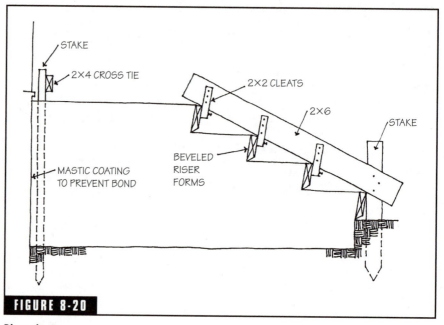

FIGURE 8-20

Riser cleats.

brick, stone, or broken concrete. Be sure to keep the fill at least 4 in. away from the side forms, the riser forms, and the top of the treads and landing. This will assure that you get a minimum 4-in. thickness of concrete over and around the fill material. Place a sheet of wire mesh reinforcement in the form (Figure 8-21), holding it back from the edges about 3 in. so that it will be completely embedded. Start pouring the concrete in the bottom step. Fill the next step with a shovel, tamp the concrete to fill in corners, and settle the concrete against the forms by tapping the outside of the forms lightly with a hammer.

Steps that are not supported by earth fill must be self-supporting. The bottom form should be made of 1 × 6 lumber because it will carry considerable weight until the concrete cures and attains strength. Supporting posts under the form should be 4 × 4s. To provide the structural capacity needed, steel reinforcing bars are required to add tensile strength. Reinforcing bars should be sized and spaced according to the length and thickness of the steps (Figure 8-22). Forms and shoring should be left in place for at least one week before the concrete can support itself.

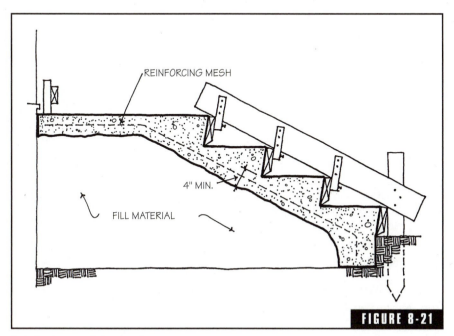

REINFORCING MESH

4" MIN.

FILL MATERIAL

FIGURE 8-21

Reinforcing mesh in step forms.

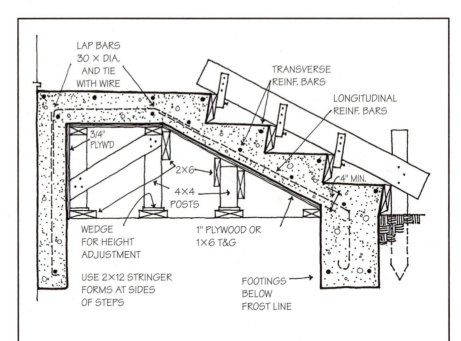

Concrete Dimensions		Reinforcing Bars			
		Longitudinal		Transverse	
Length, ft.	Thk., in.	Size	Spacing, in.	Size	Spacing, in.
2-3	4	#2	10	#2	12-18
3-4	4	#2	$5^1/_2$	#2	12-18
4-5	5	#2	$4^1/_2$	#2	18-24
5-6	5	#3	7	#2	18-24
6-7	6	#3	6	#2	18-24
7-8	6	#3	4	#2	18-24
8-9	7	#4	7	#2	18-24

FIGURE 8-22

Forms and reinforcing for self-supporting steps. *(from Dezettel, Masons and Builders Library).*

8.2.4 Patios

Concrete patios are built the same as sidewalks except that the size and shape will dictate a different pattern of control joints and a drainage slope of $1/_4$ in. per ft. away from the house is recommended. If the patio is 12 ft. wide, for instance, the total slope would be $12 \times 1/_4$

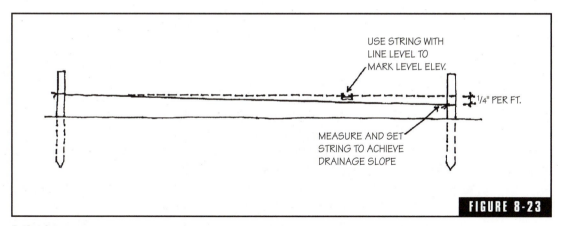

Patio slope.

in. = 3 in. Mark three in. down on the stake at the outer edge, and set the string for the side forms at this mark (Figure 8-23). The bottom of the excavation should remain level, with the concrete thickness varied to achieve drainage slope. If the ground slopes sharply, the forms may have to be deeper at the outer edge (Figure 8-24).

8.3   Masonry Paving

Clay, concrete, and stone masonry can all be used for residential sidewalk, patio, and driveway paving. There are many different types of paving units and several different methods of installation. Masonry paving systems essentially fall into two different categories and are classified as rigid or flexible, depending on whether they are laid with or without mortar. *Rigid masonry paving* is laid in a mortar setting bed with mortar joints between the units. *Flexible masonry paving* or mortarless paving is laid on a sand bed with sanded joints and contains no mortar underneath or between the units. Either type of paving can be designed to support pedestrian or vehicular traffic, and selection of the type of paving system to be used will depend to a large extent on the desired aesthetic effect.

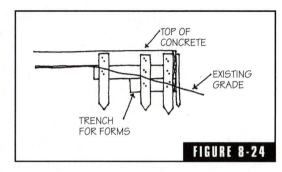

Concrete forms at raised patio edge.

Rigid paving systems with mortared joints create a formal look while flexible systems with sanded joints are more rustic in appearance. One may be more appropriate than the other on any given project, depending on the style of the house and the type of landscaping that is planned. Concrete masonry pavers are designed for and typically used in flexible paving systems. Brick and natural stone are used in both rigid and flexible paving systems.

Rigid masonry paving is laid on a mortar setting bed over a reinforced concrete base. The base may be either a new or an existing concrete slab. A Type M masonry mortar should be used for both the setting bed and the joints in outdoor paving exposed to the weather. Some authorities believe that an air-entrained mortar can improve freeze-thaw resistance in masonry paving in the same way that air-entrained concrete improves the winter durability of concrete paving. Use either an air-entrained portland cement mixed with mason's lime or an air-entrained masonry cement in the proportions recommended in Chapter 4 for a Type M mix. The mortar setting bed should be about $^1/_2$ in. thick.

Flexible masonry paving systems for residential sidewalks and patios are typically laid on a sand bed placed directly over an undisturbed soil subgrade. For driveways, a gravel base must first be installed over the subgrade to provide additional stability and moisture protection. The sand layer acts as a leveling bed which compensates for irregularities in the soil or gravel surface and provides a smooth substrate for placement of the units. A sheet membrane must be installed to prevent sand from settling into a gravel base. Sheet membranes are also installed in flexible paving systems to discourage weed growth. Roofing felt, polyethylene film, and special weedblock landscaping fabrics are all suitable because they are moisture- and rot-resistant. Pavers are generally butted together with only the minimal spacing between adjacent units caused by irregularities of size and shape. The joints are swept full of dry sand to fill between units. Even though mortarless masonry paving is flexible and has the ability to move slightly to accommodate expansion and contraction, it is recommended that expansion joints be placed adjacent to fixed objects such as curbs and walls.

8.3.1 Brick Paving

Modular paving bricks that are designed to be laid with mortar have the same 3-$^5/_8$ in.-$\times$7-$^5/_8$ in. face dimensions as ordinary modular wall brick, but they are solid and do not have holes cored through the middle. When laid with standard $3/8$-in. mortar joints, this creates a 4-in. × 8-in. module. Paving bricks that are designed to be laid butted together without mortar are a full 4-in. × 8-in. face size so that patterns will still lay out to a 4-in. module. This makes it easy to plan the dimensions of the paving based on whole and half-size units to minimize the amount of cutting. It is important to use the correct size unit for the type of paving planned. All bond patterns can be achieved with *actual* 4 × 8-in. units laid dry and tight, or with *nominal* 4 × 8 in. units laid with $3/8$-in. mortar or sand joints. Patterns that require the width of the unit to be exactly one-half the length may not be laid dry and tight using nominal dimension units designed for mortar joints, and vice versa.

Many different effects can be achieved with standard rectangular brick pavers by varying the bond pattern in which the units are laid (Figure 8-25). For driveways with units laid in a sand bed, choose a pattern that does not have continuous joints in the same direction as the path of travel. These will be unstable because the units will have a tendency over time to slide forward or backward because of the repeated braking and acceleration of cars. If you use a pattern such as the running bond, be sure the continuous joints are laid perpendicular to the path of the vehicles. A pattern with the units laid in a more intricate design like the herringbone or basketweave will usually prove to be most stable against sliding, displacement, and the formation of ruts.

Concrete slab bases for rigid brick paving should be 4 in. thick and reinforced with welded wire fabric as for a driveway, sidewalk, or patio slab as described above. Existing concrete slabs can also be used to support rigid brick paving as long as there are no major structural cracks. Minor cracks will not be harmful, but they should be patched. If you pour a new concrete slab to serve as a rigid paving base, make sure that it slopes $1/4$ in. per foot to drain water. Depending on the size and shape of your project, and the contour of the ground around it, the surface can slope to one side or be crowned in the middle to shed water off both sides. Be sure to excavate deep enough to allow for the thickness of the concrete slab plus the thickness of the mortar setting bed and the pavers. Relocate any existing downspouts that would drain onto the paving, or use flexible drain pipe to route the water runoff around the paving. Finish the concrete surface with a wood float finish so that it

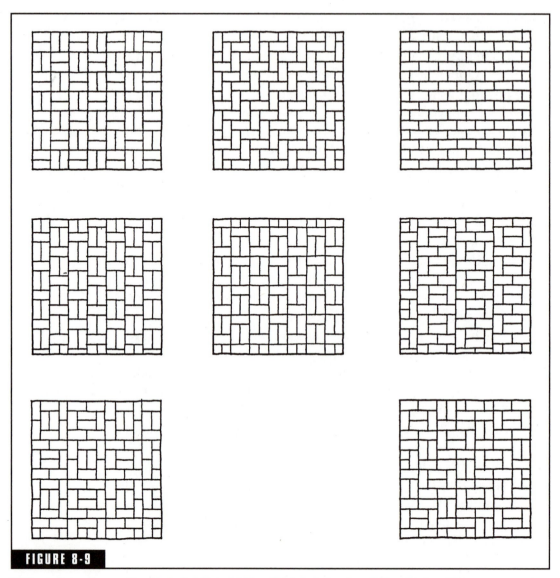

FIGURE 8-9

Brick paving patterns. *(from* Technical Note 14 Rev., *Brick Industry Association, Reston, VA).*

will form a good bond with the mortar setting bed. Always allow a new slab to cure for several days before laying the mortar bed.

For rigid brick paving, lay out the length and width of the area in a dry run without mortar to check the spacing. Use your finger or a piece of $3/8$-in. plywood to allow for the thickness of the mortar joints. Adjust the spacing if necessary to make a better fit. Expansion joints must be provided in rigid masonry paving to accommodate thermal and moisture movements. Joints should generally be located parallel to curbs and edges, at 90° turns and angles, and around interruptions in the paving surface (Figure 8-26). Fillers for brick masonry expansion joints must be compressible to accommodate the natural expansion of brick units as they absorb moisture (Figure 8-27).

Clean the top of the concrete slab and apply the mortar setting bed. This setting bed will not only hold the pavers in place, but it will also help to compensate for minor irregularities in the slab surface. If you are working on an existing slab and it is not properly sloped to drain water, you can use the mortar setting bed to achieve some drainage. Maintain a minimum thickness of $3/8$ in. and a maximum thickness of 1 in. Place the mortar, then smooth the surface using the flat side and score the surface using the notched edge of a metal trowel. Place the pavers and mortar joints in one of three ways.

- Using a conventional mason's trowel, butter two sides of each paver and set them firmly into the mortar setting bed. If necessary, tap the pavers down with the trowel handle and use a mason's level to check the surface to make sure it is level. Remove excess surface mortar with the edge of the trowel.

- Place the units on the mortar setting bed, leaving the joints open. After the pavers have been installed and set up for a day or two, wet them with a garden hose and fill the joints with a thin mortar mix about the consistency of sour cream. Use a coffee can or other small container that can be squeezed to form a spout, and work the mortar into the joints with the point of a trowel. Use a wet sponge or cloth to clean excess mortar off the brick surfaces before it dries.

- Instead of the usual mortar setting bed, lay the units on a cushion of 1 part portland cement and 3 to 6 parts damp, loose sand. Leave the joints open, spacing the units apart with your finger. After all the pavers are in place, sweep the open joints full of the same dry portland cement and sand mixture. Be careful, especially at first, not to dislodge the pavers as you sweep. Sweep excess material from the surface and spray the paving with a fine water mist until the joints are completely saturated. Keep the paving moist for at least three days to assure proper curing of the cement.

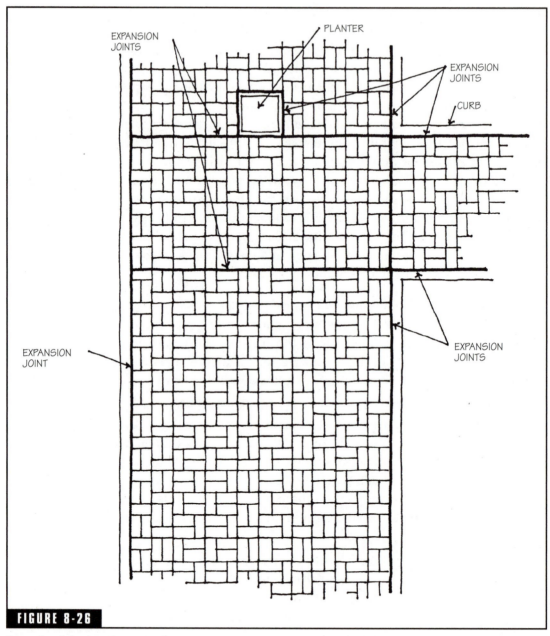

Expansion joint locations.

Use a string line to maintain the coursing in straight lines. Wrap nylon line or string around a brick, stretch the line across the working area, and wrap the other end around another brick (Figure 8-28). On small projects, lay the pavers in complete courses working across the slab. On larger projects, lay the pavers in smaller, rectangular sections. To allow for normal expansion and contraction, rigid brick paving should be isolated from fixed objects and other construction such as curbs, planters, and concrete paving. A

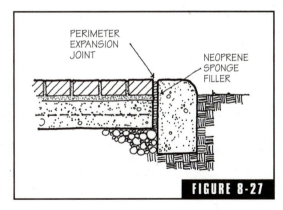

Perimeter expansion joint.

soft expansion joint filler should be placed between the two elements to allow them to expand and contract independently. If you use either of the wet mortar methods of setting the pavers, you will need to tool the joint surfaces. The joints are ready for tooling when the mortar is "thumbprint" hard. That is, when you can press your thumb against the mortar and leave a print impression without mortar sticking to your thumb. Use a rounded jointer to produce a concave shaped joint.

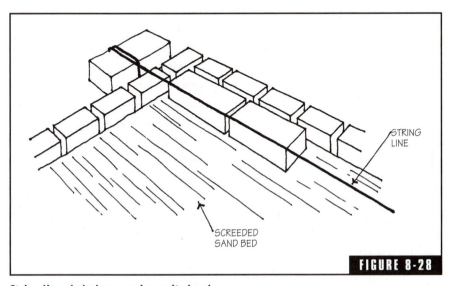

String lines help keep paving units level.

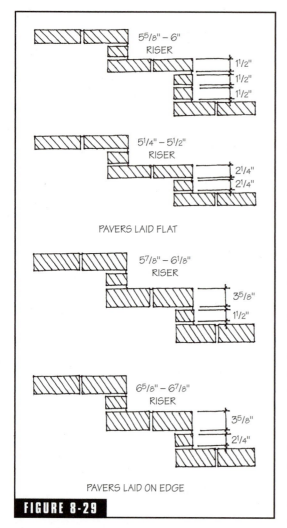

55/8" – 6"
RISER

11/2"
11/2"
11/2"

51/4" – 51/2"
RISER

21/4"
21/4"

PAVERS LAID FLAT

57/8" – 61/8"
RISER

35/8"

11/2"

65/8" – 67/8"
RISER

35/8"

21/4"

PAVERS LAID ON EDGE

FIGURE 8-29

Riser height variations for brick steps.

If a brick walk or patio includes a sharp change in grade, it may require the construction of a set of steps for access. For maximum stability, the steps should be installed on a mortar setting bed over a concrete base, even if the walk or patio itself is laid as mortarless paving on a sand bed.

The size of brick pavers you use will have some effect on the height of risers created when the bricks are stacked up. Figure 8-29 shows four different ways of creating risers using different paver thicknesses, either laying the brick flat or setting it on edge, and by varying the mortar joint thickness from $3/8$ in to $1/2$ in. This will give you some flexibility in achieving the exact riser height you need so that they add up to the correct overall height. The exposed length of the pavers as shown produces a tread width of 12 in. Steps should be at least as wide as the sidewalk leading up to them. A width that is a multiple of 8 in. will accommodate the use of 2-$1/4$-in. pavers that are either laid on edge or laid flat (Figure 8-30). A 4-in.-thick stepped concrete base reinforced with welded wire fabric or reinforcing bars should be used to support the brick pavers (Figure 8-31). Form and pour the reinforced concrete base as described elsewhere in this chapter for concrete steps. Finish the concrete surface with a slightly rough texture so that it will form a good bond with the mortar setting bed. Allow the concrete to cure for several days before laying the mortar bed. Either slope the surface of the treads on the concrete base for drainage, or pour the concrete flat and slope the brick treads by varying the mortar bed thickness.

Mortarless brick paving can be laid either on a sand bed over a compacted gravel or soil base (Figure 8-32). The sand acts as a cushion and

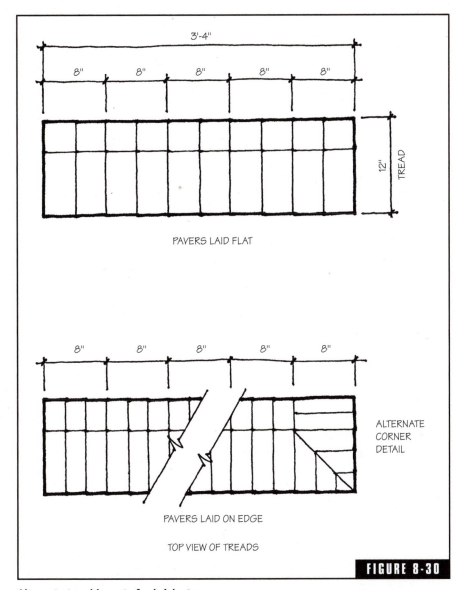

3'-4"

8"   8"   8"   8"   8"

12" TREAD

PAVERS LAID FLAT

8"   8"   8"   8"   8"

ALTERNATE
CORNER
DETAIL

PAVERS LAID ON EDGE

TOP VIEW OF TREADS

FIGURE 8-30

Alternate tread layouts for brick steps.

a leveling bed to compensate for minor irregularities in the base. If the soil is naturally well drained and stable, the sand bed for sidewalks and patios can be placed directly on the excavated subgrade. If the natural drainage is poor or the soil is soft, you will need a gravel drainage base below the sand bed. The required thickness of the gravel

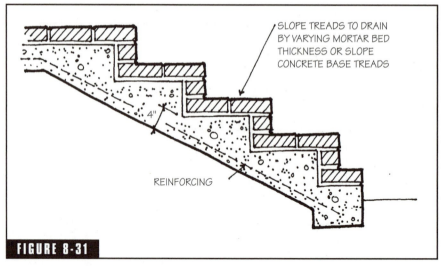

FIGURE 8-31

Concrete base for brick steps.

base depends on the strength of the underlying soil, the thickness of paver that will be used, and whether the base must support foot traffic or cars and light trucks. For residential driveways, a 4-in. thick gravel or crushed stone base plus a 2-in. sand setting bed is required, and for patios or sidewalks a 2-in. gravel base plus a 2-in. sand bed. Mortarless paving systems can also be laid on existing asphalt if a 2-in. sand leveling bed is added.

Mortarless brick paving requires some method of containment at the edges to keep the units from sliding. A soldier course of bricks set

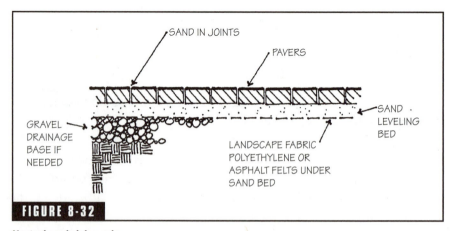

FIGURE 8-32

Mortarless brick paving.

on end, landscape timbers, concrete curbs, or one of the newer metal edging systems will all provide the required stability (Figure 8-33). The metal edging is a simple and easy method, and the metal is concealed below the ground, so it does not change the normal appearance of the masonry paving. Edging should be installed before the paving units, and the pavers worked toward the established perimeters. Modular planning in the location of perimeter edging can eliminate or reduce the amount of cutting required to fit the units. To install a brick soldier course edging, stretch a string line between the wooden stakes to act as a guide for the height and alignment of the edging. If your pavers are 2-1/4 in. thick, make the trench about 2-1/2 in. wide and about 4 in. deep. If your pavers are 1-1/2 in. thick, make the trench about 2 in. wide and about 5 in. deep. Put a little sand in the bottom of the trench, and place brick pavers on end with the flat side against the string line (Figure 8-34). Tamp the pavers down with a trowel handle to get the right height. Fill in around the edging with soil. The units should stick up above the slab high enough to cover the depth of the 2-in. sand setting bed plus the thickness of the

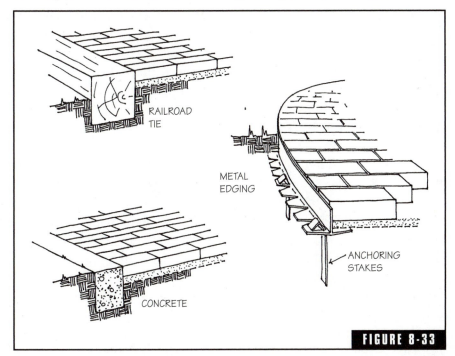

RAILROAD TIE

METAL EDGING

CONCRETE

ANCHORING STAKES

FIGURE 8-33

Edging for brick pavers.

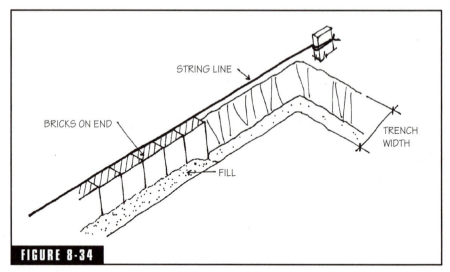

STRING LINE

BRICKS ON END

TRENCH
WIDTH

FILL

FIGURE 8-34

Brick soldier edging.

pavers when they are laid flat (2-$\frac{1}{4}$ in. or 1-$\frac{1}{2}$ in.). Butt the edge pavers snugly against one another. To install metal edging, follow the manufacturer's instructions.

To keep weeds from growing up between the unmortared paving joints, install a layer of polyethylene or asphalt-saturated felt building paper over the soil subgrade or the gravel base. Lap adjoining sections over one another at least 2 in. Fill the paving area inside the edging with ordinary construction sand. Use a straight length of 2 × 4 with a length of 1 × 4 nailed to it to "screed" the sand to a uniform 2-in. thickness (Figure 8-35). Place the pavers on the sand bed, butting them tightly together and tamping them into place with a rubber mallet or a trowel handle. Use a string line to maintain the coursing in straight lines. If you have to kneel on the sand bed at first to lay the brick, put down a piece of plywood to keep from making depressions in the surface. After you have laid a few courses, you should be able to move around and kneel on the pavers instead. Periodically check the surface of the paving with a mason's level to assure that the pavers are level or are sloping uniformly in the correct direction. When all the units are in place, sweep the joints full of sand to stabilize the brick. Fill the joints again in a few days if the sand settles a little.

8.3.2 Concrete Masonry Paving

Bond patterns for concrete masonry pavers are dictated by the shape of the units. Different manufacturers have patented designs, usually available in a variety of colors (Figure 8-36). Concrete masonry

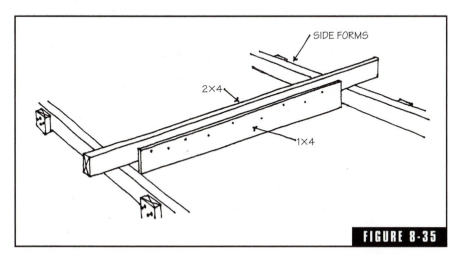

SIDE FORMS

2×4

1×4

FIGURE 8-35

Screeded sand.

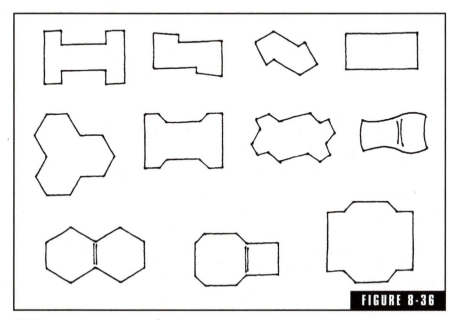

FIGURE 8-36

CMU pavers.

pavers are always laid on a sand setting bed, but the installation method is a little different than for mortarless brick paving. If the soil is naturally well drained and stable, the sand bed for sidewalks and patios can be placed directly on the excavated subgrade. If the natural drainage is poor or the soil is soft, you will need to add a 4-in. gravel drainage base below the sand for driveways, or a 2-in. gravel base for patios or sidewalks.

Like mortarless brick paving, concrete masonry pavers require some method of containment at the edges to keep the units from sliding. Some alternative solutions include landscape timbers, concrete curbs, or a metal edging system as shown above for brick paving. Some paver manufacturers make a special curb unit which is used to form the edges of the paved area. To install the paver edging, stretch a string line between wooden stakes to act as a guide for the height and alignment of the edging. Paver curbs are usually set even with or slightly higher than the finished surface of the paving. Make a trench alongside the excavated area that is the same width and full depth of the curb unit. Put a little sand in the bottom of the trench, and set the pavers on end with the flat side against the string line. Tamp the pavers down with a trowel handle or rubber mallet to get the right height. Butt the edge pavers snugly against one another.

Place a weed-block membrane as described above for mortarless brick paving. Fill the excavated area inside the edging with a loose layer of well-graded fine and coarse sand. Allow about one cubic yard of sand for every 150 sq. ft. of paving area. Keep the sand stockpile and any exposed sand in the paving bed dry during wet weather by covering it with plastic sheeting. Screed the sand to a uniform thickness of about 1-3/4 in. using a straight length of 2 × 4 with a length of 1 × 4 nailed to it. Do not stand or kneel on the sand bed before setting the pavers. Beginning in one corner, place the pavers on the sand bed leaving only about 1/8 in. between units. Use a string line to maintain the coursing in straight lines. At the end of each work day, tamp or vibrate the units to compact the sand bed and settle the pavers into place making a single pass over the pavers with a vibrating plate compactor (Figure 8-37). Spread dry sand over the pavers and fill the joints by sweeping the sand around. Make a second pass with the vibrating plate to complete compaction, and sweep excess sand from the surface.

FIGURE 8-37

Vibrating plate compactor.

8.3.3 Natural Stone Paving

A flagstone patio or walk is simple to build and is much like fitting the pieces of a puzzle together. Flagstone paving may be set on a 2-in. compacted sand setting bed or on a mortar setting bed.

For a sand bed installation, fill the excavated area with ordinary construction sand screeded to the correct thickness. Starting in one corner, place the stones on the sand and tamp them into place with a rubber mallet or a trowel handle. Make sure that the stones are solidly bedded and do not wobble. Some stone can be very brittle, and if it is not solidly supported can crack at points of high stress concentration. If necessary, dig out a little sand to make the bedding on uneven stones more solid. Arrange the straight edges of the stone toward the outside perimeter, and fit the irregular edges together, leaving about $1/2$ in. to $3/4$ in. between the stones (Figure 8-38). Trim individual stones with a hammer and chisel if needed, and use a mason's level to maintain the paving roughly level. When all the stones are in place, sweep the joints full of sand. Wet the sand with a garden hose to compact it and then sweep more sand into the joints. Fill the joints again in a few days if the sand settles a little.

FIGURE 8-38

Flagstone walkway edge.

A mortar set flagstone walk or patio must be set on a reinforced concrete base and is installed in much the same way as rigid brick paving. A Type S or Type M mortar works best. After the stone has been set into the mortar bed and allowed to cure for a day or two, fill the joints with a thin mortar mix using a coffee can or other small container that can be squeezed to form a spout. Work the mortar into the joints with the point of a trowel and use a wet sponge or cloth to clean excess mortar off the stone surfaces before it dries. Flagstone can also be laid on a dry cushion of 1 part portland cement and 3 to 6 parts damp, loose sand with the joints filled with the same dry cement and sand mixture. After removing excess material from the surface, spray the paving with a fine water mist until the joints are completely saturated. The paving must be kept moist for at least 3 days to assure complete cement hydration.

Masonry Garden Walls

A freestanding masonry wall can provide privacy for a patio, define the perimeters of a lawn or garden area, or act as a buffer to street noise. Masonry garden walls add an elegant touch to high-end homes and require far less maintenance by the homeowner than ordinary wood fences. Freestanding walls do not have a building frame or stud wall to provide lateral stability, so they must resist overturning forces with a wide footing, a height that is proportional to the wall thickness, and the stiffening effect of piers or pilasters.

9.1   Footings

Concrete footings provide stability against overturning for freestanding masonry walls. An inadequately sized footing or one that is set too shallow in the ground can cause the wall to lean. The bottom of a garden wall footing must be below the winter frost line to avoid displacement by frost heave (refer to the frost depth map in Figure 6-3 or consult your local building department). In warm climates where the frost depth is close to the surface, the bottom of the footing should be a minimum of 12 in. below grade so that it is supported on firm, undisturbed soil. For footings that must be set very deep, it will be more economical to build a concrete "stem" on the footing rather than building several courses of brick below the ground level. The soil under the footing must be of

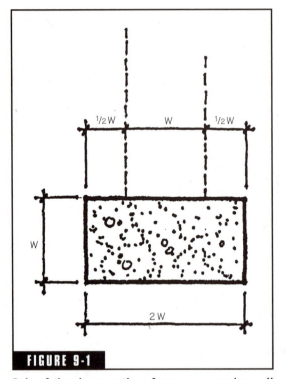

FIGURE 9-1

Rule-of-thumb proportions for masonry garden wall and screen wall footings.

sufficient strength to withstand the weight of the wall without uneven settlement. If the soil under the footing is soft or unstable, or if the area is not well drained, a 6–8-in. layer of compacted gravel should be placed in the bottom of the footing excavation. If the ground slopes substantially along the length of the wall, both the concrete footing and the wall may have to be stepped to follow the slope. For flatter slopes, build a footing that is deep enough so that its bottom is below the frost line but at the same elevation for the full length of the wall. Refer to Chapter 6 for details on concrete footings.

Industry rules of thumb recommend that the footing thickness should be the same as the width of the wall it supports, and the footing width should be a minimum of two times the thickness of the wall it supports (Figure 9-1). For an 8-in.-thick wall, this would mean a 16-in.-wide footing, 8 in. thick. Minimum concrete strength should be 2,500 psi. Formwork should be constructed in the same way as formwork for foundation wall footings. Where piers or pilasters are incorporated into the design of a wall, the footing must be wider as well (Figure 9-2).

9.2   Brick Garden Walls

Brick walls can be built in many sizes, shapes, and styles. The most common type of brick garden wall is a double-wythe wall with a finished thickness of about 8 in. Most building codes require that for lateral stability, maximum wall height should not exceed 18 times the wall thickness. An 8-in. wall can be a maximum of 12 ft. high (18 × 8 in. = 144 in. = 12 ft.). In most instances, residential walls will not exceed 6 or 8 ft., and some building codes and subdivision ordinances restrict wall heights to 6 ft.

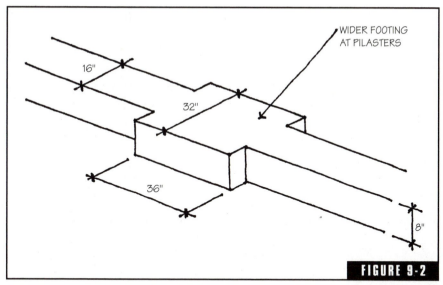

WIDER FOOTING
AT PILASTERS

16"

32"

36"

8"

FIGURE 9-2

A wider footing is required at pilasters.

Nominal Wall Thickness (t), Inches	Maximum Distance Between Piers or Pilasters (18 t), feet
4	6
6	9
8	12
12	18

FIGURE 9-3

Recommended pilaster spacing for masonry screen walls and garden walls.

Supporting piers or pilasters are used to provide additional lateral stability for freestanding masonry walls. The usual limitation is the same as the height-to-thickness ratio, or 18 times the thickness of the wall (Figure 9-3). This means that an 8-in.-thick wall would require pilasters every 12 ft. Pilasters are basically just thicker wall sections which add stiffness. They can be used as decorative features even when they're not needed for extra strength because they give the wall a different look. Small pilasters can be built to project on only one side

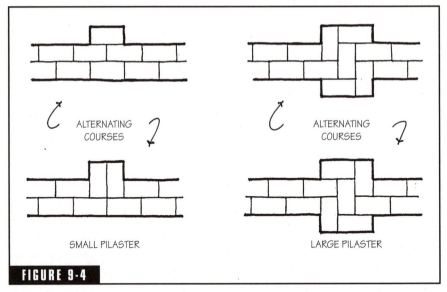

ALTERNATING
COURSES

ALTERNATING
COURSES

SMALL PILASTER

LARGE PILASTER

FIGURE 9-4

Masonry wall pilasters.

of the wall, and larger pilasters to project on both sides (Figure 9-4). The small pilasters are adequate for walls up to 4 ft. high, and the large ones for walls up to 6 or 8 ft. high. Alternating courses of brick in the wall must overlap the brick in the pilaster to form a strong interlocking structure. If you live in an area that is subject to earthquakes, you must use a special seismic design and will need the services of a structural engineer.

Brick walls are usually laid in a running bond pattern, and the two wythes are tied together with $3/16$-in.-diameter galvanized steel wire Z-ties or corrugated sheet metal ties (Figure 9-5). Corrugated ties are less expensive than the wire ties, but they have to be spaced closer together, so more are needed. Most building codes require that rigid wire ties support a maximum of $4\text{-}1/2$ sq. ft. of wall area and be spaced a maximum of 24 in. on center vertically (every 9th course of brick) and 36 in. on center horizontally. Corrugated ties or flexible ties may support a maximum of $2\text{-}2/3$ sq. ft. of wall area and the spacing should be reduced to a maximum of 16 in. on center vertically (every 6th course of brick) and 24 in. on center horizontally. Every other row of ties should be offset so that a staggered pattern is created (Figure 9-6). The ties must be properly embedded, with mortar completely surrounding

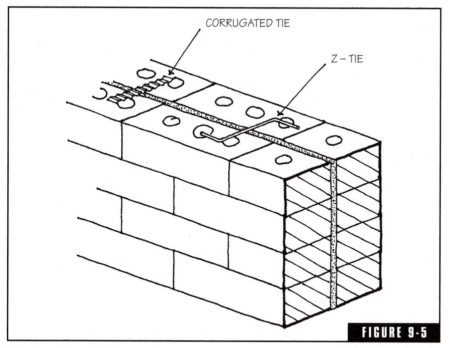

Double-wythe wall with metal ties.

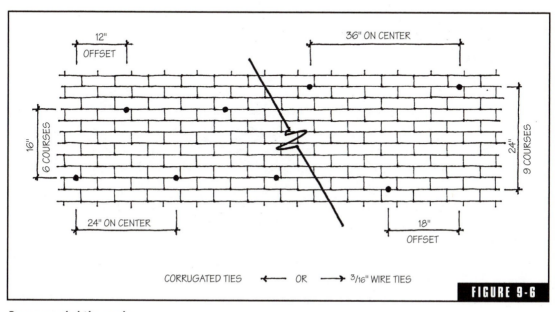

Recommended tie spacing.

them on all sides. Spread the mortar first and then place the ties, pressing them down into the middle of the mortar.

Double-wythe brick walls can also be laid up in a number of other bond patterns by turning some of the units crosswise in the wall as masonry headers. Different patterns can be created by alternating the header and stretcher units in different ways. The Flemish bond, English bond, and common or American bond are simple patterns (refer to Figure 5-7). In addition to the decorative effect they add, the header units hold the two wythes of the wall together instead of steel ties, so there is no metal in the wall to corrode over time. These decorative bond patterns recreate the look of historic masonry buildings, so the style goes well with older homes and with new homes of traditional design. The English bond pattern uses alternating courses of headers and stretchers, and the Flemish bond pattern uses alternating stretcher and header units in each course. There are two alternate ways of forming the corner pattern for Flemish and English bond walls. One is called a Dutch corner (Figure 9-7) and uses field-cut ¹/₂- and ³/₄-length units. The other is called an English corner and uses a field-cut closure

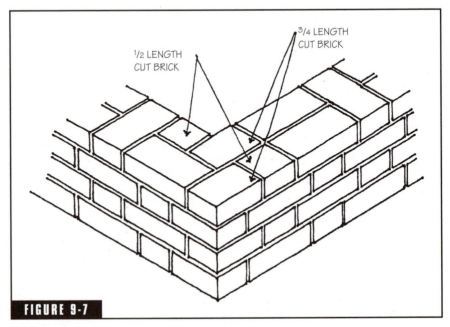

FIGURE 9-7

Dutch corner bond.

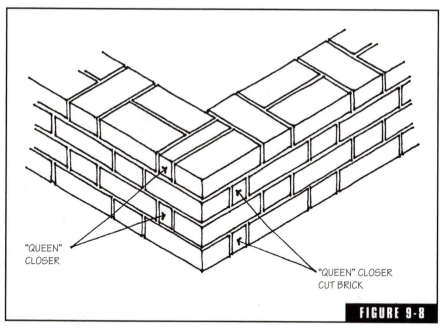

FIGURE 9-8

English corner bond.

brick called a queen closer (Figure 9-8). The common or American
bond pattern uses header units in every sixth course. With common
bond, it is customary to begin with a header course at the base of the
wall, and field-cut $3/4$ closure units are required to make the corner
pattern (Figure 9-9). The inside and outside wythes of double-wythe
walls must be laid at the same time so that the ties or header units can
be set in place. The collar joint between stretcher wythes should be
completely filled with mortar so that water does not collect in the
voids, where it could cause freezing and thawing damage.

A masonry wall cap is called a coping. The appearance of a wall is
affected by the type of coping that is used (Figure 9-10). Some manufacturers produce special-shaped brick copings that are sloped or con-
toured to shed water and project beyond the face of the wall $1/2$ in. on
both sides. Brick copings can also be made of solid bricks laid as headers or of cored bricks laid as rowlocks. Stone or precast concrete copings can also be used to cap a brick wall. The top of a masonry wall
exposed to the weather requires special care and attention. Since
water can penetrate through the joints in a masonry coping, extra

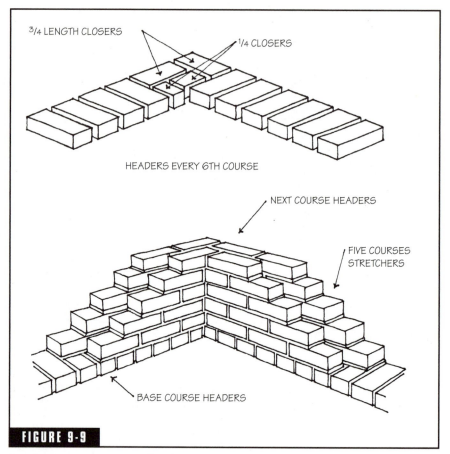

3/4 LENGTH CLOSERS

1/4 CLOSERS

HEADERS EVERY 6TH COURSE

NEXT COURSE HEADERS

FIVE COURSES STRETCHERS

BASE COURSE HEADERS

FIGURE 9-9

American or common corner bond.

measures must be taken to protect the wall, especially in cold climates with a lot of rain or snow. Water that is trapped in a wall and then freezes can expand and cause physical damage to the brick and mortar. The course immediately below the coping should either be solid brick without cores, or the cores should be solidly filled with mortar. It is also very important that the collar joint between wythes be solidly filled to eliminate voids in which water could collect and freeze. For maximum weather protection, flashing should be installed immediately below the wall coping. Crimped copper or stainless steel is very durable and comes in sheets about 1 in. narrower than the wall width. The crimped shape allows the mortar to form a mechanical bond with

Brick garden wall copings.

the metal even though the mortar won't stick to it (Figure 9-11). Smooth metal or plastic flashings do not provide any bond and should be used only if the coping is of large stone or precast units because the weight of the units will be the only thing holding them in place.

9.3   Brick Screen Walls

Solid brick can be used to build what are sometimes called "pierced" screen walls by omitting units to form a pattern of openings (Figure 9-12). A screen wall can provide privacy while still allowing light and air through the wall. There are several different styles of brick screen wall. One of the most attractive and simple to build consists of two wythes of brick laid in an English bond pattern with every other header brick omitted to form the openings (Figure 9-13). The remaining headers tie the two

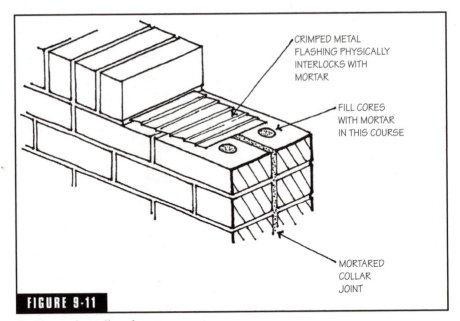

FIGURE 9-11

Flashing under wall copings.

FIGURE 9-12

Brick screen walls.

Brick screen walls.

wythes together and provide support for the stretcher units. The first three courses can be laid as a solid wall to form a good base. The middle courses are then laid in the open pattern, and the upper portion of the wall is finished with three more solid courses and a coping. To help protect against damage caused by freezing and thawing of trapped moisture within the wall, use only solid bricks without core holes. If the bricks have a "frog" or indention on one side, make sure it is on the bottom of the unit so water will not collect in the depression.

Standard height-to-thickness ratios for conventional exterior solid brick walls limit the span or height of 8-in.-thick walls to 12 ft. Brick screen walls should probably be built more conservatively, though, because the open head joints and intermittent bed

Brick screen walls.

ENGLISH BOND
WITH EVERY
OTHER HEADER
BRICK OMITTED

ENGLISH BOND

FIGURE 9-13

English bond pattern screen wall with headers omitted to form pierced wall.

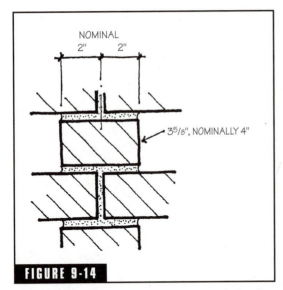

NOMINAL
2"   2"

3⅝", NOMINALLY 4"

FIGURE 9-14

Provide adequate mortar bedding for load distribution in brick screen walls.

joints reduce the wall's flexural stability against wind loads and prevent the use of joint reinforcement. An 8-in.-brick screen wall should probably be limited to a maximum height of about 6 ft., with solid piers or pilasters spaced about every 8 ft. The coursing in the panel should overlap the coursing in the pier for maximum stability (Figure 9-4). Regardless of the exact design of a brick screen wall, the bond pattern should provide continuous vertical paths for distributing loads to the foundation (Figure 9-14).

Clay screen tiles are decorative units used to build masonry screen walls (Figure 9-15). These units are often available in both cream-colored and red clays and patterns that vary among different manufacturers. Although no longer widely available, these special units can create a unique wall design. A running bond pattern which interlocks the individual units is stronger than a stack bond pattern (Figure 9-16). Walls made from screen tile should not exceed 6 ft. in height, and they should be connected to piers or pilasters every 12 ft. or so with galvanized metal ties laid in the bed joints.

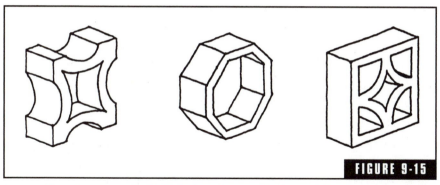

FIGURE 9-15

Screen tile units. *(from Beall, Christine,* Masonry Design and Detailing, *4th edition, McGraw-Hill, New York).*

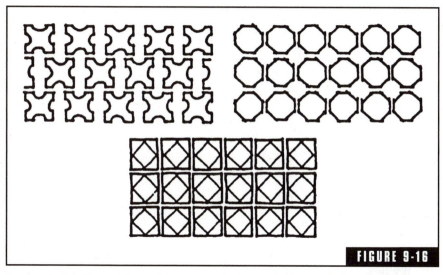

FIGURE 9-16

Screen tile bonding patterns. *(from Beall, Christine,* Masonry Design and Detailing, *4th edition, McGraw-Hill, New York).*

9.4   CMU Garden Walls

Concrete block garden walls are usually built with a single wythe of 8-in.×16-in. block and reinforced with steel wire joint reinforcement (Figure 9-17). You can use ordinary gray utility block or decorative "architectural" block which come in a variety of colors and textures. Architectural block (such as split-faced or ribbed units) have only one decorative face, so a wall with a decorative finish on both sides requires

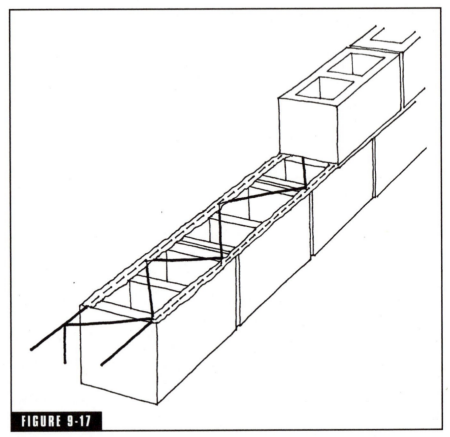

FIGURE 9-17

Single-wythe CMU wall.

two wythes of 4-in. block (Figure 9-18). Concrete block walls need wire joint reinforcement to help minimize shrinkage cracking. The two wythes of a double-wythe wall can also be tied together by the joint reinforcement. For best performance, joint reinforcement should be installed in every second or third bed joint throughout the height of the wall, beginning with the second course. Like metal ties, joint reinforcement must be completely embedded in the mortar to develop its full strength. If it is laid on dry units and mortar is simply spread on top, the joint reinforcement will not be properly bonded and cannot provide adequate restraint. Where joint reinforcement must be overlapped to splice two sections, lay the wires side by side in the joint and overlap them about 16 in. The width of the joint reinforcement should be about 1 in. less than

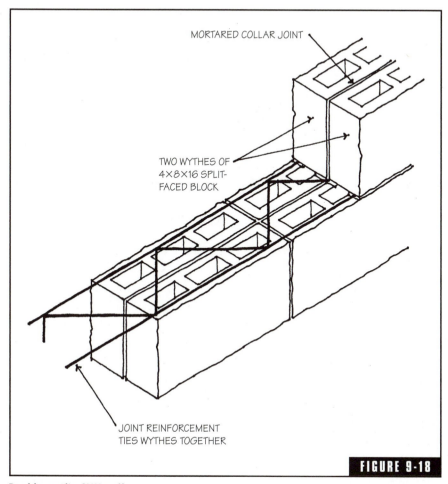

MORTARED COLLAR JOINT

TWO WYTHES OF
4×8×16 SPLIT-
FACED BLOCK

JOINT REINFORCEMENT
TIES WYTHES TOGETHER

FIGURE 9-18

Double-wythe CMU wall.

the actual width of the units or the wall so that it is protected by a good cover of mortar on both faces of the wall. Joint reinforcement spacing affects recommended control joints spacing. The table in Figure 9-19 shows that control joints must be spaced closer together as the amount of joint reinforcment decreases and may be spaced further apart as the amount of joint reinforcement increases. Joint reinforcement should stop on either side of control joints to allow shrinkage cracking to occur at the joints. The grout fill or the interlocking shape of a control joint block links the two adjacent sections of wall together so that they move together when lateral loads are applied (Figure 9-20).

Recommended Spacing of Control Joints	Vertical Spacing of Joint Reinforcing			
	None	24 inch	16 inch	8 inch
Expressed as ratio of panel length to panel height, L/H	2	2½	3	4
With panel length (L) not to exceed, feet	40	45	50	60

FIGURE 9-19

CMU control joint spacing. *(from NCMA, TEK 10-1, National Concrete Masonry Association, Herndon, VA).*

The height of freestanding CMU garden walls is limited by the same height-to-thickness (h/t) ratio as brick walls. Maximum wall height should not exceed 18 times the wall thickness. An 8-in. wall can be a maximum of 12 ft. high. Lateral support must be provided at the same ratio of 18 times the thickness of the wall (Figure 9-3). This means that an 8-in.-thick wall would require pilaster stiffening every 12 ft. With hollow CMU walls, vertical reinforcing steel can be grouted into the cores of the units, which essentially creates an integral pilasters where the wall thickness remains the same (Figure 9-21c). Alternatively, projecting pilasters may be created with standard units bonded into the wall (Figure 9-21b) or with special pilaster units (Figure 9-21a). Projecting pilasters may be hollow, grouted, or grouted and reinforced, depending on the lateral loads and the height of the wall. In seismic areas and coastal areas subject to hurricane winds, grout and reinforcing steel will be required to meet code requirements for load resistance. Ungrouted hollow pilasters should project from the wall a distance equal to approximately $1/12$ of the wall height, and their width should be equal to approximately $1/10$ of the horizontal span between supports. Using either standard or special units based on the 8×16 module will produce an 8-in. projection with a 16-in. width, which is adequate for wall heights of up to 8 ft. and pilaster spacings of up to 12 ft.

The course of block just below the coping in a CMU wall should be filled solidly with grout. Lay pieces of screen wire in the bed joint below this course so the grout will not flow down into the rest of the wall. Cap the wall with flat coping block or stone and install flashing in the same way as for brick walls (Figure 9-22).

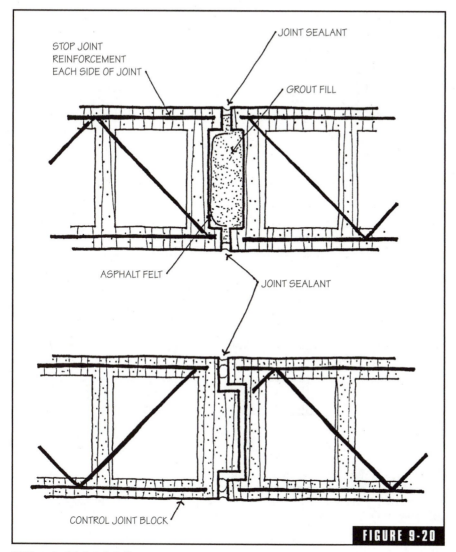

STOP JOINT
REINFORCEMENT
EACH SIDE OF JOINT

JOINT SEALANT

GROUT FILL

ASPHALT FELT

JOINT SEALANT

CONTROL JOINT BLOCK

FIGURE 9-20

CMU control joint details.

Concrete block is often treated with paint, plaster, or clear water repellents, particularly in climates with large amounts of rainfall or cold weather. Many manufacturers produce colored and textured architectural block which are integrally treated with a water-repellent admixture so that they may be exposed to the weather without any additional protective coating. When block treated with an integral water-repellent admixture are used, the block manufacturer should

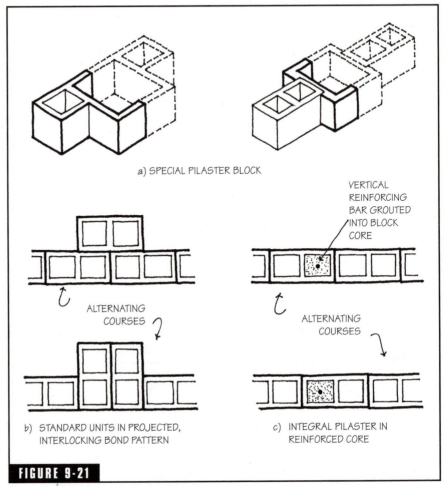

a) SPECIAL PILASTER BLOCK

VERTICAL
REINFORCING
BAR GROUTED
INTO BLOCK
CORE

ALTERNATING
COURSES

ALTERNATING
COURSES

b) STANDARD UNITS IN PROJECTED,
INTERLOCKING BOND PATTERN

c) INTEGRAL PILASTER IN
REINFORCED CORE

FIGURE 9-21

CMU pilasters *(from Beall, Christine,* Masonry Design and Detailing, *4th edition, McGraw-Hill, New York).*

supply a chemically compatible admixture for use in the mortar. When treated units are not used, a clear water-repellent coating may be field applied, but the wall will need to be recoated every few years to maintain its water repellency. Neither integral nor surface-applied water repellents protect against water penetration through shrinkage cracks or joint separations.

Gray block can be painted with any type of breathable coating such as acrylic latex house paint. The masonry should be allowed to cure for at least 30 days before it is painted. Portland cement plaster or *stucco*

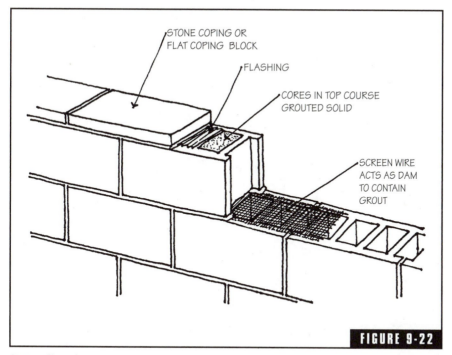

STONE COPING OR
FLAT COPING BLOCK

FLASHING

CORES IN TOP COURSE
GROUTED SOLID

SCREEN WIRE
ACTS AS DAM
TO CONTAIN
GROUT

FIGURE 9-22

CMU wall copings.

as it is usually called, is also a popular finish for gray block walls, and the block's rough texture provides an excellent substrate with good adhesion. When applied over concrete or concrete block, stucco can be applied in two layers rather than the usual three required over metal lath and studs (Figure 9-23). There are four types of metal accessories used with stucco applications over concrete block: corner "beads" for making corners sharp and true to a line, drip screeds used at the bottom of a wall to stop the plaster just above the ground, control joint strips, and casing beads for working up to window and door frames, gate posts, or other abutting surfaces (Figure 9-24). Stucco accessories are attached to CMU walls with masonry nails. For a softer and less contemporary look, corner and casing beads can be omitted and the stucco edged by hand with an intentional imperfection of line.

Stucco, like any portland cement product, shrinks as it cures and dries out, so control joints must be incorporated in the finish. For applying stucco over concrete block, control joints should be formed using a hot-dip galvanized or zinc control joint strip. Wherever there are control

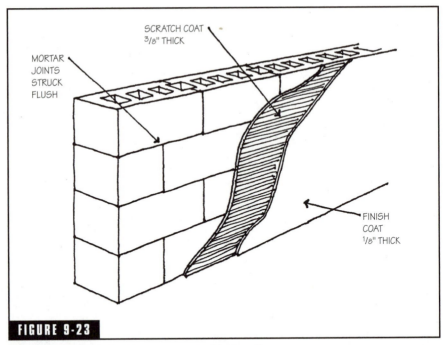

FIGURE 9-23

Two-coat plaster application on concrete block wall.

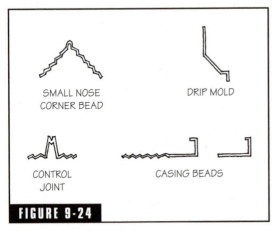

FIGURE 9-24

Plaster accessories.

joints in the concrete block wall, form a stucco control joint in the same location. When applying the plaster to the wall, spread the mix up to either side of the control joint, leaving the metal slot empty.

One of the most important things in mixing plaster is consistency from batch to batch. Always use a container for measuring ingredients so that the proportional volume of materials is the same each time. For both the base coat and the finish coat, measure one part portland cement, one part lime, and six parts sand or one part masonry cement and three parts sand. The amount of moisture in the sand will influence how much water is needed in a plaster mix to get a good workable consistency. Bags of sand bought for small projects will be dry. Bulk sand bought by the ton for larger projects will probably be damp or wet. The sand should be kept covered so that the moisture content will not change drastically because of rain or drying. Within the first two hours after mixing, the plaster mix can be retempered with water to replace evaporated moisture and restore proper consistency. In hot and dry weather, the time limits on retempering may need to be shorter. Plaster that has begun to harden must be discarded.

Before plastering begins, the wall should be moistened by misting it with a garden hose sprayer and the surface moisture then allowed to dry. The scratch coat should be applied and screeded to about a $^3/_8$-in. thickness, then scratched to improve bond with the finish coat. Cure the scratch coat for at least 24 hours before proceeding, but keep the wall damp by misting with a garden hose. This will assure a strong surface and minimum shrinkage and is particularly important on hot or windy days. Plaster that dries out too quickly will have a lot of random surface cracks.

The finish coat uses the same ingredient proportions as the scratch coat. If the scratch coat is dry, moisten it again with a garden hose mist and let the surface moisture evaporate before beginning the finish coat work. Trowel on a finish coat of plaster that is about $^1/_8$ in. thick, working up to the edges of the metal control joints, corner beads, and drip screeds. For a smooth finish, trowel the surface several times as it becomes progressively harder until you have achieved the texture you want. Decorative textures can be applied to produce a variety of looks. Keep the stucco moist for several days while it cures. If the stucco will be painted, allow about a month for curing first. Choose a porous or "breathable" type of coating such as acrylic house paint, cement-based paint, or an acrylic elastomeric coating. Follow the paint or coating manufacturer's instructions for cleaning, priming, and painting over stucco.

To produce a bright white finish coat that will not need paint, substitute white portland cement and white sand in the mix. This will be more expensive than painting initially, but the stucco will never need recoating. To produce colored stucco, add liquid or powder pigments to the finish coat plaster mix. Measure the amounts carefully and exactly and make sure each batch of plaster is mixed the same or you will get uneven coloring. With white portland cement, the colors will be brighter, but the mix will be more expensive. When using colored

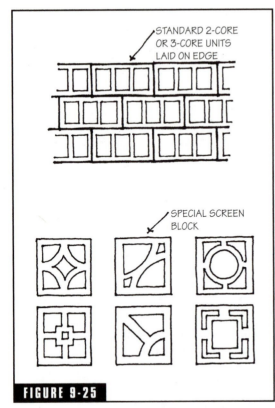

STANDARD 2-CORE
OR 3-CORE UNITS
LAID ON EDGE

SPECIAL SCREEN
BLOCK

FIGURE 9-25

CMU screen block and wall bonding patterns.

plaster, you cannot retemper the mix with water as usual because it will dilute the colors, so mix smaller batches that you can use up before the mix water begins to evaporate.

9.5   CMU Screen Walls

Concrete block screen walls can be built using either decorative screen blocks or regular two-core or three-core utility blocks turned on edge (Figure 9-25). CMU screen walls are usually built with supporting pilasters for added strength. Recommended pilaster spacing is based on height-to-thickness ratio and is the same as for brick walls (see Figure 9-3). One of the simplest ways to build CMU pilasters is to use special pilaster blocks with notches into which the screen block can be nested, and a center core for reinforcing steel (Figure 9-26). At the pilasters, the concrete footing should be widened to accommodate the extra wall thickness. For a nominal 18-in.×16-in. pilaster in an 8-in.-wall, widen the 16-in. wide footing to 36 in. × 32 in. (see Figure 9-2). No. 3 steel reinforcing bars in the footing should turn up 18 in. (Figure 9-27) and overlap the vertical steel bars in the pilaster at least 12 in. (Figure 9-28). The lap splice should be tied tightly with steel wire, and the steel in the pilaster must be held upright until it is embedded in grout. Build the pilaster up four courses at a time, and allow the mortar and units to cure overnight. Then grout the cavity solidly with a mortar mix to which extra water has been added. Stop each grout pour about $3/4$ in. below the top of the block. This will form a "key" with the next pour and make the pilaster stronger (Figure 9-29). Use an extra rebar to stir or agitate the grout slightly to make sure that all the corners and recesses are filled and that there are no pockets of trapped air. Let these first courses of the pilasters cure for a few days before building them higher.

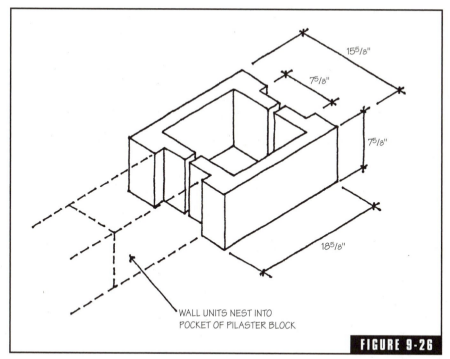

15⁵/₈"

7⁵/₈"

7⁵/₈"

18⁵/₈"

WALL UNITS NEST INTO
POCKET OF PILASTER BLOCK

FIGURE 9-26

CMU pilaster block.

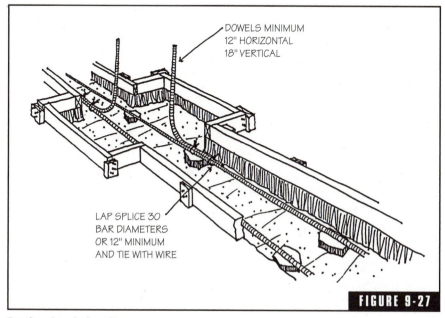

DOWELS MINIMUM
12" HORIZONTAL
18" VERTICAL

LAP SPLICE 30
BAR DIAMETERS
OR 12" MINIMUM
AND TIE WITH WIRE

FIGURE 9-27

Footing dowels for pilasters.

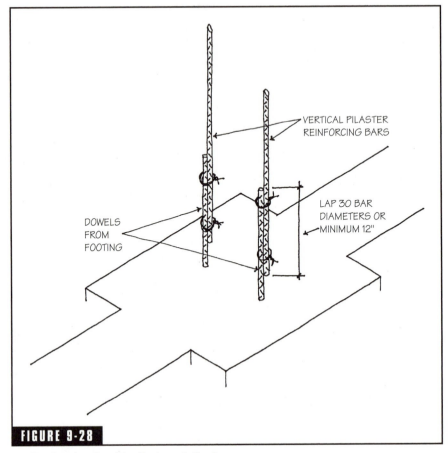

VERTICAL PILASTER
REINFORCING BARS

LAP 30 BAR
DIAMETERS OR
MINIMUM 12"

DOWELS
FROM
FOOTING

FIGURE 9-28

Lap footing dowels with pilaster reinforcing.

Cap the top of the grouted pilaster with a stone or precast coping, or with a bed of smoothly troweled mortar which is sloped from the center outward and downward to shed rain and snow. CMU screen walls require joint reinforcement to restrain shrinkage and minimize cracking. It should be installed in every second or third bed joint, beginning with the second course, just as it is in a solid wall.

Screen blocks are usually laid in a stack bond to form a grid pattern. Both head and bed joints are fully mortared, which increases the lateral load resistance of the wall and allows the use of joint reinforcement. Reinforced bond beam courses at the top and bottom of the wall (see Figure 6-19) add even greater strength. The face shells and webs of screen block should be at least $3/4$ in. thick. Type S mortar should be

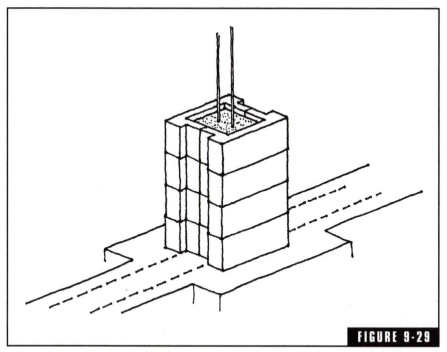

FIGURE 9-29

Grouted and reinforced CMU pilaster.

used, and truss-type joint reinforcement should be located in every other bed joint for a maximum spacing of 16 in. on center. Because of their decorative coring pattern, the way screen blocks are positioned in the wall greatly affects their compressive strength. The National Concrete Masonry Association (NCMA) tested a variety of screen block designs to determine their relative strengths when turned different ways. Figure 9-30 shows that the relative strength of the blocks tested in the position shown can vary significantly as a percentage of the same unit strength when tested with the core holes vertical. Units should have a minimum compressive strength of 1,000 psi (gross area) when tested with the holes in a vertical position parallel to the direction of the load.

Control joints in screen block walls should be located at one side of each pilaster. To form the control joint, line one end of the pilaster block with roofing felt or building paper before mortaring in the screen block (Figure 9-31). Joint reinforcement should stop on either side of the control joint and should not continue through it.

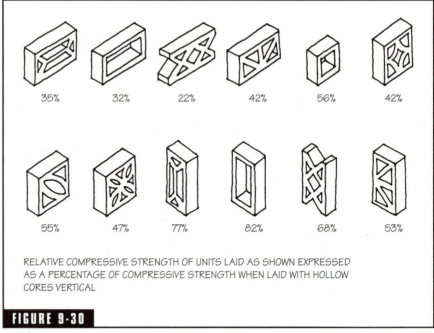

RELATIVE COMPRESSIVE STRENGTH OF UNITS LAID AS SHOWN EXPRESSED
AS A PERCENTAGE OF COMPRESSIVE STRENGTH WHEN LAID WITH HOLLOW
CORES VERTICAL

FIGURE 9-30

How screen block design, shape, and orientation influence strength. *(adapted from NCMA, TEK 5, National Concrete Masonry Association, Herndon, VA).*

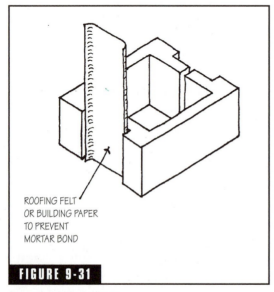

ROOFING FELT
OR BUILDING PAPER
TO PREVENT
MORTAR BOND

FIGURE 9-31

Control joint at pilaster.

9.6 Stone Garden Walls

Stone garden walls can take one of two forms. A dry-stack wall gives a very rustic appearance but is time-consuming and labor intensive to build properly. A mortared wall is more formal, especially if it is built of cut stone rather than rubble. The style of the home and its budget will dictate which type of stone wall is most appropriate.

9.6.1 Dry-Stack Stone Wall

Dry-stack stone walls are built without mortar. Friction, gravity, and the interlock of the individual stones hold the wall together. These walls are simple to build and do not require concrete footings. The stones may require considerable cutting and shaping to make a good interlocking fit. Easily workable stones like bluestone, sandstone, or limestone will usually be the best.

Dry-stack walls without a concrete footing are limited to a height of 3 ft. At the base, a 3-ft. high wall should be 2 ft. thick. Each end and face of a dry-stack wall must be "battered" or sloped inward 1/2 in. for every foot of height (Figure 9-32). The wall should sit in a 6 to 12-in.-deep trenched excavation. If necessary, 4 in. of gravel can be placed in the bottom of the trench to improve drainage. If the ground slopes, the trench may be dug in a series of flat terraces. To help assure that the wall slopes evenly from bottom to top, build a slope gauge by nailing two 1×2s together as shown (Figure 9-33).

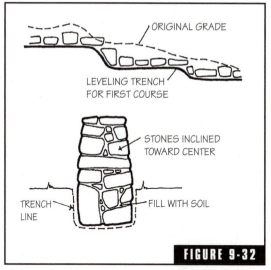

Dry-stack stone wall. *(from S. Blackwell Duncan,* **The Complete Book of Outdoor Masonry,** *TAB Books, Blue Ridge Summit, PA, 1978).*

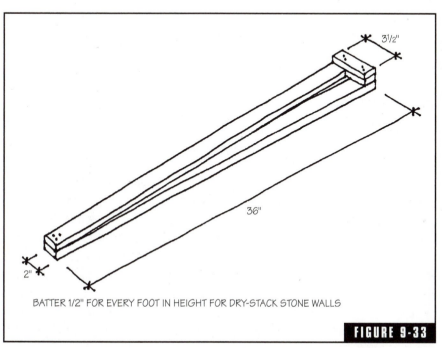

BATTER 1/2" FOR EVERY FOOT IN HEIGHT FOR DRY-STACK STONE WALLS

FIGURE 9-33

Slope gauge for battering dry stack stone walls 1/2 in. for every foot of height.

The wall should consist of two rows of large stones with their top surfaces tilted slightly downward toward the center of the wall so that they are lower in the middle than at the outside edges. The largest stones should be used for the first course, not only to create a good base, but also to avoid lifting and adjusting these heavy pieces at higher levels. Large stones should form the outside faces of the wall and smaller stones should be used in the middle. A bond stone that is the full width of the wall should be placed every 3 or 4 ft. in each course to tie the two halves of the wall together. Each stone should be chosen for the best fit, trimming and cutting as necessary to make them sit firmly in place, and shimming with small pieces of broken stone if needed. After several courses of stone are laid, the small spaces along the face of the wall are filled in by hammering in small stones. This process is called "chinking," and helps interlock the wall and tilt the stones inward. The stones in successive courses should overlap the stones above and below to avoid creating continuous straight vertical joints and to produce a stronger wall. Ends and corners should be interlocked to provide stability.

Flat stones of roughly rectangular shape work best for cap stones. The top course should be as level as possible for the full length of the wall, and in cold climates, many masons like to set the wall cap in mortar and fill the joints between cap stones with mortar to keep out some of the rain and snow. Mortar joints in the wall cap should be convex rather than concave so they will not collect water.

9.6.2 Mortared Stone Wall

Mortared stone walls are laid on concrete footings poured below the frost line. Rubble stone walls are laid up in much the same way as dry-stack walls except that the voids and cavities between stones are filled with mortar instead of stone chips. Walls less than 2 ft. in height should be 8 in. to 12 in. thick. Walls up to 4 ft. high should be 12 in. to 18 in. thick. Even though mortar provides additional strength for these walls, the same care should be used in selecting and fitting the stones together, saving the largest stones for the base course, the squarest ones for the ends and corners, and the flattest ones for the cap. Stone that is at least roughly squared on all sides will work better than rounded fieldstone or river stone or rubble that is too angular or irregular in shape. Mortared stone walls must have bond stones that extend through the full thickness of the wall spaced at a maximum of 3 ft. on center vertically and horizontally.

Mortar for stone walls is made with different proportions than that used for brick or concrete block. A mix using 1 part lime, 2 parts portland cement, and 9 parts sand, or 1 part masonry cement to 3 parts sand should perform well. The mortar joints can be raked out about $1/2$ in. deep to accent the shape of the stones, and then brushed with a whisk broom to remove excess mortar. For a joint that is flush with the face of the stones, use just the whisk broom. Do not rake out the joints in the top of the wall. Use a jointing tool to smooth the mortar, forming a convex surface that won't hold water.

Retaining Walls

Retaining walls can be used to stabilize an earth embankment and protect it from erosion, create terraces in a sloping yard, build a tree well, or build raised planting beds. Retaining walls may be built of brick, concrete, concrete block, or stone. Some designs incorporate reinforcing steel and others rely soley on gravity to resist soil pressures. Newer systems of special concrete masonry retaining wall blocks have greatly simplified the design and installation of retaining walls, and there are a number of proprietary products available.

10.1   Retaining Wall Types

Traditional retaining walls are built with steel reinforcing bars embedded in concrete, grouted between two wythes of solid brick, or grouted in the hollow cores of concrete block. A concrete footing anchors the wall and resists overturning and sliding forces. This type of wall is called a reinforced *cantilever retaining wall* because the stem of the wall is essentially cantilevered from the footing in much the same way that a beam might be cantilevered from a column (Figure 10-1). Cantilever retaining walls are rigid structures of solid construction. Allowances must be made for expansion and contraction of the materials and for drainage of soil moisture, which may build up behind the wall. The strength of these walls derives from the combination of steel

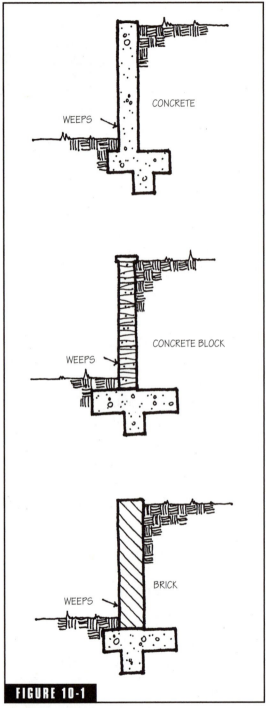

<figure>
FIGURE 10-1

Cantilever retaining walls. *(from Newman, Morton, Standard Cantilever Retaining Walls, McGraw-Hill, New York).*
</figure>

for tensile strength and concrete or masonry for compressive strength and corrosion protection.

Before steel and concrete were invented, retaining walls were built of brick or stone and used simple gravity to hold the soil in place. These *gravity retaining walls* rely on the mass of the wall to provide resistance to sliding and overturning and on the form of the wall to reduce the weight of the soil as its height increases (Figure 10-2). The wedge-shaped wall requires a lot of material, particularly for tall retaining walls. The structure is so stable, however, that it can be built of unreinforced brick or even of dry-stacked stone laid without mortar. A mortared brick gravity wall relies on the weight of the masonry and the bond of mortar to units to resist the overturning motion of the earth embankment. A dry-stacked stone gravity wall relies on its weight, friction between the stones, and the physical interlocking of the stones for its strength. Gravity retaining walls are not used much any more, but for low retaining walls or terraces in a garden, there is nothing more charming than the rustic look of dry-stack stone. Gravity retaining walls can still be fairly economical for small installations, but dry-stack stone is labor intensive, and the taller the wall the less cost-effective this type of construction will be.

One of the newest developments in the concrete masonry industry is the dry-stacked, interlocking concrete block retaining wall system. Referred to as *segmental retaining walls,* a variety of proprietary units and systems are available, each with a slightly different method of construction (Figure 10-3). The units are set back or *battered* in each course so that the weight of the wall leans inward against the soil embankment. Some types of units interlock simply by their shape, while others use pins or dowels to connect successive courses. Because they are dry-stacked without mortar, interlocking retaining wall systems are simple and fast to install, and the stepped-back designs reduce overturning stresses. Segmental retaining walls are so simple and so popular, they have virtually made cantilever retaining walls obsolete. Unless the look of a concrete, brick, or stone wall is desired for aesthetic reasons, a concrete masonry segmental wall is the fastest and least labor-intensive solution.

10.2 Reinforced Cantilever Retaining Walls

Some of the primary considerations in designing and building a cantilever retaining wall should be

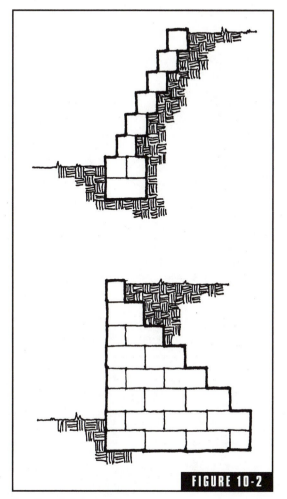

FIGURE 10-2

Gravity retaining walls.

- A stable footing

- A dampproof coating on the back of the wall to prevent soil moisture from saturating the masonry or concrete and eventually corroding the reinforcing steel or causing efflorescence

- Permeable backfill behind the wall to collect soil moisture

- Weep holes or drain lines to remove moisture and prevent hydrostatic pressure buildup

- Expansion or control joints to permit natural thermal and moisture movements

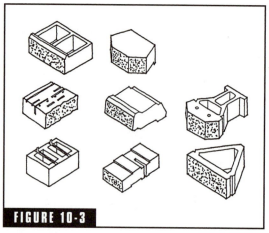

FIGURE 10-3

Segmental retaining wall units. *(from National Concrete Masonry Association,* **Design Manual for Segmental Retaining Walls,** *NCMA, Herndon, VA).*

10.2.1 Footings

The bottom of the footing must be below the winter frost line to avoid displacement by frost heave. The soil must be of sufficient strength to withstand significant pressure under the front edge of the footing, since the tendency of a cantilever retaining wall is to tip forward. Figure 10-4 shows allowable soil-bearing pressures from the CABO *One and Two Family Dwelling Code.* If the soil under the footing is soft or unstable, an engineer should design the wall and its footing. If the ground slopes, the footing should be stepped as described in Chapter 6. The frost depth map in Figure 10-5 shows long lines of equal frost depth in the central and southern states, but in the west and north shows local frost depths that can vary widely within a small area. Consult the local building official if you need more information about the frost depth in your area. In warm climates, the frost depth is very shallow, but the footing should still be set about 12 in. below finish grade so that it is supported on firm, undisturbed soil.

Retaining wall footings are a little different from foundation wall or garden wall footings. The soil pressure pushes against the wall, so to keep the footing from sliding, a bottom projection is added which sits further down in the soil. The bottom trench can be cut directly into the soil and the upper portion of the footing formed with wood in the usual way. The bottom of the main footing section as well as the projection should be below the frost line. Reinforcing bars from the footing must stick up into the wall. For walls that are relatively short, they will extend the full height of the wall. For taller retaining walls, the bars from the footing will be

Class of Material	Soil-Bearing Pressure, psf
Crystalline bedrock	12,000
Sedimentary rock	6,000
Sandy gravel or gravel	5,000
Sand, silty sand, clayey sand, silty gravel, and clayey gravel	3,000
Clay, sandy clay, silty clay and clayey silt	2,000

FIGURE 10-4

Allowable bearing pressures for various types of soil. *(from Council of American Building Officials,* **One and Two-Family Dwelling Code,** *Falls Church, VA).*

shorter, but they must overlap and be tied to separate reinforcing bars in the wall. The reinforcing dowels should be in the center of the wall. For a concrete block wall, the dowel spacing must be accurate enough to fit into the cores of the block. Minimum concrete strength should be 2,500 psi.

10.2.2 Dimensions and Reinforcement

For the cantilever wall designs given in this chapter, no surcharge load is permitted. That is, no automobile or equipment traffic should occur on the top side of the wall, and the soil slope at the top of the wall should be zero. In situations where surcharge loading is expected or cannot be avoided (e.g., next to a street or driveway, or where the slope of the retained soil is greater than zero), an engineer should be hired to design the wall for this additional loading. Walls that are taller than

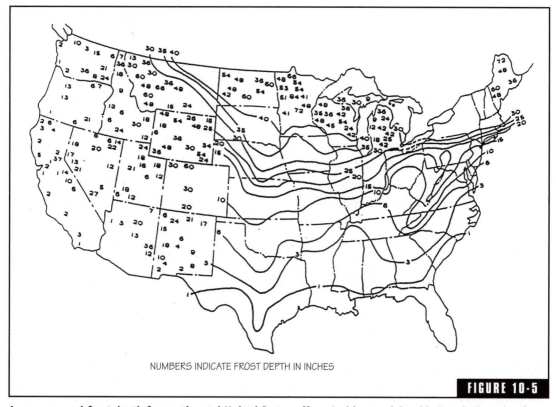

NUMBERS INDICATE FROST DEPTH IN INCHES

FIGURE 10-5

Average annual frost depth for continental United States. *(from* Architectural Graphic Standards, *9th ed).*

those shown in the design tables should also be designed by an engineer. The taller the wall, the greater the pressures exerted on it and the greater the possibility of wall failure or collapse if the design does not provide adequate strength. In situations where the embankment is high and steep, consider using a series of shorter walls with flat terraces in between so that the loads on the retaining walls are minimized. Whenever there is any doubt about the adequacy of a retaining wall to withstand the soil pressure or if there is a significant amount of soil moisture, hire an engineer. The design fees are much more affordable than the liability associated with property damage, personal injury, or life safety in the event of a failure.

Concrete retaining walls are built the same as the concrete foundation walls described in Chapter 6. Since the wall will not have the benefit of the house framing to brace it along the top edge, a retaining wall actually has to be stronger than a foundation or basement wall. Figure 10-6 illustrates typical reinforced concrete retaining walls for 3- and 4-ft. heights. Minimum concrete strength should be 2,500 psi in mild climates and 3,000 psi in moderate and severe weathering climates. Taller concrete retaining walls typically have a stem which increases in thickness from top to bottom, but the stem in shorter walls such as these is the same thickness throughout its height. Control joints should be located every 40 ft. on center. They must be saw-cut into the face of the concrete wall after the forms are removed and should be about 2 in. deep. If the wall is longer than 60 ft., it should be separated into sections with an expansion joint which fully separates the adjacent sections. The joint should be filled with a compressible material or caulked with a high-performance exterior sealant. Horizontal reinforcing bars should stop on either side of an expansion joint but may continue through a control joint.

The table and drawings for **concrete block retaining walls** in Figure 10-7 provide design dimensions for walls up to 4 ft., 8 in. in height. The reinforcing dowels in the footing must be located in the center of the wall and spaced in conjunction with the coursing layout of the block so that the dowels will line up with the hollow block cores. Using a two-core rather than a three-core type of block provides larger core spaces that are easier to align with the steel dowels. Two-core block walls also make it easier to align the cores throughout the height of the wall so that the vertical reinforcing steel fits properly. Control joint spacing in

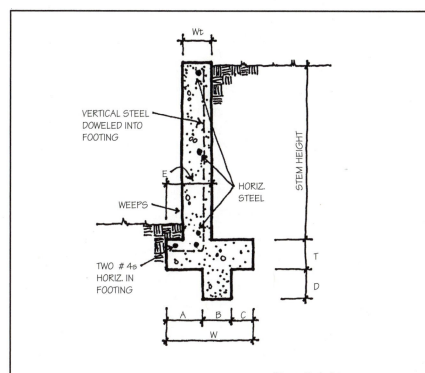

	Stem Height	
	3'-0"	**4'-0"**
A	6	10
B	8	8
C	6	6
D	8	8
E	6	8
T	8	8
W	20	24
Wt	8	8
Vertical reinforcing	#4s at 16" o.c.	#4s at 16" o.c.
Horizontal reinforcing in stem wall	One #4 top and bottom	#4s at 21" o.c.

Notes: Backfill slope at top of wall is zero, equivalent fluid pressure is 30 psf, surcharge load is zero. All required dimension are in inches.

FIGURE 10-6

Design table for concrete retaining walls. *(adapted from Morton Newman,* Standard Cantilever Retaining Walls, *McGraw-Hill, New York).*

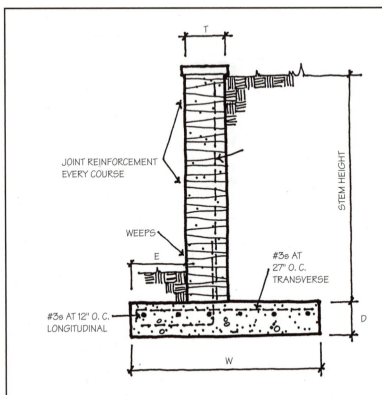

	Stem Height			
	3'-4"	**4'-0"**	**3'-4"**	**4'-0"**
E	12	12	12	12
W	32	36	32	36
D	9	9	9	9
T	8	8	12	12
Vertical Reinforcing and dowels	#3s at 32" o.c.	#4s at 32" o.c.	#3s at 32" o.c.	#3s at 32" o.c.

Notes: Soil-bearing pressure is 1500 psf, backfill slope at top of wall is zero, maximum equivalent fluid pressure is 45 psf, surcharge load is zero, masonry is fully grouted, joint reinforcement is at every course. All required dimension are in inches.

FIGURE 10-7

Design table for concrete masonry retaining walls. *(adapted from Randall and Panarese, Concrete Masonry handbook).*

concrete masonry cantilever walls will depend on the amount of pre-fabricated joint reinforcement used. Figure 10-8 shows maximum joint spacing. Joints can also be located so that they form wall panels of approximate square shape, so for a 4-ft.-high wall, control joints would be located at 4 ft. on center, and so on. This type of spacing will provide the greatest protection against random shrinkage cracks forming in the wall.

The table in Figure 10-9 gives recommended design requirements for double-wythe, grouted **brick retaining walls** up to 4 ft. high. The brick should be Grade SW with a compressive strength of at least 5,000 psi, and the mortar should be Type M. The reinforcing dowels in the footing must be located along the center line of the wall so that they will fit properly between the two brick wythes. In addition to the steel bars required by the tables, prefabricated wire joint reinforcement should be installed in the mortar bed joints every 16 in. or 6 courses. This will tie the two wythes of brick together, and it will increase the strength of the wall. Expansion joints should be located in brick retaining walls every 16–20 ft. on center. The joint should actually be a complete separation between two adjacent wall sections, and the joint should be caulked with a high-performance exterior sealant. This will allow the two sections to expand freely with changes in moisture content.

10.2.3 Drainage and Waterproofing

Drainage and waterproofing for cantilever retaining walls is similar to that required for basements. In this case, the protection is required for the wall itself rather than for an occupied space. A buildup of moisture

Recommended Spacing of Control Joints	Vertical Spacing of Joint Reinforcing			
	None	24 inch	16 inch	8 inch
Expressed as ratio of panel length to panel height, L/H	2	$2\frac{1}{2}$	3	4

FIGURE 10-8

Recommended control joint spacing for concrete masonry. *(adapted from NCMA, TEK 10-1, National Concrete Masonry Association, Herndon, VA).*

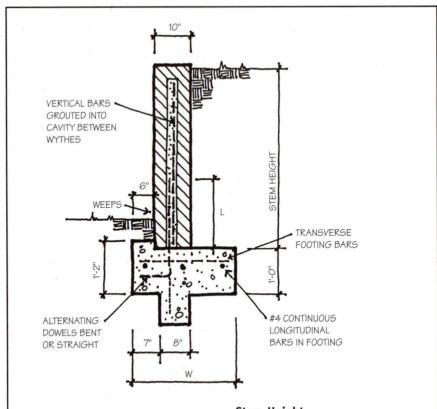

	Stem Height			
	2'-0"	**2'-8"**	**3'-4"**	**4'-0"**
W	21	21	24	28
L	12	12	12	16
Dowels	#3 at 40	#3 at 40	#3 at 40	#3 at 27
Vertical bars	#3 at 40	#3 at 40	#3 at 40	#3 at 27
Transverse footing bars	#3 at 40	#3 at 40	#3 at 40	#3 at 27

Notes: Backfill slope at top of wall is zero, equivalent fluid pressure is 30 psf, surcharge load is zero, masonry is fully grouted. All required dimensions are in inches.

FIGURE 10-9

Design table for brick retaining walls *(adapted from* Technical Note 17N, *Brick Industry Association, Reston, VA).*

behind retaining walls causes hydrostatic pressure which can significantly increase the loads on the wall. Concrete retaining walls can be drained to avoid hydrostatic pressure buildup using a length of PVC pipe placed in the bottom of the forms at a point just above finish grade. This will form an open drain tube through the concrete. To hold the tube in place during the concrete pour, drive a screw through the formwork at each side (Figure 10-10). Space the weep tubes 3 to 4 ft. on center. For well-drained soils, a 1-in. pipe diameter should be adequate. For wetter soils, a little larger-size PVC may be necessary. Use a piece of screen wire to keep the gravel backfill out of the weep tube. Weeps in brick and concrete masonry building walls are formed by omitting the mortar from head joints at the base of the wall. In a grouted retaining wall, however, a PVC tube works better. Lay the pipe across the masonry, setting the front end flush with the face of the wall, cut the brick or block to fit around it, and mortar the space in between (Figure

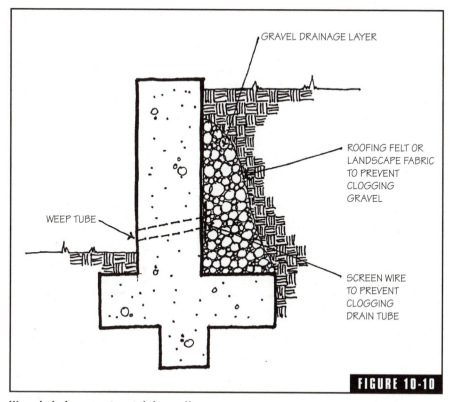

FIGURE 10-10

Weep hole in concrete retaining wall.

10-11). Space the weeps 32 in. to 48 in. on center. In areas where precipitation is heavy or where poor drainage conditions exist, prolonged seepage through weep holes can cause the soil in front of a retaining wall and under the toe of the footing to become saturated and lose some of its bearing capacity. In these instances, a continuous drain of perforated pipe should be placed behind the wall near the base but above the bottom of the footing, with discharge areas located beyond the ends of the wall (Figure 10-12).

Coarse gravel backfill behind concrete or masonry retaining walls should extend from the top of the footing to within 12 in. of finished grade, be 2 ft. wide, and run the entire length of the wall. To prevent the infiltration of fine soil, a layer of roofing felt or landscape fabric should cover the gravel. Waterproofing requirements for the back face of a retaining wall will depend on the climate, soil conditions, and type of masonry units used. Seepage through a masonry wall can cause efflorescence or calcium carbonate stains, but a waterproof membrane will keep the wall from being saturated. Walls of porous concrete block should always be waterproofed because of the excessive expansion and

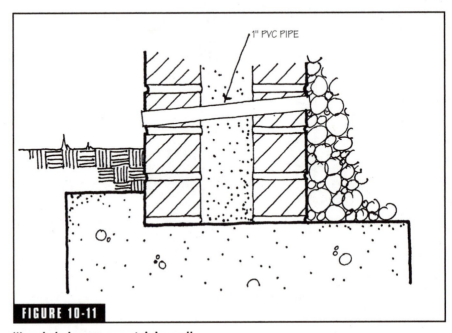

1" PVC PIPE

FIGURE 10-11

Weep hole in masonry retaining wall.

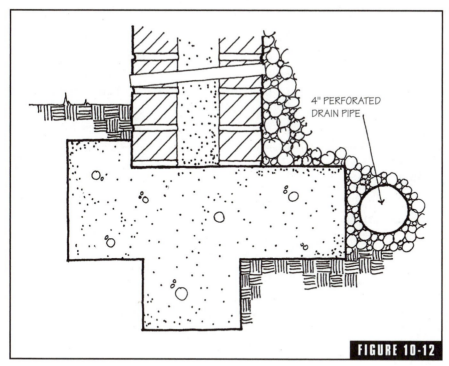

4" PERFORATED
DRAIN PIPE

FIGURE 10-12

Perforated pipe drain.

contraction that accompanies variable moisture content. In climates
subject to freezing, a waterproof membrane can prevent the potentially
destructive action of freeze-thaw cycles when moisture is present in
the units. Walls should cure for at least three weeks before backfilling
begins.

10.2.5 Construction

Concrete retaining walls are formed, poured, and cured in the same
way as concrete foundation walls. The footing should be poured and
formed first, and then the wall formed and poured in a second operation. Wall forms must incorporate snap ties or spreaders to keep the
sides from bowing. Forms can be stripped after two or three days, the
protruding wire of the snap ties broken off, and the plastic cones pried
out. Since the wall will be exposed to view on one side, the holes left
by the cones should be patched with cement paste.

Joint reinforcement should be installed every 8 in. on center in concrete masonry walls and every 16 in. on center in multiwythe brick

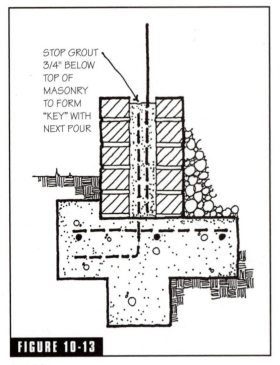

STOP GROUT 3/4" BELOW TOP OF MASONRY TO FORM "KEY" WITH NEXT POUR

FIGURE 10-13

Grout key.

walls. Masonry can be grouted course by course as the wall is laid, or several courses can be laid and the grout poured after the wall has cured for a day or two. Grout for pours up to 4 ft. in height should be mixed to a fluid consistency that will flow easily into the wall cavity or block cores and surround the reinforcing bars. Grout should be rodded or vibrated to remove voids. Reinforcing bar positioners are used to hold the vertical steel in place until it is grouted. Stop the grout about 3/4 in. below the top of the masonry retaining so that it will form a "key" with the next pour (Figure 10-13). A flashing course is installed under the coping in masonry retaining walls to protect the top of the wall from moisture.

Backfilling should not begin for at least three weeks after a concrete or masonry wall has been completed. The gravel and soil backfill should be placed in depths of 12 to 24 in. at a time to avoid large impact loads. Earth-moving equipment should be kept away from the wall a distance equal to the wall height to avoid surcharge loading.

10.3   Segmental CMU Retaining Walls

Mortarless interlocking concrete masonry unit systems make the construction of retaining walls simple and easy to accomplish even with unskilled labor. Sold under a number of different trade names, these systems are available through concrete block manufacturers, masonry distributors, lumber yards, and home centers throughout the country. The units are usually made in a rough, stone-like textures and in colors ranging from grey to buff or earth tones. These systems are called *segmental retaining walls* (SRWs), and there are two basic types. *Conventional SRWs* are structures that resist the force of the retained soil solely through gravity and the inclination or *batter* of the SRW units toward the soil embankment (Figure 10-14). Conventional SRWs may be either single or multiple unit depths. *Soil-reinforced SRWs* are composite systems consisting of SRW units in combination with a mass of retained soil stabilized by horizontal layers of geosynthetic reinforcement materials (Figure 10-15). Some systems can be laid in either straight or curved lines, but others are limited to straight walls and 90-degree corners. No mortar is required for SRW systems, but the units must be restrained against sliding by either a physical interlocking shape or a shear connector such as rods, pins or clips (Figure 10-16).

Because they are dry-stacked, segmental retaining walls are flexible and can tolerate minor movement and settlement without distress. The units are not mortared together, so they expand and contract freely and do not require expansion or control joints. SRWs also permit water to drain directly through the face of the wall so hydrostatic pressure is eliminated and weep holes are not necessary. Water drainage through the face of the wall, however, would result in staining,

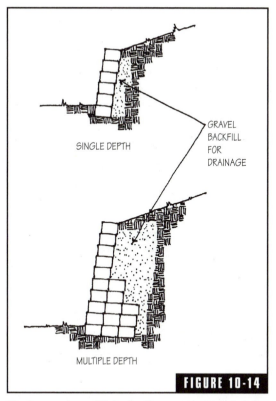

FIGURE 10-14

Single- and multiple-depth segmental retaining walls. *(from National Concrete Masonry Association, Design Manual for Segmental Retaining Walls, NCMA, Herndon, VA).*

efflorescence, and possible freeze-thaw damage if the units remained saturated from wet soil. Primary drainage is provided by gravel backfill, and in very wet areas includes drain lines at the base of the wall. This moves moisture quickly to the bottom of the wall and limits to the base course any staining which might occur. SRWs are typically supported on gravel bed foundations instead of concrete footings. The maximum height that can be constructed using a single-unit-depth conventional SRW is directly proportional to its weight, depth, and vertical batter for any given soil type and slope conditions (Figure 10-17).

The allowable height of a wall can be increased by using multiple unit depths or soil-reinforced systems. Soil-reinforced SRWs use geosynthetic reinforcement to enlarge the effective width and weight

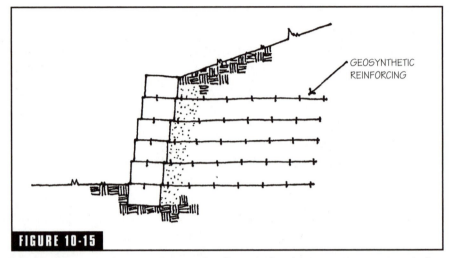

FIGURE 10-15

Soil-reinforced segmental retaining walls. *(from National Concrete Masonry Association, Design Manual for Segmental Retaining Walls, NCMA, Herndon, VA).*

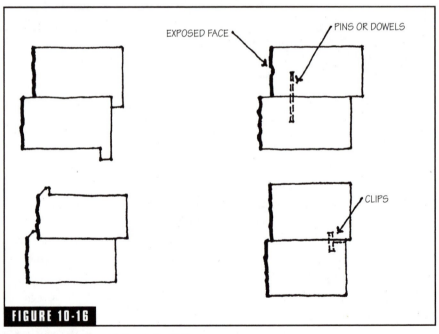

FIGURE 10-16

Units must provide resistance to sliding.

A Maximum exposed wall height (feet).

Unit Height, Inches	Soil Angle of Internal Friction (Table B) 28°			Soil Angle of Internal Friction (Table B) 34°		
	Wall battered 5°	Wall battered 10°	Wall battered 15°	Wall battered 5°	Wall battered 0°	Wall battered 15°
6	2'-0"	2'-6"	3'-0"	2'-6"	3'-6"	3'-6"
8	2'-3"	2'-3"	2'-10"	2'-10"	3'-6"	3'-6"

Notes: Backfill slope at top of wall is zero, surcharge load is zero, required wall embedment at toe is 6 inches, soil and block unit weight is 120 pcf, unit depth is 12 inches. Wall batter is for unit setback per course.

B Angle of internal friction for various soil types.

Soil Type		Angle of Internal Friction, Degrees
GW	Well-graded gravels, gravel sand mixtures, little or no fines	37–42
GP	Poorly graded gravels or gravel sand mixtures, little or no fines	
SW	Well-graded sands, gravelly sands, little or no fines	33–40
SP	Poorly graded sands or gravelly sands, little or no fines	
GM	Silty gravels, gravel-sand-silt mixtures	
SM	Silty sand, sand-silt mixtures	28–35
GC	Clayey gravels, gravel-sand-clay mixtures	
SC	Clayey sands, sand-clay mixture	
ML	Inorganic silts and very fine sands, rock flour, silty or clayey fine sands or clayey silts with slight plasticity	25–32
CL	Inorganic clays of low to medium plasticity, gravelly clays, sandy clays, silty clays, lean clays	

FIGURE 10-17

Maximum exposed height for conventional SRWs based on soil type and angle of wall batter. *(from National Concrete Masonry Association,* **Design Manual for Segmental Retaining Walls,** *NCMA, Herndon, VA).*

of the gravity mass. The reinforcement (either geogrids or geotextiles) extends through the bed joint between the SRW units and into the soil to create a composite gravity mass structure. This composite structure offers increased resistance for taller walls, surcharged structures, or more difficult soil conditions. With most systems, you can build a 3- to 4-ft. high wall in good soil without the need for soil reinforcing or engineering design. As an alternative to a single-high wall in steeply sloped areas, consider two shorter walls stepped back against the slope (Figure 10-18).

In soils that drain well, excavate a trench along the length of the wall 6 in. deep and 18–24 in. wide and place a 2-in. sand bed in the trench for leveling the units. In dense or clayey soils, or in areas that do not drain well, excavate 4–6 in. deeper and add a gravel or crushed stone drainage bed. Level the drainage bed with a rake and tamp the gravel to compact it. Place a layer of landscape filter fabric over the gravel, then add the 2-in. sand leveling bed. Getting the base course of units level is very important to the strength and stability of the wall. Use wooden stakes, a string, and a line level to maintain the correct elevation.

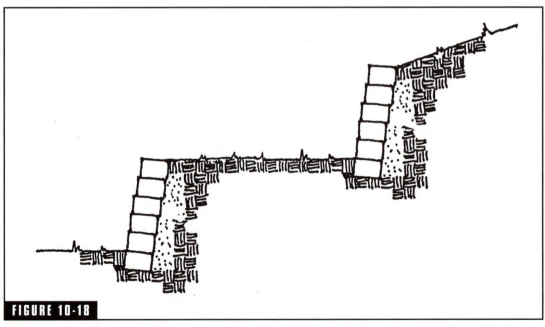

FIGURE 10-18

Two-level, terraced retaining wall.

Lay the first course of units, butting each one snugly against the next and following the string line for alignment and elevation. Complete the entire first course before starting the second, leveling each unit on its own (back to front and side to side) and to adjacent units. Offset the second course of units one-half the length of the units in the course below to form a running bond. After the first two courses of units are laid, begin adding the gravel and soil backfill behind the wall (Figure 10-19). To give the wall a finished look, some systems include special solid cap units. With other systems, cap units can be made from regular units.

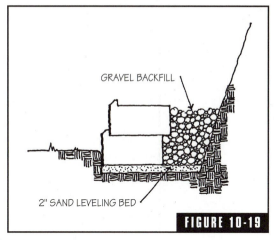

GRAVEL BACKFILL

2" SAND LEVELING BED

FIGURE 10-19

Adding backfill.

10.4   Dry-Stack Stone Gravity Retaining Walls

A dry-laid stone retaining wall may require considerable cutting and shaping with the chisel to make a good interlocking fit. Easily workable stones like bluestone, sandstone, or limestone will usually be the best. Dry-stack stone retaining walls do not require a concrete footing. They may be laid directly onto the soil in an excavated trench. In order to achieve stability, the wall must lean against the embankment slightly, being tilted or battered toward the soil 2 in. for every ft. of wall height (Figure 10-20). Dry-stack walls without a concrete footing are limited to a height of about 3 ft. At the base, a 3-ft. wall should be 18 in. thick. The wall should sit in a 6-in. to 12-in. deep trenched excavation. If necessary, 2 in. of sand can be placed in the bottom of the trench to improve drainage. Dry-stack stone retaining walls allow soil moisture to drain naturally through the open joints so they do not require weep holes.

In soils or areas that drain well, excavate a trench along the length of the wall 6 in. to 12-in. deep and 18–24 in. wide. Remove all grass, sod, roots, and large rocks, and place a 2-in. bed of sand in the trench for leveling the units. In dense or clayey soils, or in areas that do not drain well, excavate 4–6 in. deeper and add a gravel or crushed stone

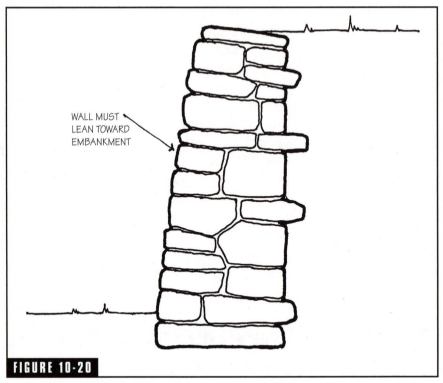

WALL MUST
LEAN TOWARD
EMBANKMENT

FIGURE 10-20

Dry-stack stone retaining wall.

drainage bed. Level the drainage bed with a rake and tamp the gravel to compact it. Place a layer of landscape filter fabric over the gravel, then add a 2-in. leveling bed of sand. Getting the base course of units level is very important to the strength and stability of the wall. Use wooden stakes, a string, and a line level to maintain the correct elevation. To help assure that the wall slopes evenly from bottom to top, build a slope gauge by nailing two 1 × 2s together as shown (Figure 10-21).

Starting at one end of the wall, lay the first course of stones, carefully fitting each one, seating it firmly in the sand bed, and following the string line for elevation. Use the largest stones for the first course, not only to create a good base, but also to avoid lifting and adjusting these heavy pieces at higher levels. Dig out under the stones or fill in under them with soil if necessary to get them to sit flat without wob-

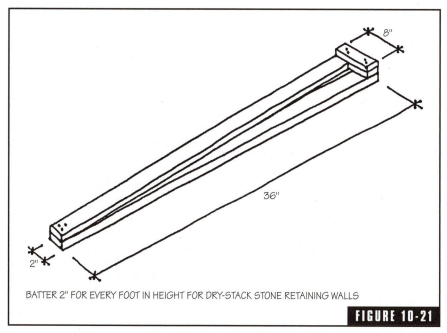

BATTER 2" FOR EVERY FOOT IN HEIGHT FOR DRY-STACK STONE RETAINING WALLS

8"

36"

2"

FIGURE 10-21

Slope gauge for battering dry-stack stone walls 2″ for every foot of height.

bling. Pack the spaces between stones in this first course with soil to give the wall a more stable base. Set the next few courses of stone on top of the first, making sure that the stones tilt in toward the earth and not outward toward the face of the wall. This will provide the stability needed to keep the soil from pushing the wall over. After the first few courses of stone are laid, begin adding the gravel drainage backfill behind the wall (Figure 10-22). Use the slope gauge to make sure that the wall tapers correctly from bottom to top (Figure 10-23). Set the remaining courses of stone in the same manner, installing long stones that stick back into the backfill about every 4 ft. in each course (Figure 10-24). Fill around these "bond" stones with the gravel backfill.

Carefully select each stone for the best fit, choosing stones that need a minimum number of shims. Check the fit of each stone as you lay it. Trim and cut as necessary for shaping using a mason's hammer or chisel. If a stone wobbles on a point or sharp corner, shape it to sit more securely. Check your work periodically with a mason's level to

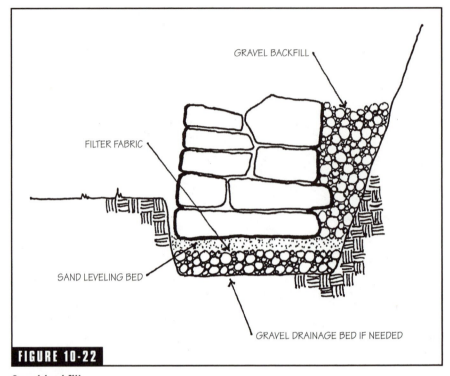

GRAVEL BACKFILL

FILTER FABRIC

SAND LEVELING BED

GRAVEL DRAINAGE BED IF NEEDED

FIGURE 10-22

Gravel backfill.

keep each course approximately level. If a stone does not sit firmly in place, use small pieces of broken stone to shim it. All of the stones should be slightly inclined toward the soil embankment so that the weight leans in on itself. After laying several courses of stone, fill in the small spaces along the face of the wall by driving in small stones with a hammer. This is called "chinking" and helps interlock the wall and tilt the stones inward. Lay stones in successive courses so that they overlap the stones above and below in a manner similar to a running bond brick or block wall. Avoid creating continuous straight vertical joints. The overlapping pattern will produce a stronger wall.

Flat stones of roughly rectangular shape work best for cap stones. The top course should be as level as possible for the full length of the wall, and in cold climates, many masons like to set the wall cap in mor-

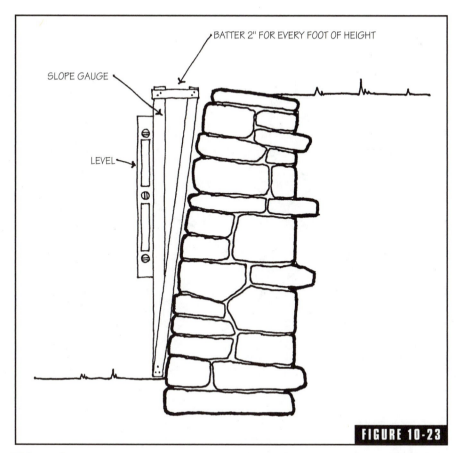

BATTER 2" FOR EVERY FOOT OF HEIGHT

SLOPE GAUGE

LEVEL

FIGURE 10-23

Using a slope gauge.

tar to protect the wall from moisture. Trowel on a 1-in. to 2-in.-thick mortar bed covering only about 2 ft. of the wall at a time. Fill in the joints between the cap stones with mortar too, making the joints convex so they will not collect water. Fill across the back of the cap stone with a little soil to secure it in place.

10.5   Tree Wells

A tree well is just a retaining wall built around the base of a tree to pro-tect it when a grade level is changed by adding soil. Tree root systems

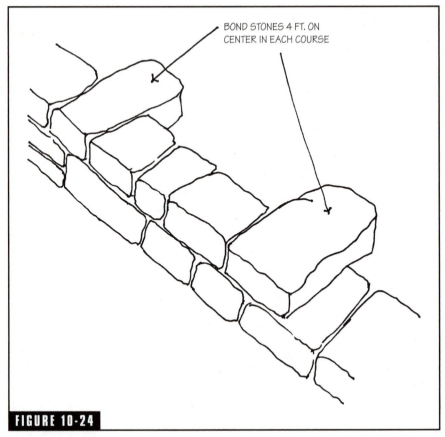

BOND STONES 4 FT. ON
CENTER IN EACH COURSE

FIGURE 10-24

Bond stones in a dry-stack stone retaining wall.

are approximately the same shape below ground as the spread of the
limbs above ground. This should be a good guideline for how wide the
diameter of the tree well should be. Make the diameter large enough so
that when you excavate for the footing, you don't cut any large roots.
Not only will this damage the tree, but it can also make the footing
unstable.

GLOSSARY

Absorption The process of moisture filling permeable pores in a porous, solid material.

Accelerator An admixture which speeds the rate of hydration of cement, shortens the normal time of setting, or increases the rate of hardening, strength development, or both, of concrete, mortar, or grout.

Actual Dimensions Exact size of masonry units, usually width of mortar joint less than nominal dimensions.

Admixture A material other than water, aggregate, or cement used as an ingredient in concrete, mortar, grout, or plaster and added to the mix either immediately before or during the mixing.

Adobe Unfired clay bricks dried in the sun.

Aggregate Materials such as sand, gravel, and crushed stone used with cement and water to make concrete, mortar, grout, or plaster.

Air Content The volume of air voids in cement paste, concrete, or mortar.

Air-Entraining Agent An admixture for concrete or mortar which causes the formation of air bubbles in the mix to improve workability and frost resistance.

Air Entrainment The introduction of air in the form of minute bubbles into concrete or mortar during the mixing in order to improve the flow and workability of fresh mixes and the durability of the hardened material against damage from repeated freezing and thawing when saturated.

Air Void An entrapped or entrained air pocket in concrete or mortar. Entrapped voids are usually larger than 1 millimeter in diameter and removed by vibration, power screeding, or rodding.

Anchor Metal rod, wire, or strap that secures masonry to its structural support.

Anchor Bolt A headed or threaded metal bolt or stud either cast in place, grouted in place, or cemented into a drilled hole and used to attach steel or wood members to concrete or masonry.

Arch A vertically curved compressive structural member spanning openings or recesses; may also be built flat by using special masonry shapes or placed units.

Abutment The skewback of an arch and the masonry that supports it.

Arch Axis The median line of the arch ring.

Camber The relatively small rise of a jack arch.

Crown The apex of the arch ring at midspan.

Depth The depth (*d*) of any arch is the dimension that is perpendicular to the tangent of the axis. The depth of a jack arch is taken to be its greatest vertical dimension.

Extrados The exterior curve that bounds the upper extremities of the arch.

Fixed Arch An arch whose skewback is fixed in position and inclination. Plain masonry arches are, by nature of their construction, fixed arches.

Gothic or Pointed Arch An arch with relatively high rise whose sides consist of arcs or circles, the centers of which are at the level of the spring line.

Intrados The interior curve that bounds the lower extremities of the arch (*see* **Soffit**). The distinction between soffit and intrados is that the intrados is linear, whereas the soffit is a surface.

Jack Arch An arch having horizontal or nearly horizontal upper and lower surfaces. Also called flat or straight arch.

Major Arch Arch with span greater than 6 ft. and having equivalent uniform loads greater than 1000 lb./ft. Typically, a Tudor arch, semicircular arch, Gothic arch, or parabolic arch. Rise-to-span ratio greater than 0.15.

Minor Arch Arch with maximum span of 6 ft. and loads not exceeding 1000 lb./ft. Typically, a jack arch, segmental arch, or multicentered arch. Rise-to-span ratio less than or equal to 0.15.

Rise The maximum height of arch soffit above the level of its spring line.

Roman Arch A semicircular arch. If built of stone, all units are wedge-shaped.

Segmental Arch   An arch whose curve is circular but less than a semicircle.

Semicircular Arch   An arch whose curve is a semicircle.

Skewback   The inclined surface on which the arch joins the supporting wall. For jack arches, the skewback is indicated by a horizontal dimension (K).

Soffit   The undersurface of the arch.

Span   The horizontal distance between abutments. For minor arch calculations, the clear span (S) of the opening is used. For a major parabolic arch, the span (L) is the distance between the ends of the arch axis at the skewback.

Spring Line   For minor arches, the line where the skewback cuts the soffit. For major parabolic arches, the term commonly refers to the intersection of the arch axis with the skewback.

Trimmer Arch   An arch (usually a low-rise arch of brick) used for supporting a fireplace hearth.

Tudor Arch   A pointed four-centered arch of medium rise-to-span ratio.

Voussoir   One of the wedge-shaped masonry units which forms an arch ring.

Arching Action   The distribution of loads in masonry over an opening. The load is usually assumed to occur in a triangular pattern above the opening extending from a maximum at the center of the span to zero at the supports.

Ashlar   Squared stones or a pattern of stonework using squared stones.

Backfill   Soil, rubble, etc., used to correct overexcavation or to replace earth in a trench or around a foundation wall.

Base Coat   Plaster coat or coats applied before the final coat.

Bat   A broken brick or piece of brick with one undamaged end. Also called a brickbat. Usually about one-half brick.

Batch   Quantity of concrete or mortar mixed at one time.

Batter   Masonry that is recessed or sloping back in successive courses; the opposite of a corbel.

Batching   Weighing or volumetrically measuring and introducing into the mixer the ingredients for a batch of concrete, mortar, or plaster.

Bed   (1) In masonry and bricklaying, the side of a masonry unit on which it lies in the course of the wall; the underside when placed horizontally. (2) The layer of mortar on which the masonry unit is set.

Bed Joint   In masonry, the horizontal joint between courses of masonry.

Bedding Course   The first layer of mortar at the bottom of a masonry wall.

Bleeding   The flow of mixing water within or its emergence on the surface of newly placed concrete or mortar, caused by the settlement of the solid materials within the mass.

Bond

Adhesion Bond   The adhesion between masonry units and mortar or grout.

Masonry Bond   Connection of masonry wythes with overlapping header units.

Metal Tie Bond   Connection of masonry wythes with metal ties or joint reinforcement.

Mortar Bond or Grout Bond   Adhesion between mortar or grout and masonry units, reinforcement, or connectors.

Pattern Bond   Patterns formed by the exposed faces of the masonry units—for example, running bond or flemish bond.

American bond   Bond pattern in which every sixth course is a header course and the intervening courses are stretcher courses.

basketweave bond   Modular groups of units laid at right angles to those adjacent to form a pattern.

blind bond   Bond pattern to tie the front course to the wall where it is not desirable that any headers should be seen in the face work.

common bond   Bond pattern in which five to seven stretcher courses are laid between headers.

cross bond   Bond pattern in which the joints of the stretcher in the second course come in the middle of the stretcher in the first course composed of headers and stretchers intervening.

dutch cross bond   A bond having the courses made up alternately of headers and stretchers. Same as an English cross bond.

English bond   Bond pattern with alternating courses of headers and stretchers. The headers and stretchers are situated plumb over each other. The headers are divided evenly over the vertical joints between the stretchers.

English cross bond   A variation of English bond, but with the stretchers in alternate courses centered on the stretchers above and below. Also call Dutch bond.

Flemish bond   Bond pattern in which each course consists of alternate stretchers and headers, with the headers in alternate courses centered over the stretchers in intervening courses.

Flemish garden bond   Units laid so that each course has a header to every three to five stretchers.

header bond   Bond pattern showing only headers on the face, each header divided evenly on the header under it.

herringbone bond   The arrangement of units in a course in a zigzag fashion with the end of one unit laid at right angles against the side of a second unit.

random bond   Masonry constructed without a regular pattern.

running bond   The placement of masonry units such that head joints in successive courses are horizontally offset at least one-quarter the unit length.

stack bond   (1) The placement of units such that the head joints in successive courses are vertically aligned. (2) Units laid so no overlap occurs; head joints form a continuous vertical line. Also called plumb joint bond, straight stack, jack bond, jack on jack, and checkerboard bond.

Reinforcing Bond   The adhesion between steel reinforcement and mortar or grout.

Bond Beam   A course or courses of a masonry wall grouted and usually reinforced in the horizontal direction serving as an integral beam in the wall.

Brick   A solid masonry unit of clay or shale, formed into a rectangular prism while plastic and burned or fired in a kiln. Similarly shaped units made of portland cement mixes are called ***Concrete Brick.***

Arch Brick   Wedge-shaped brick for use in an arch which provides uniformity of mortar joint thicknesses as the arch is turned.

Building Brick   Brick for building purposes not specially treated for texture or color. Formerly called common brick.

Clay Brick   A solid or hollow masonry unit of clay or shale, usually formed into a rectangular prism while plastic and burned or fired in a kiln.

Clinker Brick   A very hard-burned brick whose shape is distorted due to nearly complete vitrification.

Common Brick   *See* **Building Brick.**

Concrete Brick   Brick made from portland cement, water, and suitable aggregates, with or without the inclusion of other materials.

Cored Brick   A brick in which the holes consist of less than 25% of the section.

Face Brick or Facing Brick   Brick made especially for exposed use, often treated to produce surface texture. May be made of selected clays or treated to produce desired color.

Hollow Brick   A masonry unit of clay or shale whose net cross-sectional area in any plane parallel to the bearing surface is between 60 and 75% of its gross cross-sectional area measured in the same plane.

Paving Brick   Vitrified brick especially suitable for use in pavements where resistance to abrasion is important.

Salmon Brick   Generic term for relatively soft underburned bricks which are more porous, slightly larger, and lighter colored than hard-burned brick. Usually pinkish orange (salmon) in color.

Brick Grade   Designation for durability of the unit expressed as SW for severe weathering, MW for moderate weathering, or NW for negligible weathering.

Brick Hammer   A steel tool, one end of which has a flat, square surface used as a hammer, for breaking bricks, driving nails, and so on. The other end forms a chisel peen used for dressing bricks. (Also called brick ax or bricklayer's hammer.)

Brick Ledge   A ledge on a footing or wall which supports a course of masonry.

Brick Type   Designation for facing brick that controls tolerance, chippage, and distortion. Expressed as FBS, FBX, and FBA for solid brick; HBS, HBX, HBA, and HBB for hollow brick; and PS, PX, and PA for paving brick.

Buck   Framing used around an opening in a wall where a door or window will be placed.

Bug Holes   Small holes in concrete caused by entrapped air voids at the surface of formed concrete during placement and compaction.

Bulking   Increase in volume of a quantity of sand in a moist condition compared to the volume of the same quantity of sand in a dry state.

Bull Float   A tool with a large, flat, rectangular piece of aluminum, wood, or magnesium and a long handle, used to smooth concrete slabs.

Bush Hammer   Hammer with a serrated face used to roughen a concrete surface.

Buttering   Placing mortar on a masonry unit with a trowel.

Cast-in-Place   Concrete that is deposited in the place where it will harden as part of a structure; opposite of precast.

Cement   A burned mixture of clay and limestone pulverized for making mortar, grout, or concrete (such as portland cement, masonry cement, etc.).

Cement Paint   Coating made mostly of white portland cement, water, and lime.

Cement Paste   A constituent of concrete and mortar consisting of cement and water.

Checking   Development of shallow cracks at closely spaced but irregular intervals in concrete, plaster, or mortar surfaces. Also known as crazing or craze cracks.

Cinder Block   *See* **Concrete Block.**

Centering   Temporary formwork for the support of masonry arches, hearth extensions, or lintels during construction. Also called center(s).

Closer   The last masonry unit laid in a course. It may be whole or a portion of a unit. Supplementary or short-length units used at corners or jambs to maintain bond patterns.

CMU   Concrete masonry unit.

Collar Joint   *See* **Joint, Collar.**

Color Pigment   Inorganic matter used in concrete and mortar to vary the color.

Common Bond   *See* **Bond, Pattern, Common.**

Compaction   The process of reducing the volume of freshly placed concrete or grout by vibration, tamping, or rodding to eliminate voids.

Concrete   A homogeneous mixture of portland cement, sand, gravel, and water which may also contain admixtures or coloring pigments.

Concrete, Green   Concrete which has been placed and has set but is not completely hardened.

Concrete Block   A hollow concrete masonry unit made from portland cement and suitable aggregates such as sand, crushed stone, cinders, burned clay or shale, pumice, scoria, and air-cooled or expanded blast furnace slag, with or without the inclusion of other materials.

Concrete Lift   (1) An increment of concrete height within the total pour. A pour may consist of one or more lifts. (2) The height to which concrete is placed in a form without intermission.

Concrete Masonry Unit   Hollow or solid block or solid brick of portland cement, water, and aggregates.

   A-Block   A hollow unit with one end closed and the opposite end open forming two cells when laid in the wall.

   Bond Beam Block   A hollow unit with web portions depressed 1-$\frac{1}{4}$ in. or more to form a continuous channel or channels for reinforcing steel and grout. Lintel blocks are often used to form bond beams.

   Concrete Block   A hollow concrete masonry unit made from portland cement and suitable aggregates such as sand, crushed stone, cinders, burned clay or shale, pumice, scoria, and air-cooled or expanded blast furnace slag, with or without the inclusion of other materials.

   Concrete Brick   A solid concrete masonry unit made from portland cement and suitable aggregates.

   H-Block   A hollow unit with both ends open and sometimes a continuous bond beam recess at the intersecting web.

   Lintel Block   A masonry unit consisting of one core with one side open. Usually placed with the open side up like a trough to form a continuous beam, as across a window or door opening.

   Paving Block   A solid, flat unit used for road and walkway paving.

   Split-Face Block   Concrete masonry units with one or more faces having a fractured surface for use in masonry wall construction.

   U-Block   *See* **Lintel Block.**

Concrete Pour   The total height of concrete to be placed before stopping work. A concrete pour may consist of one or more concrete lifts.

Connector   Mechanical devices, including anchors, wall ties, and fasteners, for securing two or more pieces, parts, or members together. *See also* **Anchor, Fastener,** and **Wall Tie.**

Consistency   The relative stiffness or flow of freshly mixed concrete, mortar, or grout.

Construction Joint   *See* **Joint, Construction.**

Control Joint   *See* **Joint, Control.**

Coping   The material or masonry units forming a cap or finish on top of a wall, pier, pilaster, chimney, etc. It protects the masonry below from penetration of water from above. Should be projected out from the wall to provide a decorative as well as protective feature.

Core (1) The molded open space in a concrete masonry unit. (2) A hollow space within a concrete masonry unit formed by the face shells and webs. (3) The holes in clay units. Also called cells.

Corrosion The chemical or electrochemical reaction between a material, usually a metal, and its environment that produces a deterioration of the material and its properties.

Corrosion Resistant Material that is inherently resistant to, or treated or coated to retard harmful oxidation or other corrosive action.

Course One of the continuous horizontal layers of units bonded with mortar in masonry.

Crack A flaw consisting of complete or incomplete separation within a single element or between contiguous elements of constructions.

Crazing Development of shallow cracks at closely spaced but irregular intervals in concrete, plaster, or mortar surfaces. Also known as checking.

Creep Time-dependent deformation due to sustained load.

Curing The maintenance of proper conditions of moisture and temperature during initial set to develop required strength and reduce shrinkage in concrete products and mortar.

Curing Compound A membrane-forming liquid applied as a coating to the surface of newly placed concrete to retard the loss of water.

Curling The distortion or warping of an essentially flat surface into a slightly curved shape. In concrete slabs, curling is the phenomenon caused primarily by differences in moisture between the top and bottom of the slab.

Dampproofing Treatment of a surface to retard the passage or absorption of water in the absence of hydrostatic pressure.

Darby A hand-manipulated straightedge, usually 3 ft. to 8 ft. long, used in the early-stage leveling of concrete or plaster surfaces.

Deformed Bar Reinforcing bar with ridges which serve to interlock with surrounding concrete, mortar, or grout.

Differential Movement Movement of two elements relative to one another that differs in rate or direction.

Dimensions of Masonry Units

Actual The measured dimensions of a masonry unit.

Height (1) The vertical dimension of the unit in the face of a wall. (2) Vertical dimension of masonry units or masonry, measured parallel to the intended face of the unit or units.

Length (1) The horizontal dimension of the unit in the face of the wall. (2) Horizontal dimension of masonry units or masonry, measured parallel to the intended face of the unit or units.

Nominal (1) A dimension greater than the specified (standard) dimension by the thickness of one joint, but not more than 13 mm or $^1/_2$ in. (2) A dimension that may be greater than the specified masonry dimension by the thickness of a mortar joint.

Thickness (1) That dimension designed to lie at right angles to the face of the wall, floor, or other assembly. (2) Horizontal dimension of masonry units or masonry measured perpendicular to the intended face of the masonry unit or units.

Double-Headed Nail A nail with two heads used in building concrete formwork.

Dowel Steel pin or bar extending into adjoining portions of concrete to prevent shifting of the two elements relative to one another.

Durability The ability of a material or construction to resist weathering action, chemical attack, abrasion, and so on.

Dusting Development of powdered material on the surface of hardened concrete.

Dutch Bond A pattern bond having the courses made up alternately of headers and stretchers. Same as English cross bond.

Efflorescence, Water Soluble A crystalline deposit, usually white, of water-soluble compounds on the surface of masonry. Normally can be removed with water washing.

Efflorescence, Water Insoluble A crystalline deposit, usually white, of water-soluble compounds which, on reaching the masonry surface, become water insoluble primarily through carbonation (also sometimes called lime run or calcium carbonate stain). Normally requires acid washing for removal.

Expansion Joint In masonry, a continuous joint or plane without mortar or other hard materials, designed to accommodate volume increase and differential movement.

Face Shell The side wall of a hollow concrete masonry or clay masonry unit.

Face Shell Bedding   Mortar is applied only to the horizontal surface of the face shells of hollow masonry units and in the head joints to a depth equal to the thickness of the face shell.

Falsework   Temporary structures such as shoring or formwork for beams, lintels, arches, and slabs. Built to support work in progress.

Fastener   Device used to attach nonmasonry materials to masonry.

Fin   A narrow projection on a concrete surface caused by mortar flowing between the cracks in forms.

Finishing   The leveling, smoothing, compacting, and treatment of the surface of concrete or plaster to obtain the final desired finish.

Flagstone   A type of stone that splits easily into flags or slabs; also a term applied to irregular pieces of such stone split into slabs from 1 to 3 in. thick, and used for walks, patios, etc.

Flashing   A thin, impervious material placed in mortar joints and through air spaces in masonry to prevent water penetration and/or provide water drainage.

Flemish Bond   *See* **Bond, Pattern, Flemish.**

Float   A rectangular hand tool, usually of wood, aluminum, or magnesium, used to impart a relatively even but still open texture to a concrete surface.

Fog Curing   The application of a fine mist of water used during the curing of concrete, masonry, or stucco.

Form or Formwork   A temporary structure or mold used to contain fresh concrete while it hardens and cures.

Form Oil   Oil applied to the inside surfaces of concrete forms to promote the release of the form from the concrete.

Frog   A depression in the bed surface of a brick. Sometimes called a panel.

Furrowing   The practice of striking a shallow V-shaped trough in a bed of mortar.

Gradation   The size distribution of aggregate particles, determined by separation with standard screen sieves.

Grout   A mixture of cementitious material and aggregate to which sufficient water is added to produce pouring consistency without segregation of the constituents.

Grout Lift   (1) An increment of grout height within the total pour. A pour may consist of one or more lifts. (2) The height to which grout is placed in a cell, collar joint, or cavity without intermission.

Grout Pour   The total height of a masonry wall to be grouted prior to erection of additional masonry. A grout pour will consist of one or more grout lifts.

Grouted Masonry   Hollow-unit masonry construction in which the empty cores are filled solidly with grout. Also, double-wythe wall construction in which the cavity is filled solidly with grout.

Grouting, High Lift   The technique of grouting where the masonry is constructed in excess of 5 ft. high prior to grouting.

Grouting, Low Lift   The technique of grouting as the wall is constructed, usually to scaffold or bond beam height, but not greater than 4 ft.

Green Concrete   *See* **Concrete, Green.**

Green Mortar   *See* **Mortar, Green.**

Hardener   A chemical applied to a concrete floor to reduce wear and dusting.

Harsh Mix   A mixture which lacks desired workability and consistency due to a deficiency of cement paste, aggregate fines, or water.

Hawk   A tool to hold and carry plaster or mortar; generally a flat piece of metal approximately 10 to 14 in. square, with a wooden handle fixed to the center of the underside.

Head Joint   The vertical joint between masonry units, perpendicular to the face of the masonry.

Header   A masonry unit that overlaps two or more adjacent wythes of masonry to tie them together.

Initial Rate of Absorption (IRA)   A measure of the capillary suction of water into a dry masonry unit from a bed face during a specified length of time over a specified area.

Initial Set   The beginning change from a plastic to a hardened state.

Interlocking Block Pavers   Solid masonry units capable of transferring loads and stresses laterally by arching or bridging action between units when subjected to vehicular traffic.

Joint   In building construction, the space or opening between two or more adjoining surfaces.

  Mortar Joint   In mortared masonry construction, the joints between units that are filled with mortar.

    bed joint   Horizontal layer of mortar on which a masonry unit is laid.

collar joint Vertical, longitudinal joint between wythes of masonry or between masonry wythe and backing.

   concave joint A recessed masonry joint formed in mortar by the use of a curved steel jointing tool. Highly resistant to rain penetration.

head joint Vertical transverse mortar joint placed between masonry units within the wythe at the time the masonry units are laid.

raked joint A mortar joint where $1/4$ in. to $1/2$ in. of mortar is removed from the outside surface of the joint.

tooled joint A mortar joint between two masonry units manually shaped or compressed with a jointing tool such as a concave or vee-notched jointer.

Movement Joint In building construction, a joint designed to accommodate movement of adjacent elements.

   control joint In concrete, concrete masonry, stucco, or coating systems; a formed, sawed, or assembled joint acting to regulate the location of cracking, separation, and distress resulting from dimensional or positional change.

   construction joint The joint between two successive concrete pours meet.

   expansion joint A continuous soft joint or void joint to accommodate expansion, contraction, and differential movement which does not contain mortar, grout, reinforcement, or other hard materials.

Joint Reinforcement Steel bar, wire, or prefabricated reinforcement (ladder or truss type) which is placed in mortar bed joints.

Keystone The wedge-shaped piece at the top of an arch which binds, or locks, all the other members in place.

Lead The section of a masonry wall built up and racked back on successive courses. A line is attached to leads as a guide for constructing the section of wall between them.

Lime A general term for the various chemical and physical forms of quicklime, hydrated lime, and hydraulic hydrated lime.

Hydrated Lime Quicklime to which sufficient water has been added to convert the oxides to hydroxides.

Lime Mortar A lime putty mixed with an aggregate, suitable for masonry purposes.

Lime Putty   The product obtained by slaking quicklime with water according to the directions of the manufacturer or by mixing hydrated lime and water to a desired consistency.

Quicklime   A hot, unslaked lime. A calcined material, a major part of which is calcium oxide (or calcium oxide in natural association with lesser amounts of magnesium oxide) capable of slaking with water.

Slaked Lime   Formed when quicklime is treated with water; same as hydrated lime.

Lintel   A beam or supporting member placed over an opening in a wall.

Mason   A worker skilled in laying brick, tile, stone, or block.

Masonry   Brick, structural clay tile, stone, concrete masonry units, terra cotta, etc., or combinations thereof, bonded with mortar, dry stacked, or anchored with metal connectors.

Masonry Cement   Proprietary cement used in masonry mortars and plaster containing one or more of the following materials: portland cement, blended cement, natural cement, slag cement, or hydraulic lime; and in addition usually containing one or more materials such as hydrated lime, limestone, or chalk.

Masonry Unit   Natural or manufactured building units of stone, clay, concrete, or glass.

Mason's Hammer   A hammer with a heavy steel head, one face of which is shaped like a chisel for trimming brick or stone.

Mason's Level   Similar to a carpenter's level, but longer.

Mortar   A mixture of cementitious materials, fine aggregate, and water, used to bond masonry units, and which may contain additives and admixtures.

Fat Mortar   Mortar containing a high percentage of cementitious components. It is a sticky mortar which adheres to a trowel.

Fresh Mortar   The wet mix of ingredients before they begin to cure.

Green Mortar   Mortar that has begun to set but is not fully cured.

Hardened Mortar   Mortar that has fully cured.

Harsh Mortar   A mortar that is difficult to spread; not workable.

Lean Mortar   Mortar that is deficient in cementitious components. It is usually harsh and difficult to spread.

Mortar Bond   The adhesion of mortar to masonry units.

Mortar Joint   *See* **Joint, Mortar.**

Mortar Mix   A proprietary, mill-mixed, cementitious material to which only water must be added to make masonry mortar.

Multiwythe Wall   A wall composed of two or more wythes or rows of masonry.

Neat Cement   In masonry, a pure cement undiluted by sand aggregate or admixtures.

Parging   The application of a coat of cement mortar to the back of the facing or the face of the backing in multiwythe construction.

Paver   A paving stone, brick, or concrete masonry unit.

Pick and Dip   A method of laying brick whereby the bricklayer simultaneously picks up a brick with one hand and, with the other hand, enough mortar on a trowel to lay the brick. Sometimes called the Eastern, New England, or English method.

Pilaster   A column of masonry built as part of a wall.

Pilaster Block   Concrete masonry unit designed for use in construction of plain or reinforced concrete masonry pilasters and columns.

Plaster   *See* **Stucco.**

Pointing   Troweling mortar into a joint after the masonry units are laid.

  Repointing   Filling in cut-out or defective mortar joints in masonry with fresh mortar.

  Tuckpointing   Decorative method of pointing masonry with a surface mortar that is different from the bedding mortar.

Portland Cement   A hydraulic cement produced by pulverizing portland cement clinker, and usually containing calcium sulfate.

Quoin   Projecting courses of brick or stone at the corners and angles of buildings as ornamental features.

Racking   A method entailing stepping back successive courses of masonry.

Rebar   Shorthand term for steel reinforcing bar.

Reinforced Masonry   Masonry units and reinforcing steel bonded with mortar and/or grout in such a manner that the components act together in resisting forces.

Repointing   *See* **Pointing.**

Retempering   Moistening and remixing of concrete, mortar, or stucco to a proper consistency for use. Must be done within first $1^1/2$ to 2 hours after initial mixing, depending on ambient temperature and wind conditions.

Rowlock   A brick laid on its face edge so that the end is visible in the wall face.

Rubble Rough, broken stones or bricks used to fill in cores of cavity walls or columns. Also rough, broken stone direct from the quarry.

Running Bond *See* **Bond, Pattern, Running.**

Screed Straightedge used to strike the surface of concrete or stucco or to level the surface of sand.

Screen Block Concrete masonry units for use in masonry screen walls.

Screen Tile Clay tile manufactured for masonry screen wall construction.

Set A change in consistency from a plastic to a hardened state.

Shrinkage Volume change due to loss of moisture or decrease in temperature.

Single-Wythe Wall A wall containing only one masonry unit in wall thickness.

Slushed Joints Vertical joints filled after the units are laid by "throwing" mortar in with the edge of a trowel. (This method is not accepted as good practice in masonry construction.)

Soap A masonry unit of normal face dimensions, but having only nominal 2-in. thickness.

Soldier A stretcher set on end with face showing on the wall surface.

Stone

Building Stone, Natural rock of adequate quality to be quarried and cut as dimension stone, and used in the construction industry.

Cast Stone An architectural precast concrete building unit intended to simulate natural cut stone.

Cut Stone Stone fabricated to specific dimensions.

Dimension Stone Natural stone that has been selected, trimmed, or cut to specified or indicated shapes or sizes, with or without one or more mechanically dressed surfaces.

Fieldstone Natural building stone as found in the field.

Flagstone A flat stone, thin in relation to its surface area, commonly used as a stepping stone, for a terrace or patio, or for floor paving. Usually either naturally thin or split from rock that cleaves readily.

Stone Masonry Masonry composed of natural or cast stone.

Stone Masonry, Ashlar Stone masonry composed of rectangular units having sawed, dressed, or squared bed surfaces and bonded by mortar.

ashlar pattern   A pattern bond of rectangular or square stone units, always of two or more sizes. If the pattern is repeated, it is patterned ashlar. If the pattern is not repeated, it is random ashlar.

coursed ashlar   Ashlar masonry laid in courses of stone of equal height for each course, although different courses may be of varying height.

random ashlar   Stone masonry pattern of rectangular stones set without continuous joints and laid up without drawn patterns. If composed of material cut to modular heights, discontinuous but aligned horizontal joints are discernible.

Stone Masonry, Rubble   Stone masonry composed of irregular shaped units bonded by mortar.

coursed rubble   Masonry composed of roughly shaped stones fitting on approximately level beds, well bonded, and brought at vertical intervals to continuous level beds or courses.

random rubble   Masonry built of unsquared or rudely squared stones irregular in size and shape.

squared rubble   Construction in which squared stones of various sizes are combined in patterns that make up courses as high as, or higher than, the tallest stones.

Story Pole   A marked pole for masonry coursing during construction.

Stretcher   A masonry unit laid with its greatest dimension horizontal and its face parallel to the wall face.

Striking   The cutting away of mortar with the trowel; also the tooling of mortar joints.

Stringing Mortar   The procedure of spreading enough mortar on a bed to lay several masonry units.

Stucco   A mix of portland cement, portland cement, and masonry cement, or portland cement and lime with aggregate designed for use on exterior surfaces.

Tie   *See* **Wall Tie.**

Tolerance   Specified allowance of variation from a size specification.

Tooling   Compressing and shaping the face of a mortar joint with a special tool other than a trowel.

Trowel

Concrete Trowel   A flat, broad-bladed steel hand tool used to finish concrete or to apply, shape, and finish plaster.

Mason's Trowel A trowel having a flat, triangular steel blade in an offset handle used to pick up and spread mortar. The narrow end of the blade is called the "point"—the wide end, the "heel."

Tuckpointing *See* **Pointing.**

Unit Masonry Construction of brick or block that is set in mortar, dry-stacked, or mechanically anchored.

Unreinforced Masonry Masonry constructed without steel reinforcement, except that which may be used for bonding or reducing the effects of dimensional changes due to variations in moisture content or temperature.

Vapor Retarder Material or system that impedes the diffusion of water vapor.

Veneer A single facing wythe of masonry, anchored or adhered to a structural backing, but not designed to carry structural loads.

Vibrator A machine used to eliminate trapped air bubbles and consolidate freshly placed concrete or masonry grout.

Voussoir One of the truncated, wedge-shaped masonry units which forms an arch ring.

Wale A long, horizontal member on formwork used to hold studs in place.

Wall Tie Metal connector which bonds wythes of masonry walls together.

Water Absorption Process in which water enters a material or system through capillary pores and interstices and is retained without transmission.

Water Infiltration Process in which water passes through a material or system and reaches an area that is not directly or intentionally exposed to the water source.

Water Leakage Water infiltration that is unintended, uncontrolled, exceeds the resistance, retention, or discharge capacity of the system, or causes damage or accelerated deterioration.

Water Penetration Process in which water enters a material or system through an exposed surface, joint, or opening.

Water Permeation Process in which water enters, flows within, and spreads throughout a material or system.

Water Reducing Agent A material which increases slump and workability of freshly mixed concrete or mortar without increasing the amount of water.

Water Repellant A material or treatment for surfaces to provide resistance to absorption of water.

Water Saturation The maximum amount of water a material or system can retain without discharge or transmission.

Water Vapor Permeance Time rate of water vapor diffusion through unit area of a flat material or construction induced by unit vapor pressure difference between two specified surfaces, under specified temperature and humidity conditions.

Waterproof Impervious to water.

Waterproofing Treatment of a surface or structure to prevent the passage of water under hydrostatic pressure.

Weep Hole Opening in face of wall to permit the escape of moisture; usually located immediately above flashing.

Workability The property of freshly mixed concrete, mortar, or plaster that determines its working characteristics and the ease with which it can be mixed, placed, and finished.

Workmanship The art or skill of a worker; craftsmanship; the quality imparted to a thing in the process of creating it.

Wythe Each continuous vertical section of masonry one unit in thickness.

BIBLIOGRAPHY

ACI *Standard Practice for Selecting Proportions for Normal, Heavyweight, and Mass Concrete,* ACI 211.1, American Concrete Institute, Detroit.

ACI 530/ASCE5/TMS 402 *Building Code Requirements for Masonry Structures,* American Concrete Institute, American Society of Civil Engineers, The Masonry Society, 1999.

ACI *Building Code Requirements for Reinforced Concrete,* ACI 318, American Concrete Institute, Detroit.

ACI *Concrete Primer,* American Concrete Institute, Detroit, 1987.

Adams, J.T., *The Complete Concrete, Masonry and Brick Handbook,* Van Nostrand Reinhold, New York, 1979.

Beall, Christine, *Masonry: Concrete, Brick and Stone.* Creative Homeowner Press, Upper Saddle River, N.J., 1997.

Beall, Christine, *Masonry Design and Detailing,* 4th edition, McGraw-Hill, New York, 1997.

Beall, Christine, *Thermal and Moisture Protection Manual,* McGraw-Hill, New York, 1999.

Brick Industry Association (formerly Brick Institute of America), *Technical Notes on Brick Construction,* Reston, VA.

Callendar, John H., *Timesaver Standards for Architectural Design Data,* 6th ed., McGraw-Hill, New York, 1982.

Concrete Construction Publications, *Basics of Concrete,* Concrete Construction Publications, Inc., Addison, Illinois, 1986.

Connor, Harold W., *Residential Concrete,* National Association of Homebuilders, Home Builder Press, 1994.

Council of American Building Officials, *One and Two-Family Dwelling Code,* Falls Church, VA, 1995.

Council of American Building Officials, *One and Two-Family Dwelling Code, 1996/1997 Amendments,* Falls Church, VA, 1997.

Dezettel, Louis M., *Masons and Builders Library,* Macmillan, New York, 1986.

Duncan, S. Blackwell, *The Complete Book of Outdoor Masonry,* TAB Books, Blue Ridge Summit, PA, 1978.

Fine Homebuilding, *Foundations and Masonry,* The Taunton Press, Newton, Connecticut, 1990.

Kolkoski, Rynold V., *Masonry Estimating,* Craftsman Book Company, Carlsbad, California, 1988.

Kosmatka, Steven H., and William C. Panarese, *Design and Control of Concrete Mixtures,* Portland Cement Association, Skokie, Illinois, 1988.

Laska, Walter, *Masonry and Steel Detailing Handbook,* The Aberdeen Group, Addison, Illinois, 1993.

Lstiburek, Joseph and John Carmody, *Moisture Control Handbook,* New York: Van Nostrand Reinhold, 1993.

Meadows, W.R., Inc. *The Hydrologic Cycle and Moisture Migration,* Elgin, Illinois, 1989.

Mckee, Harley J. *Introduction to Early American Masonry—Stone, Brick, Mortar and Plaster,* Washington, D.C.: The Preservation Press, 1973.

National Association of Home Builders, *Residential Concrete,* Home Builder Press, Washington, D.C., 1994.

National Concrete Masonry Association, *Design Manual for Segmental Retaining Walls,* NCMA, Herndon, VA, 1993.

National Concrete Masonry Association, *TEK Bulletins,* Herndon, VA.

Newman, Morton, *Standard Cantilever Retaining Walls,* McGraw-Hill, New York, 1976.

Nolan, Ken, *Masonry and Concrete Construction,* Craftsman Book Company, Carlsbad, California, 1998.

Olin, Harold B., *Construction Principles, Materials and Methods,* 5th ed., New York, Van Nostrand Reinhold, 1990.

Portland Cement Association, *The Homeowner's Guide to Building With Concrete, Brick and Stone,* PCA, Skokie, Illinois, 1988.

Portland Cement Association, *Trowel Tips—Mortar Sand,* PCA, Skokie, Illinois, 1992.

Ramsey, Charles G. And Harold S. Sleeper, *Architectural Graphic Standards, 9th edition,* New York, John Wiley & Sons, Inc., 1994.

Randall, Frank A. And William C. Panarese. *Concrete Masonry Handbook, 5th Edition,* Skokie, Illinois, Portland Cement Association, 1991.

U.S. Army, *Concrete and Masonry,* Technical Manual No. 5-742. U.S. Government Printing Office, Washington, D.C., 1970.

Waddell, Joseph J., *Concrete Manual,* International Conference of Building Officials, Whittier, California, 1989.

Watson, Donald and Kenneth Labs. *Climatic Building Design,* New York, McGraw-Hill, 1983.

INDEX

ABOUT THE AUTHOR

Christine Beall is a consulting architect who has more than 25 years of experience in the design, specification, and construction of residential, commercial, institutional, and industrial buildings. She has written several books, including *Masonry Design and Detailing* and *Thermal and Moisture Protection Manual* (also from McGraw-Hill), and has published more than 100 articles and papers on masonry, sealants, glass, fire-resistant materials, moisture problems, and related construction topics. An active member in several professional organizations, Ms. Beall works as a consultant and expert witness in solving or avoiding design and construction problems. She has also been a contributor to *Architectural Graphic Standards,* the *Masonry Designer's Guide to the MSJC Masonry Code and Specifications* and McGraw-Hill's *Encyclopedia of Science and Technology*.